Judiciaries within Europe

An in-depth study of the careers and roles of judges in France, Germany, Spain, Sweden and England, this book is based on original-language materials and investigations of judges and judicial institutions in each country. On the basis of these detailed case studies, the book suggests factors that shape the character of the judiciary in different countries, focusing on issues such as women's careers and the relationship between judicial careers and politics. Bell's investigations offer lessons on issues which the English judiciary is having to confront in its current period of reform.

JOHN BELL is Professor of Law at the University of Cambridge. He is an Honorary Queen's Counsel and a Fellow of the British Academy. He worked previously at the Universities of Oxford and Leeds. He has written on judicial reasoning and on various aspects of French law. He has been a visiting professor in Paris, Brussels and Le Mans and a stagiaire at the Conseil d'Etat in Paris.

CAMBRIDGE STUDIES IN INTERNATIONAL AND COMPARATIVE LAW

Established in 1946, this series produces high quality scholarship in the fields of public and private international law and comparative law. Although these are distinct legal sub-disciplines, developments since 1946 confirm their interrelation.

Comparative law is increasingly used as a tool in the making of law at national, regional and international levels. Private international law is now often affected by international conventions, and the issues faced by classical conflicts rules are frequently dealt with by substantive harmonisation of law under international auspices. Mixed international arbitrations, especially those involving state economic activity, raise mixed questions of public and private international law, while in many fields (such as the protection of human rights and democratic standards, investment guarantees and international criminal law) international and national systems interact. National constitutional arrangements relating to 'foreign affairs', and to the implementation of international norms, are a focus of attention.

The Board welcomes works of a theoretical or interdisciplinary character, and those focusing on the new approaches to international or comparative law or conflicts of law. Studies of particular institutions or problems are equally welcome, as are translations of the best work published in other languages.

A list of books in the series can be found at the end of this volume.

Judiciaries within Europe

A Comparative Review

John Bell

CAMBRIDGE
UNIVERSITY PRESS

CAMBRIDGE UNIVERSITY PRESS
Cambridge, New York, Melbourne, Madrid, Cape Town, Singapore,
São Paulo, Delhi, Dubai, Tokyo, Mexico City

Cambridge University Press
The Edinburgh Building, Cambridge CB2 8RU, UK

Published in the United States of America by Cambridge University Press, New York

www.cambridge.org
Information on this title: www.cambridge.org/9780521172851

First published 2006
Reprinted 2007
First paperback edition 2010

A catalogue record for this publication is available from the British Library

ISBN 978-0-521-86072-7 Hardback
ISBN 978-0-521-17285-1 Paperback

Contents

Preface

My interest in judiciaries in different European countries was stimulated by a series of workshops I helped to run in the 1990s with Antoine Garapon of the Institut des Hautes Etudes de la Justice in Paris, Giuseppe di Frederico, Carlo Guarnieri and Patrizia Pederzoli from the University of Bologna, and José Juan Toharia from the Autonomous University of Madrid. These workshops were attended by judges from a number of countries – up to eighteen in one instance. Listening to the similarities and differences of the experiences that they related to each other, and having to produce concluding remarks for sessions, I was made not only to identify similarities and differences, but to reflect on the reasons for them. Discussion on these issues with academic colleagues and judges helped me to formulate the basis of a research project of which this is the fruit. The project was generously supported by the British Academy, which awarded me a Readership in 1999 to 2001, together with funds to undertake research visits to France, Germany, Sweden and Spain. In each of those countries, I was given generous assistance by academic colleagues and by those with responsibilities for the judiciary, as well as by judges themselves. I was able to complement reading of key materials with interviews and observation of court processes.

I owe a debt of gratitude to a large number of people who have helped in numerous ways to provide information and ideas on this research. Among the judges and judicial officials who deserve particular mention are Tora Wikström of Domstolsverket, Michael Gressmann of the German Ministry of Justice, Jacques Debû and Irène Carbonnier. Among academic colleagues, Antoine Garapon, Luis Diez-Picazo, Kjell-Åke Modéer, Torbjörn Vallinder, Ulf Bernitz, Carlo Guarnieri and José Juan Toharia were particularly helpful in providing introductions for my visits and commenting on my ideas or even drafts. In addition, I have benefited from comments arising from talks, particularly in the Universities of Cambridge and Nottingham, as well as in Hardwicke Buildings which has made me an honorary member of its chambers. Support and interest from colleagues in the Universities of Leeds and Cambridge, often through informal discussion, has been invaluable. It remains my fault if I have not made the most of these different supports and stimuli to research.

Abbreviations

Abel, *Legal Profession*	R. L. Abel, *The Legal Profession in England and Wales* (London 1988)
Abel, *Market and State*	R. L. Abel, *English Lawyers between Market and State* (London 2003)
Algotsson	K.-G. Algotsson, 'Lagrådet, rättstaten och demokratin' in T. Håstad and L. Lewin, *Politik och Juridik. Grundlagen inför 2000-talet* (Uppsala 1999), 37
Annuaire Statistique	Ministry of Justice, *Annuaire Statistique de la Justice, édition 2003* (Paris 2003)
Auld	R. Auld, *Review of the Criminal Courts of England and Wales* (2001) (http://www.criminal-courts-review.org.uk/ccr-oo.htm)
Baas	N. J. Baas, *Onderzoeksnotities 2000/8: Rekrutering en (permanente) educatie van de rechtsprekende macht in vijf landen* (Ministry of Justice, Netherlands 2000)
Baer	A. Baer, *Die Unabhängigkeit der Richter in der Bundesrepublik Deutschland und in der DDR* (Berlin 1999)
BGB	Bürgerlichesgesetzbuch
Bodiguel	J.-L. Bodiguel, *Les magistrats, un corps sans âme* (Paris 1991)
BOE	Boletín Oficial del Estado
Brown and Bell	L. N. Brown and J. Bell, *French Administrative Law* (5th edn, Oxford 1998)
CE	Spanish Constitution

CEFJC	Centre d'études et de formation des juridictions commerciales
CGPJ	Consejo General del Poder Judicial
CGTC	Conférence Générale des Tribunaux de Commerce
CSM	Conseil Supérieur de la Magistrature
Currie	D. P. Currie, *The Constitution of the Federal Republic of Germany* (Chicago 1994)
DCA	Department of Constitutional Affairs
DDR	German Democratic Republic
Diesen	C. Diesen, *Lekmän som Domare* (Stockholm 1996)
DRiG	Deutsches Richtergesetz
DV	Domstolsverket
EDCE	Etudes et Documents du Conseil d'Etat
Ekelöf	O. Ekelöf, 'Teleological Construction of Statutes' (1958) 2 *Scandinavian Studies in Law* 75
Elites	J. J. Ruiz-Rico (ed.), *Monográfico dedicado al studio sobre la 'Elite juridical española'* (1987) 53 *Documentacion Juridica*
ENA	Ecole Nationale d'Administration
ENM	Ecole Nationale de la Magistrature
French Legal Cultures	J. Bell, *French Legal Cultures* (London 2001)
Garapon and Papadopoulos	A. Garapon and I. Papadopoulos, *Juger en Amérique et en France* (Paris 2003)
GG	German Basic Law (*Grundgesetz*)
Guarnieri and Pederzoli	C. Guarnieri and P. Pederzoli, *The Power of Judges. A Comparative Study of Courts and Democracy* (Oxford 2001)
HD	Högsta Domstol
JO	Justitieombudsman
Judicial Elite	T. Vallinder, 'Who is Included in Sweden's Judicial and Legal Elite?', unpublished conference paper, Bellagio Conference Centre, 1985
JUSTICE	JUSTICE, *The Judiciary in England and Wales* (London 1992)

Kommers	D. P. Kommers, *The Constitutional Jurisprudence of the Federal Republic of Germany* (2nd edn, Durham 1997)
LCD	Lord Chancellor's Department
Les Conseils supérieurs	T. Renoux, *Les Conseils supérieurs de la magistrature en Europe* (Paris 1999)
Libro Blanco	Consejo General del Poder Judicial, *Libro Blanco* (Madrid 1997)
Lieber and Sens	H. Lieber and U. Sens (eds.), *Ehrenamtliche Richter. Demokratie oder Dekoration am Richtertisch?* (Wiesbaden 1999)
LOPJ	Ley Organica del Poder Judicial
LR	Lagråd
Massot and Girardot	J. Massot and T. Girardot, *Conseil d'Etat* (Paris 1999)
MEDEF	Mouvement des Entreprises de France
Memoria 2003	CGPJ, *Memoria Anual 2003* (Madrid 2003)
Memoria 2004	CGPJ, *Memoria Anual 2004* (Madrid 2004)
Merino-Blanco	E. Merino-Blanco, *The Spanish Legal System* (London 1996)
Modéer, *Domarkulturen*	K. Å. Modéer, *Den svenska domarkulturen – europeiska och nationelle förebilder* (Lund 1994)
Moreno	J. D. Moreno, *Los Jueces de Paz* (Madrid 1987)
Morgan and Russell	R. Morgan and D. Russell, *The Judiciary in the Magistrates' Courts* (RDS Occasional Paper No. 66, Home Office 2000)
Peach	*Report on Judicial Appointments and QC Selection, Main Report* (London 1999)
Peczenik and Bergholz	A. Peczenik and G. Bergholz, 'Statutory Interpretation in Sweden' in D. N. MacCormick and R. S. Summers (eds.), *Interpreting Statutes* (Aldershot 1991)
Precedent	D. N. MacCormick and R. S. Summers (eds.), *Interpreting Precedents* (Aldershot 1997)
Principles of French Law	J. Bell, S. Boyron and S. Whittaker, *Principles of French Law* (Oxford 1998)
RF	Swedish Constitution

RR	Regeringsrätt
Ruiz Miguel and Laporta	A. Ruiz Miguel and F. J. Laporta, 'Precedent in Spain' in D. N. MacCormick and R. S. Summers (eds.), *Interpreting Precedents* (Aldershot 1997)
Schmidt	Folke Schmidt, 'Construction of Statutes' (1957) 1 *Scandinavian Studies in Law* 155
Scholz	J.-M. Scholz, *Gerechtigkeit verwalten. Die spanische Justiz im Übergang zur Moderne* (Frankfurt am Main, 2003)
Skyrme	T. Skyrme, *The Changing Image of the Magistracy* (London 1979)
Smith, Bailey and Gunn	S. H. Bailey, J. P. L. Ching, M. J. Gunn and D. C. Ormerod, *Smith, Bailey and Gunn on the Modern English Legal System* (4th edn, London 2002)
SOU 1994:99	SOU 1994:99, *Domaren i Sverige inför framtiden – utgångspunkter för fortsatt utredningsarbete*
Statutes	D. N. MacCormick and R. S. Summers (eds.), *Interpreting Statutes* (Aldershot 1991)
Stevens, *Independence*	R. B. Stevens, *The Independence of the Judiciary. The View from the Lord Chancellor's Office* (Oxford 1993)
Stone Sweet	A. Stone Sweet, *Governing with Judges* (Oxford 2000)
TC	Tribunal Constitucional
TFN	Tjänsteförslagsnämnden för domstolsväsendet
Toharia	J.-J. Toharia, *Opinión pública y justicia. La imagen de la justicia en la sociedad española* (CGPJ, Madrid 2001)
Troper and Grzegorczyk	M. Troper and C. Grzegorczyk, 'Precedent in France' in D. N. MacCormick and R. S. Summers (eds.), *Interpreting Precedents* (Aldershot 1997), ch. 4
Vår författning	E. Holmberg and N. Stjernquist, *Vår författning* (Stockholm 2000)

1 Introduction

If you visit criminal courts in different Western European countries, judges look different and behave differently. In Sweden the young judge in the *tingsrätt* will be in ordinary clothes, sitting on a panel with lay assessors, probably even older than her parents, at the same level as the prosecutor, defence lawyer and the accused. It is more like a meeting than a common-law trial, with everyone joining in, often across the table, rather than speaking at the invitation of the presiding judge. In France, the three women judges, one middle-aged and two younger, will be in robes, on a dais raised above the accused and his lawyer. Alongside the judges, and at the same level, will be the prosecutor. The focus of the event is the discussion between the judges and the accused or the judges and witnesses, with occasional interventions of the defence advocate. The English, middle-aged trial judge is even more formal, wearing a wig, and raised above everyone. In front of him will be the advocates for prosecution and defence in robes, who do much of the talking, and the accused behind them, who says little. The lay jury will be in a separate box on the side. Such initial impressions offer a starting point for this book. People who are called 'judges' are of different ages and relate differently in the court setting to those around them. Most continental judges are women. So why the differences, and do the appearances indicate a real difference in what they are doing?

Such questions are complex, and my ability to answer them is limited by my knowledge of languages and understanding of how different legal systems work. I am content to try to take a substantial step by looking at a number of questions in relation to five judiciaries. This book aims to examine three aspects of the diversity of judiciaries in Europe. First, it aims to document and analyse four differing continental European judicial systems, to study their structures and their specific character, and to compare these with the English judiciary as a representative of the common-law tradition. These chapters will not simply document differences in the recruitment, training and functions of judges in individual countries. They aim to identify a number of features that shape the way in which the work of a judge is performed and valued within particular legal systems. These more embedded features of the systems structure what I want to label 'a judicial culture'. Judges in different systems may perform a variety of tasks, some of which are similar between systems and some of which are specific to one system. But the 'judicial culture' focuses more on the institutional context within which judges operate and the particular way in which they perform their tasks. Each chapter will focus on a number of common themes, so that comparison between the systems can be made. Secondly, the chapters are written also to enable the reader to understand the system in its own terms and the factors that make it distinctive. Thirdly, the final chapter will draw out some overall conclusions about the factors that mould the character of judiciaries. In brief, I will argue that there is no single pattern or paradigm for the judge in Europe. Each judiciary is nested within a set of relationships to a legal community, to institutions of government and to the wider society which is unique. One can comment on whether it works effectively or as claimed within its own context, but comparative judgements of worth are more difficult.

This chapter aims to explain the approach taken to the study of the topic. My perspective will be an institutional comparison, looking at the judiciary as a social organisation within a context of expectations set by legal norms and by other institutions.

The centrality of the institutional perspective

Perspectives on judicial activity

There are three major perspectives from which the culture of the judiciary can be studied. The personal perspective looks at the way individuals perceive their role and career. The institutional perspective looks at the judiciary as a collective and examines the way in which the structures of the career and organisation of judges, as well as legal processes, affect the judiciary as a social institution. The external perspective looks at the judiciary from the perspective of its impact on the wider world.

Personal

If we start with the experience of the individual *judge*, the character of the tasks assigned and the career profile will be important. The attractiveness of the career and the opportunities that it makes available form a major part of any account of the judiciary. For instance, the ability of the career to permit social advancement, to provide personal fulfilment or to enable a person to manage family commitments is of high importance to many who prefer this career over that of private practice. The experiences among different social groups of life as a judge provide diverse perspectives on a common career, and this is a major factor in any account of the judicial culture.

The literature on such personal perspectives is limited. Only where judges are personages of the state, as in Britain or Sweden, or in the French Conseil d'Etat, is there much judicial biography which can offer insights into individual motivations. On the other hand, some countries, such as France, Germany and Italy, have a substantial literature of popular books and articles written by judges for a general public in which their individual motivations and perspectives on the judicial role are articulated. In addition, there are a few opinion surveys that have looked at the views of judges.

Sapir argued that the *locus* for a social culture is always the individual. The individual does the thinking and adopts attitudes, and if there is a group perspective then it has to be located in specific individuals who can be identified.[1] In studying institutional judicial culture, my focus is less on differences between individual judges than on the way individuals work within organisations. Individual testimonies provide evidence for an institutional culture, provided they are replicated sufficiently. These individual stories enable us to explain how the ideas and practices within organisations are developed and perpetuated.[2] Attitudes that individuals share from their activity on a common task form the basis for ascribing a culture to an institution. Naturally, within an organisation, there will be diversity. Individuals have a variety of opinions, so that the ascription of a particular culture to an organisation is really to take a point along the spectrum as 'typical' or representative. One is trying to identify a recurrent or pervasive set of characteristics.[3]

[1] See E. Sapir, *The Psychology of Culture. A Course of Lectures* (reconstructed and edited by Judith T. Irvine, Berlin 1994), 141.

[2] S. Derné, 'Cultural Conceptions of Human Motivation' in D. Crane (ed.), *The Sociology of Culture* (Oxford 1994), 267, 282.

[3] G. E. R. Lloyd, *Demystifying Mentalities* (Cambridge 1990), 5; Derné, 'Cultural Conceptions', above n. 2, 284–5.

Institutional

The institutional dimension focuses on the *judiciary* as both an organisation and a collective. Within a single legal system, there may be several collective groupings of judges, which need to be discussed separately (for example, in France civil, administrative and constitutional judges differ from commercial and labour court judges). As an institution of government, the judiciary has important relationships to political and social power. As a collective, it typically has a corporate life that relates to higher authorities (for instance the Ministry of Justice and a Judicial Council) and to society in general (such as through campaigns on particular issues and through the media). Corporatism involves both associative activity, through professional associations, and socialisation.

An institutional culture involves a set of beliefs and attitudes that give shared meaning to an activity. I would adopt the view of Garapon that one must include some unconscious features of the culture which explain why actions take place: 'To grasp a culture thus involves one in trying to formulate what is so obvious for the members that "it goes without saying". The best way of abstracting oneself from one's own culture is to look at it from the outside in confronting it with other cultures.'[4] The analysis of these implicit attitudes is a matter of interpretation. It has to be recognised that such analysis is a construction of the author. The reality of such an analysis depends on the degree of correspondence between it and the perception of the actors. Because these may be implicit rather than explicit, there is no suggestion that the actors would use the author's concepts to describe themselves and how they perceive what they are doing. All the same, there needs to be sufficient evidence that they could recognise themselves in the presentation without distortion.

External

The external perspective is interested in the *social and political impact* of judicial activity, both in court and outside. Political scientists find the relationship of the judges to politics to be of major importance, even if they are also concerned about the character of the judicial career. According to Guarnieri and Pederzoli, three factors affect the character of the judiciary – the judges themselves (especially how they are recruited), the legal system (especially the ease of access to the courts)

[4] A. Garapon, *Bien juger. Essai sur le rituel judiciaire* (Paris 1997), 150.

and the character of the political system.[5] For them, the priority is to be given to the political context: 'While judicial structures are important as a starting point in understanding why some judiciaries are more politically active than others, it is not just structures but political context (historical and contemporary) that ultimately determines the level of judicialisation in any country.'[6]

The classical area for examining the relationship of judges to politics is constitutional review. It forms the subject-matter of many studies of judges.[7] Political scientists have also focused on constitutional justice and its effect of 'judicialising' politics.[8] The first focus is on the way in which political issues can be contested in court, either by politicians or interest groups (e.g. through expanded rules on standing). A second focus pays attention to the impact of judicial review on the conduct of politics, either the juridification of political discourse and action, or the self-limitation which politicians undertake to avoid judicial sanctions.[9] Stone Sweet suggests that there is a fundamental difference in discourse and justification between law and politics: 'Legal discourse, that of judges and lawyers, tends to be rule-laden, and is structured by doctrinal norms and the demands of exegesis. Political discourse, that of politicians and political scientists, tends to be interest-laden and is conducted in the language of power or ideology.'[10] So the legal understanding of what occurs in judicial activity differs from a political science perspective on the political consequences of that activity.

Apart from this political dimension, there is also the perspective of the subjects of the law, in particular litigants. Friedman[11] considers this to be a major focus in understanding legal culture. His concern is both with the impact of law on individuals in their ordinary lives and with their picture of the law and of judges. Even though I have not adopted this 'popular legal culture' approach, the public opinion of the judiciary contributes an important part of the context in which the judicial culture develops. Judges are aware of the context in which they are called upon to consider issues, and they exercise a responsibility for the

5 C. Guarnieri and P. Pederzoli, *The Power of Judges. A Comparative Study of Courts and Democracy* (Oxford 2001) (hereafter 'Guarnieri and Pederzoli'), 3.
6 Ibid., 182–3.
7 See, for example, A. Stone Sweet, *Governing with Judges* (Oxford 2000).
8 C. N. Tate and T. Vallinder (eds.), *The Global Expansion of Judicial Power* (New York 1995), ch. 1.
9 M. Shapiro and A. Stone Sweet, *On Law, Politics and Judicialisation* (Oxford 2002), 189.
10 Ibid., 187.
11 L. M. Friedman, *Law and Society: An Introduction* (Englewood Cliffs, New Jersey, 1977), 76.

development of the law. So they will respond, where they consider it appropriate, to the demands of the external context. In addition, judges individually and collectively will take note of the regard in which they are held. This will affect initial recruitment – whether the job has an attractive status – and then the deportment of judges in performing their functions and in engaging with the media.

Clearly the political science and social perspectives on the consequences of judicial activity are important. My approach in this work will be more limited. It is valuable to use the insights of these other disciplines to understand how judicial institutions operate, including how the external context has an impact upon them. But my focus will be on the internal aspects of judicial institutions and cultures.

Why adopt an institutional perspective?

An institutional perspective is useful first because it relates to the nature of law, secondly because this is how one operates as a legal actor, and thirdly because it is how the law relates to the wider world.

The nature of law: law as institutional fact

The law is something more than simply a system of rules or legal standards. Those rules operate in a context of institutions, professions and values that form together a 'legal culture'.[12] Several prominent legal theorists[13] focus their analysis of law and legal culture as a set of ideas and attitudes held by lawyers or those subject to the law. But this is only part of the picture, since law is as much about practices, what people do, as about what they think. On the one hand, legal culture is a pattern of behaviour or an activity, which Bauman would describe as 'praxis'.[14] On the other hand, there is a set of ideas and values, which are communicated through language and signs that express attitudes and values towards the activity.[15] As praxis, legal culture is observable and as ideas it interprets reality.

The most helpful way to consider the relationship between the practical and ideological aspects of legal culture is to use Searle's conception

[12] J. Bell, *French Legal Cultures* (London 2001) (hereafter '*French Legal Cultures*'), ch. 1.

[13] See, e.g., R. Cotterrell, 'The Concept of Legal Culture' in D. Nelken (ed.), *Legal Cultures* (Aldershot 1997), 22–3 and 29, and L. M. Friedman, 'The Concept of Legal Culture: A Reply' in ibid., 35.

[14] Z. Bauman, *Culture as Praxis* (London 1973).

[15] See C. Geertz, *The Interpretation of Cultures* (1973, Basic Books edn, London 1993), 5; R. Williams, *Culture* (London 1981), 11–12.

of 'institutional fact'. An institutional fact is a fact which we invest with meaning within a particular set of social relations because it performs a particular function. Thus a green piece of paper having the right design may count as a 'dollar' in money. The paper has no intrinsic worth, but rules arising from social convention confer on it the value of money.[16] The same is true with law, for law is an institutional system. As MacCormick and Weinberger point out,[17] law is not a set of 'natural facts' that can be inspected directly. Rather it is an interpretative reality under which certain physical events take on a special significance. That assignment of meaning to natural facts depends on collective intentionality, not just the wishes or views of a particular individual observer or actor.[18] In law, agreed perceptions turn a set of facts into a 'trial' – the situation in which one person sits on a raised platform while another person stands silently in front of him and two others argue facing the person seated. The legal community creates the institutional reality which individuals can then use to explain events. But the institutional system and practices precede the ideas.

Applied to judicial practice, the institutional fact analysis would focus attention on the judge as an actor whose actions are invested with meaning by the legal community through shared understandings, some of which are expressed in legal norms. Performing correctly as a judge requires that an individual performs the appropriate actions and meets the expectations of the legal community, and in particular those who have a leading role in that community, which will include the judicial community. It is not enough that an individual judge decides according to what she thinks is right, she must decide according to the legal point of view.[19]

Operating as a legal actor

Because law is an institutional fact, becoming part of a legal culture, such as a judicial culture, makes it possible to understand and act from the appropriate point of view. As Zetterholm comments: 'The social

[16] J. R. Searle, *The Social Construction of Reality* (London 1995), 47.

[17] N. MacCormick and O. Weinberger, *An Institutional Theory of Law* (Dordrecht 1986), ch. 3.

[18] Searle, *Social Construction*, above n. 16, 46.

[19] Cf. the 'Magneaud phenomenon' where a judge applied his own sense of fairness, rather than the law, in dealing with a poor woman caught stealing bread to feed her child: Amiens, 22 April 1898, DP 1899.2.329, note Josserand; F. Gény, *Méthodes d'interprétation et sources du droit positif* (2nd edn, Paris 1919), vol. II, 287–307.

group creates, through the interaction of its members and their communication and acculturation processes, the coherence necessary for individual mental and cognitive development and day-to-day cooperation, and for the intergenerational transfer of knowledge.'[20]

Whatever individuals may think privately, in order to describe and to participate in a legal activity it is necessary to adopt a legal point of view. Hart labels this as an 'internal' point of view.[21] To do this it is necessary to act as part of a tradition. Our expectations of what is a 'legal' approach to a problem are set typically by a tradition. The approach of the judge is as an institutional legal actor, whose role and authority is defined not just by rules, but by an overall institutional culture.

A tradition is a body of norms and practices that is handed down. This practice of preserving and developing a tradition gives rise to a legal community, a group that will hand on and develop authentically the tradition, and induct new people into it. Taking part in the tradition is the way a person comes to understand the law from the legal point of view.[22] My argument has two aspects. First, as a general feature, in order to interpret legal texts or undertake legal practices in an effective manner, a person needs to become part of a tradition in which a text or idea becomes accessible. Being a judge involves being able to interpret legal texts and to perform legal procedures in ways that are considered appropriate not just by her, but by the legal community and, through it, by the outside world. Bourdieu emphasises more generally this *constitutive* function of culture – a culture makes it possible for a person to be able to interpret reality and to act.[23] Culture, in his view, involves both explicit training and implicit approaches and values. This analysis is in accord with the analysis of comparative lawyers such as Rudden who suggest that there are a range of features about the judiciary (which might apply to any lawyer) which have an impact on the kinds of assumptions that underlie judicial reasoning. For him, training and recruitment and even the place of work of a judge 'create a corpus of professional habits and assumptions which affects the

[20] S. Zetterholm (ed.), *National Cultures and European Integration. Exploratory Essays on Cultural Diversity and Common Policies* (Oxford 1994), 71.

[21] H. L. A. Hart, *The Concept of Law* (2nd edn, Oxford 1994), 89–91, 254–8 and N. MacCormick, *H. L. A. Hart* (London 1981), 37–40 on the hermeneutic point of view.

[22] J. Bell, 'Comparative Law and Legal Theory' in W. Krawietz, *Festschrift for R. S. Summers* (Berlin 1994), 19 at 29. See also M. Krygier, 'Law as Tradition' (1986) 5 *Law and Philosophy* 237 at 255.

[23] P. Bourdieu, 'Systems of Education and Systems of Thought' in M. F. D. Young (ed.), *Knowledge and Control* (London 1971), 189 at 192–3.

judicial method and, through it, the legal order, and does so all the more strongly for being so rarely made explicit'.[24] The second, more specific, feature of law is that reasoning develops by analogy, such that one needs to be part of the tradition before one can select appropriate other parts of the legal system which can serve as analogies in solving legal problems.

How law relates to the wider world

In making decisions and engaging in activities, judges will be acting in an institutional, and not a personal capacity. They are expected to fulfil a role. Of course, the outside world can examine the work of judges by focusing on individuals. One can try to explain or even predict the outcomes of cases by reference to the presence or absence of particular individuals.[25] But the authority of decisions depends not so much on these personal elements as on the quality of the justification given. At that point, one is examining how far the decisions and actions can be defended in terms of what is properly expected of a person in that judicial role. The expectation relates to the institutional role, rather than the personal qualities.

The extent to which the judiciary as an institution relates and is accountable to the wider community will vary from one legal system to another. But it would be right to suggest that the judiciary as a public service could not simply be a self-authenticating community. The nature of the problem in explaining this can be illustrated by taking two issues, accountability for individual judicial decisions and accountability for performance as a whole.[26]

Lasser[27] usefully points to the way in which judges tackle accountability for the outcome of individual judicial decisions through the giving of reasoned justifications. He sees a spectrum between systems. At the one extreme, the French have a bifurcation of justification with public decisions that are formalistic, typically collegiate and offer little

[24] B. Rudden, 'Courts and Codes in England, France and Soviet Russia' (1974) 48 *Tulane Law Review* 1010 at 1014.

[25] E.g. D. Robertson, *Judicial Discretion in the House of Lords* (Oxford 1998), especially chs. 1 and 2.

[26] A. Le Sueur distinguishes accountability for content, process, performance and probity: 'Developing Mechanisms for Judicial Accountability in the UK' (2004) 24 *Legal Studies* 73 at 81. The issue of probity is important, but generally handled by discipline in the systems discussed here, and process is usually seen as part of performance.

[27] M. Lasser, *Judicial Deliberations. A Comparative Analysis of Judicial Transparency and Legitimacy* (Oxford 2004), 14–20.

explanation of the substantive reasons for the result, but very elaborate and detailed private consideration of such issues. At the other extreme, the common-law judgment offers a unitary justification, incorporating substantive, policy-based reasons for decisions into personalised opinions. He suggests that the audiences for legitimacy are different at the two extremes. For the French, detailed justification is legitimated and accountable by its acceptance by a group of technical experts who know the issues in detail. For the common lawyers, the justification needs to gain acceptance not only by the community of lawyers, but also by the wider community, and so the language and content is open to inspection by both.

We will also see later that notions of judicial independence affect ideas of accountability for the overall performance of the judiciary. Such accountability will relate to matters such as the number of cases decided, public satisfaction with the process of reaching decisions, and the use of resources. In some systems, the autonomy of the judge relates not only to individual decisions, but also to performance issues. In very crude terms, the public purse is expected to pay for the judicial service and leave the judges to manage how it delivers justice. But judges usually only manage their own courts directly. The judicial service is then managed by either a constitutional or an executive agency. The overall accountability of judges for performance lies predominantly with the judicial service agency, which, in its turn, is accountable to the wider community, especially to the political community. Linked to this accountability comes also the possibility of political authorities issuing guidelines and controlling budgets for the agency. We will see that this area of accountability is of increasing importance.

Both these issues illustrate the way in which the external community is engaged by judicial activity, as an audience to which it relates, as an influence on its decisions and activities or as a body to whom the judiciary is responsible for what it undertakes.

Objections

The institutional point of view therefore focuses on the institutions which act as guardians of the legal tradition and of authentic actions in law, that decide what is appropriate or not. They will be involved in inducting, guiding and controlling actions in law. This will apply clearly to the judicial community.

In describing the legal community within which judicial decisions or activities take place, we need to map the roles which different individuals occupy, particularly the leading guardians and developers of a tradition. Outside that community, there are the other communities and reference groups who constitute the environment within which a legal community works and with whom it enters into dialogue about both its role and what it is trying to achieve.

There are at least three objections to this approach. The first is that the notion of a legal tradition or legal culture makes the law appear rather fixed in the past and inflexible, whereas we know that the rules of law change significantly and rapidly. Whilst it is true that the deep structure changes more slowly, it would be wrong to consider legal cultures as fixed. To understand the institutional aspects of law, in my book on *French Legal Cultures*[28] I argued that legal culture should be analysed in relation to something like Kolb's reflective learning model. This applies particularly when studying a profession like the judiciary, which is organised institutionally over a long period. The key elements of the analysis are that there is an *activity*, a set of tasks and procedures that define judicial work. The reflective practitioner engages in the activity and produces outputs. He or she then reflects on what has been done. The *reflection* by individuals and by the profession as a whole gives rise to *norms and standards* for how the activity should be conducted in future. This structure of organisational learning does not deny change, but seeks to understand how deeply change operates.

It might be objected that this description of legal communities is too sealed within a particular jurisdiction. That is not the intention. Of course, in rapidly changing societies, legal systems increasingly face similar problems and are influenced by political, business and administrative trends in ideas which cut across jurisdictional boundaries. Particular legal and judicial systems are open to outside influences, but they retain their own distinctive characteristics, approaches and values. Systems are often searching for ideas, rather than authorities in the other systems, and undertake their own selection of what is suitable.[29]

It might also be argued that the approach gives too much attention to the views of lawyers, the official view of the activity of judges. Is not the perspective of the non-legal actor a better measure of the significance of what judges do? In my previous book I argued that 'understanding the

[28] *French Legal Cultures*, 21–2.

[29] See V. Gessner, 'Global Legal Interaction and Legal Cultures' (1994) 7 *Ratio Juris* 132; W. Twining, *Globalisation and Legal Theory* (London 2000), 189–93, 252–3.

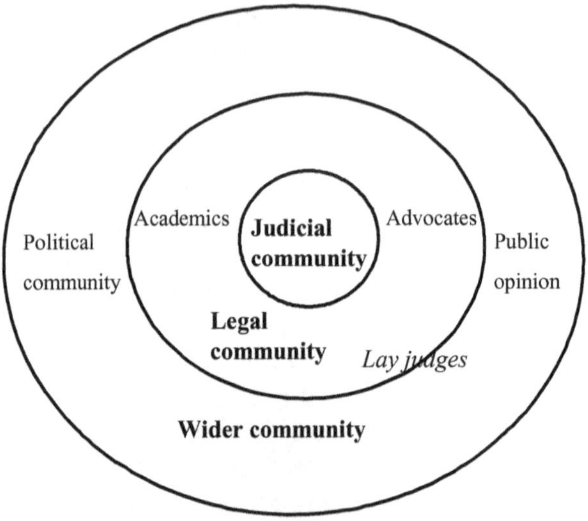

Figure 1.1 Place of the judicial community.

culture of the official system has some value in terms of explaining what officials and other legal actors are trying to achieve, even if it does not help to explain the strategic use of law by institutions and individuals who are supposedly subject to that law'.[30] That applies to this work as well.

The core method

The core method is illustrated by figure 1.1. The judiciary is located within a nest of communities, each of which is studied in turn. It focuses on the internal structure and dynamics of the judicial community in a particular country. The judiciary is then studied in terms of its primary cognate audience, the legal community, which is composed, in particular, of professional lawyers, called 'advocates' for short, and doctrinal legal writers, typically the academic community. Finally, it is examined in terms of the wider community. Clearly here the non-professional judiciary acts as a bridge, as in some systems it represents the wider community. For this reason, there will be special attention paid to lay judges. The other major areas of the wider community are the political community, for whom constitutional adjudication is particularly important, and any evidence of the wider public opinion on the judiciary.

[30] *French Legal Cultures*, 14.

Inside the judicial community

In studying the institution of the judiciary, it is necessary to look first within the judicial community. That community sets standards for judicial activity and inducts new judges into their role. It is the most immediate influence in defining what it is to be a judge. The first group of features that define the judge in this context are structural and relate to the nature of the career – who becomes a judge and by what process; how judicial activity and personnel are managed; and how they are socialised into a community. The second group relates to the values and history that shape the way in which judges perceive their role. The third group of factors relates to the roles that judges perform.

Career

The character of the judicial career affects both who becomes a judge and how he or she operates both as an individual and as part of a group. The first issue that shapes the judicial career is whether the judiciary is professional or lay, and whether the professional judge is recruited as an initial career or laterally from among other established legal professionals. Socialisation, through common training or collective action, is important in producing a common outlook among judges, as are common career opportunities, either for promotion or for diverse non-judicial activities. Finally, management structures affect the freedom of judges individually and collectively to pursue their own views about the needs of justice.

Professionalism

Within most legal systems, there is a range of different kinds of judge, with different experiences. There are two spectra on which a particular kind of judge can be located. One spectrum focuses on whether the judge is professional or lay. At one end of this spectrum is the full-time, professional career judge, the classical continental European model. At the other end of the spectrum, there is the lay person serving as a judge either in an area of her special expertise (e.g. commercial law) or as a representative of society (e.g. in criminal cases). In the middle of the spectrum is the lay judge. The use of lay people as judges has distinct rationales from the use of professional lawyers. As I have argued elsewhere,[31] at a very general level, the involvement of lay people offers an element of popular participation as a corrective to formal legal rationality. The law must reflect not only adherence to formal legality, but

[31] See J. Bell. 'Lay Judges' (2002) 5 *Cambridge Yearbook of European Law* 293 at 294–6.

also substantive standards of fairness. This is shown in the justifications offered in different countries. For example, the 2002 Swedish official report on lay judges[32] identified three contributions of lay judges:

- to guarantee effectiveness by keeping judicial decisions in line with social values;
- to maintain confidence of citizens in the effectiveness of courts;
- to keep the interest of the public in the effectiveness of justice by collaboration of lay people.

The lay judiciary serves to ensure both the effectiveness and the legitimacy of the judicial system, including as a check on the power of professional judges. At the same time, it has to be recognised that not all non-professional judges are lay people – they are often lawyers from a different professional background.

The second spectrum differentiates within the professional judiciary between what Guarnieri and Pederzoli describe as 'bureaucratic' and 'professional' models.[33] Although the 'professional' model is usually described with reference to the common law, there are a number of features that increasingly fittingly describe the lateral entry routes into continental European judiciaries. They distinguish these models as set out in figure 1.2.

The concept of the judge as 'civil servant', which is what is meant by 'bureaucrat' in this context, focuses on the idea that the judge has a lifelong career, which often has a low profile. The structure of the public service, with possibilities for career breaks, makes it attractive. The 'professional' route of lateral recruitment of judges in later career with prior experience in another profession has become a common feature of legal systems, even those with a tradition of initial career judges. Expertise as administrators, prosecutors or advocates often provides a different experience, as well as extra numbers to serve as judges. The common law has also begun to develop longer-term judicial careers or career paths. Thus the effective pattern of becoming a judge is changing. All the same, the ethos of the judiciaries may well remain within the paradigms which Guarnieri and Pederzoli have described. In a system like France, which is seeing increasing variety in routes of entry to the judiciary, it remains true that the senior positions go to those who have undertaken the career track, 'bureaucratic' judiciary. By contrast, in a

[32] *Framtidens nämndemän* (Betänkande från Nämndemannakommittén) SOU 2002:61 (Stockholm 2002), 53.

[33] Guarnieri and Pederzoli, 66–7.

Bureaucratic	Professional
Selection by exam at a young age	Appointment after professional experience
Training primarily within the judiciary	Experience as legal expert
Hierarchy determines organisational roles and promotion	No formal system for advancement
Generalist approach to tasks	Judges recruited for specific tasks and promotion not widespread
Weak guarantees of judicial independence	Strong guarantees of professional independence

Figure 1.2 Guarnieri and Pederzoli's models.

common-law country like England, the senior positions are still going to those who have been successful at the Bar, rather than those who have risen through the various ranks of the lower judiciary.

Part-time working has some importance. Within many continental civil service systems, judges are able to opt to work part-time for a substantial number of years. This often has the effect of facilitating the position of judges with family responsibilities, frequently women, even though it will slow down their career advancement. A different form of part-time working in both continental and common-law systems enables practitioners in other legal professions to work as judges on a part-time basis, whilst keeping their roles in private practice. This is seen by the English system predominantly as a stepping stone to participation in the full-time bench. In other systems, the part-time judgeship, such as in the case of the French *juge de proximité* or the Spanish *juez de paz*, is just another kind of judicial role which does not lead to a fuller judicial role. Such judges are far less integrated than the part-time career judge in those countries or the aspirant recorder in England.

Recruitment

In examining who becomes a judge, it is necessary to examine both the process of recruitment and the character of those who are recruited. Judges are universally appointed on 'merit', but the meaning of this term and the processes to achieve such an appointment vary. In particular, there is a tension between the conceptions of judging as a job or as a public office that has important implications for appointments, both for how far judges control them and for the role of politicians.

On the one hand, considering judging as a *job*, the priority criterion of 'merit' is professional expertise. On the other hand, a judge holds a *public office*, which carries responsibility as an organ of government. Now the latter requires qualities that can be assessed by a range of non-professionals. The key to success in a judicial appointments system is the recognition of the relative importance of these two conceptions of the judicial role at different levels within the judicial hierarchy.

Judging as a job The more that judging is seen as a career in which one spends a substantial part of a working life, the more it is appropriately viewed as a job. By all means, it is a profession with substantial responsibilities, but it is a job like many others. At first instance, much of that work will be routine – divorces, bankruptcies, debt actions, possession actions. There is little of high policy, but a lot of work with great importance to the parties and those who depend on them. Deciding these matters, which are often uncontested, in a sensitive and professional manner is a demanding task, but often routine. The main qualities required for the role would be expertise, sound judgement, and a good manner in dealing with the public. Just as in other professional activities, it might be thought that appointment by members of the profession is the best way to secure competent performance. But if we examine these ideas more closely, it is clear that others can take an informed view.

Judging as a public office The force of the rhetoric on judicial independence focuses not on judging as a professional job, but on the constitutional task on providing justice impartially and effectively, carrying the confidence of the people. Particularly in relation to senior positions, when difficult or controversial legal issues come to centre stage that may have consequences for society and for relations with other branches of government, professional legal knowledge is necessary, but not sufficient. The judgements required will often involve going beyond the established rules, and the interpretation offered or the guidelines laid down will be ones for which the judge must take more personal responsibility. The judge here is engaging in debates that have more social and even political dimensions. It is here that the concept of the judge's role as a public office comes to the fore. The task is to exercise a part of governmental power in an independent and responsible manner. In this context, the expertise required of the judge goes beyond professional legal competence. This has implications for the skills that are included in the notion of 'merit' when assessing a person's suitability, and it affects the composition of the body who should make the decision. In particular, it suggests that non-lawyers, including politicians, ought to have a say in who is appointed.

The two conceptions have implications both for the skills that candidates for initial appointment and promotion should demonstrate, and for the appointment process as a whole. The conception of judging as a public office has particular implications for senior appointments, and often leads to a difference in the appointments criteria and processes at this level within the judicial career. The various chapters in this book will examine the recruitment procedures in the different countries.

Appointment processes

Most European judicial appointment procedures privilege technical professional competences, because they are focusing on appointments of career judges to posts which involve routine justice (which can sometimes turn out to be very controversial). In his study, Oberto[34] offers a typology of four systems of selecting judges: (1) nomination by the executive; (2) election; (3) co-option by the judiciary; (4) appointment by a committee consisting of judges and academics following a competitive process. The typology looks clear, but, in fact, systems make use of a mix. Indeed, both Germany and France use all of them. Election is usually confined to the choice of non-lawyer judges, such as in labour or commercial courts, so it is worth noting here the main ways in which judges are involved.

In many countries, judicial appointments and promotions are made by the executive, for example in England, in many German Länder, in France and for the highest Swedish courts, but judges may be involved in *advisory bodies*. In Germany, there is a split between those Länder which have a judicial appointments committee and those which have appointments by the Minister of Justice. In either case, judges are involved in an advisory capacity through their local representative organ (the *Präsidialrat*), a local judges' council. This will offer an advisory opinion on the suitability of the candidate, focusing particularly on its knowledge of the individual's professional performance.[35] In France, the *Conseil*

[34] G. Oberto, *Recrutement et formation des magistrats en Europe. Etude comparative* (Paris 2003), 13.

[35] See below p. 113.

supérieur de la Magistrature has a stronger position. It gives its opinion on the qualifications of candidates proposed by the Minister (and on other applicants), can hear candidates and can give a negative opinion (which is binding in the case of judicial appointments, as opposed to those to the posts of prosecutor). It also recommends appointments at the senior level, the Cour de cassation. The advisory bodies perform mainly a *vetting*, rather than a *recommending* function.

In other judiciaries, judges may be involved in *decision-making bodies*. Europe has two main kinds of such executive body – a Judiciary Council and an independent Courts Administration Agency. In the former, as in Italy, the judicial involvement is focused on the judicial career.[36] In the latter, as in Spain and Sweden, judicial appointments and promotions are part of the portfolio of an organisation responsible for managing the judicial career, resources and the court system as a whole.

Who is appointed?

Important questions when examining recruitment are what type of person is attracted to the position and who is appointed. The profiles of judges that will be seen in the following chapters will be different. There are different questions to be asked about professional judges and lay judges. In relation to professional judges, the interesting questions concern the attractiveness of the judicial role, compared with other legal professional or even civil service roles. What motivates a person to apply to be a judge and to stay in the profession? Personal motivations are varied, so the research is concerned with general features of the different judicial careers that may be distinctive. There is little published research on this and so I have used three sources of information. In the first place, I have talked to a number of judges in each of the countries, as well to the relevant ministry or judicial agency or judicial union in order to ascertain their insights. Over a number of years, I have also helped to run multinational judicial workshops, which have given opportunities to confirm the solidity of these impressions. The information is largely anecdotal and will rarely be noted in this book as evidence for propositions. Secondly, sociological research has been conducted in some countries, particularly on women in legal professions, and this has provided additional support for views on the motivations of judges. Finally, patterns do emerge from the statistical data produced on the judiciary by the ministries

[36] Guarnieri and Pederzoli, 52–60.

or agencies responsible for judicial appointments and promotions. On the whole, the interpretation of these data is incomplete, but there are the beginnings of insights which correlate quite well with the other two sources.

Analysis of the social composition of the judiciary is also patchy. Empirical research is more common in the Anglo-Saxon world than in continental Europe. So the information available is incomplete. Ethnicity is a particular problem, because most ministries to which I have talked state that they could not seek such information – all citizens are equal. In many countries which do not permit dual nationality, ethnic minority residents do not have local nationality and so are ineligible for judicial posts. It is noticeable that the issue of ethnicity came to the fore in Sweden only when the nationality law was changed to permit dual nationality and thus to facilitate those from ethnic minorities becoming nationals. Thus, regrettably, little is said in this book on ethnicity. My consideration of diversity will focus on two reported features, first the position of women in the judiciary and second the extent to which the judiciary is a meritocratic elite. By and large, it is easier to analyse the judiciary as an educational elite relative to other legal professions than to say much about the social representativeness of the judiciary. Given that high educational qualifications will be a prerequisite for entry into the judiciary, it can be expected that judges, like other lawyers, will come more frequently from middle-class backgrounds.

More can be said about the social representativeness of the lay judiciary. A key justification for many lay judiciaries is that they can represent their communities. Accordingly, there have been studies in France, Germany, Sweden and England on who becomes a lay judge. As will be seen, there are very similar patterns of problems in recruiting voluntary judges, despite the different ways in which they are recruited, trained and deployed in the different systems.

Increasingly, continental European systems are recruiting not just from among recent graduates, but also from among professionals with a number of years of experience in legal activity or in the public administration. In part, this is a recognition that being a professional judge requires a blend of expertise and qualities that cannot just be found among those who wish to dedicate their lives to being judges. In part, this is simply because the pool of graduate recruits is too small to meet demand. It is necessary to examine what kind of person is attracted by such a mid-career change.

Promotion and mobility

Where individuals occupy posts in the judiciary over a long period of time, there need to be opportunities to experience different kinds of activity. The facility which makes this possible will often determine the kinds of people who occupy judicial roles and the relationship between the judiciary and other professions, legal and other. The existence of promotions procedures also has an influence on management structures. Both of these aspects are considered later in this chapter.

The organisation of the judiciary

The organisation of the judiciary is an important feature of the character of the institution and the judicial career. As a professional organisation, a judiciary has to be conceived not just as individuals judging, but as an organised and administrative unit.[37] There are two organisational features of some general significance: the existence of a unitary judicial corps or a judiciary fragmented across several corps, and the management structure of the judiciary.

Judicial corps

It matters whether one has a unified judiciary within a jurisdiction (as in Sweden) or whether the judiciary is divided into a number of groups, as in France and, to some extent, in Germany. Where the judiciary is basically generalist, then it is relatively easy to mix a range of activities over a career, and it is possible to talk of *the* judiciary within a particular legal order. Where the judiciary is divided into constitutional, administrative, and civil and criminal branches, then being a judge in each can be very different, and one cannot make straightforward statements about the judiciary in that legal order. A unified corps of judges recruited in relatively similar ways and performing common tasks, even with specialisms, creates a sense of identity and common responsibility. By contrast, as in France, a divided set of judiciaries, each performing different tasks within different organisations, can lead to a plurality of identities and responsibilities.

The unity of the judicial corps is also affected by the concentration or decentralisation of the judicial activity. Where activity is concentrated, for example in a capital city, then this may attract certain groups of people to become judges and, in particular, it will make it easier for judges

[37] For a similar analysis of courts, see H. Fix-Fierro, *Courts, Justice and Efficiency* (Oxford 2003), 139.

to operate two-career families. Where the work is decentralised then this may cause other kinds of behaviour. For instance, in order to gain promotion at an early age, a judge may be advised to seek a promotion in a remoter regional centre, which is less sought after, in order to have a good profile of experience to attain the next rung on the promotions ladder. Now such a pattern of behaviour is less likely among many women judges, whose mobility is circumscribed by domestic considerations. As a result, the promotion of women is typically hampered.[38] So even if there is a majority of women in the lower ranks of the judiciary, this is not replicated in the senior ranks, or even among applicants for senior ranks.[39] Certainly, where the judiciary is a national service, as in France and Spain, then mobility between regions is easier than in Germany, where the judge belongs to a region.

Management and governance

The management and governance of the judiciary have an important impact on its sense of identity and independence. While governance sets the broad structures of responsibility and accountability, management systems are very important in the everyday lives of judges and how they operate. This is reflected in both the internal and the external management structures. Within professional groups, such as judges, there is usually a tension between collegiality among fellow professionals and hierarchy. Often as a function of size, but also as a result of adopting a civil service culture, many judiciaries have a strong hierarchical pattern. Judges are assigned tasks and are under orders. As professionals, especially ones with claims to judicial independence and to occupy public offices, they will resist this hierarchical approach.

Internal authority will be exercised by judicial hierarchical superiors. The importance of superiors for appraisal, promotion and assignment of tasks is relevant for defining the character of a judiciary, and for the way in which judges relate to each other. To the extent that senior judges exercise managerial roles in the deployment of judges, then, hierarchical authority prevails over collegiality. This is even more stressed where, as in most countries with a career judiciary, regular performance appraisal is conducted or references are required from senior judges to establish the suitability of a judge for promotion. In relation to this internal authority, collective action by judges will wish to secure

[38] See below pp. 368–9.
[39] See especially the experiences of France and Sweden, below pp. 54, 190 and 247.

participation and representation at local level. Furthermore, this kind of managerialism identifies a new role for professional judges and offers a different career path from focusing mainly on adjudication.

External authority is exercised by those who are constitutionally or administratively responsible for the judiciary and the court service. Europe has two main kinds of executive body – the Ministry of Justice and an independent Courts Administration Agency. The decision-maker in many cases is the Minister of Justice or, for some roles such as judicial appointments, formally the head of state. In appointments, this maintains a view that something more than technical expertise is required for the role of judge. So, in Sweden, the senior judicial appointments are made by the Government. In relation to the management of justice, the authority of the Minister stresses the political character of the responsibility for delivering a fair system of justice.

Many European countries have given judges a greater role in the administration of the court system and its resourcing. Judicial independence and judicial self-government are often linked.[40] Article 6 of the European Judges Charter provides that 'The administration of the judiciary must be carried out by a body that is representative of the Judges and independent of any other authority.' For instance, in Spain, the Consejo General del Poder Judicial (the Judiciary Agency), composed of judges and politicians, makes the appointments and runs the judicial side of the court system as a constitutional agency, with another agency dealing with court administration. The English system has the latter, but not the former type of agency.[41] This idea of judicial self-government is gaining ground in countries like Denmark, whose Courts Administration Agency is responsible to Parliament for the whole organisation of justice, within the budget given by the Parliament. By contrast, in Sweden, there is a distinct agency responsible for the judicial system, including the recruitment and management of judges, composed of non-government members, some of whom are judges. It operates like any executive agency of government, with the Ministry of Justice providing its framework of principles and a budget. But then it can decide how it operates, subject to making an annual report. The agency is also involved in performance appraisal. Whether the agency is a constitutional body as in Spain or an administrative body as in Sweden,

[40] See below p. 29 and Lord Woolf, 'The Rule of Law and a Change in the Constitution' [2004] CLJ 317 at 322–3.

[41] See below pp. 321–5.

the emphasis is on judicial independence from the routine of ordinary politics.

Management of promotion is important, especially where the career lasts a long time, but there is a tension between individual and institutional imperatives and strategies that has to be managed in the running of the judicial system. Individual judges need to be assured of a transparent promotions process that offers clear targets and criteria. At the same time, judicial independence requires that judges are not simply rewarded for decisions favourable to powerful interests. Judicial management also needs flexibility to appoint the best staff. Judicial independence is normally protected by a guarantee of immovability – a judge cannot be transferred against her wishes. Promotions policies, on the other hand, create incentives for people to move to ensure that the local court system does not become too set in its ways. Mobility can be achieved either through promotion, or because judges find a secondment or transfer of functions gives them an interesting career opportunity. A tension between stability and mobility arises both for the individual, who may have domestic reasons for staying in the same location, and for the judicial administration, which needs to make use of good people in other locations. This is not the only problem of career management. Regular appraisal systems are part of a civil service structure and are increasingly applied to judges. The scores on appraisal are often used in promotion decisions. Few countries have gone so far as Italy in allowing judges to progress in grade whilst performing the same functions in the same location.[42] That system avoids a serious scrutiny of individual merits and performance in judicial promotions. On the other hand, appraisal creates power in the judicial hierarchy and in the nominating authority (often political) that makes the final appointments and assignment of tasks, often based on such performance reports. There is a serious danger that the concern to avoid undue interference with judicial independence and not to be seen to be influencing judicial decisions may lead to an abdication of responsibility on the part of those responsible for the judiciary to examine individual performance and ensure proper accountability. This abdication is most commonly seen where promotions are based predominantly on seniority. Such an approach does not favour the advancement of women or younger judges. Seniority looks at a rather narrow aspect of merit and also does not pay much attention to the overall needs of the system.

[42] Guarnieri and Pederzoli, 57–8.

Socialisation

The processes by which individuals are bonded together as part of a legal community are important for its effectiveness, especially in order that they share a common outlook on their role. There are two features that the research examines in this respect: the processes of initial and continuing training, and the existence of professional associations and networks.

Training serves not only to prepare judges for their future work, but also to establish common understandings among judges as a social community. Guarnieri and Pederzoli comment that 'The means of educating and training new judges, whether in special schools as in France or extensive on-the-job training as in Germany, partially compensate for the recruits' lack of practical legal experience. More significantly, their professional socialisation is achieved almost exclusively within the judiciary.'[43] Judicial colleges clearly establish common understandings and create networks between judges of the same generation and those who train them. Either as part of this training or as part of a post-training apprenticeship, placements in courts and other legal institutions serve also to mould recruits into the judicial or legal community. This initial formation contrasts with the socialisation of judges recruited laterally who already have a different prior professional formation. They will have their existing formation, and will usually be required to do less formal training before starting work. For them, initial postings, usually to a collegial court, will provide socialisation by training on the job. Judicial training at later points may also serve not only to ensure commonality of understandings, but also as informal networking that consolidates a common sense of identity. As will be seen later, even without a judicial college, prior and continuing training events run by the English Judicial Studies Board perform a similar role.[44] It is all the more effective because it holds events for the entire judiciary from time to time. Whereas that Board also provides initial and continuing training taking a substantial amount of time for lay magistrates, there is far less official training offered for lay judges in many of the other systems studied. Here the training is often voluntary and is organised by associations set up by the lay judges themselves.

In many judiciaries, another important aspect of the collective life of the judicial community is the role of judicial unions or professional associations. The relationships of the judiciary to judicial management

[43] Ibid., 43. [44] Below p. 319.

authorities provide one reason for collective action and the creation of associations. In some countries, typically those with a strong Ministry of Justice or Courts Administration Agency and a civil service judiciary, the unions can play an important role in representing the interests of judges to hierarchical superiors. They may well be welcomed as part of the collective bargaining structure, but relations can also be confrontational, especially where the unions have political differences with the government of the day. Associations serve the purposes of representing the judiciary as a body of professionals and expressing their collective interests not only to local and central management, but also in wider political debate on matters such as law reform and civil liberties. But the associations also contribute to professional development and socialisation.

The existence of professional associations was a twentieth-century phenomenon. Many legal systems started off with a single judges professional association which represented judges in discussions with government about terms and conditions of employment as well as the work of the courts. But elections within the judiciary of members to their judicial appointments commission have caused different views to surface. Most starkly, these are reflected in Italy by different 'correnti' or currents of opinion, each of which succeeds in getting its members elected to the supreme judicial council.[45] In France and Spain, the single judges association has fragmented into several clearly political associations, which compete to obtain nominations.[46] On an election by proportional representation, the different judges' views are reflected. Such judicial associations are even more active when the judges council (or Courts Administration Agency) has an important role in allocating resources, as in Spain. Here priorities for justice are a legitimate subject for debate, and disagreement among the judges and different conceptions of justice are reflected in the different orientations of associations. In Sweden and Germany, where politicians have a stronger role, these judges associations exist but are less markedly political.

The reasons for the existence of professional associations demonstrate the importance of a kind of internal 'judicial politics' in setting out and debating different views on the character of justice. Not all countries have this phenomenon. The French members of the Conseil d'Etat are

[45] For a list see Guarnieri and Pederzoli, 56, table 1.3; C. Guarnieri, 'Appointment and Career of Judges in Continental Europe: The Rise of Judicial Self-Government' (2004) 24 *Legal Studies* 169 at 187.

[46] Below pp. 63 and 195–6.

sufficiently few in number and close to power not to need this way of articulating views and having them heard. They are already part of the elite. In England, the existence of the Bar, senior judges sitting as members of the legislature, the House of Lords, and the role of the Lord Chancellor as a senior judge have all contributed to the absence of professional associations among the higher levels of the judiciary, though these structures are all subject to radical change as this book is being written. To some extent, the existence of professional associations of judges is a sign of relative powerlessness in the face of those in authority. The existence of such judicial associations can be viewed as both a symptom of judicial self-perception and a way of life for the judiciary.

Values: independence

The conception of judicial independence adopted in a particular judiciary is an important indicator of its place within the institutions of government. It is complex and involves the status and ways of working of judges as much as the formal mechanisms by which judges are appointed and removed. As I have explained in more detail elsewhere,[47] judicial independence involves characteristics such as impartiality and political neutrality far more centrally than ideas such as the irremovability of judges.[48] The independence of the *judiciary* focuses on governance issues – the extent to which the judiciary controls its affairs in terms of appointment, dismissal and career management, as well as in running the court system. The independence of *individual judges* pays attention to the operational freedom of the judge from the dictates of both external actors (such as ministers or the media) and internal actors (such as hierarchical superiors).[49] These are both issues of substance and of perception about how judges relate to power. The independence of the *judiciary as a whole* focuses not only on these issues, but also on its ability to do justice according to law, as it sees this.

[47] J. Bell, 'The Judge as Bureaucrat' in J. Eekelaar and J. Bell, *Oxford Essays in Jurisprudence – Third Series* (Oxford 1987), 51–3; J. Bell, 'Judicial Cultures and Judicial Independence' (2001) 4 *Cambridge Yearbook of European Legal Studies* 47.

[48] For example, the formal guarantee of judicial irremovability contained in the English Act of Settlement of 1701 was merely intended to make the judges independent of the King, not of Parliament, and certainly not to be a free actor as the third branch of government: S. Shetreet, *Judges on Trial. A Study of the Appointment and Accountability of the English Judiciary* (Amsterdam 1976), 8.

[49] See Guarnieri and Pederzoli, 21–2. R. Stevens, *The English Judge* (Oxford 2002), 79 argues that judicial independence in England is predominantly of the individual judge, rather than of the judiciary as a collective.

Freedom from interference

The idea of freedom from interference is the longest-standing idea, but it involves a number of issues. Interference in individual cases must be distinguished from interference in the judicial career, notably appointment and dismissal. In this latter area, political involvement in individual appointments has to be distinguished from political direction of the judicial and courts system as a whole.

The idea of judicial independence started from the issue of the removal of judges by politicians. The Latin model, termed the 'High Council of the Judiciary', developed by degrees from judges and others controlling the disciplining of judges, to involvement in judicial appointments and promotions, to judicial dominance of all these procedures. The term was invented in France to describe the idea of an institution which would protect the independence of the judiciary by dealing with dismissals. It arose in 1883 as a reaction to the most severe purges of judges that century (1879–80), conducted there by a democratic government, whose concern was the loyalty of the judges to the system.[50]

The involvement of such a council in judicial appointments was an idea developed in Portugal before the First World War and was operated in relation to Spanish judicial appointments and promotions by 1917. However, this was never an institution which worked effectively much before the end of the Second World War. The Latin concept of a judicial council mainly composed of judges failed obviously to work in the face of dictatorships, keen to ensure that their loyalists were represented in all positions of authority. It only works within a context in which the ruling elite is prepared to accept some restriction on its power.

France and Italy created judicial councils in their post-dictatorship constitutions of 1946 and 1948 respectively. The purpose was to insulate the judiciary from political interference and to ensure that one of the major institutions of society was not capable of being manipulated by anti-democratic forces (as it had been in the very recent past). But there was a major difference in the two arrangements. For the French, the Council was essentially a body to decide on judicial discipline, but only to advise on judicial appointments. The decision about appointments remained with the Government. The Council was composed of a mix of both politicians and judges. The Italians moved more quickly to a body

[50] C. Charle, 'Etat et magistrats. Les origins d'une crise prolongée' (1993) *Actes de la recherche en sciences sociales* 39.

wholly nominated by the judiciary.[51] In part, this was a compromise to deal with a politically divided country. This strongly independent institution has gained favour in a number of countries emerging from dictatorship, such as Spain and Portugal.

The problem in Germany was different. The experience of dictatorship led to strengthening judicial involvement without giving anything approaching judicial autonomy. The past concern was that judges had been too remote and unresponsive to the increasingly democratic character of society.[52] Most judicial appointments are made by ministries, after the advice of the appointment committees composed of judges and politicians, or at least the local judicial Präsidialrat.

In more recent years, pressure towards the consolidating of judicial independence and judicial control over the justice system has been influenced by judges' experience of the criminal prosecutions of politicians for corruption (political or financial), for example the Italian 'clean hands' investigations by Judge Del Pietro.[53] Judges have come under great pressure from the politicians to drop charges or they find that politicians use their powers in an abusive way. There is obviously a concern that politicians will seek to take revenge on judges who take unpopular decisions.

Concerns about systematic or individual pressure on judges by politicians are not hypothetical. At the same time, they do not preclude legitimate political questions about the direction in which a judge's exercise of power might take society (politics with a small 'p'). In a divided society, there are different views about the way in which society should go. Having judges who are aware of these and even who reflect together a variety of tendencies in society may be one way in which judicial decisions can come to terms with the political dimensions of decisions. As has been noted, these are reasons why most systems include politicians in the judicial appointments process.[54]

In brief, freedom from improper political interference in individual cases or in the career paths of particular judges does not necessarily justify banishing politicians from the whole process. Banishing politicians from the process does not banish political issues. They will surface in debate about the composition of the judiciary, and might be reflected in

[51] Guarnieri and Pederzoli, 52–7.

[52] H. H. Rupp, 'Die Bindung des Rechters an das Gesetz' NJZ 1973, 1769 at 1770; also H. Rottleutner, 'The Conformity of the Legal Staff' (1993) *Rechtstheorie, Beiheft 15*, 441. For the continuing importance of the contrast between the *Obrigkeitsstaat* idea and democracy, see J. Limbach, *Im Namen des Volkes* (Stuttgart 1999), 10.

[53] Guarnieri and Pederzoli, 175–6.

[54] Above pp. 16–17.

a role for associations of like-minded judges and lawyers who will seek to secure representation of their ideas in the judiciary through membership of the judicial appointments commission or Courts Administration Agency.

Independence to serve justice

Judicial independence also involves a freedom to take responsibility for serving justice. It is here that the public office concept has its strongest impact. Judges are responsible first to their oath to dispense justice. This idea of judicial independence goes beyond judges being free to determine the list of cases for hearing. In many European countries, there has been a move to give judges a greater role in the administration of the court system and its resourcing. This has been noted in discussing judicial management.[55] In this context, judicial independence and judicial self-government are often linked.[56] All the same, the concern has really moved away from the classical areas of judicial independence (mainly protecting judges from political interference) to issues of the effectiveness of the judicial system.[57]

Roles

The character of the judiciary is affected significantly by the tasks that it has to perform. As I have suggested elsewhere, a legal culture is shaped by professional reflection on the tasks that the law performs – there are rules that define the tasks and how they are to be performed, there is the performance of those tasks and then there is reflection by legal actors and non-legal actors on the outcomes, which may lead, in turn, to a redefinition of the tasks and how they are to be reformed.[58] The nature of the tasks affects the character of the role. Of particular note is the issue of creativity, because this impacts on the standing of the judiciary in legal development in relation to other actors in the legal community and also in relation to the political community.

Judicial tasks: routine

Even if the institutional arrangements dealing with the organisation and career of judges have developed in a particular way, the actual

[55] Above p. 22.

[56] See the German judges union's resolution of 15 November 2002 on its website: http://www.drb.de/pages/html/texte/beschluss_sv.html.

[57] L. Philip in T. S. Renoux, *Les Conseils supérieurs de la magistrature en Europe* (Paris 1999), 61.

[58] *French Legal Cultures*, 21–2.

performance of judges will be strongly affected by the operational context in which the judges have to work. This context is composed of a number of elements, but it is worth highlighting perhaps three: the material conditions, the workload, and the interactions with legal and non-legal actors.

The character of the judicial role depends heavily on where tasks fall along the spectrum from routine to scope for individual imagination and initiative. The processing of large numbers of routine cases that involve barely more than registering a divorce, a debt, a mortgage default or a bankruptcy is very different from having to decide an issue on a disputed point of law or one that has wide social ramifications. The workload of the courts in which judges work provides a good indicator of where on the spectrum a particular judicial role lies. Clearly, in lower courts with hundreds of thousands of largely uncontested cases, or where the outcome is overwhelmingly a conviction or a divorce or a repossession order for a house, the work is routine. Courts with very few cases that have been filtered for importance play a totally different social role. Some supreme courts, such as the House of Lords in England, have this latter character, with barely seventy substantive cases to decide a year. Other supreme courts, like the Cour de cassation in France, deal with about 30,000 cases a year, many of which are routine rejections. In order to find the small group of creative cases, it is necessary to examine the work of the highest formations of that court, the Assemblée plénière and the chambres réunies, where one finds a similarly small number of cases to the House of Lords. A further indicator of the character of the role is the number of judges involved in a decision. Although continental courts have traditionally favoured panels of judges, they are increasingly resorting to single judges to decide routine cases, or at least to delegating the bulk of the work to a single judge.

Not all lower court judges are predominantly performing routine tasks. For example, in family and children's cases, the judge may have an ongoing involvement in the affairs of particular households in ensuring maintenance, access to children, or the improvement of a child in need of special measures. Even in criminal cases, sentencing will not always be a routine and bureaucratic task. Here the work is described by Ost as that of a trainer, rather than a dispute settler.[59] In such circumstances,

[59] F. Ost, 'Juge-pacificateur, juge-arbitre, juge-entraîneur. Trois modèles de justice' in Ph. Gérard, F. Ost and M. Van de Kerchove, *Fonction de juger et pouvoir judiciaire* (Brussels 1983), 1.

the judge may be able to exercise more imagination and initiative. Such work makes the judicial role more satisfying for many judges. The availability of such roles at the lower levels may be an important feature of the character of the judiciary. For example, in Spain and France, the role of investigating judge in serious criminal cases offers such a task involving personal initiative.

It is important to note not only which tasks are assigned to judges, but also how they are performed. An important feature in this regard lies in the material conditions under which they work. Poor conditions, either in pay or in the character of the workspace and support for judicial tasks, contribute to a sense of low status. Judicial unions will often focus on this in relation to lower courts. But the absence of offices may also contribute to the isolation of judges, especially where they might have other incentives, such as the family situation, to work at home.

Guarnieri and Pederzoli[60] stress the importance of access to justice – who is able to bring litigation before judges – in determining the character of the judicial role. Their concern is primarily with the kinds of political cases that are brought to court through judicial review, but the analysis applies to ordinary civil litigation. Where there is wide access to financial support for litigation or where the costs of bringing a case are low, then the judges will be dealing with a wide range of ordinary problems. Where there is more limited access, then the judges will be performing a different kind of role, perhaps more oriented to important cases or commercial cases. The research has not spent much time in documenting this aspect of the role of courts. It is a feature that will serve to explain the relative caseloads of courts in different countries and also the prevalence of arbitration or mediation. There are, however, longstanding studies in the field[61] that can still be read as a background for understanding these different legal systems.

The role of a judge will vary significantly according to the tasks which are assigned. To take two examples: the existence of a function of constitutional review undertaken by judges is identified by many commentators as an important indicator of the 'political' character of the judicial role.[62] Similarly, in the UK it was considered controversial that judges should assess the economic or social value of restrictive practices balanced against their effects on prices for consumers.[63] In my studies of

[60] Guarnieri and Pederzoli, 3.

[61] Notably M. Cappelletti and B. Garth, *Access to Justice: A World Survey* (Milan 1978).

[62] Guarnieri and Pederzoli, 1–4; Tate and Vallinder, *Global Expansion*, above n. 8, ch. 1.

[63] See J. Bell, *Policy Arguments in Judicial Decisions* (Oxford 1983), 133–4, 148–53.

France, I have drawn a distinction between the tasks of the administrative judges (particularly in giving legal advice to the government) and the tasks of the civil judges. The portfolio of tasks which any particular group of judges has will affect the expectations and character of their work, and it may well affect the way in which they are recruited. Among the facets of the judicial role, I would draw out the importance of *creativity* and *controversiality*. Creativity implies a power to shape the law. It contrasts with routine activities of law application. Where the judges have an acknowledged creative role, then their ways of working need to reflect this, as does their standing. Controversiality covers not only the political, but also the social role of the judge. To what extent is the judge expected to confront socially controversial situations and make rulings in relation to them? Where any decision involves discretion, then the role of the judge in social debate will be important. Guarnieri and Pederzoli draw attention to the role of judges in criminal prosecutions of politicians and other public figures as being a factor in identifying the social role of judges.[64] One could also point to the importance of judges in making decisions in areas such as the sterilisation of mentally handicapped people.[65] In such cases, the judge is a major arbiter of social disputes in areas where politicians are happy not to become involved.

Creativity

The creative role of judges can be limited or extensive. Creativity can take at least four major forms. In the first situation, the judge may be making a new rule. There may be a new situation which has not occurred before, but which requires a decision. A good example is the question of whether it would be unlawful for doctors to separate conjoined twins in such a way that one of them was almost certain to die.[66] A second and more common situation is where the judge has to interpret texts to find a solution to a particular case. Once we come to stating the rules, there is much merit in Radolfo Sacco's suggestion that the interpreter makes use of 'legal formants', by which he means various pieces of evidence about what the law is.[67] He makes the valuable suggestion that a statute, a textbook or a precedent case does not contain a complete statement of the rule; rather it offers information about the rule, which is more or less authoritative. The job of the interpreter is to complete the rule for this case. In that sense, the rule does

64 Above p. 28. 65 Below p. 336.
66 *Re A (Conjoined Twins: Surgical Separation)* [2000] 4 All ER 961.
67 R. Sacco, 'Legal Formants: A Dynamic Approach to Comparative Law' (1991) 39 *American Journal of Comparative Law* 1 at 21–4.

not exist until the decision has to be made. So much of the justification has to relate to the choice of formants and the way in which these are extended. The scope for manoeuvre left to the decision-maker depends on the currents of opinion within the legal community and who exercises authority within it. Where the judges are a dominant authority, then their room for manoeuvre is greater than where they are expected to follow trends of the legislator or doctrinal legal writing. A third and important creative role is played in categorising facts and developing the law incrementally through this process. The facts do not come as self-evident, but have to be turned into 'facts-in-law'.[68] The narrative of those facts will bring out these features, and it is here that different legal systems diverge. The sparse French or German narrative of facts reveals a sense that the reader only needs to understand the essential facts that are necessary to the judgment that is made by application of the rules. The English approach tries to help the reader understand how the problem arose and how the solution makes sense in that factual matrix. A final form of creativity might be applying 'indeterminate or open-textured' concepts, such as 'reasonableness' or 'the welfare of the child'. We are not able to develop precise criteria in advance to determine what the appropriate standard should be. Rather we want the decision-maker to examine the particularity of each situation and exercise judgement on how to apply the law.[69] The idea of 'the welfare of the child' is but one example of where we prefer to focus on the particular, rather than simply try to create a rule that will be unduly rigid or complex. The different forms of creativity exist in all legal systems, but different branches of the law have different degrees of creativity. Legal systems also vary in their attitude towards creativity, and how comfortable they are with the power that this involves. This work is not able to cover all these aspects of creativity in its analysis of the judicial role. It will focus mainly on rule-making in the first two areas of creativity, but the other two are also significant and will be mentioned in some places.

Extrajudicial tasks

Judges will not only be involved in adjudication or even court administration. As a judge, an individual may be involved in a number of other activities within their career. The most striking opportunity in many countries is to become a prosecutor. In other countries, this is seen as

[68] G. Samuel, *Epistemology and Method in Law* (Aldershot 2003), 125–48.

[69] On the tension between having rules and wanting to pay attention to the particular, see Z. Bankowski, *The Law of Love* (Dordrecht 2002), ch. 9.

an administrative task and constitutes a distinct profession. But even then, as in Sweden, the professions of judge and prosecutor are seen as sufficiently connected for it to be permissible for a person to move from one to the other and back again. A more inquisitorial tradition saw it as a natural progression.

The other opportunity common to most countries, though not to the UK, is the chance to enter the public administration and return. (Indeed, in some cases, the chance to enter politics and return.) Administrative tasks, particularly working in the Ministry of Justice or the Courts Administration Agency, provide a chance to contribute from experience. The professional judge could be seen as the mainstay of the judicial function working among part-time and non-professional judges. It is therefore possible to confer on this judge certain administrative roles.

The involvement of the judge in law reform is another common area of activity. It is most marked in the Conseil d'Etat in France, in the English Law Commission and in the Swedish chairing of law reform committees.

Beyond this, the judge as a public figure may perform tasks of general public service, such as presiding at inquiries. Although such activities are not part of the judicial career, the invitation to serve in this way comes to a judge because of the social standing of the judiciary, particularly its reputation of being independent of politics, but also as being a group of wise people. We will see that this is now very controversial in England.[70] In other countries, the criminal process is used more frequently (but controversially) to hold public officials and politicians to account. Therefore, the tasks that judges are invited to perform illustrate not only what judges do, but also the standing of the judiciary in the wider community.

Judges and the legal community

The judiciary is only part of the legal community. The authority, status and function of judges depend in part on their relationship to two groups within the wider legal community: the legal professions and academic lawyers.

Judges and the legal professions

There are a variety of legal professions in the different countries studied in this book. Some of them, e.g. notaries, have a very limited impact

[70] Below p. 342.

on the way the judiciary works. The most important professional group is the advocates, those who provide legal advice and conduct cases in court. In all the countries, except England, the two tasks are provided directly to the public by a single profession. In terms of work in court or in chambers, the judge interacts with this profession more than any other, except that of the prosecutor, which is often a profession connected to the judiciary in any case. In terms of competition for the best recruits, this is usually the main alternative to becoming a judge, since professions like notary are typically restricted in number.

In terms of relative status among recruits and in society, the judiciary has often occupied an elite position. In countries such as Germany and Sweden, legal education is common among all professions and its purpose in large part has been to provide a pool of trained lawyers suitable for working in the judiciary. In these countries and in Spain, recruitment as a judge has been a badge of meritocratic quality. In England, recruitment as a judge has been a badge of quality in later career as a barrister. But this picture has been changing, especially since the 1980s. The amount of national work for private practitioners has increased both with growing commercial activity and with increased individual wealth. In addition, there has been a transnational aspect to legal work. Clients, such as multinational firms, work across jurisdictions within Europe and beyond, and international law firms have been established. These are either American or English firms with offices in different countries or networks of law firms from different jurisdictions. Firms of advocates, typically restricted to regional bar areas, grew in size and importance when the restrictive rules were relaxed in the early 1990s in order to meet transnational competition. The free movement of services and freedom of establishment in the European Union also contributed to changes in the economy of law firms. As a result, the number of advocates has increased rapidly. The incomes of lawyers in commercial practice have increased and so has the social attractiveness to recruits, since this life of private practice offers international experience. The less-well-paid role of the judge, limited predominantly to national activity, has lost relative attractiveness and status.

The change in the position of the judiciary in the legal community can, in part, be illustrated by changes in the demography of the judicial and advocacy professions. In most of the jurisdictions studied in this book, the numbers of advocates rose from 1992 to 2002 by 60–70 per cent. Only Sweden had a lower increase (36.5 per cent). Looking at professional judges, the picture in the same period is much less uniform. In Sweden and Germany, the increase in numbers was around 1 per cent, but in France it was 18 per cent and in Spain 29 per cent. England has seen a much higher increase of 72 per cent, but from a much lower base. The result is that in England the ratio of full-time judges to barristers and solicitors has actually improved slightly (from 1:70 to 1:66) over the period, and so has mirrored the rapid growth in the legal professions as a whole. The ratio in Spain has declined by a small amount from 1:20 to 1:25, and that in Sweden from 1:1 to 1:1.5. The biggest changes have been in France and Germany, where the increases in private legal practice have led to a decline in the ratio of judges to advocates from just over 1:3 to about 1:5.

In some legal systems, especially in the common law, there is a close relationship between the Bench and the Bar, and this produces a different dynamic from the confrontation that exists between investigating judges and defence advocates in systems such as France or Spain.

Research into these dynamics of status and attractiveness relies heavily on discussion with professionals, legal journalism and on some academic studies. Many of the changes are too recent to have been studied in depth, but the correlation of different sources makes the analysis presented here sufficiently robust.

Judges and legal academics

The relationship between judges and professors has been an area of study for many years. Among legal historians, it is a common issue in the study of the development of legal ideas. Van Caenegem[71] wrote that the relative influence of legislators, judges and professors depended largely on which of these groups was available to provide the ideas and impetus for legal change and whether any of the other groups was active. The English common law had active judges in formative years, while Germany had active professors and France an active legislator. Applied to the modern law, there is usually an active legislator and it is recognised that judges engage in lawmaking. The question becomes one about the influences on these forms of lawmaking. Who generates the ideas about the reforms that need to be undertaken, and what are the sources that are consulted?

It is not easy to answer these questions. As Duxbury has pointed out,[72] it is not easy to trace the sources of influence on decisions. In many

[71] R. C. Van Caenegem, *Legislators, Judges, Professors* (Cambridge 1987), 84–111.
[72] N. Duxbury, *Judges and Jurists* (Oxford 2003), 17–21.

systems, the court judgment will refer to some academic authorities as a justification for decisions. In France and the European Court of Justice, such references may be found in the opinions of the advocate general or equivalent or in the report of the reporter judge, in so far as these are published. Clear cases of influence would be where there has been academic criticism of an appeal court judgment and the supreme court reverses that decision and some part of the judgment or other published proceedings includes a reference to that criticism. Further evidence can be found where judges or academics are members of law reform bodies. Sweden perhaps offers the clearest example. Yet again academics may be appointed to courts and this also gives rise to a presumption of influence. However, there is also a range of informal contacts that do not leave much trace. Perhaps the most common is the role of the academic as legal adviser or even as advocate in a case. In most systems studied in this book, the fact of being a professor qualifies an individual to give legal opinions and even to practise. Alongside the published academic writings and practice-oriented commentaries on legal developments, there will be submissions to the courts which seek to influence decisions. The relationship of this writing as 'hired gun' to academic scholarship is a matter of conjecture, but should not be disregarded.

Again, this is a phenomenon undergoing change. In England, the universities were hardly teaching law in a serious way before 1945 and legal scholarship was very thin. The expansion of the numbers of students and staff particularly since the 1960s, together with pressure to publish research, has increased scholarly activity, and this is being used increasingly by the courts.[73] By contrast, the increasing activity of French private law professors as advocates has diminished their output and influence. Established paradigms need to be examined carefully to see if they still apply.

Judges and the wider community

The relationship of judges to the wider community is found in a number of dimensions – relations with lay judges as representatives of the community, with politicians over judicial review, and with social standing as well. The relationship with lay judges will be considered in detail in each national chapter.

[73] Below pp. 301 and 327.

Judges and politics

Guarnieri and Pederzoli[74] identify the role of judges in constitutional justice as one of the major determinants of a judicial culture. To the extent that judges are involved in adjudicating on the validity of legislation, they are a check on the power of politicians. It requires a sophisticated understanding of the democratic process to explain how it is possible to assert the freedom of the people to govern itself, and yet to confer on an unelected elite the authority to act as guardians of the constitution.[75] In the countries represented in this book, there are two broad tendencies. The first represents the European tradition of constitutional courts. In this model, a separate constitutional court is created, staffed by a separate judiciary, which is specially chosen for the task. This allows for a process of judicial appointments which is more openly political and also permits some modification of the judicial process itself. The second model, represented by Sweden and England, does not differentiate clearly constitutional adjudication from other kinds of issue. There is no separate judiciary and no special process. In part this is because the systems are reluctant to confer on judges a special constitutional role. So it is necessary to identify the extent to which constitutional adjudication is regarded as separate. Some, like Cappelletti, have argued that this was an inevitable feature of modern democracies in the West.[76] Those countries that have had a constitutional rupture had to address the issue more openly. But now the European Convention on Human Rights and European Union law work together to confer on the national court the duty to enforce supranational law to some degree. The broader political debate is the extent to which this leads to a judicialisation of politics or a politicisation of the judiciary, or indeed both. This book cannot consider all such issues in depth. There is much writing on the former issue.[77] Such writing studies in depth the nature of governance and the role of judges within the overall political institutions and activities in a society.[78] Whilst benefiting from this literature, the focus of this

[74] Guarnieri and Pederzoli, ch. 3.

[75] See R. M. Dworkin, *Freedom's Law* (Oxford 1996), Introduction; J. Bell, *French Constitutional Law* (Oxford 1992), 236–9.

[76] M. Cappelletti, *The Judicial Process in Comparative Perspective* (Oxford 1989), part II; T. Koopmans, *Courts and Political Institutions. A Comparative View* (Cambridge 2003), chs. 3, 4 and 5.

[77] See, for example, Tate and Vallinder, *Global Expansion*, above n. 8.

[78] Shapiro and Stone Sweet, *On Law*, above n. 9, 19–54; J. R. Schmidhauser (ed.), *Comparative Judicial Systems* (London 1987), ch. 1.

Table 1.1 *Judicial purchasing power relative to other public positions*

Country	Purchasing power[79]	Comparison with civil servant	Comparison with Member of Parliament
France	0.83	1.03	0.6
Germany	0.95	1.01	0.73
Spain	n/a	0.93	1.1
Sweden	1.1	1.57	1.0
England	1.35	2.54	3.22

work will be more on the latter issue of how the political sensitivity of constitutional issues affects the judicial role, and what role judges are playing. Would it, in fact, be true to say that constitutional review is significantly about checking politicians, or is it really an alternative form of appeal against the decisions of courts? Some judicial decisions will be discussed as illustrations, but the workload of constitutional courts will be a principal source of evidence for their role.

Social status

The social role of the judge is reflected in her status. This has an impact on who becomes a judge and the authority accorded to judicial decisions. There are a number of different indicators of importance.

One indicator is the pay of judges. In 2001, the European Association of Judges undertook a survey of judges' salaries in twenty-nine European countries.[80] The survey shows that, rather than examining gross income, it is more useful to examine judicial salaries in terms of purchasing power and in relation to other public positions. The figures in table 1.1 suggest that there are differences in the relative status of judges, civil servants and Members of Parliament in the various countries studied. For most countries, the similarity of salary levels suggests a comparable status of judge and civil servant. This is not surprising, if the judicial career follows the pattern of other civil service careers. Sweden gives the judge a high status on a par with a Member of Parliament, reflecting in part their contribution to the legislative process. This table ignores an

[79] Ratio between net income of a forty-five-year-old judge and the purchase of a home, two cars and four personal computers in ten years.

[80] A. Peters, 'Richtereinkommen im europäischen Vergleich' (Deutscher Richterbund website, www.drb.de).

important comparator, the income of an advocate, which is much less easy to establish. Where possible, this is added in the various chapters.

A second indicator of the status of judges is their role as 'personages of the state'. In Sweden, it is common for judges to head major inquiries or law reform committees. In France, this will typically be the role of the conseiller d'Etat, less often civil judges. Thus, even on the reform of criminal procedure, the committee was made up of academics and conseillers d'Etat, rather than a majority of civil judges. The committee for the reform of the German Civil Code did not include civil judges. By contrast, the judges in France, Germany and Spain will perform the role of routine public official.

A third indicator would be the opinion of politicians and the public. This is more difficult to gauge. In relation to politicians, one can look at the kinds of criticism to which judicial decisions are subjected and the respect accorded to them. Where there is deference to the judiciary, it occupies a higher status than where decisions are contested. In relation to public opinion, there are some opinion polls, such as in Spain, that focus particularly on views about judges. But most opinion surveys, such as the regular Eurobarometer survey, relate more generally to the system of justice rather than expressing a specific view on the work of judges.

Conclusion

This work aims to use the study of the judiciaries of a number of different countries to provide a basis for identifying a number of key features shaping the character of the judiciary. Some of the themes are set out in this chapter. There are three features of this work that call for comment: the use of common key terms in relation to different legal traditions, the details of each system, and the choice of countries to be studied.

In using common terminology for the different systems, and using English language terms, I am aware of the possible distortion of the different national phenomena. To begin with, the term 'judge' has a particular cultural resonance in the English language, which is linked to the experience of the common law. In using this word to describe other legal systems, it is necessary to explain how their linguistic terms are used, and what they signify. On the whole, it has been necessary to go beyond simple linguistic equivalents of the English term to include what might be considered 'magistrates' or 'tribunal members'. Similar problems are involved with other key terms, such as 'court' and 'trial'. There is no simple function that can be identified as common to all systems, since various tasks are carried out by different people in each system. All the same, there are a number of features that, in an overlapping way, can provide us with a similarity. The criminal process is one example. At one end of the spectrum, there is the concentrated English trial that brings all the evidence together and presents it to judges or a judge and jurors who have no prior knowledge of the matter and are limited to the information as presented at trial. At the other end of the spectrum, there is the extended French process in which evidence has been collected and evaluated by prosecutor and investigating judge, before being presented to a different body of people, heavily based on the file of information already collected. The broad function may be the establishment of criminal guilt, but the processes and actors are very different. As a result, it is best to explain how the processes work within each system, and how different checks and balances work, before trying to identify similar issues.

This method of explaining how the system works in its own terms is an important feature of my approach. It shares with Lasser[81] the belief that 'immersion' in a particular legal system is an essential part of conducting comparative law, especially where one may be trying to seek out the unstated and unconscious assumptions on which those within the system operate. Accordingly, I have chosen to present each legal system in its own terms, and in ways that make sense of the particular characteristics of the way that system works. All the same, the chapters reflect a broadly common structure of issues raised in this chapter. In particular, I am concerned to identify within the particularities of each system the dynamics that shape its own judicial tradition(s). The method is therefore not strictly functional. It aims both to be faithful to the particularity of each individual legal system, and to reflect on common preoccupations and concerns in Europe. There is no claim that there are universal functions that can be found in all legal systems. Such a claim is unnecessary. It is sufficient to recognise that the common heritages within Europe and similarities in contemporary political values and social circumstances provide a basis for suggesting that there are sufficient similarities between judges in the different countries to make them usefully comparable.

Why have the different countries been chosen? In the first place, the five different countries represent diverse and longstanding traditions.

[81] Lasser, *Judicial Deliberations*, above n. 27, 10–11.

Each is relatively independent, rather than being part of another legal system. The countries represent different legal families, and thus offer contrasts. Of course, what emerges is that such a typology is of limited help. There is such an interplay between the different systems that it is really the mix of features that is distinctive in an individual system, rather than the civil, constitutional, criminal or administrative branches of law. France offers a range of different professional judiciaries, civil, administrative and constitutional, that have distinctive organisations and settings. Spain offers a mix of old and new elements, with a distinctively independent organisation of the judiciary. Sweden offers an alternative way of providing an independent judicial organisation, and a distinctive role for the judiciary in legislation, as well as a strong and distinctive lay judiciary. Germany offers the common judicial training, but a fragmentation of judges into different specialist areas. In order to keep the work within a reasonable length, I have omitted Italy, which has been well studied by Guarnieri and Pederzoli.[82] The sixth chapter offers a view of the English judiciary and its recent developments in the light of these continental European preoccupations.

There is no single pattern or paradigm for the judge in Europe. There are a variety of different traditions. But there are also some similarities in the kinds of question that need to be addressed. We think too readily of the technocratic expertise of the professional lawyer judge, and too little of the personal qualities that she shares with the lay judge. The qualities of sound judgement and representing the law to the community are shared by all involved in the judicial function. Those shared qualities help us to understand the authority and social standing of the judges and the kinds of career patterns which evolve.

In comparing the different judiciaries, it is important to understand the historical background that has shaped both the tasks that are assigned and the way in which they are performed. All the same, those tasks are not simply inherited from the past, but are part of a pattern of current decisions about the place of the judiciary among the institutions of government.

One might ask whether comparative law can identify a 'better solution' or at least lead to an assessment of whether one judicial system is performing well. The immersion method would make a comparatist cautious in forming such judgements. In order to make such assessments,

[82] C. Guarnieri, *Magistratura e politica in Italia* (Bologna 1993); also Guarnieri and Pederzoli, 3 and 56, table 1.3.

it is necessary to have benchmarks for what would be a good judicial system, which are not easy to establish. In recent times, there have been documents such as the 'Universal Charter of the Judge' produced by the International Association of Judges in 1999, and the 'Judges Charter in Europe' produced by the European Association of Judges in 1993. But both of these are basic and provide little guidance as to what should happen at an operational level. Given the interplay of different institutions within government and the legal professions, there are few generic external criteria by which to assess the performance of a judiciary. For the most part, any evaluation has to be based on whether the judiciary is performing the role which is set for it within its own legal system. Particular institutions and practices may be borrowed from time to time, but they change their character when transposed into another institutional setting.

2 The French judiciary

Unlike most European countries, France does not have a single body of professional judges. There are several corps of judges and, as I have argued elsewhere,[1] there are different legal cultures within France. If anything, the distinction of the corps has been accentuated in recent years, although the origins of many differences pre-date the Revolution of 1789. Among the professional judges, there is a major distinction between the *magistrats judiciaires*, dealing with civil and criminal law, on the one hand, and the two main corps of administrative judges on the other. Both these groups of judges are civil servants and, therefore, there are similarities in the way they are recruited, even if there are also significant differences. To these must be added a body of judges who are not strictly speaking professional judges, the members of the Conseil constitutionnel, who are appointed for a non-renewable period of nine years. There are also several bodies of non-professional judges, each of which has its own particular connections to social communities, as well as to the professional judges. It is not possible to present a picture of 'the judiciary' in France, but there is a patchwork of different features relating to the different judiciaries and their contexts.

Organisational structures

This fragmentation of the judiciary is shaped and reinforced by institutional structures. There are distinct hierarchies of courts, distinct management and distinct career structures.

[1] J. Bell, *French Legal Cultures* (London 2001) (hereafter '*French Legal Cultures*').

The court systems

The French legal system has a number of different courts, each with its own hierarchy of courts and its own judiciary.[2] This has a profound impact on the character of the different judiciaries. French court institutions are structured according to three basic principles. First, courts are *specialist* to varying degrees. Three distinctions are of fundamental importance: between public law and private law, between civil law and criminal law, and between these ordinary courts and the Conseil constitutionnel. There is no court that has even residual jurisdiction over all branches of law. Courts are then grouped between those of general jurisdiction (*juridictions de droit commun*) and specialist courts, described as exceptional courts (*juridictions d'exception*) or as courts of limited jurisdiction (*juridictions d'attribution*). Secondly, French courts are typically *regional*. Only at the highest point in the hierarchy is there a national court in any branch of law (with the obvious exception of constitutional law). Thirdly, the French adhere to the principle of the *right to an appeal* (*double degré de juridiction*). This right of appeal on law and fact creates a substantial caseload.

Civil and criminal courts

The *juges judiciaires* are the ordinary civil and criminal judges. Civil and criminal courts carry distinct names, but are co-located. This combination of functions and personnel makes it appropriate to call these courts the 'ordinary courts'.

There are two general first instance civil courts, the 473 *tribunaux d'instance* and the 181 *tribunaux de grande instance*. Cases are assigned to one or other of these courts depending on their seriousness. The tribunal de grande instance is, by tradition, a collegial court, but, in recent years, much important civil work has been carried on by single judges. In particular, the *référé* is a rapid procedure before the president of the court or his delegate, who can make orders to protect the status quo pending hearing of the case, and can order provisionally performance of an obligation or payment of damages.[3] In practice, this decision is often the definitive solution.

There are also some specialist civil courts. The *tribunaux commerciaux* have existed since 1563, and are typically staffed only by non-professional

[2] J. Bell, S. Boyron and S. Whittaker, *Principles of French Law* (Oxford 1998) (hereafter '*Principles of French Law*'), ch. 2.

[3] Ibid., 91–2.

or 'consular' judges elected indirectly by the members of the local chamber of commerce.[4] They deal with commercial matters or those which arise between commercial people (*commerçants*) or on commercial matters or things (e.g. commercial leases, companies and patents). Labour courts (*Conseils des prud'hommes*) also pre-date the Revolution, and they are staffed essentially by lay people.[5]

In criminal matters, the lowest level court, the *tribunal de police*, deals with the minor offences, the *contraventions*. Cases will be tried by a single judge, and some 98 per cent lead to convictions. More serious cases (*délits*), involving heavy fines or imprisonment, are tried by the *tribunal correctionnel*. There are 181 of these courts located in the main town of a *département* and the judges are the same as those for the tribunal de grande instance. In some cases, a *juge d'instruction* will prepare the case for trial. Here trial will usually be before a panel of three professional judges, and the conviction rate is high (95 per cent). A small number of very serious cases (*crimes*), e.g. rape or murder, are tried by the *cour d'assises*. This is located with the Cour d'appel. The trial is heard by three judges sitting with nine jurors. The cours d'assises decided 3,245 cases in 2001, of which 95.7 per cent were convictions.[6]

Young persons are tried in specialist courts, involving one or more *juges des enfants* and an assessor. The criminal jurisdiction of the juge des enfants is an adjunct to his or her main function of intervening when the health, safety or moral situation of the child is threatened.

Appeals

Appeals on both civil and criminal cases lie to the thirty-three regional cours d'appel, except that decisions of the cour d'assises are appealed (since 2001) to a differently constituted cour d'assises.[7] Apart from urgent matters, the cour d'appel is collegial with a minimum of three members, though civil cases are often heard before a single *rapporteur*. A typical cour d'appel will have a number of specialist chambers. Appeal lies on law and fact. Because there is a file on the case containing all the elements of the evidence produced by the lower civil and criminal courts, it is easy to conduct such an appeal on fact as well as law, though the court may order such additional investigations if necessary.

[4] See generally pp. 89–90. [5] Below p. 92.

[6] Ministry of Justice, *Annuaire Statistique de la Justice, édition 2003* (Paris 2003) (hereafter '*Annuaire Statistique*'), 125.

[7] See below p. 94.

In 2001, the cours d'appel heard 206,294 civil appeals and 27,314 criminal cases.[8]

A litigant may make a *pourvoi en cassation* against a decision of the cour d'appel to the Cour de cassation, created in 1790, which is the only national court in France on civil or criminal matters. As its name implies, it is not strictly an appeal court, but merely a body that quashes the rulings of appeal courts for error of law.[9] The normal cassation procedure is that the Cour de cassation merely decides the disputed question of law and then refers it to a different cour d'appel for decision on the merits in the light of its ruling. In 2001, the Cour de cassation decided 20,613 civil matters (resulting in cassation in 20.6 per cent of cases) and 9,581 criminal matters (resulting in cassation in only 5 per cent of cases).

The Cour de cassation has nearly 200 members and is made up of six chambers, five civil chambers and one chamber dealing with criminal law. The Cour sits normally in panels of five judges. More important cases may be heard by a larger panel of judges within a chamber. To resolve divergences of interpretation and case-law between chambers, there is a *chambre mixte* composed of the Premier President together with the president and three senior members of each chamber concerned. The *Assemblée plénière* deals with cases of major importance and can consist of up to twenty-five of the most senior members.[10] The Cour de cassation gives a ruling on a point of law on a preliminary reference from a lower court (*saisine pour avis*).[11] In 2001, it gave only eight *avis*.

Administrative courts

Administrative law is the branch of law that is concerned with the powers and organisation of governmental bodies, notably the state.[12] Its central characteristic is the presence of the administration as one of the parties to the dispute. The notion of the 'administration' here covers not only national government, but also local authorities, public agencies and public services. Public law has special rules governing not only the use of powers, but also the rules of contract, the liability of public authorities and employment.

[8] See *Annuaire Statistique*, 25 and 135: this does not include the 32,152 decisions of the Chambre de l'instruction.

[9] The nature of *cassation* is discussed in *Principles of French Law*, 3–4, 85.

[10] *French Legal Cultures*, 29.

[11] Art. 151-1 of the *Code de l'organisation judiciaire* from 1991.

[12] See generally L. N. Brown and J. Bell, *French Administrative Law* (5th edn, Oxford 1998) (hereafter 'Brown and Bell'), chs. 3 and 4.

The consequences of the distinction between public and private law are twofold: firstly, the applicable rules of law are not the same for public bodies as for private bodies; secondly, any public law litigation is tried by different courts according to different procedures by different groups of judges, whose background is distinct from that of private law judges. This radical separation is a feature of the French republican tradition. Set out in a *loi* of 16–24 August 1790, it was restated by decisions of the Tribunal des Conflits at the beginning of the Third Republic. More recently, it has been declared a fundamental principle recognised by the laws of the Republic by the Conseil constitutionnel.[13] The precise allocation of disputes to either public law or private law does pose some difficulties, and there is a special court, the Tribunal des Conflits, which exists to resolve them. It is made up of equal numbers of judges from the Conseil d'Etat and the Cour de cassation, and the Minister of Justice has the casting vote.[14] In 2001, it decided fifty-two cases.

The oldest of the public law courts is the Conseil d'Etat, set up by Napoleon in 1799. It was originally a court of first and last instance, but since the creation of the tribunaux administratifs in 1953 and the cours administratives d'appel in 1987, the Conseil has increasingly become a supervisory court, with a role as an appeal court in a small number of areas. Its jurisdiction is typically to review the decisions of the lower administrative courts and to quash them where the law has been wrongly applied. Since 1989, it also gives advisory opinions on the law during litigation when requested to do so on a reference from those courts.[15] It retains some matters as a court of first and last instance.[16] In 2001, the Conseil d'Etat decided some 12,480 cases.

The judges of the Conseil d'Etat form a distinct corps of the administration.[17] The Conseil is not only a judicial body, it is a major adviser to the Government. Only one of its six sections is concerned with litigation (the Section du contentieux).[18] This section is then further sub-divided into

13 Ibid., 127–8; CC decision no. 86–224 DC of 23 January 1987, *Competition Council*, Rec. 8.

14 His casting vote is rarely required, but was used, for example, in TC 12 May 1997, *Préfet de Police de Paris*, D 1997, 567.

15 Brown and Bell, 79–86.

16 For a summary of the current jurisdiction of the Conseil d'Etat, see Brown and Bell, 54–5. In 2001, the jurisdiction in first and last instance covered 21.7 per cent of decisions: *Rapport Public 2002*, EDCE vol. 53, p. 59.

17 The term 'administration' is preferred to 'civil service' since the latter is much narrower in meaning than the French term 'fonctionnaire'.

18 The other sections are Finances, Intérieur, Travaux Publics, Sociale and the Section du Rapport et des Etudes: see Brown and Bell, 64–78.

different levels, depending on the importance of cases. Important cases of principle will be decided by the whole Section du contentieux. Very important cases are reserved to the Assemblée du contentieux, presided over by the Vice-President and involving the presidents of all the sections of the Conseil.[19]

The tribunaux administratifs and the Cours administratives d'appel are staffed by a separate corps of judges from the Conseil d'Etat. At the bottom of the pyramid of courts are the thirty-six tribunaux administratifs spread across France. In 2001, the tribunaux administratifs decided 134,560 cases. Above these are the seven cours administratives d'appel, which hear appeals on points of law and fact from the tribunaux administratifs. The presidents of these courts are members of the Conseil d'Etat. In 2001, they decided 15,105 cases.[20]

In addition to the ordinary generalist administrative courts, there are a number of specialist public law courts, each with their own staff of judges. These are often called *commissions* and have competence only in respect of particular issues. Such commissions are usually chaired by administrative judges. Among the most important of these commissions is the Commission des réfugiés.[21]

The Conseil constitutionnel

Technically, the Conseil constitutionnel is not a court, but a 'council'.[22] It was not originally conceived as a court, striking down legislation and protecting civil liberties. It was a body for resolving disputes on the boundaries between the legislative competence of the executive and Parliament and on disputed parliamentary elections. The current role of the Conseil has changed markedly from that original brief, but neither the structure nor the procedure has changed to make it more like a court. Only in dealing with the several hundred national election cases does it really behave much like a court in procedural terms.

This national Conseil constitutionnel does not hear applications from individual citizens concerning the constitutionality of *lois* passed by Parliament in relation to concrete fact situations, nor can it receive references from the administrative or civil and criminal courts. Rather it reviews the constitutionality of *lois* in abstract before they are signed by the President. References are made by the President of the Republic, the

[19] *French Legal Cultures*, 31. [20] *Annuaire Statistique*, 269.

[21] On the commissions, see Brown and Bell, Appendix D.

[22] See generally, J. Bell, *French Constitutional Law* (Oxford 1992), 48–56, and below p. 94.

Prime Minister, the President of the National Assembly or the President of the Senate, or, more commonly, from sixty deputies or senators (usually from opposition parties). In this way it does not deal with 'cases', but rather reaches 'decisions' about the constitutionality of the *loi* taken as a whole. As will be seen later, the members of the court do not need to have legal qualifications and are not drawn necessarily from the ranks of the various judiciaries. Although not integrated into the hierarchy of courts, the Conseil does carry authority in its interpretations of the Constitution. Its rulings on the constitutionality of a *loi* must be followed by the private and public law courts, and its interpretations of provisions of the *loi* are typically followed as authoritative statements.

Management of the judiciary and courts

The contrasting management structures of the ordinary and administrative courts reflect different models. The Ministry of Justice has a direct role in relation to the ordinary courts, with judicial self-government limited to appointments and promotions, whilst the Conseil d'Etat really operates like an executive agency managing the budget, resources and personnel of the administrative courts.

Ordinary judges

The management of the ordinary judiciary and the courts is primarily the function of the Ministry of Justice. It receives the budget for the ordinary courts and is responsible for the running of the courts, the budget for the justice service, including the judicial salaries, and the nomination of judges and prosecutors. The Ministry is also responsible for the judicial college, the *Ecole Nationale de la Magistrature* (ENM). Since the Ministry is also responsible for many aspects of the policy affecting the courts, it is the dominant force shaping the work of the judges. Although its minister is a politician, many of its staff are judges on secondment.

Since 1946, the role of the Ministry has been constrained by the existence of the *Conseil Supérieur de la Magistrature* (CSM) which has acquired increasing roles in the discipline and promotion of judges. The CSM was created originally to ensure the independence of the judiciary. Initially it had a power of recommendation over the promotions of the lower judicial grades, but it became gradually less effective in this role and, when reconstituted in 1958, it was given only an advisory role. Gradually this role has been increased so that, since a constitutional amendment of 1993, it is now a dual one. In relation to the ordinary grades of judge, it is required to give a favourable opinion on promotions to postings in the sitting judges (*siège*) or the prosecutors (*parquet*) that are recommended by the Ministry of Justice. In the cases of the highest postings, such as procureur, president or member of the Cour de cassation, the CSM makes proposals. The CSM is made up of a number of external members, together with judges elected onto one of two panels, either the siège or the parquet.[23] In its present structure, the CSM is strongly representative of the judges and offers a limited judicial self-government, confined to appointments.

Presiding judges do have management roles in relation to staff within their court, but this is confined mainly to acting as hierarchical superiors (e.g. in monitoring performance and promotions and as persons responsible for ensuring cases are properly distributed among judges). They have no significant responsibility for budgets.

Administrative judges

The administrative judiciary is more independent. Although under the Ministry of Justice, its budget is sent direct to the Conseil d'Etat, and that body organises recruitment and training, as well as career development and promotion. In many ways, the Conseil operates like an administrative agency that manages this branch of the judiciary. It controls both itself and the lower administrative courts.

It is only since 1900 that the majority of promotions to senior posts in the Conseil have come from within the ranks of the corps.[24] The internal promotion system has gradually come to dominate, creating a real career track in judicial work within the Conseil, even if many, in practice, will also serve outside as part of their career. Since 1986, there has been an independent *Conseil supérieur des tribunaux administratifs et des cours administratives d'appel* presided over by the Vice-President of the Conseil d'Etat and administered by a secretary-general adjoint from the Conseil d'Etat and on which members of the lower administrative courts and the Conseil d'Etat are represented.[25] This body deals with appointments, training and promotions. It is managed from within the Conseil d'Etat.

[23] There is one member of the parquet on the siège panel and similar cross-membership on the parquet panel.

[24] J. Massot and T. Girardot, *Conseil d'Etat* (Paris 1999) (hereafter 'Massot and Girardot'), 36.

[25] Brown and Bell, 88. See more generally, P. Fanachi, 'Les tribunaux administratifs de 1953 à l'an 2000' in *La Revue Administrative, numéro spécial: Le Conseil d'Etat avant le Conseil d'Etat* (Paris 1999), 115.

The process is less formal and more within the control of judges than the equivalent process for the ordinary judiciary.

On the whole, promotion within the Conseil d'Etat works by way of seniority. The Vice-President will play a significant role in determining the future career of individuals within the Conseil, but the demands of the wider government machine (and increasingly international organisations) for the highly skilled individuals within the Conseil reduces his options as to the availability of individuals for judicial tasks.

Career structure

Ordinary judges

Recruitment and selection

Ordinary judges are recruited through both student entry and lateral entry. If one includes secondment, there are now some thirteen different entry routes. The main entry takes place through three *concours*,[26] which lead to the professional training college, the ENM. The profile of the 2003 entry is typical. Of the 220 admitted through the first concours, designed for those leaving university, 82.7 per cent were women.[27] The second concours is for civil servants of at least four years' standing aged under forty-six years and five months. Only twelve were admitted, of whom seven (58 per cent) were women. The third concours is for those of at least eight years' standing in a private sector profession (including being an *avocat*) and who are under forty. Only five were admitted in 2003, of whom three were women. The typical portrait of an entrant is that she is twenty-five years old, with a Master's degree in law, coming from the Paris area and prepared for entry at the Institut des études judiciaires of the University of Paris 2.

To keep pace with the need to appoint more judges particularly for criminal justice and to reduce delays in other areas, various exceptional recruitment rounds have been held, and this was formalised into a complementary competition in 2002. This competition recruits people from legal backgrounds who are at least thirty-five with ten years of professional experience. They have to undergo written and oral examinations. Of the eighty-four people admitted in 2003, forty-seven were women (56 per cent). Finally, there can be a secondment for a number of years

[26] The *concours* is seen as increasing the democratic character of the judiciary: see H. Dalle, 'Le recrutement et la formation des magistrats: Une question de légitimité' (1991) 57 *Revue de l'Administration Publique* 53.

[27] Statistics from ENM website (http://www.enm.justice.fr).

where individuals are recruited often for their expertise. For example, some members of the Cour de cassation are drawn from among university professors. The profile of judges in 2002 showed that only 72 per cent had entered through graduate recruitment to ENM.[28] The multiplicity of recruitment routes enables a balance of age and experience. Thus not all judges belong to the cohort of lifelong judges.

Despite this increasing diversity, experience in the ENM is meant to provide an element of initial socialisation for the majority of judges. Initial socialisation is assisted by the familiarity with the career that many recruits already have because of their family background. According to Bodiguel's research, one judge in ten is from a family of judges, one in five is from a family of lawyers, and one in two is from a family in the public service.[29] In addition, nearly half in his survey (43.6 per cent) were married to another judge. He concludes that family links are an important influence in the choice of this profession.

Women now constitute the majority of the profession, above all at lower levels, though they are less strongly represented at the most senior levels. There has been a gradual feminisation of the profession since the 1960s. Boigeol attributes this to a view that 'The judiciary appeared . . . as a respectable position for the daughters of the middle classes who hesitated longer to place their sons in it.'[30] In 1959, of 255 candidates, 116 (45.5 per cent) were women, but among those who were successful, only nine out of thirty-eight (23.7 per cent) were women.[31] By 1982, 28.5 per cent of ordinary judges were women and in 2003 there were 7,312 judges of whom 52.2 per cent were women.[32] All the same, Boigeol[33] has also pointed out that, in more senior posts, men still predominate and

[28] Figures from personal communication from Hubert Dalle.

[29] J.-L. Bodiguel, *Les magistrats, un corps sans âme* (Paris 1991) (hereafter 'Bodiguel'), 139. But, according to Bancaud, 26.2 per cent of top posts in the Cour de cassation in the period 1945–85 went to children of judges and the figure rises to 47.7 per cent if one includes all who have a family connection with the judiciary. The latter figure is similar to the figure for members of the Cour de cassation with a family member in the judiciary in 1901 (44.6 per cent): see A. Bancaud, *La haute magistrature judiciaire entre politique et sacerdoce* (Paris 1993), 21–2.

[30] A. Boigeol, 'La magistrature française au féminin: Entre spécificité et banalisation' (1993) 25 *Droit et Société* 489 at 492.

[31] ENM colloquium, October 2002, ENM website (http://www.enm.justice.fr).

[32] CSM, *Rapport d'activité 2003* (Paris 2004), 12 (this figure includes 480 judges working outside the courts).

[33] See A. Boigeol, 'Male Strategies in the Face of the Feminisation of a Profession' in U. Schultz and G. Shaw (eds.), *Women in the World's Legal Professions* (Oxford 2003), ch. 22 at 412–13.

women are not proportionately represented among the applicants for senior posts in the judiciary. This is supported by the analysis presented by the CSM in 2004.[34] It noted that, while women made up 63.4 per cent of the lowest (second) grade of judges, and 48.8 per cent of the middle (first) grade, they constituted only 20.15 per cent of the highest grade (*hors hiérarchie*). The position is worse among the senior management positions – women made up 8.9 per cent of heads of courts or chief prosecutors and 14.8 per cent of local presiding judges or prosecutors. A particular problem is that women constituted only 17.9 per cent of applicants for these senior management posts. The CSM tried to analyse these results, but was unable to offer much explanation.[35] It pointed to the fact that women also occupy only 14 per cent of higher civil service posts and 14 per cent of managerial positions in the private sector in general. But it is likely that the need for a judge to move geographically in order to achieve promotion to senior positions is a significant influence on the decision not to apply.

Training and career

The basic career pattern since the 1960s has been that a judge is trained through the ENM based in Bordeaux. Training involves not only courses, but also placements in different organisations involved with the law, including in a cabinet d'avocat, and the prefecture (and even possibly abroad). There are also a number of practical exercises. Such a period of training over two years, often working in groups, socialises the year group (*promotion*) with each other, and integrates it into the judicial world. Following the exit examinations, the ENM also serves to prepare the judges for their initial posting. Candidates from the complementary competition also have a short orientation programme organised by the ENM before they begin training on the job by way of a placement. As an organisation involved with continual professional development, it offers courses that are taken up by a significant number of judges. (Some events can involve several hundred judges.) The activities of the ENM facilitate both formal and informal dialogue on a regular basis among judges from different parts of France.

The promotion of private law judges is secured through a single framework. Before 1946, political influence and recommendation was particularly important.[36] Promotion is first determined by a person

[34] CSM, *Rapport d'activité 2003*, section 2. [35] Ibid., section 3, 2e.

[36] Bodiguel, 113. For an example of the process, see A. Bancaud, 'Une nomination judiciaire sous la IIIe République' (1997) 26 *Genèses* 154.

being placed on the *tableau d'avancement*, where seniority is the principal determinant, although performance is also a factor. The Commission d'avancement is chaired by the Premier Président of the Cour de cassation, with sixteen elected members from the different grades of the judiciary and two members of the Ministry of Justice. In these elections, the judicial unions play a significant role. This degree of self-government is important for the character of the judiciary. In November 2000, there were over 800 judges on the tableau d'avancement, who would take years to be promoted. The promotion system was reformed by an organic law of 26 June 2001. Now a judge cannot be promoted within a court in which she has served for more than five years, and judges cannot serve by way of transfer for longer than six years. Judges often choose to stay in a particular area for domestic reasons, so they may have to trade off promotion and mobility.

But it has to be acknowledged that promotion for most judges is recommended by the Ministry of Justice. Candidates make their requests known to the Ministry and the CSM, and this will typically trigger the process. There are usually only sufficient recommendations made to fill the places. This means that the CSM is not called upon to select, but to approve or disapprove. The CSM does reject proposals, even if they are not contested by the individual or by others who consider they have a better claim.[37] The CSM reports the reasons for its rejection in its annual report. For example, in its annual report for 2000,[38] the CSM justified the rejection of some candidates on grounds of lack of experience, and in other cases personal characteristics made them unsuited to the post. The CSM will sometimes prefer another candidate, perhaps because of his or her seniority or family situation, where the profile is otherwise similar to the candidate proposed by the Ministry of Justice. Indeed, a judge can insist that the Minister and the CSM take into account his family situation at the time of an application for promotion.[39] This makes the career particularly attractive for families with two professional careers. Only about 2 per cent of Ministry proposals were rejected in 2000 and 2001. This is not surprising, since the combination of judicial involvement in determining those eligible for appointment and experience of the CSM's reasoned decisions in rejecting applicants enables an

[37] CSM, *Rapport d'activité 1999* (Paris 2000), 15.

[38] CSM, *Rapport d'activité 2000* (Paris 2001), 6–10.

[39] See CE 6 August 2002, *Ozoux*, AJDA 2002, 1408 (quashing of a decision to transfer other judges from Metropolitan France to la Réunion in preference to the applicant, whose wife and children remained there). This right dates from a *loi* of 1921.

understanding to develop within the Ministry of the kinds of candidate who will be acceptable.

The judicial career is very diverse. The 2,881 judges studied by Bodiguel had followed 683 different career paths! All the same, the majority will remain within the judiciary for their full career, but will change functions or locations from time to time. Classically, they will engage in three kinds of 'judicial' activities. First, the most traditional activity is for the judge to adjudicate on individual cases (as a *magistrat de siège*). Bodiguel[40] estimates that about half of all judges will spend their whole career on this activity. Naturally, a judge will have a number of postings, both geographical and in terms of task. The work as an adjudicating judge at first instance can include work as a juge des enfants, or as a judge of civil or of criminal matters. Women are over-represented among the *magistrats de siège*. In 2003, 75 per cent of women occupied posts as magistrats de siège 25 per cent were prosecutors. In part the former role is attractive because it offers the possibility of relatively solitary work with limited numbers of fixed appointments in a day, thus permitting flexible working patterns.[41] But Boigeol comments that, given the substantial number of women in the profession, it is no longer appropriate to consider them as a homogeneous group and the reasons for individual career paths will be varied.[42]

Secondly, a substantial number of judges will choose to become members of the parquet whose role is essentially as public prosecutor. More than half of these will return to become adjudicating judges.[43] Equally, those who start in the parquet will typically go to the siège (only 11 per cent did not), and just over 40 per cent of these return to the parquet.[44] Traditionally, this second route has been taken by those who attain the highest places in the Cour de cassation. A posting in the parquet ensures that one is known. The 1999 report of the CSM notes that fewer people are applying for this route. In part, the reason lies in the greater public responsibilities to negotiate with the mayor, the police and with local associations and others. This has made the work focus more on criminal justice policy and administration and has changed the legal aspect of

40 Bodiguel, 110.

41 CSM, *Rapport d'activité 2003*, 13; Boigeol, 'La magistrature française', above n. 30, 501 and 522.

42 Boigeol, 'Male Strategies', above n. 33, 417. 43 Bodiguel, 111.

44 CSM, *Rapport d'activité 2001* (Paris 2002), Appendix 4 reports that from 1 January 2001 to 20 March 2002, 92 individuals moved from parquet to siège and 102 moved in the opposite direction out of a total of 2,065 appointments made.

the work. It has also made it perhaps less flexible in terms of time commitments.[45] Until 1994, posts in the parquet were decided by political authorities and they were essentially part of the political spoils system. Nowadays, the CSM exercises a reviewing role and does reject candidates proposed by the Ministry as unsuitable for the proposed posting.

Thirdly, a posting as juge d'instruction can be seen as attractive to some. This role is emblematic of judicial independence and the service of justice.[46] The judge is individually and publicly a focus of attention in the fight for justice, in finding the wrongdoer. Whether deciding on the investigation and prosecution of murder, a sudden death or political corruption, this is the individual who will be the public image of what the law is doing. This investigative process has gradually given way to defence rights. The roles of the juge d'instruction thus pull in different directions. As Samet puts it, '[The very character of the role of the *juge d'instruction*] thus surprises and misleads, and it has become common to ask oneself whether the *juge d'instruction* is Salomon or Maigret, judge or investigator, defender of rights or pursuer of wrongs.'[47] But the fundamental idea of a judge who investigates and who also judges is very distinctive in the French form of criminal process. The freedom of the juge d'instruction is limited by the fact that he or she must act on a referral made by the procureur.[48] The public reputation of the juge d'instruction comes from the fact that he or she is not subordinated to the Ministry of Justice, unlike the procureur, and can be seen as a more impartial champion of the rights of the individual, as well as of the public interest. That said, the effectiveness of the juge d'instruction as protector of rights is questioned by Hodgson's empirical research.[49]

The *instruction* process is a rather solitary one for the judge. Despite the publicity given to the criminal 'affaires' in the 1990s, the research conducted by Roussel[50] suggests that there was little contact between judges dealing with similar kinds of issue. The character of this role differs from the trial judge. The juge d'instruction has to maintain an ongoing relationship with the accused, his lawyers and witnesses over

[45] CSM, *Rapport d'activité 1999*, 77.

[46] See A. Garapon and I. Papadopoulos, *Juger en Amérique et en France* (Paris 2003) (hereafter 'Garapon and Papadopoulos'), 156–7.

[47] C. Samet, *Journal d'un juge d'instruction* (Paris 2000), 33.

[48] P. Chambon, *Le juge d'instruction. Théorie et pratique de la procédure* (4th edn, Paris 1997), paras. 43–4.

[49] J. Hodgson, *French Criminal Justice* (Oxford 2005).

[50] V. Roussel, *Affaires de juges* (Paris 2002), ch. 2; also L. Greilsamer and D. Schneidermann, *Les juges parlent* (Paris 1992), 41ff and 69ff.

many months. This development of a personal relationship is closer to the juge des enfants and the juge des affaires familiales. As Garapon points out, this office-based, bureaucratic justice (*justice du cabinet*) is not neat and clear-cut in reaching a decision at the end of a debate between parties; rather it is a process of coming to a decision on the basis of a more fluid set of inputs, and differs from the *justice de l'audience*.[51]

Administrative judges

Administrative judges have a different background to private law judges. They are administrators recruited predominantly from among those who have been through the various concours to enter the ENA, and they have chosen the tasks of administrative judge as their posting. Administrative judges belong, however, to two distinct corps, which themselves have distinct cultures.

In 2001, there were nearly 1,300 administrative judges. On the one hand, some 300 judges belong to the *grand corps* of the Conseil d'Etat, which is one of the elite groups of administrators. These highly talented individuals are likely to have a variety of postings within government and in the public administration during the course of their career. By contrast, the 981 judges of the Cours administratives d'appel and tribunaux administratifs fit the more classical model of a judiciary and will have predominantly judicial functions once they enter the corps, although a few may spend some time on secondment to various branches of the administration. There is the possibility of nomination to the Conseil d'Etat from the corps of lower administrative judges, so the two corps are not totally separate. All the same, their status, careers and functions are significantly different.

Members of corps of the tribunaux administratifs and the Cours administratives d'appel enjoy similar status to private law judges in that, since 1986, they cannot be moved against their will and their promotions are organised by the *Conseil Supérieur des tribunaux administratifs et des Cours administratives d'appel*. Substantial networking and visiting occurs to ensure that the Conseil d'Etat is well aware of the career aspirations and situations of candidates for promotion, and the corps of the lower judges is still small enough to rely on personal knowledge, compared with the more formal procedures for promotion and career development that exist among the 7,000 and more *magistrats*.

[51] A. Garapon, *Bien juger. Essai sur le rituel judiciaire* (Paris 1997), 257–9.

This combination of diversity of corps within the administrative judiciary and the lead role of the Conseil d'Etat as both the administrative court and the agency responsible for the court system and the training and careers of judges makes the administrative judicial system different from that in civil and criminal law.

Recruitment and selection

The administrative courts have always had a distinctive recruitment within the civil service, but the distinctiveness of careers in relation to the civil judiciary has been accentuated in recent years. Whereas in the nineteenth century, the members of the Conseil d'Etat would have been educated largely in the law faculties, as would civil judges, [52] at the beginning of the twentieth century, distinct competitive examinations for the two careers encouraged separate educational paths.

The Ecole des Sciences Politiques has educated almost all the members of the Conseil d'Etat in preparation for the entrance examination, and since its foundation in 1945, the ENA has become the training college for the civil service of which administrative judges form a part. The number of places at the ENA is strictly controlled by the Government. For example, in 2002 there were 116 places, of which only 58 places were for those coming out of higher education.[53] ENA training is generalist, with no specialist formation for those who are going to become administrative judges. The two-year training involves courses in Paris and Strasbourg and placements in various parts of the administration or even abroad or in the private sector. The training is thus in different locations and separately organised from that for the ordinary judges. All trainees have courses on public administration and public law. At the end, there is an exit examination that produces a ranking of students in order of merit. According to their place in this order of merit, candidates have their pick of the postings available in that year. The Conseil d'Etat, like the Inspection générale des finances and the Cour des Comptes, is chosen by bright and ambitious recruits not merely because of its work, but also because of the opportunities which joining this corps will have for their future career.[54] Those lower down the order might well choose to become members of the corps of the tribunaux administratifs and the Cours administratives d'appel. Whereas

[52] C. Charle, *Les élites de la République 1880–1900* (Paris 1987), 109–10.
[53] The success rate for university entrants was 1 in 10.4: ENA website (http://www.ena.fr).
[54] Massot and Girardot (p. 36 note 55) state that of the sixty-seven *majors* (top of the class) up to 1998, thirty-one had chosen to belong to the Conseil d'Etat and thirty the Inspection générale des finances.

to join the Conseil d'Etat is considered to be one of the elite posts, joining the other judicial corps does not have much more prestige than becoming an *administrateur civil*. The new members of the Conseil d'Etat typically will not expect to devote their career exclusively to judicial work.

The ENA route now accounts for a limited number of judges. Perhaps five a year might enter the Conseil d'Etat and a further dozen the administrative courts. Particularly since 1983, there has been an effort to supplement the recruitment of young people through the ENA with the recruitment of more experienced people at a later stage in their career. Two major groups are recruited into the Conseil d'Etat through the *tour extérieur*. The first are members of the corps of the tribunaux administratifs and the Cours administratives d'appel. Since 1985 one post of conseiller in six and one post of *maître des requêtes* in four has been reserved for members of that corps, and indeed since 1992 half the appointments for the latter post have been filled by members of the lower administrative courts. Secondly, at the level of *conseiller* in the Conseil d'Etat, individuals are likely to have performed at a high level in another civil service corps. Nominations are made by the Minister, but since 1994 the Vice-President of the Conseil has had to give a public opinion on all proposed nominations to the *tour extérieur* except for individuals coming from the lower administrative courts. This is clearly an attempt to put the brake on political patronage, which was so important in the past. But this still only constitutes a limited dilution of the ENA predominance. In 1998, of 141 presidents and conseillers, only 12 had come in as *maîtres des requêtes* by the tour extérieur, and 31 came in by that route as conseillers (with eight from the tribunaux administratifs). Among the 137 maîtres des requêtes, 27 came in by external recruitment (other than from the lower administrative courts).[55]

In contrast, among the lower administrative court judges, the recruitment through the ENA is complemented in four ways, which now provide the bulk of staffing. There is the *tour extérieur*, *détachement* and a recruitment among *officiers* of the armed forces, but additionally there is an increasing practice of having a complementary competition. This last route is open to ordinary judges, civil servants and graduates eligible for entry to the ENA. The age for this last category was reduced in 2002 from twenty-eight to twenty-five. This additional recruitment has

[55] Massot and Girardot, 37.

become very important for a rapidly expanding corps. In 2002, some twenty-six candidates were recruited in this way. In 2003, the number rose to forty-eight. The union of administrative judges has been concerned that the proportion of ENA-trained judges is in danger of falling below 25 per cent of the corps of the administrative judges.[56]

Rather than join the corps of administrative judges, individuals can remain within their original corps, but work *en détachement* within the various administrative courts for a fixed number of years, usually four. They are chosen for their technical expertise, which can help to feed into the experience and knowledge of the court where they work, though established members of the court may consider that these *détachés* are being trained by it. Massot and Girardot note that, in 1998, such détachés included four prefects, three administrateurs civils, three civil judges, two diplomats, two professors and two military officers.[57]

Training and career

Initial training and continuing education for such administrative judges is run by the Bureau de formation of the Conseil d'Etat, drawing on the expertise of administrative judges from the different courts. Initial training involves four elements: a number of special lectures, training in the functions of being a rapporteur within a *sous-section* of the Conseil d'Etat through work on selected (past) files, attendance at judicial hearings, and a general familiarisation with the working of the administrative sections of the Conseil d'Etat. This process of inculturation serves to achieve some kind of standardisation of expectations for the judicial role.

No such formal procedures exist for members of the Conseil d'Etat. Promotion is based on seniority and the interests of members, and is managed within the corps. New recruits are trained on the job within the Conseil, with few formal training events. The small number of recruits makes it possible to handle much of the training by way of individual mentoring.

While education at the ENA will involve some legal subjects (essentially in public law), it will not be the equivalent of a university degree. Thus much of the relevant law is acquired on the job. One former prefect remarked in interview that 'any administrator is presumed capable

56 See B. Even, 'L'ENA doit rester la base du recrutement des magistrates administratifs' AJDA 2002, 1312 at 1313.
57 Massot and Girardot, 38.

of knowing the law'. The remark was made in response to questions on why French government departments did not have many legal advisers of their own. Understanding legal rules and applying them is part of many administrative tasks, and prior legal training is not the only way to develop the appropriate methods.

A crucial part of the training of all administrative judges is the *stage* in the Conseil d'Etat. In this period, trainees are not only given lectures (typically by judges from the administrative courts), but they spend several months attached to a sous-section and follow its work. They are also taught to prepare files by way of practical exercises. This common element in formation helps to form links between individuals and encourages a standardisation of approach, achieved in the ordinary courts by the training at the ENM. The Conseil also undertakes a limited programme of continuing education. The programme is not as large as that offered by the ENA or ENM, but it is run by the central court and focuses on the judges. There is little overlap with the continuing education programme of the civil judges.

Thus the crucial role in socialisation is performed by the Conseil d'Etat. It is the guardian of the tradition and maintains the lead role within the two corps of administrative judges. That said, the Conseil has limited regular contact with the lives of the judges in the tribunaux administratifs.

Judicial corporate life

Ordinary judges

Ordinary judges are numerous, geographically scattered and engaged in a variety of tasks. Collective activity is rare. There will be occasional opportunities for presidents of courts to meet regionally or with the President of the Cour de cassation. Otherwise, judges will meet each other at continuing education events organised by the ENM. The size of the judiciary makes it difficult for concerted action without unions.

Elections to the CSM tend to give an opportunity for the judicial unions to play a role. They are able to ensure that their candidates occupy key positions. Certainly the research conducted by Bancaud into the Mitterrand period of the 1980s suggested political manoeuvres by judicial unions and political figures had not altogether disappeared from the judicial appointment process.[58] Judicial unions could not legally

[58] A. Bancaud, 'Le paradoxe de la gauche française au pouvoir: Développement des libertés judiciaires et continuité de la dépendance de la Justice' (2000) 44/45 *Droit et société* 61.

organise strikes in the 1990s but did have some form of demonstration in 1990, which coincided with the President's visit to the special session of the Cour de cassation to mark its bicentenary.[59] In 2000 and 2001, days of action led to the Minister of Justice holding round-table discussions with the unions.

The involvement of the various judicial unions is significant. About 60 per cent of the ordinary judges belong to one of the judicial unions. Of these about 60 per cent belong to the Union Syndicale de la Magistrature, 30 per cent belong to the left-wing Syndicat de la Magistrature and 9 per cent to the right-wing Association Professionnelle des Magistrats.[60] Their concerns are both to protect the status, terms and conditions of employment of their members, and to campaign for improvements in the quality of justice, particularly the infrastructure of courts and the policies which have to be implemented. For instance, the Syndicat de la Magistrature promoted a broader conception of the judicial responsibility for justice, by encouraging talks on social and philosophical themes in relation to judicial activity.[61] The judges wanted to be seen not just as technicians of procedure, but as taking an active part in defining and achieving a just society.[62] In the 1990s, the union developed an increasingly confrontational relationship with the Government. One particular trigger was the amnesty for Members of Parliament involved in funding irregularities voted for by Parliament in 1990. This led some judges in Le Mans to release some petty criminals as a gesture of complaint against what they saw as a failure to deal with political corruption.[63] The unions also defended judges and prosecutors under attack from politicians about investigations into political corruption in the 1990s. As a result, confrontation was set up between politicians and judges, with a desire on the part of the latter to be freed from political authority. The realignment of the relationship between judges and political institutions expanded the range of the work of judicial unions.[64] Concerns about the quality of the resources available to judges to perform their tasks also led to the strikes and confrontations between judges and the Minister of Justice in 1990, 2000 and 2001 that have already been mentioned.

[59] Roussel, *Affaires*, above n. 50, 112–18.

[60] See Vacarme, art. 391 (on http://www.vacarme.eu.org).

[61] See D. Applebaum, 'The *Syndicat de la Magistrature* 1968–1978' in W. Wesley Pue and D. Sugarman (eds.), *Lawyers and Vampires. Cultural Histories of Legal Professions* (Oxford 2003), 269 at 278; and Roussel, *Affaires*, above n. 50, 169–70.

[62] Roussel, *Affaires*, above n. 50, 152–3. [63] Ibid., 113.

[64] Applebaum, '*Syndicat*' above n. 61, 285; Roussel, *Affaires*, above n. 50, 279–80, 293–4.

Administrative judges

The *grands corps* are elites within French public life, and it is well known that they retain this corporate solidarity whatever spheres of life they work in. This is symbolised by the use of 'tu' in conversation. These grands corps serve as a platform for other types of career in the public and private sectors, often in managerial roles. A member of the Conseil d'Etat can also seek a placement within the ministerial office, either in a technical function, as adviser on particular issues, or more generally as a policy-maker. Particularly at the higher levels, these are politically sensitive posts and rely on an individual having some political commitment.

The corps of the administrative courts is based provincially, which often suits individuals, just as the provincial character of the civil courts suits members of the ordinary judiciary. There will be training events where individuals from the different administrative courts will meet each other. There are also more regular contacts between the presidents of courts, either in a region or across the country, especially at events organised by the Conseil d'Etat. But the size, diversity of background and its geographical spread make the corps of judges of the administrative courts less cohesive than the Conseil d'Etat. Because of the lead role of the Conseil, there are fewer opportunities for the administrative judges to have their say in proposals for reform. They do, however, have a professional association, more like the ordinary judiciary and in a way that is not felt necessary within the Conseil d'Etat. All the same, this association does not have the same political profile as the unions of ordinary judges, precisely because it lacks the most senior ranks of administrative judges. It does, however, have representation within the Conseil supérieur des tribunaux administratifs et des cours administratives d'appel.

Values: conceptions of judicial independence

Judicial independence in France is debated in relation to different issues and with different intensity in relation to the different corps of judges. There is neither a set of overarching legal provisions covering all judges, nor an overarching debate. Article 64 of the Constitution makes the President of the Republic the guardian of the independence of the judiciary, but this provision and the subsequent ones on the Conseil supérieur de la magistrature and the protection of civil liberties apply only to the ordinary civil and criminal judges. They do not apply to constitutional judges, nor to administrative judges, nor to the large variety of lay judges. In terms of substance, there are two main generic areas of debate of varying importance in the different areas. The first area is the relationship of judges to politics, both in individual decisions and in the freedom of the judicial career, and the second is the ability to carry out the mission of the judge to do justice.

Freedom from political interference

The relationship of ordinary judges to politics involves both hierarchical subordination in terms of the organisation of justice, and the interference by politicians in the handling of cases. Much of this debate focuses on criminal law and on two figures in the pre-trial process. On the one hand there is the juge d'instruction who is a single judge who is often able to develop a personal profile in the media and among the professions.[65] Single-minded fidelity to the law and independence from the powerful in politics or in society constitute the ideal of this judge around which the integrity of the criminal prosecution process is built. Freedom from external instructions in individual cases, either from the Ministry of Justice or from hierarchical superiors, has been one of the key elements in recent debates. In the end, politicians had to withdraw from trying to exercise influence on the conduct of cases.[66]

On the other hand the procureur is much more of a state official, who requires independence in some individual decisions, but needs to be under direction in relation to the broader role he plays. Michèle-Laure Rassat argues that, at the heart of the complexity of the procureur's role, is a confusion between the parquet as representative of the nation, of the sovereign power, and as representative of the executive.[67] The procureur is trained as a judge and is considered as such. For example, the Conseil constitutionnel considered that the extension of detention by the parquet was perfectly permissible, given that 'the judicial power, which under art. 66 of the Constitution ensures respect for individual liberty, includes both the *magistrats du siège* and the *parquet*'.[68] On the other hand, the parquet is subordinated to the Ministry of Justice because it is

[65] See below pp. 101–2. [66] *French Legal Cultures*, 121–3 and 137–8.
[67] Conference speech, Nancy, November 1997, 'Indépendance du Parquet, opportunité des poursuites', to be found on http://jurispole.univ-nancy2, p. 5 of the report.
[68] CC decision no. 93–326 DC of 11 August 1993, Rec. 217, considérant 5. See further T. Renoux, 'Le Conseil constitutionnel et l'instruction pénale: Juges ou magistrats?' (1998) 10 *Justices: La Justice Pénale* 75.

carrying out criminal law policy[69] and, in most periods, this has involved a right for the Ministry to give instructions on the prosecution of individual cases. All the same, any *juge du parquet* is free to plead according to his convictions, even if those are contrary to the governmental guidance.[70] However, the written submissions must conform to the wishes expressed by the Government. The Minister gives general orders through circulars. This role of the parquet and his relationship to the Government was controversial as a result of prosecutions of politicians in the 1990s.[71]

The cases of political corruption in the 1990s[72] were particularly testing for the independence of judges. The criminal prosecution of politicians for corruption (political or financial) led to direct conflicts with the judiciary over individual cases. The juges d'instruction and the procureurs then came under great pressure from the politicians to drop charges or they found that politicians used their authority in an abusive way, e.g. to send a helicopter to the Himalayas in order to bring back an investigating judge.[73] There was a long investigation of the President's party which led to the conviction of former Prime Minister, Alain Juppé, and an investigation ordered by the Prime Minister into improper pressure put on judges.[74] In other cases, criticism by politicians in the media prompted the President of the Cour de cassation to write a public defence of judges.[75]

There is not the same concern in the area of administrative law. As Loschak notes, there is an ambiguity in the role of the administrative judge. In her view, 'the administrative judge who, despite his independence, remains close to power, is willing to pay attention to the problems which the Government encounters in sensitive and serious

[69] Art. 5 of the ordonnance 58-1270 of 22 December 1958 states that they are under the direction of the Minister of Justice.

[70] See further E. Mathias, *Les procureurs du droit* (Paris 1999), 197–205; art. 33 of the Code de procédure pénale.

[71] J. Pradel and J.-P. Laborde, 'Du ministère public en matière pénale. A l'heure d'une éventuelle autonomie?' D 1997 Chr. 141 who argue that independence is 'a great necessity of our times'.

[72] See *French Legal Cultures*, 119–24 and J. Bell, 'The Criminal Liability of Politicians in France' (2000) 3 *Cambridge Yearbook of European Legal Studies* 65 at 68 and 70–2.

[73] J. Ardagh, *France in the New Century* (Penguin, London 2000), 45.

[74] See Avis of the Conseil Supérieur de la Magistrature, 28 April 2004, on the CSM website (http://www.conseil-superieur-magistrature.fr); see also Bell, 'Criminal Liability', above n. 72.

[75] See further *French Legal Cultures*, 121–4.

situations'.[76] The members of the Conseil d'Etat serve as legal advisers to the government in both formal and informal ways. As such, they are drawn into the process of policy formulation. There is inevitably an overlap between the advice given at the stage of policy or legislative preview, and the judgments given when there is a review of administrative decisions or legislation. At the same time, questions of the merits of decisions are not directly the concern of the administrative courts, and the duty to set and uphold standards for the administration is part of the role of the administrative judge. Since the 1889 decision in *Cadot*, the decisions of the courts have been fully independent.[77] In particular, the *commissaire du gouvernement* gives public and independent opinions in court. Thereby the structure has an important degree of independence.

The independence of the judicial career from improper political interference has been the main constitutional focus of attention. The creation of the *Conseil supérieur de la magistrature* (CSM) in 1946 and its involvement in judicial appointments, as well as reforms of the institution in 1993 to strengthen this role, have weakened political involvement in judicial appointments. All the same, the French system retains a significant role for politicians in judicial appointments, especially to posts as procureur, which are very much in the gift of the Government. As has been seen, political involvement has been limited, but not curtailed, in relation to ordinary judges.[78]

The CSM is also the guardian of independence in the later career. Judges cannot be moved against their will, though recent reforms on the need to move to gain promotion show an attempt to limit this inflexibility. Even more importantly, the disciplinary function is in the hand of the judiciary, not politicians.

It is interesting to note that this effective independence of administrative justice has been recognised as a constitutional value by the Conseil constitutionnel, rather than by legislation.[79] The value was institutionalised in relation to the judges of the tribunaux administratifs by the *loi* of 6 January 1986 which makes them irremovable and places their promotion and discipline under an independent national council similar to that which exists for private law judges. There is no equivalent for the Conseil d'Etat. As a grand corps of the state, it feels it does not need it,

[76] D. Loschak, *Le rôle politique du juge administratif français* (Paris 1972), 241–2.
[77] Brown and Bell, 82. [78] Above p. 55.
[79] Decision no. 80-119 DC of 22 July 1980, RDP 1980, 1691 and decision no. 84-179 DC of 12 September 1984, Rec. 73.

though there was a purge in 1879 and there have been later threats to the freedom of opinion of individuals at times of national emergency.[80] As Garapon and Papadopolous note, the lack of hierarchy and of the limited career structure in the Conseil d'Etat, as well as its proximity to government power, has not been seen as a problem for judicial independence.[81] The Conseil is effectively the bastion of independence for the whole administrative court system.

In relation to the members of the Conseil constitutionnel, there is clear political involvement in nomination, but this is counterbalanced by the absence of any direct way in which politicians can influence its operation, since the members are appointed for a nine-year fixed term, without the possibility of renewal, and they give decisions in which individual opinions cannot be identified. Politicians often make strong criticisms of decisions by the Conseil constitutionnel in the media or in political debate.[82] This does occasionally cause members or its Secretary-General to defend the institution in the press, but it is more normal for the Conseil to rely on others to put its point of view.

Freedom to do justice

The debate on judicial independence among ordinary judges is often focused on the material ability of the courts to do justice. Two main areas raise concerns in relation to civil and criminal justice more than other areas. First, there is the issue of judicial salaries. Are they high enough to attract good candidates? Should salaries give greater economic independence so as to forestall the possibility of corruption, e.g. by judges making themselves attractive for careers outside the judiciary? It is clear that French judicial salaries are not keeping pace with those of *avocats* and the attractiveness of the career relies on other benefits. Secondly, and more importantly, there are concerns about the number of judicial posts and the quality of judicial infrastructure. There have been constant complaints that there are not enough judges, so delays occur and judges are put under pressure. There are also concerns about the quality of the facilities, such as courts, in which judges work. Without a rationalisation of the number of court centres, the budget of the Ministry of Justice is stretched, and criminal justice takes precedence over civil justice. To address this problem, the judicial unions argue that judges should be able to run their own budget and thus decide on the priorities for justice. By contrast the Conseil d'Etat and Conseil

[80] See Brown and Bell, 85. [81] Garapon and Papadopoulos, 170–1.
[82] *French Legal Cultures*, 225–34.

constitutionnel already have such powers and ensure that public law courts have the sort of independence that ordinary judges desire.

Judicial roles

Judicial creativity

French attitudes to judicial creativity are marked by history and contradiction. Article 4 of the Civil Code prohibits the judge from from refusing to decide if the law is obscure, and so forces her to undertake a normative role. On the other hand, article 5 prevents the judge from making regulatory decisions and thus overstepping the scope of the judicial power. As David put it,

> judicial decisions are not a source of law in France. Strictly speaking, they never create legal rules. Their role is always understood to be the application of preexisting statutes or customs. In the absence of an applicable statute or custom, decisions can be based on principles of equity, reason, justice, or tradition. It is never enough, however, simply to refer to a prior judicial decision.[83]

Living within this (obscure) tension is something with which all judges have to struggle, but there is a broad consensus on the extent of an appropriate level of activism in different areas.

The original ideas on judicial creativity were developed in relation to civil law before the Civil Code was enacted, but these have remained the benchmark for both judicial creativity and style.[84] Even the Cour de cassation cannot formally make the ruling binding in subsequent cases. For that reason, case-law is described as 'une autorité' (albeit a privileged authority), but not binding.[85] Yet, the Code is over 200 years old and new problems arise, so the judges and doctrinal writers have had to admit that policy decisions are necessary to keep the law up to date, even if judges have to work within the conceptual structure which they inherit from the Code.[86] Although cases are only, at least formally, illustrations of the Code, in practice, even in civil law, there is an acceptance of the concept of 'a leading case', such that particular

[83] R. David, *French Law* (Baton Rouge 1972), 181.

[84] See generally M. Troper and C. Grzegorczyk, 'Precedent in France' in D. N. MacCormick and Robert S. Summers (eds.), *Intérpreting Precedents* (Aldershot 1997), ch. 4 (hereafter 'Troper and Grzegorczyk').

[85] See J. Carbonnier, 'Sources and Methods of French Law' in J. Dainow (ed.), *The Role of Judicial Decisions and Doctrine in the Civil Law* (Notre Dame 1971), 91 at 97.

[86] See generally S. Belaid, *Essai sur le pouvoir créateur du juge* (Paris 1974); E. Serverin, *De la jurisprudence en droit privé. Théorie d'une pratique* (Lyons 1985); *Principles of French Law*, 25–33.

lines of legal principle are commonly described by reference to the name of the leading case which established them.[87] The informed reader uses a multiplicity of indicators to determine the importance given to its decision by the Cour de cassation,[88] and the Cour de cassation uses its annual report to identify both its achievements and the areas in which it would like to see developments by the legislator. The tension in its role is seen from these two extracts from annual reports:

> we are pleased to emphasise that . . . whilst remaining within its role, our Court contributes to the gradual creation of the new state of law which will shape the society of tomorrow.[89]

> Numerous decisions bear witness to the desire not to be closed off from the world and not to be content with the cult of 'precedent'. Even though it is careful to avoid hasty reversals of case-law, which would not be compatible with the need for legal certainty, the Cour de cassation does not hesitate to correct its most settled doctrines when these no longer seem to it to correspond to social and economic realities or no longer are in accord with the development of ideas and morals.[90]

The Cour de cassation can develop the law radically, most famously in creating no-fault liability in delict from an introductory sentence in art. 1384(1). It can use its decisions to provoke the legislator to action, as in the area of motor vehicle accidents. It can also refuse to act and await the legislator, as in the case of civil partnerships similar to marriage.[91] The delicate nature of this position can be seen by the furore created when the Cour de cassation gave damages to a child for the expenses of its upbringing after a doctor had failed to diagnose a pregnancy, thus depriving the mother of a chance to have the plaintiff aborted.[92] The legislator intervened immediately to reverse the case-law.

Because higher court precedents do not bind, lower courts can offer 'legitimate resistance' to them. The refusal of the lower courts to

[87] Troper and Grzegorczyk, 131–2.

[88] For a full discussion in a framework which makes comparison possible with other legal systems, see ibid., 119–25; *French Legal Cultures*, 67–8 and an illustration of judicial creativity on pp. 78–88.

[89] Cour de cassation, *Rapport annuel 1975* (Paris 1976), 101.

[90] Cour de cassation, *Rapport de la Cour de cassation: Années judiciaires 1976 et 1977* (Paris 1978), 119. See also Cour de cassation, *L'image doctrinale de la Cour de cassation* (Paris 1994), 123–68.

[91] See *French Legal Cultures*, 68–9 and 71.

[92] The *Perruche* case: Cass. ass. plén., 17 November 2000, JCP 2000 II 10438; B. Markesinis, 'Unity or Division. The Search for Similarities in Contemporary European Law' [2001] *Current Legal Problems* 591.

follow a ruling of the Cour de cassation has sometimes led the latter to reconsider its views and to come up with a different solution.[93] In a colloquium organised by the Cour de cassation, judges at all levels acknowledged that the role of the lower court judges is to be a rebel, but not too often.[94] On the one hand, they are very respectful of decisions of the Cour de cassation and seek them out as the first point of reference (as far as they can be known). On the other hand, they have to follow what they believe to be the right interpretation of the law. In interviews for this research, lower judges suggested they will often only do so where they think that the Cour de cassation might well reverse its case-law or where other courts are moving in the same direction. In other words, they seek out evidence of criticism from practitioners, academics or other courts to support their personal opinion that the Cour de cassation was wrong.

In criminal law, the scope for judicial creativity is more limited. In particular, the principle of legality, i.e. the requirement that crimes and penalties be established by legislation, requires a more strict approach to interpretation of the Code.[95] Furthermore, the legislator is more active in this area.

The position of administrative law is different. There is no overarching substantive code. There are a number of very specific codes and, in recent years, a codification of procedural rules. But these are at best consolidations, rather than statements of general principle. As a result, the general principles of substantive administrative law are judge-made law, and continue to be developed by the judges.[96] Since the Conseil controls the publication of its own decisions, this process is also used to signal whether the decision is marking an important development in the law, or is merely routine or confined to its facts. The cult of the 'leading case' is even more marked, and cases are cited regularly by name and included in the judge's case file. Nevertheless, most of the law governing the administration is set out in very detailed *lois* and *règlements*, so the principal rule-maker is the legislator, except in areas such as judicial review of administrative action and administrative liability.[97]

93 For example, on the civil liability of children (Cass. ass. plén. 5 May 1984, D 1984, 525 note Chabas), liability for things (Cass. ch. réunies 13 February 1930, *Jand'heur*, S 1930. 1. 121), and on the dismissal of teachers in religious schools (Cass. ass. plén. 19 May 1978, JCP 1978 II 19009).

94 Cour de cassation, *L'image doctrinale*, above n. 90, 188–90, 191.

95 *French Legal Cultures*, 133–4.

96 See ibid., 175–85; Brown and Bell, 24–5.

97 On these two areas, see Brown and Bell, chs. 8 and 9.

In constitutional law, there is even less structure to the law. To begin with, the constitutional texts are fragmentary and incomplete. The 1958 Constitution deals with institutional matters in a general way, leaving principles on areas such as civil liberties to be worked out on the basis of the Declaration of the Rights of Man and of the Citizen of 1789 and the Preamble of the 1946 Constitution, which also refers to 'fundamental principles recognised by the laws of the Republic'. The whole edifice of constitutional civil liberties has been constructed by the Conseil, and lawyers have to refer to its decisions as the principal source of the law.[98]

The current Vice-President of the Conseil d'Etat and former Secretary-General of the Conseil constitutionel, Genevois, comments that

> Experience shows that the particularity of certain methods of interpretation is . . . a function of the idea that each court has of its place within the institutions [of the state] and the conception that it has of its functions. But, on the other hand, we are aware that, at least in domestic law, our supreme courts refer to the methods of interpretation that draw on the same legal culture.[99]

There is a significant commonality in the approaches to creativity and interpretation of law within the different French judiciaries. There is also a similarity in the relative importance of creativity in the judicial role. With a vast bulk of routine cases to process, there is limited scope for creativity at lower levels of the judiciary. It will only be at the Cour de cassation, Conseil d'Etat or Conseil constitutionnel level that there will be a regular creative element in the work of the judge. Of course, there will be some occasions at lower levels when something novel comes up. But for the most part, the tradition of the rather uncreative role of the judge is characteristic at those levels. All the same, the place of the different supreme courts in the institutions of the state and 'the conception that [each] has of its functions' does lead to different degrees of creativity.

The European dimension of the judicial role has given a new direction and status to the ordinary judge that many find attractive. The Cour de cassation has had to challenge existing French legislation in order to implement both European Union legislation and especially the European Convention on Human Rights.[100] Though excluded from challenging domestic legislation because it is incompatible with rights

[98] See Bell, *French Constitutional Law*, above n. 22, and *French Legal Cultures*, 202, 216–19.

[99] B. Genevois, 'Le Conseil d'Etat et l'interprétation de la loi' RFDA 2002, 877, 888.

[100] See G. Canivet, 'Une responsabilité supplémentaire vis-à-vis de L'Europe' in A. Garapon, *Les juges. Un pouvoir irresponsable?* (Paris 2003), ch. 7; *French Legal Cultures*, 58–63.

protected by the French Constitution, the judiciary is able to challenge legislation by reference to these supranational standards. Somewhat later, the administrative judge has also taken on the role of applying both European laws to administrative action.[101] The Conseil constitutionnel has found its role more limited by the existence of a supranational legislature and a superior court.[102] Although 'dialogue' is a popular word to describe the relationship between these different national judges and the judges of Strasbourg and Luxembourg, the principal mechanisms highlighted by the judges themselves are judicial decisions made affecting France and their reception.[103] The other suggested routes are invitations to the European judges to speak at conferences, sometimes organised by the higher French courts, and doctrinal writing.

Judicial style and reasoning

The style of French judgments is particular. It claims authority and aims to present an outcome, but without deeper explanations. It is impersonal and is typical of a civil service style, which appeals to the authority of the rule, rather than the authority of the decision-maker.[104] Properly understood in its institutional context, the style reveals much about the character and approach of judicial lawmaking.

The style of French justification can be seen from a relatively simple case.[105] The Dean of the medical faculty at the University of West Brittany refused to renew permission for one of his staff, M. Lejeune, to serve on an external agency dealing with quality assurance in health studies. The immediate cause of these actions was a successful complaint from students about exams in which 150 out of 400 students had been given a mark of '0' on his course (PCEM 1). It was alleged that M. Lejeune did not double-mark the scripts and an administrative court annulled the results. In the Conseil d'Etat, the commissaire du gouvernement, Schwartz, argued that the Dean's action was a disciplinary measure and should have been taken only after Lejeune had been given the safeguards of a disciplinary procedure. But the Conseil d'Etat upheld it, because the reasons given by the University were public interest justifications – the

[101] Brown and Bell, 283–6; more generally J. Bell, 'French Administrative Law and the Supremacy of European Laws' (2005) 11 *European Public Law* 487.

[102] See J. Bell, 'French Constitutional Council and European Law' (2005) 54 ICLQ 735.

[103] See, for example, F. Lichère, L. Potvin-Solis and A. Raynouard (eds.), *Le dialogue entre les juges européens et nationaux: Incantation ou réalité* (Brussels 2004), 96, 98 and 124.

[104] Garapon and Papadopoulos, 162–3.

[105] CE 11 June 2003, AJDA 2003, 1992, concl. Schwartz.

need for M. Lejeune to spend more time in the University, given both the absence of a colleague and the consequences of the annulment of the examinations. The decision did 'not have the character of a disguised disciplinary sanction', and so it did not have to be taken in a manner similar to a disciplinary procedure. There is a clear clash of interpretation between the commissaire and the Conseil, yet no attempt is made to discuss this clash in the judgment. The relevant section is a good example of French style:

> Considering that the argument that the challenged decision is not justified is unfounded; as, even if this decision, justified by the public interest in the greater presence of M. Lejeune in the University owing to the absence of his colleague, also mentions the particular circumstances to the events surrounding and to the situation resulting from the PCEM 1 competition of 1998–9, it does not have the character of a disguised sanction; as the argument that the decision should have been preceded by the exercise of guarantees applicable in disciplinary matters must, in consequence, be rejected;
> Considering that it follows from what has been said that M. Lejeune is not justified in requesting the annulment of the decision of 4 December 1999. . . .

The style simply gives us a result, which follows from the rule. The style shows the function of the judgment is to provide a brief explanation of the outcome, but not to provide the reasons behind that justification. Unlike the commissaire du gouvernement, who used some 700 words to justify his argument, the Conseil merely provides some 275 words to deal with the point. The lack of engagement with the arguments either of the parties or of the commissaire du gouvernement means that it does not really seek to explain the decision. Rather it seeks to provide an answer to the lower court.

Bancaud[106] described this form of decision as a 'pious hypocrisy' – making law, while appearing to deny that this is happening. But it would be a gross mistake to think that judges are really denying that they make law or that anyone in France is deceived into believing that they do not. The form of the judgment is actually more like the minutes of a committee meeting, which do not attempt to summarise the debates that went on before the decision was reached.[107] Lasser helpfully identifies a 'bifurcation' in judicial debates – the judgment is formalist, whilst the substantive, policy-focused justification occurs in another place.[108]

[106] A. Bancaud, 'Considérations sur une "pieuse hypocrisie": La forme des arrêts de la Cour de cassation' (1987) 7 *Droit et Société* 373.

[107] See *French Legal Cultures*, 78.

[108] M. Lasser, *Judicial Deliberations. A Comparative Analysis of Judicial Transparency and Legitimacy* (Oxford 2004), 16, 44–61.

He has looked at the files in the Cour de cassation and I have done the same and attended judicial deliberations in the Conseil d'Etat and tribunaux administratifs.[109] Both of us separately have observed that the oral debates among judges and the individual expressions of opinion by the reporter judge and the avocat général in the Cour de cassation or the commissaire du gouvernement in the Conseil d'Etat[110] undertake a serious and developed consideration of policy issues and the possible interpretations of the law. These debates are also reflected in the arguments made by the avocats au Conseil d'Etat et à la Cour de cassation,[111] who have a monopoly of cases before the two courts, and in doctrinal commentaries, produced by a small number of regular academic authorities. From the common lawyer's perspective, what is missing is a public presentation of policy reasons. In part, this does occur in the annual report of each court, where selected decisions are commented upon. But, in part, this is not considered necessary. Lasser is right to identify a kind of elite debate conducted within the court and the legal community, but which does not engage the wider public directly: 'The Cour de cassation's legal process thus boils down to some one hundred judges in one large court annually deciding tens of thousands of appellate cases argued by some one hundred attorneys, resulting in necessarily brief judgments that are published alongside the comments of a very small number of academics.'[112]

The regular relationships within the court and within the legal community ensure accountability for judicial creativity. This is reinforced by the possibility that lower courts will refuse to follow decisions with which they disagree profoundly. The legitimacy of this role comes from a basic French confidence in a technocratic elite, among whom a frank

[109] See J. Bell, 'Reflections on the Procedure of the Conseil d'Etat' in G. Hand and J. McBride (eds.), *Droit sans frontières* (Birmingham 1991), 211.

[110] The avocat général and the commissaire du gouvernement are judges who act as representatives of the public interest in litigation, offering advice to the court. They are not parties to litigation, but part of the court and so are considered to be unlike a common law *amicus curiae*: *Principles of French Law*, 31–2. This is a view not appreciated by the European Court of Human Rights: see J. Bell, 'The Role of the Commissaire du Gouvernement and the European Convention on Human Rights' (2003) 9 *European Public Law* 309.

[111] These ninety avocats au Conseil d'Etat et à la Cour de cassation belong to a different profession to the ordinary avocat. They are described as not part of the 'club' with the judges of these two courts, but as 'good companions as interlocutors', trusted at an informal level and having relations with the courts much closer to those of the English Bar than the ordinary French avocat: see P. Gonod (ed.), *Les avocats au Conseil d'Etat et à la Cour de cassation* (Paris 2002), 81–2, 94–5.

[112] Lasser, *Judicial Deliberations*, above n. 108, 187.

and serious debate about legal policy is undertaken away from the political and media spotlights.[113] The acceptability of decisions is not to be assessed in relation to individual decisions, but in relation to the trends, *la jurisprudence constante*:

> The French legal and judicial process therefore consists of a long-term dialogic process in which high-ranking judicial *magistrats* and doctrinal writers respond to each other over time, each incorporating, informing, framing, recasting, and redirecting the past, present, and future work of the others. As a result, French judicial decisions emerge as deeply collaborative products resulting from the long-term consultation between *la jurisprudence* and *la doctrine* at the highest levels.[114]

The comment applies to all the different French court systems, even though, as will be seen,[115] the balance between these actors differs between each system.

Extrajudicial roles

Ordinary judges

A frequent and classical external posting is an administrative role within the Ministry of Justice (the *Chancellerie*). Since the administrative posts in this Ministry are held by judges, rather than by ordinary civil servants, there are opportunities to be posted here and to influence the formulation and implementation of policy. It is argued that, to gain advancement, it is necessary to be known by those in authority. A posting in the Ministry of Justice ensures this. The top third of ENM candidates choose this as their first post and it is seen as the 'royal route' to a higher judicial career. Certainly a very substantial number of the senior judiciary have spent at least some time in the Ministry during their careers. In contrast to members of the Conseil d'Etat, members of the private law judiciary are not seconded frequently to other parts of government or the public sector.[116] The majority of those seconded are men (68 per cent), mainly in the early part of their career. In addition, a number of people are placed on *disponibilité*, mainly to take up posts in other organisations, such as international bodies or ministerial private

[113] Ibid., 327–9. [114] Ibid., 193. [115] Below pp. 82–8 and 106.

[116] See A. Boigeol, 'Les magistrats "hors murs"' (2000) 44/45 *Droit et société* 225. She notes that their most frequent external posting is as a sous-préfet. Secondment has become more frequent in the Fifth Republic and was facilitated by a *loi* of 1992. Annex 4 of the CSM's *Rapport d'activité 2001* records that 191 requests were examined from June 1998 to March 2002, 29 to posts in the ENM and 28 to the Ministry of Justice. Over 50 per cent of those on detachment are in the lowest judicial grade.

offices. A small number become Members of Parliament or even of the Government. The ordinary judiciary is not a grand corps and so is not seen as a source of public servants occupying major positions.

Administrative judges

The wide variety of potential career paths for administrators is predominantly relevant to the Conseil d'Etat, which is one of the grands corps of the public service. The corps of judges of the tribunaux administratifs and the Cours administratives d'appel has less prestige and is less often called upon to perform wider roles. France has a much more technocratic government than the UK. Ministers cannot serve as deputies at the same time, and many have not served in Parliament. Civil servants, including administrative judges, can have a political activity.[117] If they seek to enter Parliament, they can remain in their corps whilst campaigning for election, and are put on *disponibilité* when elected. When they cease to hold elected office, they can rejoin the activity of their corps. Major electoral defeats lead to large numbers of civil servants rejoining their corps while others enter Parliament or Government. Many members of the grands corps have served as Minister or Prime Minister. The Conseil d'Etat has a significant role in this respect, with members such as Laurent Fabius serving as Prime Minister, President of the National Assembly and Minister of Finance. Noëlle Lenoir headed the commission on bioethics, served as member of the Conseil constitutionnel from 1992 until 2001, and then in 2002 became a government minister.

Members of the Conseil already have non-judicial tasks as an integral part of its functions. Costa argues that the advisory function has more practical importance for the Government and the administration than the judicial function.[118] The Conseil gives its advice on all *projets de loi* before they are presented to Parliament. This role essentially involves helping with the drafting of the text or commenting on any text produced by the administration.[119] It also advises the Government on proposals for European Community decisions having a legislative

[117] On the politicising of the civil service, see L. Rouban, *Les cadres supérieurs de la fonction publique et la politique de modernisation administrative* (Paris 1994), ch. 6.4.

[118] J.-P. Costa, *Le Conseil d'Etat dans la société contemporaine* (Paris 1993), 49; N. Questiaux, 'Administration and the Rule of Law: The Preventive Role of the French Conseil d'Etat' [1995] PL 247.

[119] See J. Bell, 'What is the Function of the Conseil d'Etat in the Preparation of Legislation?' (2000) 49 ICLQ 661.

character.[120] Its comments are mainly on legal issues in the broadest sense, but the Conseil is also concerned to ensure that a measure will be workable. It feels competent to make such comments because its members have a wide experience of the administration.[121] The second function of the Conseil is to provide legal advice at the request of specific government departments. Such advice avoids potential censure before the courts in France or in Luxembourg or Strasbourg. The close connection between such advisory and judicial functions within the Conseil d'Etat ensures that the law is created and interpreted within an environment of dialogue with the administration, a feature that is distinctive to France. This establishes and reinforces relationships between the 'active' administration and its judge.

The impact of these advisory functions on the Conseil's judicial work is much acknowledged. If the Conseil has given advice on proposed legislation or on a question referred to it by the Government, then it is conventional that only the highest judicial formation of the Conseil can depart from that opinion.[122] Advice can be both legally and politically important. For example, in 1989, to defuse the politically live issue of the Islamic headdress worn by girls in state schools, the Minister of Education sought an *avis* from the Conseil on the rules that schools could legally adopt. In a prudent decision,[123] the Conseil interpreted the law as permitting freedom of expression, but with limits that ensured respect for the secular nature of the Republic enshrined in the Constitution. The advice was duly promulgated and implemented by the administration and subsequently by the Conseil in its judicial capacity.[124] When the issue became live again in 2003, the President of the Republic set up the Stasi Commission, which was composed this time of leading social and political figures, but it did contain a member of the Conseil d'Etat and was staffed by it.[125]

[120] The pre-legislative opinions of the Conseil d'Etat are sent systematically to the Conseil constitutionnel: Questiaux, 'Administration', above n. 118, 256.

[121] M. Letourneur, J. Bauchet and J. Méric, *Le Conseil d'Etat et les Tribunaux Administratifs* (2nd edn, Paris 1970), 181. See generally N. Questiaux, 'Do the Opinions Expressed by the Conseil d'Etat in its Capacity as Legal Advisor to the Government Influence Policy?' (2000) 49 ICLQ 672.

[122] Massot and Girardot, 84–5.

[123] Avis of 27 November 1989, RFDA 1990, 6; J. Bell, 'Religious Observance in Secular Schools: A French Solution' (1990) 2 *Education and the Law* 121 and C. Wiener, 'Les foulards noirs et la République', in *L'Etat de droit* (Paris 1995), 761.

[124] See CE 2 November 1992, *Kherouaa*, Leb. 329; CE 27 November 1996, *Khalid and Sefiani*, Leb. 460; Avis of CE Ass. 3 May 2000, AJDA 2000, 602.

[125] 'Commission de réflexion sur l'application du principe de laïcité dans la République'. Stasi was the Médiateur de la République (Ombudsman).

Finally, the Conseil d'Etat is a government 'think tank', rather like the English Law Commission. For example, the Section du Rapport et des Etudes has produced reports on topics such as the internet and computer networks (1998), and a review of bioethics law (1994 and 1999).

Membership of external bodies in a more legal capacity is common, just as it is for common-law judges. A member of the Conseil may be asked to chair or be part of a departmental inquiry into a problem or issue. For example, Bernard Tricot chaired the inquiry into the Greenpeace affair in 1985–6, and Jean Massot produced the report on the criminal liability of elected officials in 1999. The Conseil d'Etat operates as a resource of personnel for the rest of the administration. Advisory roles may be as much informal as formal, so that there is a request for advice that comes to people with known expertise. The relatively small number of ENA graduates enables informal networks to be set up.[126]

The advisory role of the administrative judge is almost exclusively confined to the Conseil d'Etat. The lower courts are not in the habit of giving advice to the local prefect or administrative authorities, and their judges do not have the same career opportunities to work at a policy level in government.

Professional judges and the legal community

Judges and advocates

Like much of what has been described about French law, there is no single answer as to who counts as a professional lawyer.[127] For the purposes of this chapter, it is sufficient to concentrate on *avocats* and the *avocats au Conseil d'Etat et à la Cour de cassation*. To assess their relationships to judges and their relative importance, it is necessary to examine the role of these lawyers in court and out of court, their collective representative functions, and their ability to recruit the best lawyers.

The distinction between private law judges and avocats is of very long standing, and again it pre-dates 1789.[128] Until modern times those recruited as judges had to have already completed a two-year period of traineeship in a *cabinet* of an avocat. But since 1959, there has been a sharper separation between the careers of judges and avocats, since training is totally distinct.

126 See B. Latour, *La fabrique du droit* (Paris 2002), 39ff. This is a generally useful book to gain an impression of the working of the Conseil, but the structure makes it difficult to use as a work of analysis for the workings of the Conseil.

127 See *Principles of French Law*, 69–73; *French Legal Cultures*, 44–6.

128 L. Karpik, *French Lawyers* (Oxford 1999), 32–5.

The avocat is both a legal adviser and a representative in court. The Bar has been fragmented and this has contributed to its limited influence. Avocats have traditionally worked in small offices. In 2003, outside Paris, 43.5 per cent of avocats worked on their own.[129] They are members of regional bars and only since reforms in 1991 have they been allowed to have national-level firms. There are a number of different types of firm, each with a different relationship to judges. The defence lawyers, often working individually and regionally, will have particular relationships with the few local prosecutors and juges d'instruction. But the relationship is typically confrontational. Reforms in the sixteenth and seventeenth centuries creating the King's prosecutors and the juge d'instruction left avocats to make their reputation by defending private clients.[130] The avocat not only advises the client and presents his case in court, but also orchestrates public opinion in favour of his client, e.g. by giving media interviews. As Merle explains,

> When a case has a certain public reputation, the *avocat* cannot restrict himself to his office and to the corridors of the courts. If he wants to defend the cause of his client fully, he must necessarily play the game, give interviews, reply to attacks, correct mistakes. But he is obliged to respect the secrecy of the *instruction*, to observe the deference to which he is bound with respect to the judges.[131]

The role of the avocat is one which is completely separated from the judge and can lead to incomprehension and antagonism.[132]

The commercial firms are different, but struggle in a competitive market. Uetwiller[133] distinguishes four types: the Anglo-American firm, the larger French (typically Parisian) firm that tries to participate in international networks, the niche French firm and the local firm. He notes that a 2002 study revealed that small businesses were more likely to consult accountants than avocats for legal advice.[134] Since commercial matters are likely to go to the commercial courts or arbitration, commercial firms participate little in professional life and in dealings with the ordinary judges. All the same, it is this part of the profession that is increasing in income and numbers. Between 1988 and 2004, the Paris Bar grew from 6,294 avocats to 16,336.[135]

[129] B. Chambel, 'Vers l'initié du Barreau français' in L. Marlière (ed.), *L'avocat en France* (Paris 2004), 22.

[130] See Karpik, *French Lawyers*, above n. 128, 26.

[131] R. Merle, 'Défense pénale' (1998) 10 *Justices* 91, 93; *French Legal Cultures*, 142–4.

[132] See e.g. Samet, *Journal*, above n. 47, 17.

[133] J.-J. Uetwiller, 'Le Barreau d'affaires' in Marlière, *L'avocat*, above n. 129, 30–3.

[134] Ibid., 33. [135] C. Lussan in Marlière, *L'avocat*, above n. 129, 37, 39.

The avocats au Conseil d'Etat et à la Cour de cassation have the monopoly of litigation before the two highest courts (except in certain matters, notably criminal appeals), but can act as general legal advisers. There are a restricted number of these lawyers, but their regular relationship with the highest-ranking judges enables them to exercise formal and informal influence on judicial perceptions of appropriate legal development. They thus have quite high standing within the legal community. Because their work includes many difficult legal issues, they are likely to consult academics, and younger academics may even be employed in their offices.

A number of the members of both groups of avocats are politically active and avocats are frequently members of public commissions, such as the Stasi Commission.[136] Indeed, the latter commission had an avocat, but no ordinary judge member, even if it did have a conseiller d'Etat. The voice here is individual and is stronger in political circles than the voice of ordinary judges, but less so than conseillers d'Etat and members of the Conseil constitutionnel. Whilst, on criminal justice issues, the avocat is a prominent voice in the media, on other matters both ordinary and administrative judges will play a prominent part in debates.[137]

In terms of collective representation, the fragmented bars have difficulty in expressing a common voice and their association is rightly called the *Conseil national des Barreaux*.[138] Where they do express opinions on matters such as criminal justice, they are likely to be on the same side as the judicial unions and carry much the same weight. Avocats au Conseil d'Etat et à la Cour de cassation do not need collective representation, but will have sufficient individual authority to be heard by politicians or by judges when engaging in law reform.

In terms of recruitment, the profession of avocat is in competition with that of judge. The number of *études* for the avocats au Conseil d'Etat et à la Cour de cassation is fixed, and so entry into this kind of firm is usually by inheritance or by working at an assistant level, a post carrying limited status. The rapid increase in the number of positions as avocat since the mid-1980s reflects trends in the commercial world, and especially in the globalisation of lawyer firms found in other countries. Salaries in this branch of the law have increased. There has not been the same increase in the number of posts as judge. In the ten years

[136] Above p. 78. [137] *French Legal Cultures*, 98 and 117–24.

[138] See the remarks of their president M. Benichou in Marlière, *L'avocat*, above n. 129, 7ff.

from 1992 to 2002, the number of posts as ordinary judge rose by 17 per cent and those as administrative judge outside the Conseil d'Etat by 54 per cent, and neither rate of growth matches that of the avocats. In 2002, there were 39,454 avocats in 181 bars,[139] of whom 5,893 were in training. Of these, 46.4 per cent were women. The number of women in practice grew from 12,715 in 1999 to 14,750 in 2002, whilst the number of men rose from 17,562 to 18,811. But, in the same period, the number of women in training rose from 2,926 to 3,567, whilst the number of men was smaller (2,067 in 1999 and 2,326 in 2002).[140] The growth of the profession and, in particular, the Paris Bar, has made inroads into the attractiveness of the judicial career, which has not grown in numbers or income in the same way.

By and large, these developments have little impact on the growth of the administrative judiciary, which draws heavily from the public sector.

Judges and academics

As I have stated elsewhere, the importance of doctrinal legal writing varies between the different branches of French law.[141] In reading judgments, the skilled interpreter is forced to rely on certain institutional practices in order to determine the importance of a decision, for example that decisions of different formations of the highest courts carry different authority.[142] Within the supreme courts of the ordinary and administrative systems, there are documents produced by individual judges, the reporter and the *conclusions* of the *avocats généraux* and the *commissaire du gouvernement*, though most of these are not published. These conclusions are the nearest equivalent to a common-law judicial speech and offer a focused effort to persuade the court to develop the law in a particular direction. They have the ambition to survey the law, but also to offer a personal perspective. These conclusions are regularly cited, and have formed the model for the Advocate General in the European Court of Justice. The long discussion of case-law, writings and principles they contain provides evidence both of the reasons for judicial lawmaking and of the influences on judicial reasoning. Because the judgments of the courts are not fully reasoned, the academic writer is particularly important as a skilled interpreter using these signs and sources in

[139] C. Moreau (ed.), *Statistique sur la Profession d'avocat* (Ministry of Justice, Paris 2002: http://www.justice.gouv.fr/publicat/statsavocats/statsavocatssomm.htm), tables 1–3.
[140] Ibid., table 7. [141] *French Legal Cultures*, vii–viii, 245–6.
[142] H. Le Berre, *Les revirements de jurisprudence en droit administratif de l'an VIII à 1998 (Conseil d'Etat et Tribunal des Conflits)* (Paris 1999), 297; Bell, 'Reflections', above n. 109, 229.

explaining the decision to the wider legal community, and then commenting upon and even shaping legal development.[143] Doctrinal writers are typically members of the academic profession. Some may also be avocats or judges, but their interest in going beyond the individual case persuades them to produce reflections on legal developments and on the law in general. Although much of *la doctrine* is produced by academics, judges have a major place in public law. Whilst it is easy to say who writes doctrinal work, it is more difficult to track the sources of ideas and the routes of influence. The influence and status of academics in relation to judges is seen not only in doctrinal writing, but also, less tangibly, in their place in networks.

The body of writers who constitute academic *doctrine*, especially in private law, is relatively narrow. The authors are predominantly academics, particularly *professeurs agrégés*.[144] Both leading textbooks and commentaries are provided by them. Of course, younger academics (particularly through their theses) and some notes by judges or avocats do also contribute to the body of doctrine, but the authoritative writing comes from certain established names. The *agrégation* serves to confirm the status of the academic as a recognised authority.[145]

The classical form of commentary and influence is the *note d'arrêt*, a brief commentary explaining the otherwise cryptic decision of the court and situating it within trends in legal development. This is typically the place for expressing critical comments. Since these notes are attached to the commercially published case report, they are widely read within the legal community. Most of the law reviews aim at a practitioner audience as well as academics.[146] Major academic textbooks and treatises will also be recognised points of reference for judges and practitioners. Major law firms may be producing their own internal updating systems, but this does not diminish the role of the academic in the public sphere.[147] There is clear evidence in the *rapport* and the conclusions in

143 *French Legal Cultures*, 93–4, 98–9; see also N. Duxbury, *Judges and Jurists* (Oxford 2003), ch. 4.

144 P. Jestaz and C. Jamin, 'The Entity of French Doctrine: Some Thoughts on the Community of French Legal Writers' (1995) 18 LS 415, 429, estimate that 90 per cent of doctrinal writers are professors or maîtres-assistants, and the remaining 10 per cent of judges and avocats are usually occasional lecturers.

145 Ibid., 430 and 434.

146 G. Wiederkehr, 'La culture des revues françaises de droit privé' (1988) 29 *Quaderni fiorentini per la storia del pensiero giuridico* 9 at 23.

147 Cf. Y. Dezelay, 'La production doctrinale comme objet et terrain de luttes politiques et professionnelles' in Y. Poirmeur (ed.), *La doctrine juridique* (Paris 1993), 230.

the Cour de cassation that academic views are considered carefully, and many legal doctrines adopted by legislators and the courts have their origin in the work of academics. For example, the reform of road traffic law in 1985 owed much to the work of Professor Tunc and his 1965 project.

Academics often play an important role in legal practice either directly as avocats or in giving consultations to practitioners. As a result of the need to supplement their low pay, these are major parts of their working life, and this reduces the quantity and quality of doctrinal legal writing. Much of their writing is for the use of private practitioners. But their contribution to pleadings in cases offers an indirect, but significant, route through which their ideas influence judges.

Some academics are recruited as either temporary or permanent members of the Cour de cassation. At any one time there may be three of these among the hundred or so conseillers. Such members of the Cour continue academic writing and also bring to bear their expertise on decisions of the Cour. Some of the most serious reflective work on current legal issues takes place in committees established by government to reflect on major issues of the day. A good example is the *Comité consultatif national de l'éthique pour les sciences de vie et de la santé*. Its publications on bioethical issues have been influential in stimulating debate and legislation. Its president was invited by the Cour de cassation to present arguments to it during the case on surrogate mothers.[148] A similar role is played by other leading academics, for example on bodies dealing with consumer protection.[149] The extent of contributions in these situations is difficult to assess, because it is typically not made public. Ordinary judges are less frequently members of such commissions.

In administrative law, the role of generating ideas and publicly discussing the direction of the law is shared between academics and judges. To a significant extent, this results from the fact that there is no administrative code and the general principles, especially of judicial review and government contracts and liability, have been developed by case-law of the Conseil d'Etat. There are administrative codes dealing with specific branches of law, but they are more like English consolidating statutes. The relative position of doctrinal writing and case-law in administrative law is well expressed by Gaudemet in his seminal work on legal method:

148 See JCP 1991 II 21752 note Terré; J.-C. Galloux, 'Le comité consultatif national de l'éthique pour les sciences de vie et de la santé est-il une autorité de doctrine?' in Poirmeur, *La doctrine juridique*, above n. 147, 240.

149 This point was reinforced by interviews with a range of academics and judges.

The situation is very different . . . for doctrinal writing in private law, whose activity has, to a great extent, to be exercised through an understanding and evaluation of the substantial and established written law; now, faced with this written law, doctrinal writing found itself, in a manner of speaking, on equal footing with the judge. By contrast, the commentary on administrative legislation has always been shown, except in certain specific fields, as a fastidious task and above all of limited value; a true doctrine of administrative law was only able to prosper through the study of case-law.[150]

Rivero noted that one consequence of this situation was that, whereas private law doctrinal writing and case-law corresponded to two groups which are professionally distinct – the professors and the judges – in public law the roles are more closely connected. From the very beginning 'the judge writes and the judge teaches'.[151] Historically, the first writers on administrative law were members of the Conseil d'Etat who engaged in teaching and published their courses in Sciences Politiques as texts, in much the same way as the professors of private law published their courses. Both these judge-teachers and the commissaires du gouvernement share with the professor the concern to introduce order and system. Indeed, the leading writers in the field have been both judges like Laferrière, Odent and Braibant and professors such as Hauriou, Duguit, Jèze, de Laubadère, Vedel and Chapus. At the same time, the focus of this doctrinal work is described by Hardy[152] as 'more practitioner than academic. It is more preoccupied with the good administration of the law than concerned to produce an academic theory about its genesis.'

A particular importance attaches to the conclusions of the commissaire du gouvernement in the development of administrative law. These are not just pleadings, but part of an ongoing survey and analysis of the law, arguing that it should develop in particular ways. They are points of reference, just as much as any seminal article of a professor, and much like a leading judgment in the common law. For this reason, Deguergue assimilates the commissaire du gouvernement to doctrinal legal writers.[153] But, as a judge, he or she can often have the power of

[150] Y. Gaudemet, *Les méthodes du juge administratif* (Paris 1972), 148; *French Legal Cultures*, 182–5.

[151] J. Rivero, 'Jurisprudence et doctrine dans l'élaboration du droit administratif' EDCE 1955, 27, 29.

[152] J. Hardy, 'Le statut doctrinal de la jurisprudence en droit administratif français' RDP 1990, 453, 467.

[153] M. Deguergue, *Jurisprudence et doctrine dans l'élaboration du droit de la responsabilité administrative* (Paris 1994), 731–2 and 738.

initiative, to recommend the formation of the court before which cases are decided and thereby to dictate the pace of legal change to some extent. In this way, the commissaire has a stronger influence on legal development than the professor.

The influence of doctrinal legal writing can be both formal and informal. In formal terms, the influence of writings can be seen in the conclusions, which often draw inspiration from academics.[154] A leading member of the Conseil d'Etat, Stirn, notes that the conclusions of the commissaire du gouvernement have the dual function of providing an explicit link between the judicial decision and doctrinal writing and also contributing directly to the latter.[155] Where the author is a member of the Conseil, he is likely to be cited by name. Where the author is an academic, then this is not always the case. Famously, Romieu adopted in a leading case the arguments of Professor Hauriou by saying 'on a proposé . . .'.[156]

Additionally, as Gaudemet[157] noted, there are informal contacts between doctrinal writers and judges. Certainly, among key writers, there are numerous contacts and some writers, such as Jèze, have even become members of the Conseil d'Etat, though this is rarer than in the civil courts. Several professors were among the committee which drew up the 2000 *Code de justice administrative*, which illustrates a further form of connection between doctrinal writers and administrative judges.

Doctrine in criminal law has received less attention, but has a long history. There have been journals that digested and disseminated case-law, especially of the Cour de cassation since 1829. Poncela notes that, in recent years, there has been a marked decline in the proportion of articles published by judges and avocats.[158] The academic interest has

154 Ibid., 729–30. Gaudemet, *Les méthodes*, above n. 150, 151–61 offers a number of examples of how there has been borrowing from doctrinal writing in coming to judicial decisions in administrative law.

155 B. Stirn, 'Les commissaires du gouvernement et la doctrine' *La Revue Administrative 1997: numéro spécial: Le Conseil d'Etat et la Doctrine*, 41.

156 CE 6 February 1903, *Terrier*, S 1903 3. 26 at 28. M.-A. Latournerie notes in her article 'La doctrine vue par le Conseil d'Etat' *La Revue Administrative 1997: numéro spécial: Le Conseil d'Etat et la Doctrine*, 46 that

> I could say that, according to the epoch, the *commissaires du gouvernement* know that it is more or less appropriate to lay weight on quotations from doctrinal writing in their *conclusions* and that, to carry conviction with the judging court, it is sometimes preferable to be more allusive and less exhaustive in doctrinal references in their *conclusions*.

157 Gaudemet, *Les méthodes*, above n. 150, 158.

158 See P. Poncela, 'Pour une histoire d'une revue de droit pénal' (1988) 29 *Quaderni fiorentini per la storia del pensiero giuridico moderno* 31 at 35.

been strongly in the fields of criminal policy and penology. All the same, with editors such as Marc Ancel who was both an academic and a judge of the Cour de cassation, there has been quite a dialogue between the practitioner and academic writers. The extent of influence is, however, much less well documented than in other branches of law, as the rate of publication of the conclusions of the procureur-général is lower than that for private law. The kinds of routine case presented to the Cour de cassation leave less room for doctrinal discussion. Interviews conducted for this research and examination of the (few) published rapports in criminal law give little evidence of much use by judges of the writing of professors.[159]

Doctrine is clearly read and can be an argument for reform. Commentaries on cases give a clear sense of both doctrinal and judicial debate. In addition, recent first presidents of the Chambre criminelle have organised colloquia involving judges and academics on issues of the moment. Furthermore, there is typically an academic serving as a conseiller of the Chambre. A range of judges in different courts commented that they did not think that there was a strong body of academic writing in criminal law. They would typically mention the same two or three leading authors, but did not consider that there was the same number of good scholars compared with branches of the civil law. All this builds into a picture where doctrinal writing does not, in general, have a very major influence on judicial decision-making. It also seems to have a limited place in the other forms of legislation.

In constitutional law, doctrinal writers carry different authority and can influence in different ways. The absence of established case-law in the early period made the writings of doctrinal writers particularly important as a source of inspiration for constitutional arguments. Stone notes how doctrinal writing created the climate for the decision by the Conseil in the *Associations Law* case to recognise the right of association as constitutional and to engage in judicial review of legislation.[160] The Conseil may also draw directly upon law professors as advisers.[161] The informal and confidential dialogue conducted in this role provides ample opportunity for a strong influence of a well-briefed doctrinal writer.

On the other hand, the judges themselves will be leading influences on the Conseil.[162] Some will be academics, such as Luchaire, Vedel, Badinter and Robert, whilst others will be leading figures in other spheres,

159 *French Legal Cultures*, 146–7.
160 A. Stone, *The Birth of Judicial Politics in France* (New York 1992), 70.
161 *French Legal Cultures*, 224–5. 162 See below p. 100.

such as the protection of human rights. They will have their own ideas on how the Conseil should develop the law. Equally, within the Conseil, the Secretary-General will provide legal support and can suggest legal solutions. By assisting with drafting, the Secretary-General can help in the formulation of the development of the Conseil's case-law, even if he cannot, in principle, influence the specific outcome of the decision. The last three Secretary-Generals – Genevois, Schrameck and Schoettl – have been active commentators on constitutional law during their period in office. They were members of the Conseil d'Etat and already had reputations as commissaires du gouvernement. This enabled them to have outlets for their commentaries well established before they started. As a result, there has been a kind of dialogue between academics and judges that is common in administrative law, as indeed in some aspects of the English common law.

Doctrinal writers may also influence constitutional law in other ways. The writing of the text of the reference made by politicians to the Conseil constitutionnel is often contracted out to a law professor who may introduce ideas that he hopes will influence the Conseil. For example, Stone carefully documents the roles played by doctrinal legal writers during the parliamentary debates on the Nationalisations legislation of 1981.[163] The small number of professors in this subject have effectively become a kind of alternative bar.

Furthermore, academics play an important part in public constitutional debate in which members of the Conseil constitutionnel may be precluded from taking part. The relevant writings are not just in academic works but, importantly, include writings in the quality press and now on associated internet sites. Writers such as Luchaire, Favoreu, Maus, Vedel, Avril, Duhamel, Gicquel, Rousseau and others have frequently written articles in the press commenting on constitutional issues, especially activities of the Conseil. Such writing has an important impact on public opinion, particularly where the individual is a past member of the Conseil.[164]

Thus academics have an influence through their writings, their membership of courts as judges (or in the Conseil constitutionnel as advisers), their legal advice to avocats in individual cases (or to politicians in constitutional law), and their membership of committees. They are important actors both within the legal community and beyond. Relative to judges, the academics have greater influence in private law.

[163] Stone, *Birth*, above n. 160, 130, 145–8 and 153–4.

[164] Ibid., 164; P. Jan, *La Saisine du Conseil constitutionnel* (Paris 1999), 483.

Lay judges

France has a long tradition of lay involvement in the judicial process. Apart from the minor role played by the criminal jury, this has not taken the form of popular representation in the decision-making panel. Rather, it has taken the form of the engagement of the social partners in the operation of key areas of justice that affect them. In many cases, there are conflicting social groups and, rather than the judiciary arbitrating between them on their own, the system has sought to involve the groups in the decision-making with the judge as the ultimate (but infrequently used) tie-breaker.

Commercial judges

Commercial courts operate in a way that is substantially different from other courts. A major difference is that most of the first instance commercial courts are staffed by lay judges. In 2001, there were 191 courts staffed by lay judges, compared with 35 tribunaux de grande instance with jurisdiction in commercial matters.[165] Tribunaux de commerce are composed of three lay judges sitting without a professional judge, but with a *greffier*, who has some legal training. They have a substantial caseload. In 2001, the tribunaux de commerce received some 207,431 new cases on the substance, as well as 47,616 requests for interlocutory orders (*référé*). Simple cases are heard by the president alone, so only 30 per cent of judgments were handed down by a collegial court.[166] The rate of appeals is low and in 1997 only 2.8 per cent of appeals were successful. Indeed figures suggest that in matters that are common to the tribunal de grande instance and the tribunal de commerce, the latter is reversed less often than the former.[167]

There has been a broad consensus for some time that the number of commercial courts should be reduced to ensure an efficient use of resources. But there has been less consensus on the future of the lay judges. Courts have anything from six to 172 judges, who are unpaid.[168]

[165] There is no difference in the importance of the work done by the tribunal de commerce and the tribunal de grande instance with commercial jurisdiction, nor in the workload: see the comparison made between the tribunal de grande instance of Valence (population 270,000) and the tribunal de commerce of Romans-sur-Isère (population 30,000): *Commission d'enquête sur l'activité et le fonctionnement des tribunaux de commerce* (AN rapport no. 1038 of 2 July 1998), vol. 1, part 2, section I A, p. 4.

[166] Ministry of Justice statistics cited in Conférence Générale des Tribunaux de Commerce, *Vademecum* (October 2002), 8.

[167] Ibid., 9.

[168] See *La mixité dans les juridictions commerciales* (Report to Ministry of Justice, Paris 1999), §1.2.2.

A third of the judges are in courts with over twenty-five members. Not surprisingly, Paris is the largest court, having 22.2 per cent of all the référé cases in 1997. On the other hand, the 112 smallest courts, which made up nearly 50 per cent of all courts, accounted for only 11.8 per cent of judicial business, dealing with an average of 260 cases a year.

Recruitment and selection

Commercial judges are elected indirectly by their peers every four years through the chamber of commerce. To be eligible, a person must be at least thirty years of age and have been listed on the commercial register for at least five years.[169] The jurisdiction of the commercial courts covers contract and company cases, including insolvency issues. There were concerns in the 1990s about the way in which this system places local businessmen as judges over issues such as the winding up of other businessmen in their locality, who may even be trade rivals. Accordingly, the 1999 report on mixed composition[170] proposed reforms to introduce a professional judge as president of commercial court panels concerned with insolvency and other such sensitive issues. The idea had been mooted at various times since 1975, but made little progress, not least because it required the recruitment of over 300 professional judges, when recruitment was needed for other purposes.

The 1999 proposals thus led to the resignation of 700 of the 3,200 commercial judges. To be fair, the Conseil du Patronat de France (now MEDEF, Mouvement des Entreprises de France) in its 1997 report on the tribunaux de commerce[171] had already found a reduction in the number of business leaders who were acting as commercial judges. It found that, of the commercial judges, 23 per cent were administrators (*cadres*) (54 per cent in Paris), 15 per cent were self-employed business people and 62 per cent were managers. The lack of availability of business leaders was confirmed by figures produced by the presidents of the commercial courts showing that 45 per cent of judges were aged over sixty, and this percentage rose to 66 per cent for those occupying the post of president of a court, among whom forty were over seventy years of age.

Training

Since there is no career (except possibly to be elected president of one's court) and since the judges are volunteers, there has been no systematic

[169] Art. L-413-3 of the Code of Judicial Organisation. These rules result from changes introduced by the *loi* of 16 July 1987.

[170] *La mixité dons les juridictions commerciales*, Above n. 168. [171] Cited in ibid., §3.1.1.

training. It remains voluntary. This was criticised as unacceptable in the modern day by the 1998 parliamentary inquiry.[172] It wanted both preliminary training and continuing training, linked to the ENM. For the inquiry 'The lay judge ought to acquire a real legal culture and, above all, the mastery of procedural techniques without which a person cannot be worthy of the name of "judge". Voluntariness should not be equated with amateurism. The lay judge should be a justice professional.'[173]

In 1989, the Conférence Générale des Tribunaux de Commerce (CGTC) helped to create a training centre in Tours for commercial judges, the *Centre d'études et de formation des juridictions commerciales* (CEFJC). This runs a series of training workshops. It works in collaboration with the ENM, but has its own sources of funding, mainly from business and local authorities. Events are also organised by the CGTC in local areas. The programme comprises both initial training and continuing education, including for new presidents of courts.[174] Some of the events are held jointly for ordinary judges and commercial judges, but the 1999 commission on mixed composition thought this could be extended. From 1989 to 1996, 1,635 lay judges took part in the thirty-five sessions of the CEFJC, attendance at which is entirely voluntary.

Corporate life

The commercial judges are already corporatist, since they are elected from among the members of the Chamber of Commerce. As such, they are part of the business community. This is illustrated by the joint appeal by the president of the CGTC and the president of the MEDEF to encourage more business people to become judges of the commercial courts.[175] The CGTC is the association of commercial judges and dates from 1898. It is organised regionally and holds both national and regional events. Its political influence is seen in the fact that, since 1972, a number of Presidents of the Republic have spoken at its national conference and it has been closely involved in debates on the reform of commercial courts since the 1970s. It was successful in blocking proposals in 1975, 1983 and 1999. Its involvement was also important in the major reforms of insolvency law in 1985, not least because the reforms had to be implemented by its members. It has managed to obtain public funding for training of its judges. This corporatist structure reinforces the distinctiveness of

[172] *Commission d'enquête*, above n. 165, vol. 1, part 2, Section I B, p. 14.
[173] Ibid.
[174] See *Vademecum*, above n. 166, 43–5.
[175] Charter of 25 October 2002, MEDEF website (http://www.medef.fr).

the commercial judges and their authority in their field, especially their respect within the business community.

Conseillers des prud'hommes

Created in 1806 and composed of equal numbers of employers and employees since 1848, the composition and geographical spread of these courts was reformed in 1979. These courts decide in final resort on claims under €4,000. They sit in two formations: a conciliation panel of one employer and one employee, and a judgment panel of two from each group. In about 10 per cent of cases a professional judge is called in to chair a session where there is no majority for any solution. In 2000, 98 per cent of claims were brought by the employee. There were 160,747 cases decided, of which 47,488 were by way of référé. The appeal rate of decisions was 50 per cent, but only 30 per cent were reversed. Of the cases, 50 per cent concerned the contract of employment and 40 per cent non-payment of salary or other aspects of remuneration, but increasingly cases are dealing with harassment and discrimination at work. According to opinion polls of 2001, 58 per cent of French people had a good opinion of these courts.[176]

Recruitment

Employee members of the Conseil des prud'hommes are not appointed by trade unions, but are elected by workers over the age of sixteen registered in the appropriate employment categories on a list maintained by the local registry. The candidates must be aged at least twenty-one and be of French nationality (which is, of course, a serious limitation among the plurinational workforce). Employers are elected similarly from those in the appropriate employer categories. They are elected for five years and this can be renewed. In December 2002, participation in the employee elections was under 33 per cent for the first time, compared with 66 per cent in 1979. Taken together with the number of non-unionised workers, this provides a low level of legitimacy. The elections are dominated by the large trade union confederations, with the big three (CGT, CFDT and FO) taking 75.64 per cent of the votes. Among employers, participation was even lower (26.64 per cent), with the list presented by the major employers associations taking over 80 per cent of the vote. These elections, with over 16 million employees and 750,000 employers

[176] Figures from La Documentation française website: http://www.ladocumentationfrancaise.fr/dossier-actualite/electionsprudhomales/chiffres.htm.

registered, are major tests of the unions and their popularity, so there is strong campaigning between them. The unions also receive funds from the Ministry of Employment to train their union representatives.

Training

The Labour Code provides that the state organises and finances the training of labour court judges. The Ministry approves appropriate training providers and the training programme of each institution. Such institutions may be public bodies involved in training, higher education bodies or private bodies (in practice bodies set up by unions of employees or employers).[177] A labour judge has to undertake six weeks of training during his mandate, and continues to be paid by his employer during this time.

Collective identity

The labour law judges are appointed as representatives of their constituencies, and within those are representatives of particular movements. As a result, there is no great sense of common identity as a labour judge that unites people from different backgrounds. There is no collective association of labour law judges, and national debates will take place principally with representatives of the unions and employers.

Other lay judges

Election by appropriate peers characterises a number of other lay judge appointments, in particular the assessors of the *tribunal paritaire des baux ruraux*. Others are appointed, especially the assessors for the *tribunal des enfants*. In these latter cases, the legal system is not seeking representatives of conflicting social interests, but wishes to appoint people with experience who can offer a view that enables the court to represent the opinion of society. They are drawn from a wide range of sections of the community and from different professional backgrounds. There are about 1,600 assessors for all the children's courts, and about six available for each judge (two as official wing members and four as substitutes). The lay assessors are only involved when there is a public and collegial decision to be made. This means that they are not involved in the ordering of special education, the most simple or the most serious criminal cases.

[177] Art. DL 514.3 and art. 514-1 Code du travail.

The *jurés* of the *cour d'assises* are simply community representatives involved in the most serious criminal cases. Chosen by lot from the electoral register, these citizens are intended to introduce popular common sense into the judgments of facts and sentence.

The *loi* of 26 February 2003 created a new category of non-professional judge, the *juge de proximité*. Appointed for a non-renewable period of seven years, these part-time judges will deal with small civil cases (up to €1,500) and petty crimes, especially traffic offences, involving fines but not imprisonment. They are permitted to work up to 132 days a year and are remunerated at a daily rate. The Government hopes to recruit up to 3,300 over five years and began with thirty-three appointments in July 2003. There are a range of possible routes to becoming such a juge, notably for those over thirty-five with at least four years' professional experience in law and who are qualified to apply to become a judge, or those who have worked for twenty-five years in a legal environment. Of the first thirty-three, eleven were professional lawyers (avocats, huissiers, notaires), ten had law degrees, seven were retired ordinary or administrative judges, four had worked for twenty-five years in a legal environment (e.g. a former secretary-general of the Suez bank group) and three were conciliators in civil courts. The typical appointee was a retired lawyer in his sixties.[178] The character of the appointment is thus not like a lay magistracy, but much nearer the Spanish juez de paz – lawyers not appointed to full judicial posts but deciding routine civil and criminal cases as a single judge.

Judges and the wider community

Constitutional judges

Members of the Conseil constitutionnel are not formally judges. They do not belong to a specific corps, nor do they have a career in this role, since they are appointed for a non-renewable term of nine years. They are 'wise people' appointed by political figures to perform a role that controls political life.

Because the Conseil was not originally conceived as a court, but as an independent commission, there are no specific criteria established for its membership. All the Constitution lays down is the power of the nominators. The President of the Republic, the President of the National Assembly and the President of the Senate nominate one member each

[178] *Le Monde* 21 July 2003.

every three years for a fixed term of nine years. Former presidents are also members of the Conseil, and Giscard d'Estaing was the first since 1962 to be so in June 2004 after having retired from active political life. The *ordonnance* of 7 November 1958 does set out certain functions that are incompatible with membership of the Conseil (notably membership of Government or Parliament), and this will restrict the field of potential candidates. These prohibitions on occupying major political positions for a period of nine years are sufficient to make membership of the Conseil unattractive to politicians, save at the end of their careers. Thus many politicians are appointed well into their sixties or even seventies. For those from other backgrounds, this may be less of a handicap. All the same, the first member of the Conseil to complete her period of office under normal retirement age was Noëlle Lenoir in February 2001, and she then became Minister for Europe in June 2002.

Although there are no formal criteria for such an office, it is well understood that the body of judges should contain legal, parliamentary and government expertise, though not every individual will have all three. Since fields of work include parliamentary procedure and elections, some experience of Parliament is useful, either as a member of the National Assembly or Senate, or as a member of their secretariats. The Conseil also controls the permitted scope of legislation that the Government may introduce as well as the prerogatives of the Government in parliamentary procedure. In this context, experience as a minister or as an adviser in a ministerial *cabinet* will be useful. Of course, the decisions of the Conseil constitutionnel have to be based on law, and this will require the interpretation of quite complex legal rules. There will also be the creation of new legal rules. To this end, experience of legal analysis and drafting is also useful. The portfolio of experience has to be met within the membership of the Conseil, but there is no formal way in which this can be ensured.

When one analyses the sixty-two appointments from 1959 to 2004, there have been sixteen avocats, seventeen members of the Conseil d'Etat (including two former Vice-Presidents), three members of the Cour de cassation, two of the Cour des Comptes, one former member of the European Court of Human Rights and one of the European Court of Justice. At some periods, especially since 1986, the majority of members have been lawyers. A number of others have had law or political science degrees. Legal expertise is seen as valuable, but not a prerequisite. For example, Schnapper, appointed in 2001, has a doctorate in sociology. Over half the members of the Conseil have served in Parliament as politicians, and others, such as Abadie, Lenoir and Pezant, have served in the secretariat of the Parliament. In terms of government experience, nineteen have been ministers and a further fifteen served as advisers in ministerial *cabinets*. Most of all, appointees have to have personal authority. Decisions delivered by a group of political hacks in the midst of active political debate would be resented. Indeed a number of the Conseil's decisions have been criticised for being political,[179] but the quality of both political and legal members has been such that this has not tarnished the standing of the Conseil as a whole. The appointment of presidents of the Conseil has been controversial. Mitterrand's choices were particularly disputed.[180]

Given that the three nominators are politicians and the task is politically sensitive, it is not surprising that most members have been politically active before their appointment. But this focus on the political past is not a good basis for predicting decisions. After all, the great activist leap forward in the *Associations Law* decision of 1971 involved an overwhelmingly right-wing Conseil quashing a *loi* voted by a right-wing Parliament and Government to disband left-wing political organisations. Rousseau argues that entry into the Conseil, the intellectual quality of its debates and the more general feature of 'the serenity of old age' limit the importance of past political convictions.[181] This is not to argue that people lose their strong political convictions, but that they share the common enterprise of coming to decisions on 'the rules of the political game'. The strength of debates on fundamental values does not always follow party political allegiance. Personality has a much more important role.

Institutional practices reinforce the focus on personal, rather than political qualities. In the first place, the work of the reporter is rather solitary. Secondly, the ability to participate effectively in the discussions will depend on personal features such as knowledge of the field, prior preparation (often at their own initiative), and general levels of health and concentration. Thirdly, the personal knowledge and authority of an individual may be able to influence the Conseil. For example, Rousseau makes much of the personal standing and argumentative abilities of Georges Vedel, who had been a leading constitutional law professor for over forty years before his appointment to the Conseil.

[179] *French Legal Cultures*, 228–30, 233–4. [180] Ibid., 238.

[181] D. Rousseau, *Sur le Conseil constitutionnel. La doctrine Badinter et la démocratie* (Paris 1997), 42.

Given that the appointment is for a fixed term, and that normally three individuals are appointed at once to a small collegial court, there is no specific training for the role. Members are assisted by the secretariat to the extent that they need such support. The body is collegial, but the individuals are not all based in Paris. Some will come in only for meetings of the Conseil. The body can act collectively when necessary, notably in the case of the criminal investigation of their President, Roland Dumas. But the extent of cohesion depends on individuals who are there from time to time. Individuals have had a variety of previous activities. Academics can continue their activity whilst in office, whilst others may at least be able to return to their previous activity after leaving office. Academics such as Vedel, Luchaire and Robert have continued to teach in subjects with which the Conseil is concerned. Former members of the Conseil frequently talk about its work, but they retain no specific link to the Conseil when their term of office comes to an end.

Constitutional adjudication

Since the Conseil is not formally a court, its procedures are not fully judicial and in many ways resemble those of an administrative inquiry. Outside the area of electoral law, there is no set of procedural rules. The obligation of secrecy on members of the Conseil about their deliberations has led to an air of secrecy about the way in which it functions, but the procedure has become increasingly 'contradictoire'. The procedure is described at greater length elsewhere, and it varies significantly depending on the task in hand. [182] It is most judicial when dealing with electoral disputes, but even here a Secretary-General of the Conseil has remarked that 'the Conseil intervenes both as adviser, player and judge in an environment of political tension and high stakes with strong resonance in the media'.[183]

In dealing with the constitutionality of legislation, there are two main procedures – the constitutionality of laws and treaties before they are enacted, and the declassification of enacted laws. In the case of ordinary *lois*, a reference depends on the motivation of the interested political groups. There may be some subjects where the opposition may feel too politically embarrassed to make a reference, even though there might

[182] *French Legal Cultures*, 207–16.

[183] O. Schrameck, 'Le Conseil constitutionnel et l'élection présidentielle de 1995' AJDA 1996, 3.

be some constitutional issues to be discussed.[184] Treaties may also be referred before they are ratified, and the Conseil has to rule whether the treaty is compatible with the Constitution or whether it can only be ratified after a constitutional amendment. Examples are the various amendments to the EU treaties.[185] When the Conseil considers a reference concerning a *loi* or a treaty, there is no prescribed procedure, and the member named as *rapporteur* can choose to act as he thinks appropriate. Quite sensibly, but unlike a normal court, the Conseil has developed a practice of starting work on a case before it is submitted. This aspect of the process also seems more akin to an inquiry than to a judicial process. The decision is collective and individual opinions are not known.

The reference process is an instance of *abstract constitutional review*, since there is no specific dispute. Since the decision must be taken within a short period of time (usually a month), immediately after a parliamentary debate and before the President's signature, the whole process takes place at a moment of high political sensitivity. The contrast with the legalistic procedure in abstract constitutional review cases in Germany is marked. It was generally thought that the Conseil only had competence to censure a text referred to it. But in a decision of 1999, the Conseil declared as unconstitutional a provision in a *loi* on which it had already pronounced in 1985 and which it had not then declared unconstitutional.[186]

There is a reciprocal relationship between the Conseil and the political process. Political commentators note a self-limitation by the Government in the face of particular lines of decision by the Conseil.[187] In addition, there is much legal technicality in the motions of unconstitutionality raised at the beginning of the parliamentary debates. Furthermore, the Conseil d'Etat in its advisory role exercises a pre-legislative scrutiny. As a result, the Conseil constitutionnel is often deciding at a moment when there has been significant political and legal controversy about the issues raised in the reference. Jan argues that

[184] For example, laws following 11 September 2001. The major issues in relation to the banning of religious symbols in schools under the *loi* of 15 March 2004 were never submitted to the Conseil.

[185] Bell, 'French Constitutional Council', above n. 102.

[186] Decision no. 99–410 DC of 15 March 1999, *New Caledonia*, Rec. 51: see D. Rousseau, 'Chronique de jurisprudence constitutionnelle', RDP 2000, 19 at 39.

[187] See A. Stone Sweet, *Governing with Judges* (Oxford 2000), 194–203, and Jan, *La Saisine*, above n. 164, 481.

> The reference to the Conseil constitutionnel is a parliamentary weapon in the sense that for those who seise the constitutional judge, in most cases, it continues a battle lost in Parliament on the text. That is why the law remains an instrument of political battles and the reference to the judge is a means of fighting the majority politically rather than being at the service of the law, whether it involves ensuring that the Constitution is respected or if it constitutionalises new principles. Law has laid hold of politics, but the politicians make use of the law for purposes which are not exclusively legal.[188]

For this reason, Stone Sweet prefers to locate the centre of gravity of the Conseil constitutionnel within the political process, as a kind of third chamber of Parliament, rather than within the legal system. Jan prefers to consider that there is effectively a dual control over government, by Parliament and by the Conseil.[189]

A reference is usually reasoned, and these days the argument is very full, and is often based on legal arguments drawn up by consultants (often professors of constitutional law). Although these texts are eventually published with the decision, there is no publication of these documents to the other side, as in criminal or civil proceedings. As a result, there is a system of blind pleadings.[190] Unlike in the administrative courts where arguments raised by the court of its own motion must be put to the parties,[191] there is no equivalent in the procedure of the Conseil constitutionnel. These *moyens soulevés d'office* have particular importance in constitutional law. The Conseil constitutionnel takes the view that the whole text is referred to it for review, not merely the specific articles contained in the reference. It is not trying to resolve a dispute between parties. Jan claims that of the 282 provisions censured by the Conseil from 1974, when Members of Parliament were first given the power to make references, until 1996, 37.2 per cent were on grounds raised by the Conseil itself, while only 15.8 per cent were at the instance of the Members of Parliament.[192] The ability of the Conseil to select its own grounds of review in this way has the potential to make its decisions even more unexpected and more likely to be criticised as political.[193] In his study, Di Mano[194] argued that the function of such grounds is to ensure enforcement of the basic guarantees which the Constitution affords both in relation to fundamental rights and in relation

[188] Stone Sweet, *Governing*, above n. 187, 508. [189] Jan, *La Saisine*, above n. 164, 513.
[190] G. Carcassonne, cited in ibid., 514. In 1986, Badinter did propose that there be a proper debate before the Conseil, but this idea came to nothing.
[191] See Brown and Bell, 100–1. [192] Jan, *La Saisine*, above n. 164, 506.
[193] For example, in the *Feminine Quotas* case of 1982: *French Legal Cultures*, 226–8.
[194] T. Di Mano, *Le Conseil constitutionnel et les moyens soulevés d'office* (Paris 1994), 156ff.

to rights of participation. In this he is supported by a former member of the Conseil, Vedel, and its former Secretary-General, Genevois.[195]

When the Government wishes to legislate by way of decree, using its powers under article 37, it may need to ask the Conseil to declassify a provision contained in a *loi* enacted after 1958. The procedure is entirely *ex parte* in that nobody other than the Government and the Conseil is involved. Similarly, there is no kind of judicial hearing when the Conseil approves changes to the standing orders of the National Assembly or of the Senate. Here the Conseil is an arbitrator between the Parliament wishing to protect its freedom of action and the Government wishing to protect its prerogatives to ensure legislation progresses.

Overall, the culture of the Conseil constitutionnel is unlike other courts. It is a constitutional authority in its own right, which means that it performs a regulatory function in relation to political and administrative institutions. It has to act in controversial political situations, with little possibility of delaying decisions until a less politically sensitive moment. The culture is one of both understanding and balancing political and administrative requirements. The Conseil interacts with the political process and engages with political actors in both a distanced and a reactive way. Like a court, it does not choose its agenda. It has issues referred to it. But it has a role as a constitutional authority of not just resolving a dispute, but taking a more general view of the situation. It deals with legislation in abstract, and thus as a whole, and it provides some guidance through the form of its decisions. Its procedure is becoming increasingly judicial as is its membership, but the strong mix of political and legal understanding marks it out from other bodies. The lack of a career, and the smallness of the membership, creates a team atmosphere, but with the limited duration of a team.

The public image of judges

The public image of the judge is dominated by the centrality in the media of the criminal process. In this field, the most public judges are the juge d'instruction and the procureur dealing as individuals in the pursuit of serious crime. This is a distorting mirror for the judicial process, but is significant.

The traditional view, supported by the judicial establishment, is that the case should not be the subject of comment, and even if lawyers talk

[195] See ibid., 169 and 170.

to the press, the juge should remain silent.[196] But the development of investigative journalism in the 1980s and the media attention to the criminal process has made this less sustainable as a position. The 'open secret' of the instruction process brings the juge d'instruction and the procureur to the public's attention. This media impact has expanded since the Urba case of 1991.[197] The case involved illicit financing of the Socialist Party (then in government). The juge d'instruction at Le Mans who uncovered the scheme, Thierry Jean-Pierre, took a number of steps in the investigation which were unorthodox and which breached conventional practice, e.g. by driving up to Paris to catch the managing director of Urba on a Sunday and to search at his head office. The Minister of Justice concurred with the prosecutor in seeking for him to be removed from the case. But Judge Jean-Pierre then went to the press and became a folk hero.[198] His apparently unauthorised actions were upheld on appeal to the Cour de cassation.[199] The case ultimately led to the conviction of the former treasurer of the Socialist Party, then the president of the National Assembly, Henri Emmanuelli, and the Minister of Justice was forced to renounce any involvement by his ministry in giving instructions to procureurs on the conduct of investigations in political financing cases. 'It was', the minister remarked, 'the judicial institution itself, supported by the media, which managed to paralyse any action by the Ministry of Justice in the political-financing cases.'[200]

Other judges in charge of high-profile cases have used the press to support their attempt to flush out high-profile crime. For instance, Eric Halphern is said to have connived at leaks to the press, which enabled them to follow him to Xavière Tiberi's doorstep when he was conducting a search of the house of the wife of the Mayor of Paris.[201] Many juges d'instruction, especially those involved in the Elf Acquitaine scandal, became household names.[202] Likewise, the procureur Yves Bot gained

196 See P. Drai (former Premier Président of the Cour de cassation) in Greilsamer and Schneidermann, *Les juges parlent*, above n. 50, 125 at 134.

197 On the Urba case and the judicial investigation, see Ardagh, *France in the New Century* (Viking, London 1999), 48–9; C. Samet (ed.), *Justice, transparence et démocratie* (Paris 1997), 24.

198 See his interview in Greilsamer and Schneidermann, *Les juges parlent*, above n. 50, 237. He was elected as a member of the European Parliament in the 1994 elections.

199 Samet, *Justice*, above n. 197, 24.

200 H. Nallet, *La Tempête sur la justice* (Paris 1992), 123; *French Legal Cultures*, 122–4.

201 See Ardagh, *France in the New Century* (Penguin, London 2000), 45–6 and 315: Mme Tiberi was subsequently tried for corruption, but acquitted on the ground that the evidence had been obtained unlawfully: see *Le Monde* 16 December 1999.

202 For further examples, see my *French Legal Cultures*, 121–3.

publicity in refusing to call the President of the Republic as an assisted witness.[203]

In part, the focus on the juge d'instruction arises because the defence lawyers seek to exploit the pre-trial process to influence public opinion. Her work is also individual, and so is easier for the media to report in an interesting way. There is also the temptation for the individual judge to exploit this.[204]

More generally, ordinary judges have a mixed reputation among the public. In 1997, an opinion poll found that, while 71 per cent of those questioned thought them to be competent, and 57 per cent thought they were courageous in their work, and even 77 per cent thought they were overworked, only 21 per cent thought they were independent of economic influence and 17 per cent thought they were independent of political influence. They had a higher score for honesty than avocats (47 per cent), but only 39 per cent of those questioned thought they were fair. The survey concluded that the judges 'lack credibility'. The survey also noted that left-wing supporters had markedly less confidence in the judiciary than right-wing voters.[205] A 2001 survey found that the legal system ranked the lowest among fifteen public services.[206] Judges are mainly held responsible for decisions reached, with allegations of bias brought by those who lost.[207]

The picture of members of the Conseil d'Etat and the Conseil constitutionnel is different. They are part of the administrative and governing elites and carry authority, as well as attracting criticism. As has been seen, constitutional adjudication particularly attracts comment and criticism.

Conclusion: what shapes French judicial cultures?

Ordinary judges

The culture of the ordinary judiciary involves a strong commitment to justice in individual cases and to implementing the law. The ordinary judiciary at all levels is preoccupied with a large bulk of routine

203 Bell, 'Criminal Liability', above n. 74, 68.

204 See further the prosecution of the former president of the Conseil constitutionnel, Roland Dumas: *French Legal Cultures*, 124.

205 CSA survey, 'Les Français et la justice' (1997), p. 6, published on the GIP Mission de Recherche Droit et Justice website (http://www.gip-recherche-justice.fr).

206 Mission de Recherche Droit et Justice website, ibid., May 2001.

207 Ibid., 13–14.

cases, as is seen from the caseloads of the civil and criminal courts already noted.[208] Among the activity of the judicial corps, one should also include the work of the juge d'instruction (51,420 persons under investigation and 37,363 cases terminated) and the 4,944,721 cases handled by the prosecutors. This is an impressive workload for 7,144 judges. It means that a large number of routine decisions are handed down, even in the Cour de cassation.[209] It is not surprising that the creativity of the role of the prosecutor or juge d'instruction is often preferred to the more routine and confined role of the trial judge.

In consequence, the judge cannot spend many days in a week dealing with oral hearings. These are batched and well prepared. The judge needs to spend time working on the files and writing judgments, often at home. The attraction of the trial judge role (*magistrat de siège*) is that it has a few fixed hours in a week and the rest is flexible, though there is a lot to do. The civil judge is more file-based, while the criminal judge is necessarily more engaged with the litigants and witnesses. There are individual roles, such as the juge des enfants, the juge d'instruction and the juge de l'application des peines, who work individually with parties, typically in their office. Trial judges in the upper courts and appeal judges will act more collectively in decision-making and in hearing the parties, even if there is a lot of individual work.

The normal focus on implementing the law fits well with the civil service character of the career and the structures within which civil judges work. Recruitment, promotion and training follow civil service patterns. The collective action of the judicial unions follows a similar pattern, and they often express solidarity with the industrial action of the unions in the wider public sector. At the same time, they are not a leading corps within the civil service.

The close connection between the prosecutor and the judge is distinctive. Many individuals will perform both roles in the course of a career. The prosecutor is more closely connected with political life, in that criminal justice policy is negotiated at local level and priorities for enforcement have to be implemented with a degree of discretion. In many ways, this provides most judges with a better alternative to secondment to an external organisation, particularly as it can be achieved whilst remaining in a particular locality.

[208] Above p. 45.

[209] The author was present at one sitting of the Criminal Chamber of the Cour de cassation at which eighty cases were decided, no lawyers bothering to be present for what would, for the most part, be obvious rejections.

The life of the Cour de cassation is more set apart from this routine, even if the caseload is heavy. Particularly the avocats généraux focus on developing directions for the law. But the burden of administering the routine cases, even at this level, does not facilitate effective deliberation. Overall, the Cour shares with the rest of the ordinary judiciary the burden of being the workhorse of the justice system.

Administrative judges

By contrast, the Conseil d'Etat has been able to maintain a higher profile in its judicial, legal advice and general public service roles. In part this is because a lower order of workhorses has been created in the tribunaux administratifs and in the Cours administratives d'appel, who deal with much of the routine caseload. The judiciary of these courts has come increasingly to be similar to the ordinary civil and criminal judges, and resembles the Conseil d'Etat only in some key aspects of its working methods. By contrast, the social role of member of the Conseil d'Etat is considered sufficiently important to feature in studies of social elites in France, but this is not the case for ordinary judges, even in the Cour de cassation. The recruitment pattern of the young recruits does not establish a 'career judiciary' at the higher levels, equivalent to that seen in the civil and criminal courts. A closer approximation is the ambition of the ordinary judge who wants to be a procureur or to enter a ministerial office. (Though, even then, the members of the Conseil d'Etat are less often *conseillers techniques* and more often occupy senior policy-making posts.[210])

Despite the closeness of administrative judges to the administration, there are few suggestions that they succumb directly or indirectly to pressures from the administration or are tempted to adopt views too closely associated with it. This effective independence of administrative justice has been recognised as a constitutional value by the Conseil constitutionnel.[211] The value was institutionalised in relation to the judges of the tribunaux administratifs by the *loi* of 6 January 1986, which makes them irremovable and places their promotion and discipline under an independent national council similar to that which exists for private law judges.

210 See Massot and Girardot, 37.

211 CC decision no. 80-119 DC of 22 July 1980, RDP 1980, 1691 and CC decision no. 84-179 DC of 12 September 1984, Rec. 73.

There are thus two administrative judicial cultures. The social status and the broader advisory and policy-making role of its members on the wider governmental and political stage sets the Conseil d'Etat apart. Unlike members of the House of Lords, they are not from the same corps as the rest of their judiciary and so the cohesion and solidarity of the administrative judges is more limited.

A French judicial culture?

The judges of the different courts have different structures and different training and careers. As a result, it is legitimate to consider that there are distinct judicial cultures. The distinctive nature of tasks and the size of a corps help to shape the character of the different parts of the judiciary. However, the whole idea of a corps is important in French society. Typically based on educational achievement, rather than social origins, the corps provides a basis for identity and status.[212] The tasks of the corps provide responsibilities and scope for initiative, and they call for respect. D'Iribane[213] argues that respect for the corps and appeal to its sense of responsibility are more important than command in managing relationships between professional groups in France. So it is not surprising that there should be a sense of distinctiveness among the different corps of the French judiciary, recruited through different routes and operating within different institutional structures. There is no single body which is the judiciary, as in Germany or Sweden. There is little passage between the corps of ordinary judges and that of the administrative judges. There is limited movement between the different corps of administrative judges. Members of the Conseil constitutionnel are a further distinct group. Professional and lay judges are more clearly distinct. It is only recently that the different judiciaries have come under the same ministry.[214] Recruited in separate competitions, trained in different institutions and even different cities, working in separated court systems, with separate buildings, responding to separate administrative superiors, with promotion determined by separate institutions, there is much to reinforce the distinctiveness of each corps.

Apart from the idea of a corps, the key features which shape the culture of the judiciary are the tasks to be undertaken, the recruitment

[212] See *French Legal Cultures*, 34–6.
[213] P. D'Iribane, *La logique de l'honneur* (Paris 1989), 58.
[214] Previously, the administrative courts came under the Minister of the Interior.

base and career prospects of judges, the social standing of judges in that corps, and their relationships to appropriate constituencies.

In terms of *tasks*, it is obvious that those judges undertaking the mass of routine litigation have a different focus from the members of the Conseil constitutionnel or even the Cour de cassation. In this way, members of the latter institution have more in common with the Conseil d'Etat than with other civil and criminal judges. The scope for creativity and its place in their workload is radically different at these higher levels. Even where judging involves creativity, there are differences between the limited creativity of the criminal courts and the broad creativity of building a base of constitutional principle.

Once one goes outside judicial tasks, there is a substantial difference between the work of the Conseil d'Etat as a high administrator and the work of the ordinary judge. The difference is not simply in quantity or quality, but really in nature. To act as the government legal adviser and as a distinguished public servant is a different kind of role to being an ordinary judge, even in the Cour de cassation. Only where both are seconded to ministries do the roles become similar.

The *recruitment base* for the ordinary judiciary remains predominantly among university law graduates, who are then trained through the ENM. The Conseil d'Etat recruits mainly ENA high fliers, drawn from all academic disciplines. By contrast, the lower administrative judges are increasingly drawn from other parts of the administration, rather than directly recruited from ENA. Only the Conseil d'Etat is clearly an elite, as, in other ways, are the members of the Conseil constitutionnel. Lay judges have a totally different background. Different kinds of people are being recruited to perform judicial roles in the different parts of the legal system, and this is in contrast with, for example, the German system.

Of major importance is the *nature of the career*, both its variety and promotion prospects. Nothing in training or career serves to blend these judges into a kind of common judiciary. The position is closest to that in England, though without a common experience of practice as an advocate beforehand. In the ordinary judiciary, the movement between the prosecutorial and trial judge roles provides a variety within the service, and also creates a close connection between the individuals. Administrative judges will often move from judicial to administrative tasks. The constitutional judiciary has no career and a fixed tenure, so there is change in membership, and members will move on to other public roles. The career patterns of the different judges are distinct, though particular individuals, e.g. in the lower ordinary and administrative judiciaries, may have some similarities of career pattern if they concentrate on judicial activities.

Social standing is a difficult criterion. In terms of standing within the legal communities, one has to distinguish the branches of law. The standing of the ordinary judges relative to both the avocats and the academics has traditionally not been high. The profession of judge here has been thought of as respectable but not prestigious among university graduates. To make a mark, one would have to be a member of a 'grande école', such as ENA, or be an avocat in the public eye. Roussel notes the importance of wanting to make a difference among those who have come into the ordinary judiciary laterally.[215] To achieve this, the more individual roles are sought out, such as juge d'instruction. Within the administrative judiciary, the Conseil d'Etat has standing as a grand corps. It shapes its field and the academics have to look up to it. The lower administrative judiciary has a similar status to the ordinary civil judiciary. On the whole, public standing will only be given to senior judges. Media personalities are rare in the very large corps of ordinary and administrative judges. The presidents of the Supreme Courts will be major public figures and will speak out on particular issues that affect justice. In particular, they will defend their institutions and their judges. The Conseil constitutionnel has a high standing and shapes its own field. But, to a great extent, the individuals appointed already had a high social standing and their nomination does not add a great deal to their reputation. Being a lay judge has some standing within the professional community that elected him or her, but does not have the broader social status of the lay magistrate in England.

There are two major features that create a commonality between judges. On the one hand, there is the ideology of the judicial role, values such as impartiality, due process and limited creativity. On the other, there are common lawyering tasks, such as interpretation and the implementation of European law, which bring judges together. All the same, the French system remains fragmented.

[215] Roussel, *Affaires*, above n. 50, 94.

3 The German judiciary

The culture of the German judiciary was traditionally that of a bureaucratic elite. The modern judiciary operates within a system which has structural similarities to the past, but which has undergone radical change in values. Its place as an elite has to be reviewed in the light of contemporary changes within the legal community.

In the first place, the judiciary was a bureaucratic and moderately creative part of the governing elite. The current model of judicial training was established in the nineteenth century to train officials for the service of the Prussian Crown. It is competitive, rigorous and selective. Despite the unification of Germany in 1871, the legal system and judicial appointments remained predominantly in the different regions (first kingdoms and now Länder), with a limited groups of judges serving the national (federal) courts. Before there was a national civil code, judges had a significant role in establishing the principles of law to be applied or in interpreting the various codes that the different parts of the Empire had enacted before unification. National codes for civil law, criminal law and civil procedure were all enacted before 1900. These different institutional features established as part of the *Obrigkeitsstaat*, the authoritarian society, have been retained but now serve the fundamentally different values of a liberal democracy that operates in a European context.[1]

Secondly, the elite position of the judiciary is relative within the legal community and this is subject to change. The bureaucratic role gave judges a higher status within the legal community than the private lawyers, the *Anwälte* and *Notare*. On the other hand, the professors had a higher status as oracles of the law. Whilst this structure of the legal community was sustained until the 1960s, since then it has been

[1] J. Limbach, *Im Namen des Volkes* (Stuttgart 1999), 10.

gradually changing. The economic and international roles of private sector lawyers have changed their status and income. The role of the constitutional court, the *Bundesverfassungsgericht*, and now European courts has enhanced the role of judges as leading promulgators of ideas, and has had some impact on the role of professors. The standing of judges has also to be related to the lay judiciary, whose role has been enhanced in the post-1945 arrangements, but who are often not well integrated into discussions of the judiciary.

Thirdly, in relation to the wider community, as a bureaucrat, the judge should be subordinate to his political masters and should not be a publicly known figure. But the nature of the post-1945 German democracy has given a new elite role to the judiciary as guardians of fundamental rights. Caldwell describes the constitutional culture as 'distrustful of both the power of the people and the power of the state'.[2] Judges in the Bundesverfassungsgericht at least have the responsibility of holding in check political power. All constitutional authorities, governmental, legislative and judicial, are subordinated to the law, and the final arbiter of these constitutional requirements is a court. Such a function for part of the judiciary has had some limited spill-over impact on the status of other judges, whose role is reinforced by their duties as judges under the European Convention of Human Rights and the European Union.

Organisational setting and the judicial career

One professional judiciary or many?

German judges in one sense belong to a common corps in that they are recruited through a common process[3] and have a common formation, and their career is governed by the federal German Judiciary Act (the Deutsches Richtergesetz, DRiG). But there are two features which create a significant diversity among the judiciary. In the first place, once appointed, judges are allocated to one of the systems of courts and do

[2] P. C. Caldwell, *Popular Sovereignty and the Crisis of German Constitutional Law* (Durham 1997), 177.

[3] The recruitment process described here is the common route along which an entrant moves from university to traineeship and on into the judicial career. It is possible for a civil servant to enter the judiciary by a parallel route. The civil servant (who will have a law degree) can become a 'commissioned judge' (*Richter kraft Auftrags*), which is equivalent to being a probationary judge. This entrant then progresses to become a judge for life in the usual way. For a general analysis, see David S. Clark, 'The Selection and Accountability of Judges in West Germany: Implementation of a *Rechtsstaat*' (1988) 61 S. Calif. LR 1797.

not tend to move out of their original specialism. Judges are not typically generalists, nor are they very mobile between specialisms. As a result, the experience of a career judge in one branch of the law may differ significantly from a career judge in another. In the second place, the court system is predominantly a Land matter and most judges are Land civil servants. Rules on legal education, appointment and promotion are specific to a particular Land. In addition, the major legislative powers of the individual Länder will make the law to be applied differ from Land to Land. On 31 December 2002, there were only 489 federal judges, representing 2.3 per cent of the total judiciary. So judges in one Land will have different experiences from judges in other Länder. This diversity applies not only to the professional judiciary, but also to the lay judges. All the same, there are many common features, which result not only from a traumatic history and common education and institutions, but also from the common constitutional principles that apply to all public powers.

Court structures

The court system is characterised by being specialist and regional, though ultimately hierarchically integrated at a federal level.[4] In terms of specialisms, there are five basic systems of courts each with its own first instance and appeal courts at Land level, with a federal supreme court: ordinary (civil and criminal) courts, administrative courts, tax courts, labour courts and social courts. In addition, there is the Bundesverfassungsgerichtshof, the Federal Constitutional Court. The specialist groupings of courts are of very uneven size. The ordinary civil and criminal courts had 15,456 judges (74 per cent) out of 20,901 judges in 2002, whilst administrative courts had only 2,316 judges, social courts 1,274, labour courts 1,154 and tax courts 661 judges. Within generalist courts, individual tasks can be quite specialised, especially in the appeal courts at both Land and federal levels. Once appointed after common training into a specialist area, judges will tend to remain within it for the rest of their career. As a result, many will work for much of their career in a rather specialist field in which they can become experts.

A further factor in diversity is that the courts are organised predominantly on a regional basis. There are first instance courts, such as the Amtsgericht and the Landgericht in civil and criminal matters, with an

[4] See N. Foster and S. Sule, *German Legal System and Laws* (3rd edn, Oxford 2003), ch. 3.

appeal court at Land level (the Oberlandesgericht). The federal courts at the top of each system serve primarily to deal with points of law by quashing the decision of the Land court and remitting the case back to it.[5]

The consequence for the judicial career is marked. Judges and court officials are predominantly recruited and employed by the different Länder. The basic career structure is set out at federal level and so a common pattern can be described here, but the reality of the judicial career is far more regional than in any other country discussed in this book. Moving is not inhibited by the need to pass any tests in order to join a new Land, but by the availability of posts. Movement between the different court systems is possible, but is not common. As a result, an individual is likely to remain working for the same Land in the same court system for their entire career.

As a civil servant, a judge's qualifications make it possible to secure a transfer from one part of the country to another. But because the Land is the employer, a transfer requires the approval of both the transferring and the transferee Land. Obviously, there are pressures on some Länder more than others in this context. Federal civil servants will sometimes be transferred to Berlin, and a spouse who is a judge will want to secure a transfer to Berlin or Brandenburg, where there is considerable pressure on judicial posts. The complexity of this process has led the judges association, the Deutscher Richterbund, to host a website (a 'Stellenbörse') on which judges can advertise their desire to transfer and find a willing transferee.

This predominantly regional career is helped by the geography of German courts. Unlike the Latin countries, the German map of courts has been revised substantially since 1945. As a result, there are relatively few court centres and they are in major centres of population within a region. Within the 16 Länder, there is a total of only 693 Amtsgerichte located in the main town of a Landkreis and 116 Landgerichte in major population centres, with 24 Oberlandesgerichte as appeal courts. This rational pattern of courts enables judges to live and work in major centres of population, rather than in remote rural areas, as happens in France, Spain or Italy.[6] While there may be personal pressures for judges to live close to major centres of population, there is not the same demand for judges to cluster around a capital city as exists in Spain and France. As a federal country, Germany has a much greater variety of

[5] Ibid., 69–71. [6] See below p. 18.

regional centres. Furthermore, the various federal courts are located in different cities across the federation: the Bundesverfassungsgericht and the Bundesgerichtshof are in Karlsruhe, with the exception of the criminal sections that sit in Leipzig, as does the Bundesverwaltungsgericht. The Bundesfinanzhof is in Munich, the Bundessozialgericht is in Kassel and the Bundesarbeitsgericht is in Erfurt. Most of these centres are provincial towns. There is no centralisation of high-level judicial activity around one centre, comparable to London, Paris, Stockholm or Madrid.

Management of the judiciary and of the courts

Responsibility for the management of the courts and the judiciary is divided between political authorities and the judges, either those in managerial posts or through collegial decisions. There is not the same kind of agency or constitutional organ as exists in France, Spain or Sweden.

The management of the judiciary and of the courts is predominantly a Land matter. The Land Ministry of Justice organises the recruitment examinations and the traineeships, and determines the number of posts available. It is also responsible for the buildings, the equipment and the support staff for the courts. The federal Ministry of Justice plays a similar role only in relation to the federal courts. In both cases, there is a significant political and administrative control exercised over the policy and organisation of the courts service and the judiciary. The labour courts operate similarly at Land and federal level, but are typically under the Minister of Labour. The ministers from the different Länder hold regular conferences and establish common standards. For example, they set the benchmarks for the judicial workload (the *Pensenschüssel*).[7] Clearly such benchmarks can be used to assess both the performance and staffing needs of the different courts and the performance of individual judges. The importance of the ministries in relation to the budget has had an impact on judicial numbers. Compared with most other countries covered in this book, the number of judges remained static between 1991 and 2001, despite a growth of 16.7 per cent in the number of cases decided at first instance.

As far as judicial self-government is concerned, there is a distinction between managerial functions undertaken by judges and structures for collegial decision-making. On 31 December 2002, 989 judges

[7] See H.-E. Böttcher, 'The German Judiciary System' (2004) 5 *German Law Journal*, no. 10, paras. 31–5.

(4.73 per cent) were undertaking substantial administrative functions, but more will have had incidental administrative tasks. Day-to-day management of the court will be in the hands of the president and senior administrators. Such judges have both to manage the workload of the court and to relate to the relevant ministry responsible for its organisation, premises and equipment. Apart from assigning the work to members of the court, the principal administrative work of a court president lies in personnel management.

Judicial participation in governance occurs in relation both to the general operation of the court and particularly to judicial appointments, both at ministerial and local court level. Consistent with general civil service practice, there are co-decision bodies that contribute to the decision-making of the ministry, and these are elected from the judges. Under §§ 72 and 73 of the DRiG, each Land has to have a judicial council (*Richterrat*) whose role is to be involved in general and social matters concerning judges, and to take part in wider bodies affecting all who work in the court service. These are typically organised at both Land and area level. In addition, as will be seen below,[8] there is some judicial input into the appointments process. Where there are appointments commissions, judges are typically members. Within every court, there is a *Präsidialrat*, a representative organ of the local judges, which contributes to the appointment process, especially of trainee judges. The Präsidialrat is composed of the president of the court and other judges, at least half of whom are elected. It deals with ordinary organisation matters and also advises on the suitability of candidates for appointment.

The judicial career

Initial education and recruitment

In Germany, the judicial career forms the central part of initial legal education with its concept of the 'Einheitsjurist' or 'Volljurist', the single generalist lawyer. Zimmermann suggests that '[i]t owes its existence to the need to train a homogeneous, highly qualified and loyal body of executive and judicial officers to administer a far-flung and fairly heterogeneous territory' (namely eighteenth-century Prussia).[9] Although only about 5 per cent of qualified lawyers end up as judges, formal

[8] Below pp. 120–2.

[9] R. Zimmermann, 'An Introduction to German Legal Culture' in W. F. Ebke and M. W. Finkin (eds.), *An Introduction to German Law* (The Hague 1996), 1 at 28.

training has traditionally been built around the requirements of becoming a judge. Students study for at least four years at university, collecting the certificates (*Scheine*) required to present themselves for the first state examination (*erstes Staatsexamen*) organised by the Ministry of Justice in each Land (rather than by the universities or by the Ministry of Education). The examination board will consist of both academics and practitioners, and it tests academic knowledge of the law. Normally, a student not only will undertake the requisite eight semesters (or longer) of university study, but will then take courses with a private crammer school (*Repetitorien*).[10] As a result, the average period taken from the beginning of university study until passing the erstes Staatsexamen in 2002 was 9.6 semesters. Although university study is free, most students will be funding their own maintenance throughout university and will certainly have to fund private crammer training themselves. In 2002, 15,056 students presented themselves for this erstes Staatsexamen and an average of 70 per cent passed.[11]

Following this, successful students are paid as trainees[12] for two years during which they will have placements in the civil courts, the criminal courts and the administrative courts, as well as with a public prosecutor and a private Rechtsanwalt. The payment of all trainees provides a modest but adequate standard of living. It is argued that this feature provides help to students from less well-off backgrounds to become judges. But, of course, that is only true provided the student has been able to fund the early years. Following their traineeship, students then sit the second state examination (*zweites Staatsexamen*), which 85 per cent of candidates passed in 2002. This examination is run by a panel consisting of judges and senior civil servants. At this point, they are eligible to be appointed judges, but may have to wait some time before a suitable vacancy occurs (during which time they may engage in further study). Taking the 2002 entry as a sample, 2.6 per cent of successful second state examination candidates became judges, 3.4 per cent

[10] Ibid., 29–31.

[11] Figures from the Federal Ministry of Justice. To gain some sense of the size of the student body, it should be noted that in 1997 (ten semesters before the 2002 exam) 19,210 students enrolled for the first semester of law studies.

[12] In 2001, 10,240 Referendar placements were made from among the 11,139 who passed the erstes Staatsexamen. These placements are a great expense for the Länder, since most of the successful trainees will go into the private sector, rather than into the judiciary, the prosecution or other public service. Land funds limit the number of training placements available: N. Baas, *Rekrutering en (permanente) educatie van de rechtsprekende macht in vijf landen* (The Hague 1999), 77 at 94.

prosecutors, and 76.6 per cent became Rechtsanwälte, many of whom will become lawyers within commercial firms. Others will enter the public administration.

The judges who are recruited will spend typically three years on probation (*auf Probe*). The DRiG enables the probationary judge to be dismissed relatively straightforwardly within the first two years, but with increasing difficulty thereafter. Although the training process is long, the newly qualified judges still have much to learn. A 1995 study of lower courts in Stuttgart examined the satisfaction of Rechtsanwälte and litigants with the way cases were handled by judges. In reply to all the questions, younger judges performed significantly worse than more experienced judges. For example, judges with under ten years of experience were described as arrogant by 28 per cent of respondents compared with similar criticism for only 16 per cent of judges with over twenty years of experience.[13] The study recommended that younger judges needed mentoring to enable them to manage their work and to avoid errors in decisions and behaviour.[14]

The character of training for lawyers has come under considerable criticism over many years as being both too theoretical, especially in the years up to the erstes Staatsexamen, and unrelated to the kind of practice most students will actually enter.[15] The traditional predominance of preparation for the judicial career within the education of the *Einheitsjurist* has been altered significantly by the 'Law on the Reform of Legal Education' of 18 July 2002. Since July 2003, legal education at university has included a number of key skills (*Schüsselqualifikationen*), such as rhetoric (advocacy) and languages, which are more attuned to the needs of the advocate, though other skills in case management, negotiation, communication and mediation are of general application. In addition, there will be earlier specialisation. The two-year practical stage will include a compulsory nine months spent with a Rechtsanwalt.

[13] G. Schedler, W.-D. Treuer, B. Legler and A. Kobler, 'Arbeitsplatz Gericht. Die Arbeitsweise des Zivilrichters am Amtsgericht' (September 1995, Institut für Rechtstatsachenforschung, University of Konstanz, http://www.uni-konstanz.de/rtf/praktfg/praktfg.htm), 59–62. The findings of their Oberlandesgericht study confirm that experience produces a performance that satisfies lawyers more: W.-D. Treuer, D. Ditten, H. Hoffmann and W. Gottwald, *Arbeitsplatz Gericht. Die Arbeitsweise der Zivilrichter am Oberlandesgericht* (Baden-Baden 2002), 135.

[14] Schedler et al., 'Arbeitsplatz Gericht', above n. 13, 122–3.

[15] See Zimmermann, 'Introduction', above n. 9; N. Horn, H. Kötz and H. G. Leser, *German Private and Commercial Law. An Introduction* (Oxford 1982), 35–7. For the new system, see Foster and Sule, *German Legal System*, above n. 4, 83–8.

Three months each will be spent in a civil court, a prosecutor's office and a public administration. This new legal education is far less focused on preparing the next generation of judges.[16] There is also an emphasis on lawyers having a broader range of social skills than come from traditional technical legal education.

The increasing importance of the Rechtsanwalt can be seen from the changing demography of the different professions. Whereas in 1973, judges made up 31.9 per cent of the combined total of these professions, by 2002 they made up only 15 per cent. The principal reason was that the rapid expansion of the number of Rechtsanwälte, and the absence of any significant increase in the number of judicial posts since 1990 (other than in the immediate aftermath of unification). When proper account is taken of the number of judges and prosecutors from East Germany, then the number of judges rose by about 15 per cent between 1980 and 1990, and the number of prosecutors by nearly 26 per cent. The number of posts for judges has been almost static since 1993, and this is in line with the static number of students starting law studies and those passing the second state examination. By contrast, the number of Rechtsanwälte doubled between 1990 and 2002.

The judiciary has traditionally had a high social status and high academic marks have been required for entry. This has made it attractive. But the 1990s saw a significant change. Salaries failed to keep pace with salaries in the private sector.[17] Legal education gives candidates a real experience of working in different legal professions and the chance to make an informed choice between them. But the judicial role has other attractions. Judges interviewed for this research stressed the importance of flexibility of judicial work compared with that of the Rechtsanwalt. The Rechtsanwalt is working at the behest of the client, while the judge has more freedom both to organise work and to decide when the job has been done satisfactorily.[18]

[16] See speech of the Minister of Justice to the Bundesrat, 26 April 2002, Ministry of Justice website (http://www.destatis.de).

[17] The Deutscher Richterbund has claimed that salaries in the years 1993–2003 barely kept up with inflation, and have fallen in real terms because of changes in taxation and social security contributions. By contrast, private sector salaries rose in real terms by well over 10%: J. Gnisa, in the DRB-Nordrheinwestfalen newsletter, 31 July 2003, pp. 4–5, DRB press release February 2004 on DRB website (http://www.drb.de). See also http://www.al-online.de/beruf_web.html.

[18] See also the survey noted by U. Schultz, 'Women Lawyers in Germany: Perception and Construction of Femininity' in U. Schultz and G. Shaw (eds.), *Women in the World's Legal Professions* (Oxford 2003), 281.

Table 3.1 *Numbers of Lawyers*[19]

	1980 (West Germany)	1990 (West Germany)	1993 (All Germany)	1998	2002
Rechtsanwälte	36,077	56,638	67,120	91,516	113,055
– of whom lawyer notaries	6,633	7,877	8,616	8,930	8,365
– of whom only notaries	942	1,013	1,562	1,663	1,654
Judges	16,657	19,115	20,668 (18,913 from old Bundesländer)	20,969	20,901
Prosecutors	2,800	3,200	4,920	4,998	5,150
Tax advisers	21,030	39,997	43,939	53,193	60,999
Students passing 1st Staatsexamen	5,750	8,127	9,781	12,153	10,838
Students passing 2nd Staatsexamen	4,123	6,853	7,796	10,397	10,330

[19] Statistics from the Federal Statistical Office.

It is possible for a Rechtsanwalt to apply to become a judge. Such lateral entry is not very common, but it was important in the early 1990s to staff the courts of the old East Germany. It is very rare for a judge to become a Rechtsanswalt. It is possible for civil servants with appropriate qualifications to become judges, especially in areas like social law where their experience is particularly relevant. In certain Länder, such as Bavaria, it is more common to have a transfer between the Staatsanwalt (prosecutor) and judicial careers. The disadvantage of later entry is that a candidate cannot advance quickly, so a person is less likely to reach a senior position than someone who joined the judiciary directly. For budgetary reasons, it is expensive to appoint an older person to a judicial role and there will be a reluctance on this ground to appoint people over forty-five as newcomers to judicial positions. There might also be some resentment among established judges if others are brought in with less experience and are promoted above them. The one group of people able to do this are university professors. They can retain their chairs and be appointed for up to a third of their time. They are usually appointed to positions in the higher courts. The traditional authority of the professor facilitates the acceptability of this.

Diversity in the judiciary

As in most of Europe, law is a subject studied for the major part by women, and the career judiciary now reflects this, though less so in Germany than in many Latin countries. Women were allowed to become judges only in 1922, but they were barred during the Nazi period. Whilst the percentage of women may appear small generally, the proportion of women among the younger age group (e.g. among the trainees) is significantly higher. In Germany, the proportion of women in the judiciary is similar to that in other legal professions. In 1970, women accounted for 6 per cent of judges, 5 per cent of prosecutors and 4.5 per cent of Anwälte.[20] In 2002, women accounted for just over 30 per cent of judges and 33 per cent of prosecutors. But women constituted 53.55 per cent of the newly qualified judges (*Richter auf Probe*). This latter figure matches the percentage of women among trainees (48.36 per cent) and among those passing erstes Staatsexamen (50.36 per cent). East Germany had a greater proportion of women lawyers than West Germany. In 1991, women made up 51.82 per cent of judges in East Germany, but

[20] U. Schultz, above n. 18, 275, table 2. She notes that the percentage is higher than for academic posts: ibid., 280.

only 19.05 per cent in West Germany.[21] The expansion of Western and multinational firms since reunification has led to a reduction in the percentage of women lawyers in the East.[22]

In the early 1990s, the proportion of women entering the judiciary was higher than the proportion of those passing the Staatsexamen. The explanation offered was that, among students with good marks, more women turned to the judiciary than men because that activity lends itself more easily to part-time and family-friendly work patterns. That pattern is no longer so pronounced, particularly as the earning power of lawyers has increased and the number of posts as judge has failed to keep pace with the number of successful law students. All the same, Schultz argues that the judiciary remains attractive to women:

> The judiciary offers ideal working conditions for women, particularly if they want to combine family and work: a reliably high income based on a fixed salary scale, a set workload, the usual paid maternity leave, the option of part-time working with a corresponding reduction of the workload (an option now guaranteed by state regulation for virtually the duration of their professional lives).[23]

She quotes a study showing that 17.3 per cent of judges in Nordrhein Westfalen work part-time. Her suggestion that judges have a more manageable workload is supported by a 1995 study of the work of lower court judges in Stuttgart.[24] The study found that judges were working on average a 43.5 hour week. As judges became more experienced, they were able to complete the work with minimal overtime. Whereas 53 per cent of judges with under five years of experience said they could only complete their tasks by working overtime, only 10 per cent of judges with more than fifteen years of experience said the same. By contrast, in the appeal courts, 40–50 per cent of judges found they needed to work overtime.[25] Schultz's view about the attractiveness of the judicial profession seems borne out further by the fact that, though over 48 per cent of trainee judges are women, women make up only 40 per cent of new entrants to the Anwalt profession.[26] Indeed, in 2002, of the

[21] Ministry of Justice figures, *Richterstatistik zum 31.12.2002*, table 2.

[22] G. Shaw, 'Women Lawyers in the New Federal States of Germany: From Quantity to Quality?' in Schultz and Shaw, *Women*, above n. 18, ch. 17.

[23] Schultz, 'Women Lawyers' above n. 18, 281.

[24] Schedler et al., 'Arbeitsplatz Gericht', above n. 13, 39–41.

[25] Treuer et al., *Arbeitsplatz Gericht*, above n. 13, 123–4.

[26] Bundesrechtsanwaltskammer, July 2004 (http://www.brak.de). Figures for 1 January 2005 state that the number of female Anwälte rose in 2004 by 7.84%, whereas the

women entrants to the main legal professions 22.33 per cent became judges or prosecutors, compared with only 15.56 per cent of men.[27] But Schultz also notes that there are difficulties in terms of promotion. As will be seen below,[28] to obtain promotion, a judge has to complete a six-month probationary secondment in an appeal court. This is often far from home. As a result, many women do not seek promotion, and childless women are more likely to be promoted.[29] Based on German empirical studies, she concludes that gender has an influence on the manner of handling cases, rather than in terms of the results: 'Differences between male and female judges are in evidence as regards working styles, but hardly as far as outcomes are concerned. The *formation professionnelle* serves its purpose leaving only marginal gender differences.'[30] In terms of ethnicity, statistics are not available. As a minimum condition, a judge must be a German citizen, and there is no scope for dual nationality. As a result, ethnic minority judges are a rarity.

Promotion and appraisal

In all cases, appointments are made by a Minister, with an opinion from the relevant council of the judges. In some Länder, the Minister makes promotions decisions on the recommendation of a judicial selection committee. So there is limited judicial self-government.

The initial appointment to a judicial position is made by the Ministry of Justice in a particular Land. The Basic Law sets out the 'performance principle', that is to say that selection should be made in accordance only with 'competence, suitability, and performance in the subject' (art. 33(2) GG). Obviously, the measure of competence for the initial appointment is principally performance in the zweites Staatsexamen, as well as performance in the period as a Referendar.

Although being a judge is a lifetime career, most judges cannot expect to gain promotion, since there are not enough senior posts. Salary may rise automatically every two years for those in the lowest two grades

number of Anwälte in general rose only by 4.56%, so the overall proportion of women is rising.

27 Based on Ministry of Justice and Bundesrechtsanwaltskammer statistics. About 94% of those who qualified in the zweites Staatsexamen for the relevant year proceeded into these three professions.

28 Below p. 122.

29 Schultz, 'Women Lawyers', above n. 18, 283.

30 Ibid., 316.

until the judge reaches forty-nine, but this merely compensates for the fact that the number of promotion grades is limited.

When a vacancy in a promotion grade occurs, e.g. as president of a Landgericht, the post is advertised and suitably qualified judges may apply. In many Länder, the recommendation for such appointments is made by a Richterwahlausschuss (judicial selection committee).[31] This committee will be composed of eleven to fifteen members drawn from the Land Parliament and judiciary. It has been settled that the final decision is made not by this committee (made up of judges and politicians), but by the Minister of Justice of the Land.[32] Since this is a genuine election, the committee does not have to give reasons for its decision.[33] In other Länder, the decision is simply made by the Minister of Justice. Giving the Minister of Justice the final say necessarily introduces a political element into appointments. Kötz argues that 'The Minister of Justice will always choose the one who belongs to, or is in sympathy with, his party or an allied party. It is by no means unusual for judges to belong to a political party, but it is uncommon for them to be very active.'[34]

At federal level, there is a judicial selection committee for initial appointments to the highest courts in the ordinary, administrative, social, labour and tax courts. But the federal judicial selection committee does not advise on promotions. The relevant Präsidialrat gives its advice on the basis of its assessment of the trial secondment which the candidate has undertaken in that court. There has been controversy over the clash between professional and political judgements of a candidate's suitability. In 2001, a judge, Neskovic, with a record of controversial statements and judgments in the field of illegal drugs was proposed by his Land Minister of Justice for promotion to the Bundesgerichtshof.[35] Its Präsidialrat rejected him and another nominee on the grounds that they did not have sufficient judicial experience. Another Minister of Justice made these opinions known, alleging that the relevant nominations had been made because of the political views of the candidates.

[31] Currently eight of sixteen Länder have such an arrangement.

[32] See T. Gas, 'Les institutions de gestion et de discipline de la carrière des magistrats' in T. S. Renoux, *Les Conseils supérieurs de la magistrature en Europe* (Paris 1999), 134.

[33] For example, it was held that reasons did not have to be given in the case of a pacifist judge who was refused a promotion on a re-vote in the selection committee: BVerfGE 24, 274.

[34] Horn et al., *German Private and Commercial Law*, above n. 15, 39.

[35] 'Judicial Selection Controversy at the Federal Court of Justice' (2001) 2 *German Law Journal*, no. 8.

The candidate's appointment was successfully challenged by a competitor for the post, but Neskovic was re-proposed and finally appointed to the court.[36] This shows that the function of the judges is a check, not a final decider as in some other countries. Appointment to the Bundesverfassungsgericht is by a separate procedure which is transparently political in character.[37]

Prior to the decision of the judicial selection committee or the Minister of Justice, an opinion on the suitability of candidates is delivered by the Präsidialrat, a representative organ of the local judges. This judgement of competence is based on the 'performance principle', a demonstration of effectiveness in post. Evidence of effectiveness can be found from the regular appraisal conducted every four years for lifetime judges. Appraisal is conducted by the court president and, among other sources of evidence, he will participate in a hearing led by the appraisee. A particularly important part of the evidence is the *Erprobung*, an evaluation made of a trial period as *Beisitzer* in the work of a grade to which one wants to be promoted. For example, a person wanting to work at appellate level would be seconded for a year, and the president of the court would sit with him in a case where the probationer was taking the lead, and judge the performance. Thus, peer evaluation will be a strongly influential factor in deciding on promotions, though seniority also is significant. The peer judgement on competence by the Präsidialrat will usually determine the success of a candidate. Kötz remarks that: 'In reality, there is a more subtle threat to judicial independence. It lies in the fact that in a career system a junior judge's chances of life appointment or promotion are determined to some extent by his senior's views on his qualifications and competence.'[38] So the system involves a limited degree of judicial self-government, even if politicians often retain important ultimate decision-making powers in many Länder.

Even if judges do not move out of their grade very frequently, they may well undertake a number of different tasks. Since courts are often large organisations, there are many roles which involve administrative, as well as judicial, competence. In addition, a judge may look to be seconded to another court, for example at federal level. In such a role, often as a kind of assistant (*wissenschaftlicher Mitarbeiter*), the judge will be able to perform a number of different tasks. For example, the judge in

[36] Ibid., OVG Schleswig, 15 October 2001; but also the successful renomination reported in *Hamburger Abendblatt*, 1 August 2002.
[37] See below p. 159.
[38] Horn et al., *German Private and Commercial Law*, above n. 15, 39.

a federal court or in the European Court of Justice may well be involved in the shaping of legal policy.

If individuals are going to remain in their grade a long time, there might appear to be less incentive to undertake professional development. In their early years, judges are appraised every two or three years (depending on the regulations of the particular Land). Once they become judges appointed for life, then the appraisal, conducted by the presiding judge of the court or a deputy, is every five years. Appraisal does not take place after one reaches fifty. The performance principle works in relation to appraisal. If a person is performing satisfactorily, it may be possible for them to apply to take on outside work, such as a part-time professor in a Fachhochschule (technical college).

A judge may also seek a transfer to work in an administration. It is common for judges to work in court administration or in the Ministry of Justice. It is rarer for a judge to work in other administrations, especially those with a strong party political mission.

Continuing education and appraisal

By law, all judges are bound to take part in continuing education, but they are free to decide how they go about this task. As one judge put it, 'judicial independence both in respect of the cases they handle and personally is unthinkable without the right of self-determination in their work and in the way they choose their advanced training'.[39] Baer reports that in 1993, 54 per cent of German judges had attended some form of continuing education within the past two years.[40] The Deutsche Richterakademie (the German Judicial Academy) runs events on a national level and other events are organised by the Länder. The Richterakademie was based since 1973 in Trier and now (since 1993) in Wustrau (Brandenburg) and organises over 140 courses a year with about 5,000 participants. The themes are strongly of a professional kind and courses may be given by non-lawyers, e.g. on psychology or medicine. They can include introductions to French and English law, European law, as well as court management. Some themes go beyond the immediately practical and cover historical or other themes of interest, e.g. 'the break-up of a justice culture'. Even with this level of provision, judges may have to wait several

[39] S. Schmidt-Schondorf, 'In-Service Training of Judges and Public Prosecutors in their Professional and Ethical Obligations' in *Themis no. 3, The Training of Judges and Prosecutors* (Strasbourg 1996), 89 at 91.

[40] A. Baer, *Die Unabhängigkeit der Richter in der Bundesrepublik Deutschland und in der DDR* (Berlin 1999) (hereafter 'Baer'), 97.

years before they have the chance to participate in a conference organised by the Richterakademie. Much of the training is provided by judges and prosecutors (about 60 per cent of lectures), whilst university teachers provide about 20 per cent, other legal professions about 10 per cent and the remaining input comes from non-lawyers.[41] In addition, there are conferences at Land level for local judges.

The relatively loose structure of continuing judicial training can be compared to the more programmed structure of competence training for initial education and as preparation for promotion that is provided for the civil service.[42]

Discipline

Like any person within a bureaucratic organisation, a judge is subject to internal service supervision. This is usually conducted by the president of the court. One role is simply to ensure that work is being conducted properly and to draw attention to deficiencies. A fault by neglecting to take the necessary remedial action may give rise to discipline.

In order to preserve the independence of the judge, discipline is organised in a highly structured way. The core judicial functions of deciding cases and making orders cannot be the subject of discipline. Only external features, such as delay in coming to decisions or the way in which parties were treated, can be the subject of discipline. Discipline and supervision are controlled by a special formation of the higher courts, both at Länder and federal levels, which ensures uniform conditions of treatment. A judge can complain to the service court (*Dienstgericht*) if she wishes to contest the permissibility of a direction given by a superior. More rarely, the court will also deal with serious disciplinary matters. In a large Land, these may only amount to perhaps three cases a year. They will mainly involve penalties such as suspension and loss of grade. There have been very few instances of judges being dismissed. Even a judge who expressed sympathy for neo-Nazis was not dismissed, but merely moved and allowed to retire through ill-health.[43] Discipline essentially follows civil service lines, reflecting the way judges are seen as a branch of the civil service.

[41] Schmidt-Schondorf, 'In-Service Training', above n. 39, 95; Baas, *Rekrutering*, above n. 12, 89.

[42] See the programme of the Bundesakademie für öffentliche Verwaltung: http://www.bakoev.bund.de.

[43] Schmidt-Schondorf, 'In-Service Training', above n. 39, 99–100.

Article 30 of the German Judges Law specifies very narrow grounds on which a permanent judge can be transferred to another office or can be removed from office. Similarly, the grounds for suspension for incapacity are regulated tightly. A federal judge may be removed by a resolution (*Richteranklage*) passed by two-thirds of the Bundesrat and Bundestag, but only on the ground of breach of the democratic duties of office. The protection offered to judges reflects a strong commitment to judicial independence and to avoid the problems of the Nazi era.

Conclusion

The structures of the judicial career are longstanding, but the status and attractiveness of the role are rapidly changing. The career of the ordinary professional judge is marked by a series of aptitude tests. There is entry by a competitive examination and then a lifelong career path with appraisal, committees for promotion and discipline in a hierarchical setting. These structures were designed to make judges an elite within a bureaucratic career carrying a high status. The role remains very selective, especially as numbers have not increased in the last ten years. But the growth of other professions, particularly in the private sector, has diminished the relative status of the judiciary. Being a judge offers certain advantages, particularly in relation to managing one's time, but this now has to be set against a lower salary. The increasing role of women reflects the distinct advantages of the career and public sector employment generally as 'family friendly', as well as the interest of the work. The regional character of the judiciary carries certain advantages, but offers less flexibility and interest for the really high fliers than the increasingly international top law firms do.

The structure of the career gives quite a lot of individual freedom, which is different from a typical bureaucratic role. Promotion prospects are limited, especially because of the specialist and regional character of many of the posts available. But there is the chance for secondment, or undertaking some limited teaching role in the universities or Fachhochschulen. The powers of the hierarchy are limited. For historical reasons, there are strong protections against removal and interference. There are strong collegial elements in the management of careers, which limit purely managerial or ministerial direction. Evaluation through appraisal plays a limited role. At the same time, there is a strong culture of continuing education and self-direction, taking advantage of opportunities for enjoying the role more.

Judicial corporate life

The judicial life is, in important ways, individual within a collegial court environment, but not as corporatist as in many other countries. In interviews with a range of judges, it was clear that there are few horizontal contacts between judges in different courts. Predominantly the contacts are between the presidents of courts who will meet together from time to time with the appeal court. Naturally, there are personal contacts which supplement this, including contacts through the judicial unions. If the workplace provides a comfortable context for exchanging views, then this might occur at an informal level. Baer contrasts this with the more formal structures which existed in East Germany. The West German tradition depended on more informal contacts, arising on a voluntary basis, since this could be seen as more compatible with the prevailing conception of judicial independence.[44] Links with federal courts are limited to formal contacts between presidents and the informal contacts that arise as a result of individual judges from a Land going to work on secondment as *wissenschaftlicher Mitarbeiter* in a federal court. Judges will learn from academic or publishing databases, rather than directly, what are the developments in the case-law of the higher courts.

German-speaking judges are linked by private e-mail lists, but these arise from private initiative. Judges do not generally form links with the press. It is for individual judges to decide whether to give press interviews. Prosecutors will often do so, but judges will not comment on decisions in which they have been, or may be, involved, and are generally reluctant to discuss more general legal matters. On the whole, links with the press are left to the court press service. Judicial unions may make statements. The Bundesverfassungsgerichtshof has refused to allow court proceedings to be televised.[45]

The major judicial union is the Deutscher Richterbund, which was founded in 1909 and refounded after the War in 1949. There are other, left-wing unions, such as the Neue Richterverein, and the national public sector union has a judicial section. In addition, there are some associations of judges belonging to specific categories, such as administrative judges (the Verwaltungsrichterverein). Although there was a lot of activism in the 1960s, associated with both social change and coming to terms with the Nazi past, the unions have a lower public profile. Their major roles are in suggesting names for the promotions panels, the

[44] Baer, 101–2. [45] See (2001) BVerfGE 103, 44.

Richterwahlausschuss. They also respond to consultations on reform of the law or of judicial administration. There are also associations within political parties. But the profile of the judicial associations is much lower in Germany than in Latin countries such as France, Spain and Italy. They have the character of professional associations, rather than trade unions. They do not lead demonstrations and are not involved in cross-sector issues in the public sector.

History and values

The judicial role and past tyrannies

Contemporary conceptions of judicial independence and the judicial role are shaped by reaction to the experience of two dictatorships within living memory. In each, many judges collaborated in enforcing the values of the dictators, and there were substantial purges when democracy was restored. The system of the Federal Republic has tried to learn lessons by requiring a different kind of commitment from its judges. As a President of the Bundesverfassungsgerichtshof said, 'knowledge of the reasons for totalitarian leadership is a guarantee for the continuity of civilised society'.[46]

Legal positivism and the Weimar and Nazi periods

A traditional account suggests that the pre-Nazi German judiciary was wedded to a rigorous form of legal positivism, an uncritical obedience to norms enacted by the legislator and an unwillingness to reflect professionally on the social impact of law. This explains in part why judges failed to resist the undermining of the Weimar Republic. Radbruch wrote in 1946 that 'positivism should be overcome since it had destroyed all possibilities of defence against the abuses perpetrated under the national socialist legal order'.[47] This popular view is challenged by Ott and Buob[48] who suggest that the cause of the anti-liberal and

[46] Limbach, *Im Namen des Volkes*, above n. 1, 39.

[47] G. Radbruch, 'Gesetzliches Unrecht und übergesetzliches Recht' (1946) 1 *Süddeutsche Juristenzeitung* 105 at 107 (trans. Berti).

[48] W. Ott and F. Buob, 'Did Legal Positivism Render German Jurists Defenceless during the Third Reich?' (1993) 2 *Social and Legal Studies* 94. H. Rottleutner, 'The Conformity of the Legal Staff' (1993) *Rechtstheorie, Beiheft* 15, 441 comments that, by simply taking over the judiciary from the German Empire, the Weimar Republic was left with strained relations between 'authoritarian-minded judges and the democratic parties, which never succeeded in making the Republic something dear to the hearts of the legal staff and legal scholars'.

submissive attitude of the judiciary is better traced to the purges of liberals in the judiciary conducted by Bismarck in 1878. (Lawyers and judges had played a leading part in the liberal Frankfurt constitutional convention of 1848–9.) The new criteria for selection to the judiciary ensured that only the upper middle class could be appointed, and insecurity of tenure during the training period ensured that 'a rigorous attitude of submission to authority' could be secured.[49] On this view, the judges were committed to certain substantive, authoritarian views about the way the law should be interpreted (the *Obrigkeitsstaat* mentality),[50] which was anti-democratic. For example, the high point of judicial creativity was the invention of the 'good faith' principle in art. 242 BGB to permit judges to revalue mortgage debts which had been undermined due to rampant inflation.[51] But this case, and the subsequent attitudes of the judges, favoured the protection of property rather than following the legislator's desired solution to inflation and the move from the gold standard.[52] Similarly Rupp argued that, during Weimar, it was not so much legal positivism as anti-constitutional attitudes which led judges to allow the system to be undermined.[53] The driving force was therefore not the positivist methodology adopted by judges, but the substantive values they shared.[54]

The difficulty of the new Germany in coming to terms with this legacy was illustrated by the *Rehse* case in 1968.[55] Judge Rehse had taken part in the decisions of the Volksgericht, which had passed seven death sentences in blatantly rigged trials at the end of the Nazi period under pressure from the court's Nazi president, Freisler. Rehse had been charged with murder and attempted murder and convicted by the Berlin Schwurgericht.[56] The conviction was quashed by the Bundesgerichtshof,

[49] Ott and Buob, 'Did Legal Positivism', above n. 48, 93.

[50] For a discussion of this idea, see R. Wiethölter, *Rechtswissenschaft* (Frankfurt am Main 1968), 37.

[51] RGZ 107, 78 (23 November 1923), cf. RGZ 101, 145, which had ruled the opposite.

[52] B. Rüthers, *Die unbegrenzte Auslegung. Zum Wandel der Privatrechtsordnung im Nationalsozialismus* (2nd edn, Tübingen 1973), 69ff and 76–7. See below p. 158 on the 1924 vote by judges in favour of judicial review of legislation to protect property.

[53] H. H. Rupp, 'Die Bindung des Rechters an das Gesetz' NJZ 1973, 1769 at 1770; R. Eckertz, 'Was heißt "Politische Jurisprudenz"? Eine Aufhebung' (1976) 7 *Rechtstheorie* 153.

[54] V. Curran, 'Formalism and Anti-formalism in French and German Judicial Methodology' in C. Joerges and N. S. Ghaleigh (eds.), *Darker Legacies of Law in Europe* (Oxford 2003), 205 at 225.

[55] 5th Strafrechtskammer, BGH, 30 April 1968, NJW 1968, 1339; M. Stolleis, *The Law under the Swastica* (Chicago 1998), 161–4.

[56] DRiZ 1967, 393.

which held that 'In casting his vote as a member of a collegial court, the defendant was independent and had equal rights according to the then valid law, subject only to the law and responsible to his conscience. His duty demanded that he should follow his legal convictions alone.' Relying on the text of art. 336 of the Criminal Code, the Bundesgerichtshof held that a judge could only be guilty of murder if he had knowingly acted contrary to what he believed was the law. The defendant had raised the defence of 'legal blindness' (*Rechtsblindheit*) to the charges. In his enthusiasm to carry out the law, he had made a legal mistake in approving the death sentences, which were to be exemplary in order to dissuade defeatism. As a result, the Bundesgerichtshof held that he should be acquitted unless it were shown that he did not act according to his convictions about what was legal. On a retrial, the judge was acquitted. Indeed, no judge was ever convicted for his part in Nazi judicial atrocities. The acceptance of this defence was strongly criticised by left-wing judges. Wassermann argued that the judges were simply conceiving their role as 'impersonal, non-political, legal technicians, for whom the judicial life had no responsible risks, but was a task of subsumption'.[57]

The *Rehse* case and the discussion of Weimar and Nazi judicial attitudes to law show why many have attached such importance to a more militant democratic approach,[58] which requires judicial commitment to promote actively constitutional democratic ideals, rather than just to comply with the wishes of the legislature. Although the separation of law and morals involved in legal positivism has a place as part of a liberal political agenda, the dominant judicial philosophy is a version of positivism tempered with 'a legal policy awareness' and an acceptance of judicial creativity.[59]

East German law

The influence of the German Democratic Republic (DDR) has been both as a system against which the emerging West German system sought to differentiate itself in ideas such as judicial independence and the rule of law and as a legacy that had to be eradicated upon

[57] R. Wassermann, *Richter, Reform, Gesellschaft* (Karlsruhe 1970); also T. Rasehorn, 'Das Verfahren gegen Rehse und die Problematik des §336 StGB' NJW 1969, 457.

[58] On this concept, see S. Michalowski and L. Woods, *German Constitutional Law. The Protection of Civil Liberties* (Aldershot 1999), 18–25.

[59] J. Rödig cited in K. Adomeit, 'Positivismus, Gesetzgebung und Methodenlehre' NJW 1978, 1 at 3.

unification by positive action. For the lawyer in the unified Germany, the DDR was a constitutional legal order with a properly functioning legal system. In that respect, it is not to be compared to the Nazi period.[60]

There were a number of explicit core values which distinguished the Democratic Republic from the Federal Republic. At root was the belief that all political power was the instrument of the working class to realise its policy and so all organs of government, including the judiciary, should be subservient to this.[61] In the words of art. 45 of the General Courts Act, 'Judges and lay assessors are obliged to give effect to Socialist justice.' In achieving Socialist justice, the Sozialistische Einheitspartei Deutschland (SED) played the leading role, as the self-proclaimed instrument of the working class.

Two features of the East German legal order ensured that Socialist justice was achieved. The first was the directed nature of the legal system, which reflected the concept of 'democratic centralism'. Under art. 93(2) of the Constitution, the Supreme Court (Oberste Gericht) was entrusted with 'guiding' decisions of the courts and ensured the unity of application of the law. That court was formally an organ of the Parliament (*Volkskammer*), so that there was close collaboration between the judiciary and legislature.[62] Apart from deciding appeals, the Oberste Gericht issued guidance (*Rechtlinien*) and less formal statements of its judges were published in the main legal journal, *Neue Justiz*. The higher courts could also call in decisions from lower courts of which they did not approve.[63] In addition, each court had a 'director' who was responsible for its operation to the higher court and, in the case of the Bezirksgericht (appellate court), to the Ministry of Justice. He had to report on its decisions and problems weekly. In turn, he would receive weekly workplans from the judges.[64] Whilst interference by superiors in the decision of individual cases was not allowed, judges might be called in afterwards by the director or president of the court to be told how they should decide such cases in the future.[65] Judicial independence was seen as operational independence in individual cases, but within a framework of a fundamental commitment to achieve socialist legality. Judicial conformity was secured institutionally through legal education, the choice of

[60] Limbach, *Im Namen des Volkes*, above n. 1, 48–9.
[61] See art. 47(2) of the East German Constitution of 1968.
[62] See Baer, 199–201. [63] Ibid., 55–7 and 64–9. [64] Ibid., 75–81.
[65] Ibid., 89. Some judges did complain that informal pressure was put on them: ibid., 241.

teaching staff and teaching materials, then the recruitment and discipline of judges and the framework within which they worked.[66]

The second feature was that judging was closely connected to the political process. As Schüßler expressed it, 'The anchoring of law in politics means above all that the development of the state and the law are always embedded within the development of the whole of society and in the realisation of the total policy of the working class.'[67] Law was instrumental and not separate from social planning, even if it did have a distinct place from politics. The Constitution did not create a separation of state and party. Judges were elected to their posts for limited periods by local councils or the Volkskammer, and they could be removed by the latter at any time. The role of the SED in the promotion of judges was accepted, and judges had to demonstrate commitment to the ideals of the working class and, thus, to those of the party.[68] A survey in 1981 found that 94.5 per cent of judges in the Bezirksgericht belonged to the SED and in 1986 96.4 per cent did. This contrasted with a 1972 survey in West Germany where under 20 per cent of judges belonged to a party.[69] Party discipline over its members tried to secure conformity to its overall policies. It was also born of the view that judges needed to look beyond the rule of law to take note of its social function (as the party saw it).[70]

These two characteristics of direction and party allegiance created a very different sense of judicial independence. Conformity was an ideal and there were day-to-day mechanisms to achieve it. In the East German conception, the work of the judge was a collective activity linked to the political direction of the country, rather than the more individualist independence granted in West Germany. It was unsurprising that, on reunification, East German judges were not absorbed directly into the united German judiciary. Only between 30 and 40 per cent were retained.[71] They were subject to individual scrutiny and most of the older judges were not re-appointed. Their history as committed members of the SED made them unsuited to operating in the liberal democracy of the Federal Republic, with its different notion of judicial independence. To this extent, the approach of the unified Germany was more thorough

[66] Rottleutner, 'Conformity', above n. 48, 443–4; Limbach, *Im Namen des Volkes*, above n. 1, 101.

[67] G. Schüßler, 'Politik und Recht bei der Gestaltung der entwickelten sozialistischen Gesellschaft' *Staat und Recht* 1977, 797 at 800.

[68] Baer, 224. [69] Ibid., 232–3.

[70] Rottleutner, 'Conformity', above n. 48, 446 and 448.

[71] Ibid., 443.

than that of the post-war western allies, for whom pragmatism required the re-appointment of many judges with a questionable past with little re-education for the new order of values.[72]

It is noticeable that the decision of the Bundesgerichtshof in relation to the East German border guards who shot someone who was trying to cross to the West[73] focused on interpreting the East German law applicable at the time, rather than holding the border guards to a higher moral standard. They were convicted for failing to comply with the restrictions on the use of coercive means. The West German approach has been to treat the German Democratic Republic as a valid but flawed legal order, and to undo the structural defects that made it an oppressive regime.

Judicial independence

In the light of the Nazi experience and in contrast to East Germany, the modern German conception of judicial independence centres on the separation of powers. Independence remains functional, rather than the privilege of a particular elite. It ensures that the judge is committed to the protection of rights under the law and the achievement of its requirements. Any idea of external pressure is to be resisted. A (then) Vice-President of the Bundesverfassungsgerichtshof distinguished the 'core area' of judicial independence, the interpretation and application of the law and associated judicial activism, from the 'external organisational area' which deals with the setting within which the judge operates.[74] This opinion is a gloss on art. 97 I of the Basic Law (GG) which says that judges are independent as regards specifically judicial tasks, subject only to the law.

In the 'core area', a judge must be free and not under the dictates of other judges, and must merely follow his sense of what 'statute and law' (*Gesetz und Recht* in the sense of art. 20 III GG) require.[75] Rulings of superior courts bind as general directions, rather than as specific solutions to decisions. There might be 'guideline' decisions from some higher courts or, more likely, reported custom and practice of particular superior courts, such as on sentencing, but this is very much 'soft

72 Cf. Stolleis, *Law under the Swastica*, above n. 55, 169–70.

73 BGHSt, 3 November 1992, BGHSt 39, 1; A. J. McAdams, *Judging the Past in Unified Germany* (Cambridge 2001), 33–4, 167–8.

74 H.-J. Papier, 'Die richterliche Unabhängigkeit und ihre Schranken' NJW 2001, 1089.

75 Baer, 48–50.

law'.[76] Former Bundesverfassungsgerichtshof President and then Federal President, Roman Herzog, commented that the history of the last fifty years of the twentieth century demonstrates an increasing drive to independence from the legislator within the judicial branch.[77] He points to the increasing freedom taken in the interpretation and development of legal texts as a reaction to the increasing mass of legislation and the changing self-understanding of the legislator's role. The judge is to be given more freedom in elaborating the details of legislation, but she is expected to adhere to the policy direction established. This co-operative role involves a commitment to the legislative policy and so a substantial degree of subordination to the legislature. But Herzog suggested that this is only tolerable in the context of judicial review of legislation – to ensure that the orders from the legislature are consistent with basic values. As he suggested, 'Judicial independence and judicial subordination to the law can no longer be sensibly thought about without judicial review.'[78] This is a more independent role than was experienced under the Nazis or in East Germany.

Restrictions on external activity focus on perceptions of impartiality and the degree of activism involved. Active roles in politics or administration are seen as incompatible because of their effect on the judicial role and also on the other branches of government. For example, the Bundesverwaltungsgericht held in 2000 that art. 4(1) of the DRiG prohibited a judge from also being a representative of the executive of a local authority, since this affected the self-administration of communes.[79] The application of the civil service code to judges by art. 46 DRiG, unless specifically contradicted, imposes a restriction on active participation in politics. The oath of judicial independence also requires, in the German perception, a clear distancing from active politics for the ordinary judiciary (and for the constitutional judge in active service). All the same, a 1995 survey estimated that 47 per cent of Bundesgerichtshof judges were members of a political party, and clearly this has some influence on appointments, if only to secure political balance.[80] Clearly the role of the Minister of Justice in the promotions process could be seen to put pressure on judges to please political masters, but this is limited, as

[76] Ibid., 94–8.
[77] In T. Maunz and G. Dürig, *Grundgesetz. Kommentar* (Munich 2001), art. 97(18).
[78] Ibid., art. 97(20).
[79] BVerwG 2B 47.99 of 29 March 2000, DRiZ website (http://www.Leymanns.com/servlet/PB/menu/1181827/index.html).
[80] Baer, 238–41.

has been seen by the role played by peer review in the Präsidialrat. In addition, judges may go on to have a political career.[81]

Within the court, management decisions and codes of conduct can legitimately affect the way in which the judge performs his or her functions. Supervision by superiors (*Dienstaufsicht*) in relation to performance of duties, such as on the number of decisions given in a particular time period, and general court management do not affect the core area. To that extent, the models of new public management that apply to courts and judges are not seen by senior judges as interfering with judicial independence, since judges are controlling the day-to-day activities of individual judges.

More recently, and in line with judicial developments across Europe, there has come to be demand for more judicial self-government, both in managing careers and in organising the justice service. This led the Deutscher Richterbund to pass a resolution on 'self-determination' at its annual congress in November 2002, and to agree to work to develop models which would fit the German system.[82]

The judicial role

The character of the judicial role affects those who are attracted to it and how they perform its tasks. For example, the significant difference between the role of the Rechtsanwalt and the judge may contribute to the limited movement between the professions.

Functions of judges in the legal process

Zimmermann argues that 'the working courtroom style of the German lawyer is radically different from that of the common lawyer: there is less confrontation and more desire to help the judge arrive at a conclusion'.[83] The German judge has more responsibility for ensuring justice is done, though this comes primarily through following procedure, rather than the judge taking positive steps to investigate the truth. The function of the judge varies according to the kind of court in which she is operating. In civil cases, a judge will control the progress of the case as an *Ermittlungsrichter*. The role here is to facilitate the identification of issues

[81] See, for example, the account of the career of Judge Schill in Hamburg who went on to found his own political party following his notoriety as a hard-line 'law and order' judge: *Frankfurter Allgemeine Zeitung*, 23 December 2003.

[82] See the Deutscher Richterbund website (http://www.drb.de).

[83] Zimmermann, 'Introduction', above n. 9, 17.

and the evidence that needs to be adduced or prepared by the parties. This traditional role has been reinforced by powers to give directions to the parties conferred in the 2001 reforms of the Civil Procedure Code. Those reforms included powers for a civil court to entrust the decision to a single judge in most fields. Where there is no legal or factual difficulty, the matter is heard by a single judge, but she can always refer the matter back where she meets an unexpected complexity.[84]

As a result, the oral hearing will be focused on specific issues, is judge-led and can be brief. Typically, one member of a collegial court is appointed as *Berichtserstatter* to prepare a summary of facts and proposals for a solution. The judges thus arrive at the hearing with some ideas of a potential solution which they will put to the parties often in a hypothetical form. Questions to witnesses (if any) will typically be posed by the judge. The judge does not have a power of independent investigation – he or she depends on the parties for evidence. The judge is more of an agenda setter for the issues that will be raised at trial. Given that the case will depend on written documents for the most part, there is only a limited amount of new information to be elicited at trial. A key aspect of recent reforms has been for the judge to ensure that the parties are present, both as a mechanism to improve the work of the lawyers and to reconcile them to the outcome of the case (§ 278 ZPO in its 2001 version).[85] Such reforms represent a shift away from a model of bureaucratic decision-making, focused on achieving the right legal answer, and towards the satisfaction of the litigant and his grievance. The pattern in administrative cases is similar to the more traditional model, though these decisions are based on written submission. As a result, oral presentations by lawyers are brief – often under ten minutes. The procedure is, thus, judge-led in important ways, even if the parties determine the issues and the evidence which they will lead. The result is that a judge will only attend one or two sitting days a week. On appeal, the judges may well meet before the hearing and even have a draft judgment prepared.[86]

In criminal cases, the hearing is livelier. Judges have a limited role in the investigation process, which is led by the prosecutor with the police.

[84] §§ 348 and 348a ZPO.

[85] The study by Schedler et al., 'Arbeitsplatz Gericht', above n. 13, at 66–74 found that in 1994 settlements accounted for 12–20% of decisions, but left the litigants less satisfied than with a judge's decision. See also Treuer et al., *Arbeitsplatz Gericht*, above n. 13, 97ff for a similar analysis of appeal courts.

[86] Treuer et al., *Arbeitsplatz Gericht*, above n. 13, 81–8.

A judge will have to authorise invasions of individual rights (searches, detention, etc.) during that investigation. As in civil cases, there will be a pre-trial review to identify the issues at trial and decide whether a trial is justified. At trial, the judges (lay and professional) come fresh to the issues.[87] There will be a written file, but there will need to be a full rehearsal of evidence. The witnesses will be heard. All the same, there is a heavy caseload for the courts. The Berlin criminal court at Moabit deals with 180,000 cases a year (about 700 a day), with 330 prosecutors and 200 professional judges.[88]

In all but the highest courts, judges do not have assistants, though they may be able to draw on the services of a court library. In some courts, there may not be room for them to have an office. The work of preparing a judgment and researching legal questions will, therefore, be an individual task.

The individual judge preparing the draft judgment (the *Votum*) will play the most significant role in focusing the discussion. The absence of an individual opinion by each judge leads to a different role for the other judges hearing the case. They are more involved in checking the proposed outcome as a supervisor or reviser, rather than redoing the work of the first judge. Particularly since the full file is read only by the Berichtserstatter, the concept of collective decision-making is different from that in the common law. Each judge is given a chance to have their say, and this gives precedence to those who have not prepared the judgment.

Judicial creativity

Judicial style

As Markesinis points out, the German judicial style admits creativity, but focuses on limited and predominantly legal justification.[89] He points to the fact that civil law judgments are abstract and conceptual and seek to use a relentless, scientific logic to demonstrate that a particular outcome is the best interpretation of the law and justifies a result. A typical judgment would be 2,000 to 2,500 words long, and would contain references to previous decisions, but not great discussion. Thus, although

87 M. Delmas-Marty and J. S. Spencer, *European Criminal Procedure* (Cambridge 2003), 310–17.

88 *Der Spiegel-TV* programme, 3 June 2002, available from Spiegel Online (http://www.spiegel.de).

89 B. S. Markesinis, *Foreign and Comparative Law Methodology* (Oxford 1997), ch. 11.

substantive reasons may be offered, the fuller systematisation is offered by scholarly legal writing. As Alexy and Dreier put it,

> In general, the German legal culture is substantive and value-oriented to a significant degree. Its basic values are . . . defined by the constitution. However, German legal culture also is to a high degree characterised by the systematizing achievements of the writings of legal dogmatics, and in this sense it has a pervasive formal feature.[90]

Dissenting opinions appear only in constitutional court decisions. Since 1945, the courts have been more willing to provide fuller reasons for decisions. But their style, outside the Bundesverfassungsgericht, is limited to the justification of the decision, rather than the fuller style of expert reasoning.[91] For routine decisions, in an effort to speed up decision-making, § 313a of the Code of Civil Procedure provides that judgments can be brief, simply referring to uncontested factual matters contained in the case record (*Protokoll*) and even dispensing with reasons where the parties agree.

The nature of judgments shows that they are primarily written for the legal community, in particular other judges and academic commentators.[92] They are designed to give the parties a clear decision and the legal basis on which this was reached, but not to debate legal alternatives in the way that the attorneys would have argued the case. They are not designed to engage the attention of the wider community. The style of the argument in the *Rehse* case is typical of a decision that barely acknowledges the wider concerns that a decision raises, but focuses very much on doctrinal consistency. Controls are internal to the decision-making panel and the legal community, but the decisions require significant interpretation to be comprehensible to the wider community.

Judicial creativity and the Grundgesetz

The German attitude dating from the mid-eighteenth century has been against judicial creativity. The Prussian *Allgemeines Landrecht* of 1794 provided that judges should submit cases of doubtful interpretation to a Law Commission for a ruling. In the absence of a law, the judge was to apply general principles of the law or analogy from other legal

[90] R. Alexy and R. Dreier, 'Statutory Interpretation in the Federal Republic of Germany' in D. N. MacCormick and R. S. Summers (eds.), *Interpreting Statutes* (Aldershot 1991) (hereafter '*Statutes*'), ch. 4, 117.

[91] *Statutes*, 103.

[92] Schedler et al., 'Arbeitsplatz Gericht', above n. 13, 89–93.

provisions.[93] Only in the early part of the twentieth century did the judges conceive of a more expansive function for themselves. In a judgment of October 1933, the Reichsgericht stated:

> A statute is not enacted on its own account, but it is so determined, to regulate the relationships of the personalities participating at that time in a fair and sensible manner. Beyond the wording of the statute stands its sense and purpose. The task of the judge is to make this usable in the application of the law to individual cases and accordingly to lead to fair and just solutions of current litigation with regard to good faith (*Treu und Glauben*).[94]

Such an expansive role was applied especially in the Weimar and Nazi periods to different effect. In the former, it tended to bring the law into line with contemporary needs, in the latter to bring it into line with the policies of the ruling party. Even when faced with a recent and comprehensive Civil Code passed in 1896 and coming into force in 1900, the Reichsgericht was willing to fill what it perceived to be gaps in the law. For example, in 1911, the Sixth Civil Senate held that a department store owed a pre-contractual duty to a customer to take care of his health and safety. This evaded the restrictions on the employer's vicarious liability for the delictual faults of employees under § 831 BGB, under which the employer could escape liability provided he showed that he had taken all reasonable care in selecting and instructing his employees.[95]

If the judicial role had been narrowly conceived in the past, constitutional adjudication has affected judicial creativity in two ways. First of all, the very role of the Bundesverfassungsgericht makes its judges proactive in safeguarding democracy and developing the requirements of the constitution to a contemporary situation. The judges of that court are deliberately set against the elected chambers to prevent the excesses of a democratic majority. The judges sense the tension between the 'fidelity to norms' model (*Normgebundenheit*) and a more creative model to describe what they are doing.[96] The above quotation from the

[93] S. Vogenauer, *Die Auslegung von Gesetzen in England und auf dem Kontinent* (Tübingen 2001), 29.

[94] RGZ 142, 36 at 40f.

[95] RG 7 December 1911, RGZ 78, 239; B. Markesinis and H. Unberath, *The German Law of Torts* (4th edn, Oxford 2002), 788. A similar broad interpretation was given to the phrase 'or other similar right' in § 823 I BGB so that limitations on recovery for economic loss did not apply to damage to an established business: RG 27 February 1904, RGZ 58, 24; Markesinis and Unberath, ibid., 372.

[96] See D. P. Kommers, *The Constitutional Jurisprudence of the Federal Republic of Germany* (2nd edn, Durham 1997) (hereafter 'Kommers'), 43–5.

Reichsgericht was adopted by the Bundesverfassungsgericht in one of its early decisions.[97] As the court's role has been more accepted, and as it has been faced with updating the Grundgesetz to meet contemporary political conflicts, then it has become more willing to be open about its creativity, and the public has been more ready to see the creation of norms.[98] The tension has been resolved by the way in which both constitutional judges and scholars have developed a theory of judicial decision based on the reasoned and logical application of concepts, whilst recognising that these must be implemented with an eye to the policy implications.[99] Alexy distinguishes three levels of justification in which the extent of the controlling powers of the constitutional court should be analysed.[100] On a substantive level, the court makes the arguments of individual rights depend on its assessment of the weight of substantive constitutional principles. A functional or competence level looks at the relative position of different institutions and their credentials in upholding the democratic order. As Caldwell notes,[101] German history has led to a scepticism in relation to both legislative and popular sovereignty. The judiciary is given a special role as guardian of the democratic order. Finally, the methodology of the court can be criticised in terms of its uses of sources and rational argument. At each of these three levels, there is scope for interpreting the role of the judges and the limits of their creativity.

Secondly, the philosophy of the Grundgesetz encourages all judges to seek to do justice and not just apply the law in a narrow, positivist fashion. Judicial creativity by ordinary judges is now seen as encouraged and supported by the Bundesverfassungsgericht, since the Grundgesetz provides private law with principles which determine its future development, and it sets standards both for judicial and for legislative reform.[102] For instance, in the leading *Soraya* decision of 1973,[103] art. 253 BGB provided that damages could only be awarded in delict for non-pecuniary injury in cases where statute so authorised. The

[97] BVerfGE 3, 225 at 233.

[98] See Kommers, 44–5. R. Scholz describes this as the 'juridification of the Constitution': 'Verfassungsgerichtbarkeit in gewaltenteiligen Rechtsstaat' in U. Karpen, *Der Richter als Ersatzgesetzgeber* (Baden-Baden 2002), 20 and see below pp. 167–8.

[99] See Kommers, 41, 48 and 57.

[100] R. Alexy, *A Theory of Constitutional Rights* (Oxford 2002, trans. J. Rivers), 367–8.

[101] Caldwell, *Popular Sovereignty*, above n. 2, 177.

[102] K. Larenz, *Allgemeiner Teil des deutschen bürgerlichen Rechts* (7th edn, Munich 1989), 74–5, 87.

[103] (1973) BVerfGE 34, 269; *Statutes*, 80.

Bundesgerichtshof decided that, even in the absence of a specific statutory provision, the duty to protect constitutional rights of personality justified awarding damages for non-pecuniary loss in such a case. This was upheld by the Bundesverfassungsgericht on the ground that judges were bound under art. 20(3) GG to respect both statute and justice. They thus had to respect the constitutional legal order as a whole and could fill gaps in the law 'according to common sense and general community concepts of justice'.[104] In its view,

> The interpretation of a statutory norm cannot forever remain as at the time of its enactment. One must consider what is its appropriate function at the time of interpretation. The norm stands constantly in the context of social relations and the socio-political perspectives on which it should operate. Their content can and must change and alter with the circumstances.[105]

It has also held that fundamental rights were relevant not only to the vertical relationship between the citizen and the state, but also to horizontal relationships between citizens (the so-called *Drittwirkung*).[106]

Judicial lawmaking as a source of law

The classical position of German law is stated by Larenz:

> Because their results express the current actually applicable law and, furthermore, have some claim to rightness in their own right, judicial decisions are a *source of knowledge of the law*, and an unavoidable one at that. But they are not to be considered as a 'source of law' like a statute or custom.[107]

Judicial decisions are authoritative as interpretations of the law, but are not authorities in their own right. Judges are free to depart from precedents when circumstances change or they think it is right to do so. As Zimmermann puts it,

> A doctrine of *stare decisis* does not, in general, exist in German law. But, of course, decisions of the Federal Supreme Court have a very high persuasive authority for the lower courts. The Federal Supreme Court, too, is not bound by its own previous decisions, but it tends to overrule them only rarely. Occasionally, the Court hints at a future change of opinion in order to reduce possible surprise and embarrassment for potential litigants.[108]

104 See D. P. Currie, *The Constitution of the Federal Republic of Germany* (Chicago 1994) (hereafter 'Currie'), 117–19.

105 BVerfGE 34, 288.

106 See also the *Lüth* decision, (1958) BVerfGE 7, 198; Kommers, 301–9; Currie, 178, 181–8.

107 Larenz, *Allgemeiner Teil*, above n. 102, 12.

108 Zimmermann, 'Introduction', above n. 9, 21.

In one famous instance, decisions of a lower court were quashed a total of 160 times until it finally gave way to an interpretation of asylum law laid down by a superior administrative court.[109] But this formal position gives a misleading impression of the importance of precedent. In their study of precedent, Alexy and Dreier point out that all the supreme courts cite precedent cases in over 97 per cent of their published decisions.[110] Many of these references will be brief, and a fuller discussion will occur in scholarly writing. But lawyers who appear in the courts know that they will be expected to know, cite and discuss precedent cases.[111] Although there may be no *stare decisis*, precedents carry substantial weight. Concerns about legal certainty effectively establish case-law as a subsidiary source of law.[112]

Given this creativity that is embedded in the constitutional and practical function of the judges, in what way are the decisions controlled and how is the creative function of the judges made accountable?

In the first place, the creativity will be transparent to the judges and lawyers involved. When courts make decisions in hard cases, they are conscious of making rules. In some cases, this will go against the letter of the law in order to apply established legal principles to changed circumstances.[113] As a control, there are procedural rules within collegial courts such as the Bundesgerichtshof, under which if one panel wishes to depart from a previous line of decisions from another panel, then the case is heard by the Grosse Senat, the full court, and similar procedures exist in other courts. Alexy and Dreier comment that '[t]hese procedural regulations show that precedents – in spite of their missing formal bindingness – are taken rather seriously in Germany under the aspect of unity or coherence in the administration of justice'.[114] Because cases are cited in judgments, the court will be clear where it is departing from previous decisions.[115] The formation of the court will ensure that the process is taken seriously.

Academic commentaries on legal methodology focus predominantly on the proper justifications to be offered for interpretations of legal

[109] R. Alexy and R. Dreier, 'Precedent in the Federal Republic of Germany' in D. N. MacCormick and R. S. Summers (eds.), *Interpreting Precedents* (Aldershot 1997) (hereafter '*Precedent*'), ch. 2, 37–8.

[110] Ibid., 23, also 49–50. [111] Ibid., 24.

[112] F. Bydlinski, 'Richterrecht über Richterrecht' in Bundesgerichtshof, *50 Jahre Bundesgerichtshof. Festgabe aus der Wissenschaft* (Munich 2000), 1 at 28–31.

[113] See BGHZ 85, 64 at 67, cited in *Precedent*, 25–6.

[114] *Precedent*, 32.

[115] For clear illustrations of overruling and distinguishing, see ibid., 55–6.

texts, rather than the process by which the judge or lawyer should go about discovering the law. These commentaries offer exemplars of justification, rather than commenting to any great extent on how judges should set about their task. This focus on justification follows from the fact that German courts apply the principle *curia novit legem*, and so the judge will find the relevant law in her own time, and in her own way. As a result, the doctrinal commentaries perhaps underplay the use of precedent by judges. Once the lawyers have made their submissions, the judge is expected to produce a formal justification. The accountability exercised through the decision remains confined to the lawyers.

The scope for judicial flexibility is seen in the interpretation of codes and statutes. There is no strict priority identified in relation to any specific kind of argument. In his extensive study, Vogenauer identifies a prima facie priority for the grammatical meaning of the words used in the text (the *Eindeutigkeitsprinzip*), but research by Überlacker suggested that this argument was deployed in only about a quarter of Bundesgerichtshof civil judgments.[116] Courts are strict, particularly in relation to criminal and tax matters, where considerations of legal certainty are particularly prominent. All the same, the courts are prepared to give an extensive interpretation to the meaning of words where this falls within the purpose of legislation.[117] Analysis of the case-law of the highest German administrative, civil and finance courts suggests that the purpose of legislation is a frequently cited reason for a particular interpretation. Although, in the early years after the Second World War, the courts adopted a more limited and literal approach, a more expansive approach has been followed since then.[118] Indeed, a more extensive teleological approach is shown by the application of statutes by analogy, for example the application of provisions of the Civil Code to fill gaps in public law, especially in the area of employment, and where the norms of one legal provision are integrated into the rest of the body of the law, creating an argument of consistency.[119]

The higher courts are predominantly the place for determining new or controversial norms. The lower courts are much more concerned with routine decisions applying the rules to facts. But they seek to do justice

[116] Vogenauer, *Die Auslegung*, above n. 93, 53.

[117] See ibid., 90–1, citing the example of criminal liability for using animals as 'weapons'. Vogenauer argues that, since 1983, the German courts have been less strict in their approach to taxing statutes: ibid., 97–100.

[118] Ibid., 155–9. [119] Ibid., 146–8, 33 and 218–19.

through the evaluation of facts and the concretising of legal norms.[120] In many cases, this involves using open-ended norms. The norm is incomplete and needs further refinement as it is applied to individual cases. A study made by Henf on the use of 'fairness' (*Billigkeit*) in Bundesgerichtshof decisions illustrates the scope for this form of judicial creativity, which is openly acknowledged.[121] Looking at samples of decisions over a twenty-year period, he found that this concept was used as a justification for the decision in about 40 per cent of cases, predominantly relating to the substance of the case.[122] In certain subject areas, the use was much greater. Thus it appeared in 56 per cent of family law cases, and 50 per cent of those concerned with inheritance, but in a far smaller percentage of commercial law cases. In over 70 per cent of cases, the discussion of 'fairness' occurred as part of the application of general clauses in the Code or statutes.[123] The concept provides a bridge between legal ideas expressed in rules and the broader sense of justice within the community.[124] Such an approach moves away from classical legal positivism and requires more justification.[125] But the decisions themselves provide merely the outline. Accountability is mediated through doctrinal legal commentators who will publish criticisms of decisions. Through these comments, there will be a wider dissemination into the legal community as a whole.

Conceptions of the judicial role

Underlying the debates on judicial creativity and on legal positivism is a concern to identify a role for the judiciary that copes with the practical need for law reform consistent with the rule of law and promoting a democratic society. As we have seen, a substantial agreement emerged in the 1950s and 1960s that the Federal Republic required its laws to be interpreted in the light of ethical considerations, such as those which were set out in the list of fundamental values in the first twenty articles of the Grundgesetz.[126] But the consequences of this 'ethical legal order'

120 T. Rasehorn, 'Rechtsfindung und Gerichtspraxis' NJW 1972, 81, 82–3.

121 F. Henf, *Billigkeit und Zivilrichterliche Argumentation* (thesis Kiel 1978).

122 Ibid., 83–7. 123 Ibid., 95.

124 Ibid., 351. For instance in BGHZ 54, 106 at 109, the court talks of how it is applying the standards of 'fair and right-thinking people'.

125 See Rupp, 'Die Bindung', above n. 53, 1773; R. Zippelius, 'Rechtsnorm und richterliche Entscheidungsfreiheit' (1970) 25 JZ 241, 244.

126 See, for instance, K. Zweigert, 'Zum richterlichen Charisma in einer ethisierte Rechtsordnung' in T. Eschenburg et al. (eds.), *Festgabe für Carlo Schmid* (Tübingen 1962), 299, 303; A. Arndt, *Das Bild des Richters* (Karlsruhe 1957), 9–12.

were strongly debated. Although it authorised judges to revisit and annul decisions made under the Nazis and even to prosecute people for acts which were formally lawful in that era,[127] there was a natural reluctance to challenge contemporary legislators and government in the formative and unstable years of the Republic. The debate changed in the 1960s and 1970s. Events such as the *Spiegel* case[128] in 1962 revealed the authoritarian tendencies of government behind appeal to 'state necessity'. The *Rehse* case[129] seemed to emphasise a bureaucratic and non-ethical view of the judicial role by accepting the defence of 'legal blindness'. The substantive values behind the judicial role were more debated in a stable and prosperous society.

A number of models were the focus of such debates. The traditional Prussian model was seen as essentially authoritarian and elite, imposing rules and decisions by an exercise of power. This *Obrigkeitsstaat* was not considered compatible with the democratic legal order, under which the judge had to militate in favour of democratic legal values.[130] But another aspect of the Prussian tradition was shared with many other legal systems, the ideal of the bureaucratic judge.

The ideal of the bureaucratic judge has both positive and negative elements. Positively, he is willing to commit himself to operating the system in which he works. It is this aspect of the ideal that was stressed by Weber at the beginning of the twentieth century. The bureaucratic, rational and impartial decision-maker applied the rules in a predictable and even-handed way.[131] In a democratic society, this involves a commitment to the separation of powers and the priority of the democratically elected legislature. Negatively, the idea contains values of impersonality and a lack of critical judgement with respect to the orders that are given.[132] This latter aspect was supported by ideas of legal positivism and *Begriffsjurisprudenz*. The bureaucratic idea was reflected in the traditions of judicial appointment and judicial life. It was a public service position and many of the rules applying to *Beamten* applied to judges, unless specific provision was made. The impersonality of the collegial decision (broken only in the Bundesverfassungsgericht) emphasised the

127 See Stolleis, *Law under the Swastica*, above n. 55, 161–4.

128 (1996) BVerfGE 20, 162; Kommers, 397–400.

129 5th Strafrechtskammer, BGH, 30 April 1968, NJW 1968, 1339.

130 For the continuing importance of the contrast between the *Obrigkeitsstaat* idea and democracy, see Limbach, *Im Namen des Volkes*, above n. 1, 10.

131 A. T. Kronman, *Max Weber* (London 1983), 50–61.

132 See generally, J. Bell, 'The Judge as Bureaucrat' in J. M. Eekelaar and J. Bell (eds.), *Oxford Essays in Jurisprudence* (3rd edn, Oxford 1987), ch. 3.

role of the institution, not the person, in coming to decisions, and the individual could escape blame. The idea of the *Rechtsstaat* as the rule of law and not men seemed to reinforce this.

Critics took the view that judges could hide behind the bureaucratic model and escape the engagement necessary to realise the social state ambitions, which they saw in the Grundgesetz. For Arndt, the political dimension of judicial decision-making was not an 'irritating itch', which one could get rid of, but it was rather an integral part of democratic judging:[133]

> there is no law that is comprehensible without political understanding for its specific task and without a view of the whole . . . The universal structural principle of partnership in constitutional democracy must rather lead to judging being not a process free from political responsibility, but that the judge identify himself responsibly with the legally correct decision which he has shared in making.

In a word, the roles of the judge and the legislator were complementary – the legislator sets out general principles and the judge renders these concrete. But in this relationship, the personality of the responsible judge comes more to the fore.[134] The litigant is confronted not so much with a judicial institution as with a responsible person, just as she would be if she went to an ombudsman. She then has to have confidence in the charisma of the judge.[135] Such a system is more transparent and accountable, as is appropriate in a democratic society.

The alternative, which many on the left proposed, was the model of the social judge, taking responsibility to achieve justice in individual cases and prepared to stand up against public authorities in defence of individual freedoms.[136] For some this meant that there should be changes in the process of appointment and operation of the judiciary in order to institutionalise the way the law was supposed to reflect views in the community.[137]

At root, there are two conceptions of what is meant by 'political' and how judges relate to them.[138] The broad conception proposed by the

[133] Arndt, *Das Bild*, above n. 126, 17, also 12.

[134] Ibid., 11; T. Rasehorn, *Im Namen des Volkes* (Neuwied 1968), 15–25.

[135] See Zweigert, 'Zum richterlichen Charisma', above n. 126, 309–10.

[136] See R. Wassermann, *Justizreform* (Neuwied 1970), ch. 1.

[137] See H. Ostermeyer, *Die Juristische Zeitbombe* (Munich 1973), 143–9.

[138] See T. Mayer-Maly, 'Die politische Funktion der Rechtsprechung in einer pluralen Gesellschaft' DRiZ 1971, 325 at 326.

more left-wing writers sees any policy judgement as 'political'. In the words of Judge Wassermann:[139]

> Judging (*Richten*) has the function of giving direction (*Richtunggeben*). Whoever pronounces the law, exercises power and shapes individual relationships. Because this has been true at all times, judicial activity has always been political . . . The judge should become aware of the political function of his office and see through the dominance of those collective prejudices, which would make him into a servant continually ready to obey changing powers.

As a result, the individual judge must take responsibility for decisions. In particular, he has to be transparent about the political choices which he makes, and to offer justifications for them.[140] It is not sufficient to rely on the authority of his position or on the text which he interprets and applies. The Bundesverfassungsgericht recognised the importance of judges being aware of the policy dimensions of the law.[141]

The more traditional conception of 'political' would confine it to areas where there is party political or social conflict. The complementarity of judicial and legislative developments of the law gives the primary responsibility and freedom to the political legislator. More traditional commentators criticised Wassermann and others by arguing that to go beyond normal judicial development of the law in line with legal values went too far into the role of the social engineer, creating a new kind of society, which was not a proper role.[142] Judges had to anchor themselves firmly in legal texts to justify their creativity, rather than ideals of the better society. At core, the judges, especially in the Bundesverfassungsgericht, argue that the Basic Law establishes a kind of consensus. The role of the judge, in the view of Smend and later constitutional judges, is to contribute towards a process of social integration.[143] Compromise and consensus are the social processes by which this is achieved. As Limbach put it, 'even though it is not the primary task of the Bundesverfassungsgerichtshof to create consensus in society, equally it cannot be its task to release productive unrest in society'.[144] An understanding of society and an ability to contribute to building consensus are seen here as ideals. It is not that there is an actual consensus that the judges are reproducing,

[139] Wassermann, *Richter, Reform, Gesellschaft*, above n. 57, 97.
[140] R. Wassermann, *Der politische Richter* (Munich 1972), 17–18, 85.
[141] (1954) BVerfGE 7, 198 (*Kuppelei* decision): 'the Constitution consists not only in individual sentences, but also in general political guiding ideas, which stand behind the individual rules and have shaped them'.
[142] W. Richter, 'Die Rolle des Richters in unserer Zeit' (1974) 29 JZ 345, 348.
[143] Limbach, *Im Namen des Volkes*, above n. 1, 151–6. [144] Ibid., 157.

but they are working with the grain to fashion a consensus. The task is to create the conditions for social stability, and to generate acceptance of the decisions.[145] But this role of emphasising foundational values also means that the constitutional judges, at least, have the task of resisting the majority. On the other hand, if the judges ignore the sense of justice in the community, they create a gulf between the judge and the community. This leads to a delicate balance. In Limbach's view, the job of the court is to lead a long-term policy role, not simply to be guardian of the Constitution.[146]

This conflict of views among judges is reflected in the academic literature. Alexy has provided the most sophisticated modern theory of legal reasoning, the 'special case thesis'. In brief, this suggests that 'the claim to correctness [in a legal argument] is indeed . . . raised in legal discourse, but this claim, unlike that in general practical discourse, is not concerned with the absolute rationality of the normative statement in question, but only with showing that it can be rationally justified within the framework of the validly prevailing legal order'.[147] But this relatively closed system approach is challenged by Habermas and his procedural understanding of the Constitution in which it is the process of discussion and decision-making which is laid down, rather than the content of values.[148] Like Judge Wassermann and others, he is arguing for a deliberative process that engages the interested parties in society.[149] For the judges, it is the judge who would stand at the centre; for Habermas, it is the citizenry. Thus the debate among judges reflects broader philosophical debates about conceptions of the rule of law and democracy, and how far legal reasoning is constrained.

Within this debate, there remains a consensus in Germany that the judge then plays a creative part in giving effect to the framework thus established. To take Zweigert's term, there is an 'ethicised legal order' which affects the work of all lawyers.[150] The issue is how these values are identified and applied in a pluralistic society.[151] In this, the Bundesverfassungsgericht took a stronger lead in the 1970s in having

[145] Ibid., 172, 183. [146] Ibid., 158–62.

[147] R. Alexy, *A Theory of Legal Argumentation* (Oxford 1989), 220.

[148] See, for example, J. Habermas, *Between Facts and Norms* (Cambridge 1996, trans W. Rehg), chs. 5.3–6.3.

[149] See R. Kühne, 'Die Richter und die Politisierung der Rechtsprechung' DRiZ 1971, 113 who emphasises the principle of openness and specifically discusses the work of Habermas for a judicial audience.

[150] Zweigert, 'Zum richterlichen Charisma', above n. 126, 304.

[151] Wassermann, *Der politische Richter*, above n. 140, 52–6.

presented before it controversial political and social issues, and explaining its reasons for choices. Other judges remain more reticent to engage judicially in debates about the direction of society. But the existence of vigorous debate over many years about the judicial role is one clear way in which German judges have departed from the more formal and impersonal bureaucratic image of the past.

On the whole, the debate on the judicial role takes place within the legal community, with the exception of debate on the Constitutional Court. As a result, the broad judicial consensus about the important, but limited, direction of judicial lawmaking prevails.

Extrajudicial roles

The character of judicial independence gives only limited scope for extrajudicial roles. The possibility of secondment to the Ministries of Justice has been noted, but there is little practice of secondment to other ministries. Professional judges are focused on the legal service. It is possible for judges to take part in political life and enter Parliament. That is governed by the usual civil service rules that would allow a return in due course to the civil service function. There have been two occasions on which the president of the Constitutional Court has become Federal President, but this is predominantly a figurehead role, and perhaps reinforces the attachment of the political community to the impartiality of the law, rather than suggesting that judges have become political. There are few examples of judges heading inquiries. On the whole, judges are not personages of the state who are called upon to perform tasks outside their judicial function. The separation of powers is more strictly observed than, for example, in Britain or France.

Professional judges and the legal community

Judges and Rechtsanwälte

The earlier discussion on legal education noted the traditional priority given to preparation for the judicial function, rather than to the needs of other professions. The judges were expected to be the elite among the educated practitioners. They were responsible for legal interpretation and legal development, and also for the organisation of the trial process. That model is changing, if only because the liberalisation of legal services has enabled German lawyers to create firms across

Germany and with foreign lawyers, such as British and American firms. This was reinforced by the important role of German lawyers in the legal development of Central and Eastern Europe, following the collapse of the Berlin Wall. Even within Germany, there was a substantial increase in demand for legal services. In addition, German Rechtsanwälte were recruited to fill posts as judges for the East. Restrictions on public sector budgets, under pressure throughout the 1990s because of the costs of unification and the requirements of European economic and monetary union, have kept down the number of public sector posts as judges, prosecutors and civil servants. So the private sector has both expanded and gained in influence. The greater emphasis on mediation and arbitration in the commercial sphere has also reduced the relative importance of judges.

In terms of influence on law reform, the advocates have been able to influence the agenda for the modernisation of the legal process and of legal education to reflect their interests. The emphasis on speed and mediation focuses the judge much more on the service of the lawyer and his client, rather than the judge's own conception of justice.

Judges and professors

Traditionally the professor was the most influential member of the legal community. Before codification, the professor's view was often solicited to advise on the law in individual disputes.[152] The professor would frequently serve as a part-time judge. In law reform, professors would be called upon to be members of a committee to draft new legislation. Indeed, that is very much the case today. The reform of the Civil Code in 2000 was led by professors, rather than by judges.[153] German judges are highly influenced by academic writings and legal dogmatics. In particular the higher courts take account of, and refer to, scholarly writings – the academic spirit permeates the opinions of all courts. This shows the vast extent to which the German legal culture is an expert culture.[154] The German judgments, though longer than the French, require commentary and systematisation, and this is the role of the academic. Furthermore, the requirement that a candidate produce a very substantial work on a field (a *Habilitationsschrift*) before she or he is appointed as a

152 F. Wieacker, *A History of Private Law in Europe* (Oxford 1995, trans. Weir), 65–7 and ch. 8; J. P. Dawson, *The Oracles of the Law* (Westport 1968), 450–61.

153 See W. Ernst, 'New Rules of Breach of Contract in Germany' (2002–3) 5 *Cambridge Yearbook of European Legal Studies* 333, 334–8.

154 Alexy and Dreier, 'Statutory Interpretation', above n. 90, 118.

professor ensures that there are major works of reference to which any lawyer would refer to understand a particular field. Such works, as well as the major commentaries, ensure that the academics, rather than the practitioners, produce the major sources of reference on German law.[155] All the same, Europe and changes in the income and status of professors are leading to some re-alignment of roles.

An important change since the 1990s has been the greater role of the European Union and the European Convention on Human Rights as sources of legal change. Here, at least in the European courts, judges are involved in making decisions about the new directions of the law. National judges are then among the more important implementers of these ideas. Judicial decisions do cite the decisions of the Strasbourg Court, but they feature less prominently than the German Constitution's own list of fundamental rights.[156] Weiss argues that German judges are insufficiently aware of the Convention and of international human rights standards generally.[157] All the same, the strength of these external influences results in a decline in the relative position of the national professor as a source of law reform. The trigger for the 2000 law reforming the Civil Code was a European directive. In constitutional law, as will be seen, the Bundesverfassungsgericht is setting the agenda and the professors are then commentators.

The relative salaries of judges and professors now also favour senior judges and give them greater status. In 2004, the top of the C4 professor scale (the highest point in the career) was lower than the R4 judge and was only 60 per cent of the top judicial salary. Professors can supplement their income either in practice as a Rechtsanwalt or as a part-time judge, and judges can be part-time academics, so there is an informal intermingling between the professions.

For the most part, the professors retain their authority as commentators, and commentaries provide a major source of inspiration for legal interpretation. The traditions of the German legal system established particularly in the nineteenth century remain significant, but it is as much outside the realm of publication (in committees, on the Bench or

[155] See Zimmermann, 'Introduction', above n. 9, 35–9.

[156] N. Weiss, 'The Impact of the European Convention on Human Rights on German Jurisprudence' in E. Örücü (ed.), *Judicial Comparativism in Human Rights Cases* (London 2003), ch. 3. Up to January 2003, there had been sixty-four cases brought in Strasbourg against Germany and in thirty-seven a breach of the Convention was found.

[157] Ibid.

as a legal adviser) as through writing that the professor has an impact on law reform and on opinion in the legal community.

Lay judges

Germany has developed and expanded distinctive kinds of lay judges who provide a bridge between the professional judiciary and the wider community. They serve both to influence decisions and to provide a more popular legitimacy for decisions reached. There are three principal groups of non-professional judges: community judges, expert judges and representative judges. They can either be regular members of panels of the court or, as with the criminal law *Schöffen*, be appointed for particular cases. Lay judges are not paid, but receive reimbursement of expenses and an indemnity for loss of earnings.

Community judges: Schöffen

The largest group of non-professional judges are appointed as Schöffen in the criminal courts.[158] They are non-lawyers who represent the community and constitute a democratic element in both the Amtsgericht and the Landgericht. In administrative courts (Verwaltungsgericht and Oberverwaltungsgericht), there are also similar representatives of the community. Whereas there is a specific provision in the Constitution of Courts Law, §42 Abs. 2, that attention is paid to ensuring all groups in society (in terms of sex, age, occupation and social position) are represented among the Schöffen, there is no equivalent provision in the rules governing lay judges in the administrative courts.[159] The legal provisions do not mention religious affiliation or ethnic grouping.

In practice, it is difficult to secure a panel of Schöffen that is broadly representative of the community as a whole. Based on analysis of statistics from 1977 to 1998, Brusten suggests that public service workers are over-represented and women are under-representated.[160] Data collected

[158] A good introduction is provided on the website of the Deutsche Vereinigung der Schöffinnen und Schöffen: http://www.schoeffen.de.

[159] See, for example, the introductory booklet for lay judges in administrative courts: Senatsverwaltung für Justiz, 'Die ehrenamtlichen Richter in der Verwaltungsgerichtsbarkeit' (Berlin 2000), para. 3.2.

[160] M. Brusten, 'Wie wird man Schöffe?' in H. Lieber and U. Sens (eds.), *Ehrenamtliche Richter. Demokratie oder Dekoration am Richtertisch?* (Wiesbaden 1999) (hereafter 'Lieber and Sens'), 77.

Table 3.2 *Profile of Schöffen*

	Number	% women	% 25–40	% 41–50	% 51–60	% 61–70
Landgericht (criminal)	22,773	45.8	22	28	33.45	15.97
Amtsgericht (Schöffengericht)	19,005	47.08	23.8	29.25	31.5	14.06
Landgericht (youth court)	5,223	50.35	29.66	35.76	25.94	7.3
Amtsgericht (youth)	13,946	51.01	33.24	34.7	23.77	7.08

by the Federal Ministry of Justice[161] show that Schöffen are more heavily represented in the age groups 40 to 50 and 50 to 60. On 1 January 1997, Schöffen represented 0.08 per cent of the 25 to 40 age cohort, but 0.18 per cent of the 40 to 50 group, 0.16 per cent of the 50 to 60 group and 0.09 per cent of the 60 to 70 age cohort.[162] There has been a decline in the dependence on this middle-aged group since 1975. At that time, there was a much smaller proportion of the 60+ age group available for this work, and younger women were over-represented. Now, changes in the demography of the working population have led to proportionately fewer in the 25 to 40 age group being active as Schöffen, and more in the 60 to 70 age group. Men and women are fairly evenly represented except in the 60 to 70 age cohort, where the proportion of men is double that of women. This represents a substantial change since 1975 when there were proportionately 25.5 per cent more men than women as Schöffen (and 31.6 per cent if one only looked at Schöffen hearing adult criminal cases).

In terms of employment, 20.8 per cent of Schöffen were housewives, unemployed or retired. Of the 52.7 per cent who were employees, just over half worked in the public sector. In terms of the distribution of occupations, less has changed over the twenty-two years from 1975 to 1997. Public sector workers were over-represented by about 20 per cent and the self-employed by 6 per cent. Pensioners were substantially under-represented by over 30 per cent. There was been a decline in the proportions of private sector workers and housewives giving time to this role.

161 Bundesministerium der Justiz, 'Geschlects-, Alters- und Berufsstruktur der Schöffen im Bundesgebiet im Vergleich mit der Bevölkerungsstruktur' (report 3221-1-51 0016/97).

162 Under § 35 GVG, among the excuses for not doing service as a Schöffen is that the person selected is over sixty-five or will be over sixty-five when the period of service is over. Thus those in this age group who are serving as Schöffen are predominantly volunteers.

Statistics are not kept on ethnic minorities. In order to be a Schöffen or a professional judge, one must be a German citizen, so those of Turkish origin are rarely found among the judges, even though they are the accused in about 30 per cent of cases.[163] Richert wrote in 1983 that: 'The ideal lay judge emerges as a middle-aged man, possessing a solid education, hailing from the middle class, and preferably supporting the political party in power.'[164] This profile has changed significantly in a number of ways and is, in any case, too much of a caricature, given the other factors which determine a person's availability for this kind of work. All the same, the Schöffen system is an imperfect way of achieving popular participation in the legal system.

The Schöffen for the criminal courts are selected by a special committee based on a list of suggestions drawn up by the local community (*Gemeinde*) council. For a candidate to be placed on the list, two-thirds of the councillors must approve the name. The selection committee is chaired by a judge of the Amtsgericht and consists of an administrative official appointed by the government of the Land, as well as ten local people. These 'trusted people' are nominated from residents of the area served by the Amtsgericht and chosen by the local authority responsible for the area of the court (typically the Landkreis or town council). The way these recruitment processes work varies from area to area. Some Gemeinde seek nominations from a variety of local groups, political parties and unions, others will just rely on the list of residents and generate names randomly. Political parties feature prominently among those suggesting names. Although service as a Schöffen is a duty when you are called, the pre-selection process will not always yield a random selection of society. Some employers encourage applications, others are more reluctant to lose the time of important workers.[165] Some local authorities place advertisements in the press. There is no interview procedure similar to the appointment of English magistrates, and, by and large, it would appear that the selection committee feels better able to form a judgement on those who are known to some of its members.

The Schöffen operate in criminal cases at various levels within the system. In the Amtsgericht, there will be one professional judge sitting with two Schöffen.[166] These deal with lesser offences. More serious cases

[163] See E. Sigismund, 'Zur Funktion der ehrenamtlichen Richter im Strafverfahren in Deutschland' (Ministry of Justice, Bonn, 28 April 1999), 11.

[164] J. P. Richert, *West German Lay Judges: Recruitment and Representativeness* (Tampa 1983), 66, cited by Clark, 'Selection', above n. 3, 1839.

[165] Lieber and Sens, 78–84.

[166] The prosecution may ask for two professional judges in more difficult cases.

are heard by the Grosse Kammer of the Landgericht by three professional judges and two Schöffen. The formation for the most serious offences (e.g. homicide) is the Schwurgericht, also with three judges and two Schöffen. The 1879 Code of Criminal Procedure had established a jury of twelve Schöffen sitting separately from three professional judges to try serious offences. But this was changed during the 1930s, and the pattern established in the post-war period was for the Schöffen to be concerned with all elements of the case, not just the question of guilt.

The Schöffen are nominated for four years. Their number is such that they will typically only serve for twelve sittings a year. In 1997, there were 60,947 Schöffen. The workload is ensured by having 'Hilfschöffen' appointed for long cases, so they can step in and take over a formal role, should a nominated Schöffen be unable to carry on during the course of a case. In interviews, I encountered examples of cases lasting a long time – one had involved fifty-six hearing days and another lasted over three years. The availability of Schöffen had to be planned in advance as far as possible, and individual Schöffen had to be flexible about holidays and work to see the case to the end.

There are lay members of other courts, who are not really representatives of the community. For example, the Berlin Constitutional Court, established on reunification, has nine members – three judges, three lawyers qualified for judicial office and three lay members, sitting for a fixed seven-year term. The first group appointed in 1992 were five Rechtsanwälte, three judges and a university professor. In 1999, the new group involved three Rechtsanwälte, four judges and two university professors.[167] The so-called 'lay' element really means 'non-professional judges'.

Expert and representative judges

The lay judges in chambers dealing with commercial cases, agricultural, finance, labour, social and professional courts, are appointed because of their expertise in the subject-matter of the court's work. Judges appointed to these chambers are also appointed as representatives of particular sectional interests. This is most obvious in the labour courts, where there are representatives of both employers and employees. Labour courts were formed on the French model in the early nineteenth century with lay members. Originally, these individuals

[167] See K. Eschen, 'Die ehrenamtlichen Richter an den Verfassungsgerichter der Länder – Am Beispiel des Verfassungsgerichtshofs des Landes Berlin' in Lieber and Sens, 56–9.

functioned as assessors, but under the law of 23 December 1926, they became full judges of the court.[168] The function of these experts is to broaden the knowledge of the court,[169] but also to confer legitimacy within the community represented.[170] The extent to which the lay judges can influence the process depends on the dominant role of the professional presiding judge.[171]

Nominations to the commercial court come from the chamber of industry or commerce, and appointments are made by the Ministry of Justice of the relevant Land for three years. Similarly, nominations to the labour court and the social court come from employers' and employees' organisations to the relevant ministry, which seeks to ensure a proper balance. Nominations to the various disciplinary courts of the different regulated professions of lawyer, doctor, dentist, etc. come from organisations within the profession. In detail, the arrangements differ from one profession to another.

Training and discipline

The arrangements for induction and training of lay judges are not as well organised as for the professional judiciary. In interviews for this research and in publications, lay judges comment that they would have liked further training. This is organised on a voluntary and self-help basis by associations of Schöffen,[172] but without the kind of financial support provided in Sweden by Domstolsverket.[173] It is as if the official view was that training would somehow change the character of the lay judges and their insights. The absence of formal induction programmes leaves much to the presiding judge to ensure that the lay judges are aware of their role. This is often done as cases arise. Certainly, all the interviews with judges, officials and Schöffen conducted for this research suggested that Schöffen frequently did not receive any training, nor did they meet up with other Schöffen.

168 M. Wolmerath, 'Der ehrenamtliche Richter an Arbeitsgericht' in Lieber and Sens, 129.

169 See, for example, P. Bader, R. Hohmann and H. Klein, *Die ehrenamtlichen Richterinnen und Richter beim Arbeits- und Sozialgericht* (11th edn, Heidelberg 2004), 2–3.

170 F. J. Dürrell, 'Der ehrenamtliche Richter beim Bundesarbeitsgericht' in Lieber and Sens, 148.

171 Wolmerath, 'Der ehrenamtliche Richter', above n. 168, 133.

172 The programme offered by the Deutsche Vereinigung der Schöffinnen und Schöffen is available on its website. It involves both induction and general continuing education themes.

173 Below p. 286.

Lay judges are not within a bureaucratic hierarchy, so they have no superior to give them directions about the way that they perform their tasks. They can be removed only in limited circumstances.

Functioning of lay judges

Clark wrote that: 'Several grounds have been advanced to justify lay participation in the judicial process; it fosters democracy by checking executive despotism and ensuring independent decisionmaking; it contributes to citizenship training; and it legitimates the decision made.'[174] Published literature, confirmed by interviews conducted for this research, suggests that the Schöffen in criminal cases are meant to bring common sense to the deliberation on the outcome of the case, but are not meant to be involved in detailed analysis of the case file. In administrative law, the role of the lay judges has been limited to difficult questions of law and fact. Since 1978, it has been possible for the court to make a decision by order without the involvement of lay judges, where there are no particular difficulties of fact or law.

There are two stages to the process of decision-making. The pre-trial process is conducted in different ways, depending on whether the case is criminal or administrative. In criminal matters, it is increasingly the prosecutor who is responsible for the pre-trial process of sorting evidence and determining what is relevant. The judge will conduct some form of pre-trial review, simply to schedule the different parties. There may even be discussion about possible sentences with the defence. But the judge will have to discuss this both with the other judges and with the Schöffen before a decision is reached. So the lay judges are heavily involved in the substantive aspects of the case.

In administrative law cases, which are often conducted on paper, there will be much more preparation by the reporting judge (*Berichtserstatter*) in advance. He will have examined the file and may have decided that third parties should be joined or evidence gathered. His research of the law and requests for further factual information will focus any hearing. All this preparatory work is conducted without consultation of the lay judges.[175]

In both criminal and administrative cases, the lay judge will arrive with no prior knowledge of the case file. There will be a brief introduction by the presiding judge about the nature of the case and the

[174] Clark, 'Selection', above n. 3, 1830.
[175] See 'Die ehrenamtlichen Richter', above n. 159, paras. 4.3–4.5.

basic kinds of issue to be raised. There will then be the oral hearing. In many criminal cases, the oral hearing is spread over several days and there may be some opportunity to review progress in the middle of the case. But it is not expected that the lay judge will examine the case file. As was explained in interviews for this research and in the briefing literature for lay judges, their function is to receive the account of the factual issues and to check that the professional judges have conducted an investigation of all the issues.[176] The relationship between lay and professional judges is based on a division of functions.

The importance of the oral hearing in criminal, administrative and labour matters does give scope for participation by the lay judge. Lay judges are typically invited by the presiding judge to ask questions, but the literature suggests that Schöffen are uncertain whether this is a formality or a genuine invitation.[177] Much depends on the personal relationships between the lay and professional judges and the personality of the lay judge. A lay judge needs to have a degree of confidence in order to ask questions in a legal setting without legal training. There is certainly a danger noted in the literature and interviews that the lay judges will remain relatively passive during the hearing.

Once in the private deliberation, the lay judges can outnumber the professional judges, but the extent of this will be limited by the deference shown by the lay judges to the views of the professionals. If the views of the professionals are heard first, as was suggested in interviews, this will put pressure on the lay judges to fall into line. The professional judges also play an important role by deciding questions of law. This role will not be seen externally in terms of one decision by the judge on law and another by the lay judges on facts. But the division of functions is made clear.

There is no evidence that there is any great difference in the reasoning of professional and lay judges. Lay judges are not harder or softer in sentencing. Rather, their function is to confer legitimacy on the process and to link official approaches to a view of matters which is 'close to the citizen' (*Bürgernah*).[178] On the whole, they confer this legitimacy by their presence in the case, as representatives of the community or of

[176] Ibid., para. 4.7.

[177] See U. Vultejus, 'Schöffen in Hauptverhandlung und Beratung – Ihr Einfluβ in Theorie und Praxis', and C. Renning and S. Machura, 'Die Zusammenarbeit zwischen Schöffen und Berufsrichtern' in Lieber and Sens, at 63 and 67.

[178] Sigismund, 'Zur Funktion', above n. 163, 8.

a particular relevant section. The extent to which they have an actual influence on decisions is difficult to assess, but their presence alters the internal dynamics of the court and forces the professionals to reflect on their reasons for decisions. To that extent, the system is a success, even if there is difficulty in obtaining a sufficient social representation within the criminal Schöffen.

Professional judges and the wider community

Law and politics: constitutional adjudication

Judicial review of the legislature was traditionally viewed as unacceptable, but a movement in favour of it grew in the middle of the nineteenth century. With Weimar and the impact of inflation on property, the Deutscher Richterbund in 1924 declared that judges were empowered to protect freedom of contract and to strike down legislative attacks on property.[179] This was then followed by the Reichsgericht which declared that 'in principle courts of law are authorised to examine the formal and material validity of laws and ordinances'.[180] But this actu-ally led to little positive protection for basic rights. It took the creation in 1949 of the Bundesverfassungsgericht under the influence of Professors Nauriasky and Kelsen to really create jurisdiction in this field. Although the Weimar Constitution of 1919 had created the Staatsgerichtshof to deal with constitutional litigation within a Land which did not have a constitutional court and to deal with matters where there were differences between Länder or between the Reich and the Länder, this really did not work as an independent constitutional court.[181] The success of the 1949 institution has inspired Kommers to suggest that 'the Constitutional Court is at the epicenter of Germany's constitutional democracy'.[182] Certainly, it was argued by Smend as early as 1962 that the Constitution was really what the Bundesverfassungsgericht interpreted it to be.[183] An example would be the refusal by the Federal President in 2002 to block the signing of a law on immigration despite complaints from the opposition that it was unconstitutional. President Rau's comment was that he would be happy to have the matter tested in the courts, but, in his

[179] Kommers, 6–7. [180] (1924) RGZ 107, 377 at 379; Kommers, 6.
[181] J.-C. Béguin, *Le contrôle de la constitutionnalité des lois en République fédérale d'Allemagne* (Paris 1982), 19–20.
[182] Kommers, 55. [183] Professor Rudolf Smend, cited in Kommers, 55.

presidential capacity, he would not block the outcome of the political process.[184]

Kommers suggests that there are three versions of the Constitution that the Bundesverfassungsgericht interprets. First, there is the 'unamendable constitution', the principles of federalism and of basic rights, which art. 79(3) of the Grundgesetz declares to be unalterable. Secondly, there is the 'alterable constitution', those other provisions of the written text which are amended from time to time. Thirdly, there is the unwritten constitution, the suprapositive principles of 'justice', 'dignity' and the 'moral code' which have to be interpreted and elaborated by the courts. Thus, 'Germany's real constitution, then, includes more than the written text of the Basic Law itself.'[185] To a great extent, the Bundesverfassungsgericht has been responsible for developing this.

Court membership

The Bundesverfassungsgericht has sixteen judges, sitting in two divisions or Senates, who are appointed for a fixed term of twelve years. They are elected half by the Parliament's upper house, the Bundesrat, and half by the lower house, the Bundestag.[186] The Ministry of Justice draws up two lists of eligible candidates, one consisting of judges from the highest federal courts, and the other of all persons proposed by the parties in the Federal Parliament or by the various Länder governments. The Bundesverfassungsgericht may also suggest names that have been overlooked in this process.

The Bundestag committee is composed of twelve members drawn from all parties in proportion to their strength. It deliberates in private on the files relating to each candidate, though its work is often prepared by working groups of its members. The choice of candidates requires a two-thirds majority, so that there is general agreement among the political parties. The parties usually come to an arrangement on whose turn it is to nominate a candidate, subject to any criticism from the other parties. The Bundesrat elects the candidate in plenary session, but this is a formality. All the preparatory work of selection has been done by a committee made up of the Ministers of Justice of the different Länder.

In 2005, eight of the sixteen judges were professors, of whom three had been part-time judges, and eight were judges. Only four had held elected

[184] Speech, 20 June 2002.
[185] Kommers, 38. [186] On the election process, see ibid., 20–2.

political office, and three had held administrative posts in the public service. Five were women. The average age was fifty-eight years and eleven months. Although the website[187] does not give political allegiance, all were active in political parties in some way.

Jurisdiction and procedure

The Bundesverfassungsgericht has three broad forms of jurisdiction. First, it exercises *abstract control of norms* at the instance of the Federal Government, Länder or politicians from the Bundestag. In this way, the court can examine the validity of laws passed by Parliament soon after they have been signed, or can advise on the ratification of treaties. Secondly, it exercises *concrete control of norms* when it gives rulings on issues referred to it by the ordinary courts in the course of litigation on individual cases. Thirdly, it exercises concrete control when individuals submit petitions (*Verfassungsbeschwerde*) alleging breach of their constitutional rights. In addition, it may also rule on conflicts between Länder and the Federation or between different Länder.

Kommers argues that, 'Whereas American constitutionalism has historically entailed a creative interaction between the constitutional text and evolving political practice, German constitutionalism tends to place greater emphasis on the capacity of the formal text to influence political practice.'[188] In part, this comes from the division of powers, but also from the principles which the Grundgesetz lays down. Stone Sweet has argued that the German combination of coalition government and a strong veto power in the Bundesrat ensures that most bills which governments bring forward will reflect political compromise. There is less central control and less scope for driving through politically controversial legislation than in countries such as Britain and France.[189] As a result, the Constitutional Court is less often faced with politically controversial legislation. On the other hand, he argues that the ability of the Bundesverfassungsgericht to constitutionalise areas of private law and to control judicial outcomes depends significantly on the existence and operation of the individual complaints procedure.[190]

The Bundesverfassungsgericht itself reports that in the fifty-three years from its inception in 1951 until 31 December 2004, it dealt with

[187] See http://www.bundesverfassungsgericht.de.
[188] Kommers, 38–9. [189] A. Stone Sweet, *Governing with Judges* (Oxford 2000), 54–5.
[190] Ibid., 119.

Table 3.3 *Bundesverfassungsgericht decisions*

Type of decision	1951–91	1992–2004	Total	% of decisions
Abstract norm control	61	32	93	0.072
Concrete norm control	896	253	1,149	0.89
Bund–Land conflicts	13	12	25	0.19
Organ conflicts	45	31	76	0.59
Constitutional complaints	67,545	59,589	127,134	98.85
Consistency with international law	6	1	7	0.005
Electoral cases	62	60	122	0.95
Total of proceedings	68,628	59,978	128,606	100

149,442 cases, of which 143,879 were constitutional complaints (96.2 per cent). Of these complaints only 3,566 (2.5 per cent) were successful. In terms of actual decisions, table 3.3 confirms the overwhelming weight of the constitutional complaints, and the very minor role of the very political decisions on abstract control of legislation. The Bundesverfassungsgericht states that, between 1951 and 2004, it only invalidated in whole or in part 408 federal laws and 159 laws of Länder. Landfried calculated that this amounted to about 5 per cent of all federal laws in the period 1951–90.[191] In terms of areas, she makes the point that social policy (including family law) was the largest (31 per cent of cases), followed by finance and fiscal policy (18 per cent), legal policy (including the administration of justice) (15 per cent) and regulatory measures (13 per cent).[192] Once we examine the area of constitutional complaints, then it is clear that the function that Blankenberg describes as the 'wailing wall'[193] involves complaints mainly against courts. In 2004, 5,109 (97.5 per cent) of the 5,240 constitutional complaints were brought against decisions of the courts. The Bundesverfassungsgericht is being treated as an additional appeal court.

[191] C. Landfried, 'Germany' in C. N. Tate and T. Vallinder (eds.), *The Global Expansion of Judicial Power* (New York 1995), ch. 17 at 309.

[192] Ibid.

[193] E. Blankenburg, 'Mobilization of the German Federal Constitutional Court' in R. Rogowski and T. Gawron (eds.), *Constitutional Courts in Comparison* (New York 2002), 165–9.

The procedure is adversarial, but is normally written, with only a few oral hearings a year. As in most continental procedure, a report (*Votum*) is produced by one of the judges which then introduces discussion for the rest. There is no separate representative of the public interest, such as the Advocate General in the European Court of Justice. To handle the large number of constitutional complaints, the court works in small groups with a number of assistants.[194] The court is exceptional to Germany in having individual (concurring or dissenting) opinions. In fact, in the thirty years from 1971 to 2001, only 110 decisions with individual opinions were issued, compared with 1,640 decisions without a separate opinion.[195]

Federal relations

The most traditional role for the Bundesverfassungsgericht is to resolve conflicts between the Bund and the Länder. Each of them has distinct areas of legislative competence set out in Title VII of the Grundgesetz, as well as areas of concurrent competence. The Bundesverfassungsgericht serves as the arbiter between these different bodies, a role that has significant political implications, not least because the governments may well not be of the same party.

The innovative character of the judicial role was shown in the *First Television* case.[196] Under art. 70(1) of the Grundgesetz, any matter which is not assigned to the competence of the Bund falls within the legislative competence of the Länder. Here, the Federal Government enacted a decree creating a federal television station. The Bundesverfassungsgericht held that the decree was unconstitutional, because broadcasting was a cultural matter that fell within the competence of the Länder. Given the terms of art. 70(1), the powers of the Bund were to be strictly interpreted.

Apart from dealing with the technical issue of competence, the court also went on to rule on the manner in which negotiations between the Bund and Länder were to be conducted. The Federal Government had conducted limited discussions with the Länder, particularly those governed by the opposition SPD. It had only left just over a week between an invitation to the Länder to talks on the matter and an announcement that it was going to sign the corporate contract for the new television

[194] On the function of assistants, see Rogowski and Gawron, *Constitutional Courts*, above n. 193, chs. 8 and 9.

[195] Source: Bundesverfassungsgerichtshof website (www.bundesverfassungsgericht.de).

[196] (1961) BVerfGE 12, 205; Kommers, 79.

company which it alone had drafted. The Bundesverfassungsgericht held that: 'In the German federal state the unwritten constitutional principle of the reciprocal obligation of the federation and the states to behave in a profederal manner governs all constitutional relationships between the nation as a whole and its members and the constitutional relationships among members . . .'

The concept of *Bundestreue* (profederal behaviour or comity) is a judicial standard that renders the Constitution effective. It reflects, in a way, a concept of constitutional good faith. Developed first in the *Housing Funding* case in 1952,[197] *Bundestreue* restricts what both the Federation and the Länder can do. For example, the Länder could not hold referenda on defence policy in order to put pressure on the Federation in its exclusive area of competence.[198] This legal requirement of *Bundestreue* has proved less important in recent years, after the practical realities of federalism politically required a more co-operative attitude. The judicial requirement is a safety net.

Political parties

The role of the Bundesverfassungsgericht has not simply been that of an arbitrator; it has also used its more elaborate structure of arguments to give guidance to the legislature on the way policies promoting the Constitution could be developed. For example, in the area of financial support for political parties, the court took the view that political parties were not simply ordinary associations formed by like-minded individuals, they were an important way in which democracy was promoted. The court struck down a first attempt to provide financial support by allowing individuals to obtain tax deductions for contributions to political parties.[199] But, in the course of its judgment, the Second Senate recognised the financial plight of political parties and their need for funds in order to perform their role within the constitution. It suggested that the state itself might constitutionally fund political parties and election campaigns in order to ensure effective competition among them and to reduce their reliance on special interest groups. This suggestion was immediately taken up by the Bundestag which passed the Party Finance Act 1959, authorising the public financing of the parties' 'political education' programmes, distributed according to the number of votes cast in the previous election.

197 (1952) BVerfGE 1, 299 at 315; Currie, 77.
198 *Atomic Weapons Referenda* case (1958) BVerfGE 8, 104; Kommers, 86.
199 *Tax Deduction* (1958) BVerfGE 8, 51; Kommers, 203.

In a 1966 case,[200] the court put limits on the wide scope given to party funding by the various legislatures. It considered that parties could not be funded for everything they do. Parties were constitutionally important in helping to form the will of the people, but that process must remain free from state interference.[201] The court's conception of the role of parties within German democracy made it a major interlocutor with the legislature in determining the scope for party funding through a series of subsequent decisions.[202]

Another way in which the Bundesverfassungsgericht has served to shape democracy is by banning parties which are anti-democratic. In 1952, it banned the neo-Nazi Sozialistische Reichspartei and in 1956 it banned the communist KPD.[203] At particularly difficult early stages in democracy, the court was responsible for ensuring that all permitted parties were committed to the new democratic order. In reaction to the experience of Weimar, the court adopted the concept of 'militant democracy' (*eine streitbare, wehrhafte Demokratie*), that democracy was to defend itself against anti-democratic forces. During the Cold War, the court also upheld the so-called *Berufsverbot* under which individuals belonging to anti-democratic groups were denied positions in the civil service. The court upheld the power of the democratic state to exclude from the public service those who would seek to destroy it.[204] As Currie points out, these decisions were taken at moments of perceived crisis in an environment at least of uncertainty as to the stability of German democracy, and this may explain the severity in the restrictions on free speech and the right of association.[205] More recently, the President of the Bundesverfassungsgerichtshof commented that these decisions represented the high point of 'political justice' and that, in retrospect, the court was making a mountain out of a molehill.[206] All the same, the court was also willing to challenge government claims of a political emergency to justify restrictions on fundamental rights.[207]

[200] *Party Finance Case II* (1966) BVerfGE 20, 56; Kommers, 205.
[201] Kommers, 207.
[202] See Kommers, 212–18; Currie, 209–13.
[203] (1952) BVerfGE 2, 1 (SRP) and (1956) BVerfGE 5, 85 (KPD); Currie, 216–21.
[204] (1975) BVerfGE 39, 334; Currie, 222–3, 241–2.
[205] Currie, 242. [206] Limbach, *Im Namen des Volkes*, above n. 1, 26–7.
[207] See *Spiegel* (1966) BVerfGE 20, 162, Kommers, 397: the Government could not appeal to national security to justify a police raid on a news magazine that published information about the inadequate performance of German armed forces in NATO manoeuvres.

Fundamental rights

The Grundgesetz was designed specifically in order to protect fundamental rights, and these were seen as unalterable parts of the Constitution. The Bundesverfassungsgericht was here given the role as guardian of these rights against the contingencies of democratic majorities. As Schwarze points out, Germany has a substantive and not a formal conception of the rule of law, and the protection of this framework includes the protection of fundamental rights.[208] In the event, there is a dialogue between the court and the legislature. To the extent that political reforms involve infringements of fundamental rights, the court has an important role as an interlocutor in the legislative process.

For example, art. 2(2) GG provides that everyone has the right to life and to inviolability of the person. This has been the basis for a number of decisions. One of the most controversial issues was abortion. The Catholic influence on the conservative parties and the history of the use of abortion for eugenic purposes under the Nazis influenced a cautious approach by the legislature and the court. The respect for human dignity under art. 1 GG was used as the objective basis to outlaw abortion in 1975. The SDP–FDP coalition produced a bill that permitted abortion only for medical necessity, rape and social emergency. But backbenchers in the Bundestag added clauses permitting abortion up to twelve weeks of pregnancy and then up to twenty-two weeks if the baby was likely to be born with defects or if the life of the mother was in danger. The Bundesverfassungsgericht held that abortion could not be lawful, but could escape punishment if justified by reason of threats to the life of the mother, social hardship, rape or potential birth defects. The court was balancing the rights to life of the child and the mother, rather than relying on ideas such as the right of the mother to choose to continue a pregnancy. This decision[209] was then copied almost word for word by the Government in the bill it resubmitted to the Bundestag in 1976, which was enacted. When a bill modifying the law was passed after reunification, the Bundesverfassungsgericht continued its opposition to using stages of pregnancy to define when life began and suggested a more restrictive definition of social hardship than was proposed by Parliament. All the same, it held that art. 2(2) GG did not require that a woman should be punished criminally for an abortion during the first twelve weeks of pregnancy, if she had made her decision after

[208] J. Schwarze (ed.), *The Birth of a European Constitutional Order* (Baden-Baden 2001), 122–7.
[209] (1975) BVerfGE 39, 1; Currie, 310–11; Stone Sweet, *Governing*, above n. 189, 104–12.

counselling.[210] In a sense, abortion was unlawful, but need not lead to a criminal prosecution, provided certain conditions were met. Again, the court was suggesting solutions to a question on which politicians were strongly divided. Constitutional rights become a mechanism that determines the limits of political action, particularly where an issue is challenged, as in the abortion cases, by way of abstract review.

The cases on sex discrimination reveal a much more routine role for fundamental rights in updating the law and challenging social attitudes. Article 117(1) GG gave legislatures until 1953 to bring the law into conformity with the requirements of sex equality, and thereafter the Bundesverfassungsgericht saw its role as striking down provisions that still failed to conform. For example, in 1959 it invalidated a provision of family law giving the father the final word on childrearing,[211] and later declared invalid rules that prescribed a 'housework day' only for single female workers,[212] and it found no justification for a prohibition of night working applying only to women.[213] Fundamental rights provisions thus have a wide sweep, requiring reform in private and regulatory law.[214]

The protection of fundamental rights led to a cautious approach to the supremacy of European Union law. In the *Maastricht Treaty* case,[215] the Bundesverfassungsgericht asserted that it retained competence to ensure the application of European Union law in Germany. It recognised that it would co-operate with the European Court of Justice in protecting rights, but the Bundesverfassungsgericht would still provide 'a general guarantee of the constitutional standards that cannot be dispensed with'.[216] The case was the product of a series of decisions in which the Bundesverfassungsgerichtshof had been willing to recognise the primacy of European Community law, as long as (*solange*) the European Court of Justice generally assured an effective protection of basic rights against the acts of EC authorities. It retained the view that it,

210 (1993) BVerfGE 88, 203; Currie, 313–14. In this the court followed more the line of the dissenters in the 1975 abortion case.

211 (1959) BVerfGE 10, 72.

212 (1979) BVerfGE 52, 373. The original purpose of this legislation had been superseded by events – the working week had, in practice, become five days rather than six: Vogenauer, *Die Auslegung*, above n. 93, 69–70.

213 (1992) BVerfGE 85, 191. 214 See Currie, 328–31.

215 *Brunner v. The European Union Treaty* [1994] 1 CMLR 57; J. Kokott, 'German Constitutional Jurisprudence and European Integration' (1996) 2 *European Public Law* 237 and 413; Schwarze, *Birth*, above n. 208, 169–80.

216 *Brunner*, para. 13.

rather than the European Court of Justice, should decide whether the latter was competent according to German law. Kokott remarks that an idea of 'constitutional patriotism' pervades these decisions, tied to a basic belief that 'respect for the constitution is indispensable and has to be ensured to prevent even the appearance of a relapse into the past'.[217] On the whole, the reservations about the protection of fundamental rights and the power of the European Court of Justice to determine its own competence are reflected in the views of other courts of Member States.[218]

The scope of judicial action

A constitutional agenda is not simply determined by the intrinsic nature of the issues. Some issues are by nature constitutional, such as elections and parties. But the approach to constitutional issues will often depend on the historical contingency of how questions arise. The attitude to the Berufsverbot in Germany is in marked contrast to the treatment of the same question by the French Conseil d'Etat twenty years earlier.[219] The permissibility of discrimination on political grounds for entry into the public service is understood differently, because of the different political experiences of the two democracies. Given the decision to lift the ban on the Communist Party in 1990, it is unlikely that a similar Berufsverbot would be upheld as constitutional today. Different countries also have different sensibilities towards the funding of political parties. The Germans are clearly worried about the idea of control either by the state or by rich people in a way that is not reflected in France or Spain. The idea that the Constitutional Court could review a vote of no confidence by Parliament in the head of the Government, the Chancellor, would be unheard of in most countries. Yet in Germany, the concern that Parliament might abuse its power to vote out a Chancellor and call fresh elections by illegitimate means recalls the problems of the later Weimar and the rise of Hitler. As a result, the Bundesverfassungsgericht examined the process by which the Bundestag had declared no confidence in the recently appointed CDU–FDP Chancellor Kohl.[220] By a majority, it upheld the dissolution on the ground that there was no security that the coalition majority would continue. Two statements of former President Jutta Limbach reflect the tension in the role of the

[217] Kokott, 'German Constitutional Jurisprudence', above n. 215, 417.
[218] See Schwarze, *Birth*, above n. 208, 104 (France), 334 (Spain), 426 (Sweden).
[219] Compare above p. 73 and Currie, 326–7 with CE 20 May 1954, *Barel*.
[220] (1983) BVerfGE 62, 1; Currie, 112–16.

Bundesverfassungsgericht:[221] 'The view of the Constitution as an objective value system demands political activism from the Constitutional Court', and ' . . . the Court must be wary of juridifying politics too much, or narrowing the legislature's or the executive's creative power excessively'.

In the end, the Bundesverfassungsgericht is unique within the German system in terms of personnel and subject-matter. It has a distinct group of judges, whose backgrounds differ markedly from the profile of ordinary judges. Its remit is clearly political in a number of matters, and the importance of politics in selection reflects this. It is concerned with fundamental rights, rather than the ordinary matters of litigation with which ordinary judges have to deal. Clearly fundamental rights have become a pervasive concern of the judiciary in the post-war era, and the Bundesverfassungsgericht plays a lead role in this regard. But the role which judges are given in this area in relation to the legislature is not typical.

The public image of judges

Johnson argued that Germans prefer to resolve disputes by reference to authoritative judicial decisions, which convey an element of impartiality and objective rationality.[222] This has resulted, in his view, in a judicialisation of the administrative process. But Ardagh noted in 1995 that the place of rules in society was declining, now that the need to guide and nurture a new society had receded into history.[223] This had begun with the 1968 generation and was enhanced in the 1980s, after the threats of terrorism declined. Among Europeans, Germans have a relatively high confidence in the legal system, but there are differences between the East and West Germans. The April 2002 Eurobarometer[224] reported that 64 per cent of West Germans had confidence in their legal system, whilst only 50 per cent of East Germans expressed the same confidence. Even then, the East German level of confidence was the same as the EU average (51 per cent). The level of confidence is higher than that

[221] J. Limbach. 'The Protection of Human Rights in Germany' in B. Markesinis (ed.), *The Millennium Lectures* (Oxford 2000), 153 at 155, 162. Also Limbach, *Im Namen des Volkes*, above n. 1, 121: 'Judges must be aware that they work in a tension between requiring, on the one side, the rule of the majority and on the other side respect for the fundamental values of society.'

[222] N. Johnson, *State and Government in the Federal Republic of Germany* (2nd edn, Oxford 1983), 217.

[223] J. Ardagh, *Germany and the Germans* (3rd edn, London 1995), 520–4.

[224] Eurobarometer, Report no. 56: fieldwork October–November 2001.

reported for the civil service, the national government, the Parliament or the media. Only the Austrians and the Finns had a higher confidence in the police compared with West Germans, but the East Germans were just below the EU average. There are values that characterise the legal system as a whole, but it has to be recognised that social confidence is based more on experience and perception, and is not broadly shared in Germany, especially between East and West.

German judges have a limited presence in the media and so they have a limited role in developing confidence in the legal system. The Stuttgart study in 1995 found that press coverage in national papers was much more critical than positive of the legal system and of individual judicial decisions. About one-third of reports and comments were negative, and only 7 per cent were positive.[225] The study found that the experience of litigants and lawyers in decided cases was much more positive. Of litigants, 80 per cent considered that the judge handled the oral hearing well and 70 per cent felt the case as a whole was well handled.[226] Admittedly, the Rechtsanwälte had a much more positive assessment of the judge's performance, but the overall position was favourable.[227]

Conclusion: what shapes German judicial culture?

In one sense, there are a number of features that contribute to a German judicial culture – common legal education, a deep commitment to constitutional values, judicial independence and subordination to the law. Common education and a common framework provide the basic context within which the diversity operates. But judges actually form distinct groups. There is the obvious distinction between lay and professional judges, as well as that between the ordinary judges and those of the Bundesverfassungsgerichtshof. Furthermore, among professional judges, ordinary judges work typically in their different branches (administrative, civil and criminal, finance) as well as in their different Länder, which may well characterise their whole career. As a result, their post-qualification experience will be diverse. It is only at a certain level of abstraction that one can genuinely talk of a common judicial culture.

[225] Schedler et al., 'Arbeitsplatz Gericht', above n. 13, 89–93.

[226] Ibid., 59.

[227] It is perhaps typical of the focus of judges on the legal community that this study did not ask litigants about the quality of judgments, compared with the views of the professional lawyers: ibid., 75, and also the questions asked in the study by Treuer et al., *Arbeitsplatz Gericht*, above n. 13, 135–8.

In part, the validity of the characterisation lies in the contrast with the experiences of judges in other countries, rather than among German judges, though the European influence is something to which Germans have contributed and which is shaping all legal systems.

The culture of the German judiciary was traditionally that of an intellectual elite. The conception that underlies the pattern of education is that of a highly educated group trained at the public expense from which the judges are selected. This idea of an intellectual elite works only if the best lawyers want to become judges or prosecutors. With the massive rise in the number of Anwälte and their improved status due to internationalisation, and the relative stagnation of the numbers and salaries of judges, this aspect of an elite culture is under threat. There is certainly a tension between what makes the job of a judge attractive to those who join the profession and the ideals that the state demands in terms of high calibre and committed judge–civil servants.

The second feature of the elite is its function. During the period of the Obrigkeitsstaat, the elite civil service was a part of the governing class. With the shift to democracy, particularly after 1945 and since 1989, the judiciary has to be servant of the legislature. At the same time, the German conception of democracy placed a heavy emphasis on fidelity to the Constitution and, through it, on the rule of law. Both of these constraints on the freedom of the legislature and of the executive provided a special status for the judiciary and especially the Bundesverfassungsgericht. In an important sense, it is an elite role, but at the service of democracy. The national and constitutional importance of this elite role may explain some of the difficulties of the German courts in accepting claims to sovereignty from European courts. Having been given the role as guardians of national democracy, they could not conceive this as capable of being ceded to another body.

More generally, the judiciary has an important creative role in ensuring the law is kept up to date and applied consistently with Community standards of fairness. Recent Bundesverfassungsgerichtshof presidents such as Herzog and Limbach have pointed to the extent of judicial creativity, not simply in constitutional law, but also in other fields. There is a strong commitment to respecting the decisions of the legislator entailed in the constitutional subordination of the judge to 'statute and law'. But much of the creativity has involved filling gaps either by way of analogy or by correcting the law to bring it into line with commitments to constitutional values. These techniques represent the importance given to systematic or coherence-based interpretation of the law.

The priority is that the law should operate coherently and consistently in relation to the citizen, but major changes are the responsibility of the legislator. The specific role of the courts in relation to fundamental rights follows from the importance that these have in the 1949 constitutional settlement. In other areas, basic principles are not contained in codes (as in administrative law) or the codes require very substantial interpretation (as in the civil law of delict). Here the effectiveness of the system requires judicial activism beyond the field of human rights. Within this conception, the judiciary does not have a major reforming role; it is very much an operational creativity. Indeed, in relation both to professors and to European institutions, the judges have a limited influence on the shape of the law.

A major feature of the judicial culture is the German conception of judicial independence. The independence of the individual judge is paramount, which entails an independence to form his or her own view on the merits of the case without pressure from legislative or executive bodies, or even other judges. This strict conception leads generally to a reticent relationship to the media. This conception is tied to a strict understanding of the rule of law (*Rechtsstaat*) in reaction to the experiences of the past, in the Nazi era and in the DDR. On the other hand, unlike in Spain, Portugal or Italy, political authorities retain a strong role in the selection of judges and political affiliation remains a significant factor in the choice of candidates. The administrative structure within which courts work also introduces restrictions on individual action. With the Präsidialrat and the role of the president of the court in appraisal, there is a delicate balance between a judge's autonomy and her proper subordination to the purposes of the state. Herzog's linking of judicial independence and judicial review provides a distinctive perspective.[228] The Germans do not want an autonomous judiciary, merely one that is impartial and will look at individual cases on their merits. In the case of constitutional law, the arrangement is different on account of the special position that fundamental rights play in the constitutional settlement.

Conceptions of creativity and independence focus on a conception of the task of the judiciary as a function of stability that is fundamentally apolitical. In the 1950s, there was a need to secure the foundations of democracy and so the constitutional judges did allow or require some positive actions to ensure fidelity to the Constitution. But the failure of

[228] Above p. 133.

the movements among some judges in the late 1960s and early 1970s to undertake a more radical agenda for a social state reflects the emphasis on stability and not on judicial reform. Apart from the constitutional judges, the rest of the judiciary has been engaged primarily in incremental law reform. In such law reform, it is not the only inspiration for change. There is a strong influence from the professors, and it is notable that judges were not well represented in key law reform commissions. The apolitical nature of the judiciary (compared with others studied in this book) can be seen in the character of collective action. There is a strong collegiality and professionalism in continuing education and in collective representation to the ministries, but there is not the same depth of political divergence in associations that is found in the Latin countries.

There is a tension between the role of the judge as an active guardian of the consensus values on which German society depends and the essentially bureaucratic character of the judiciary. Each branch of the judiciary constitutes a hierarchically integrated corps within overarching Länder and federal regulation. The rules for appointment, promotion and conditions of service are similar to those in the civil service, and many of the same rules apply. The traditional collegial decision-making and absence of individual opinions represent a kind of impersonal approach, which emphasises the importance of the law, the rational and impartial authority, rather than the personality of the judge. The style of judgments offers reasons to the legal community, but there are few fora in which the judiciary is accountable for its conception of the social consensus. Much depends on ideas of judicial self-regulation.

The idea of a 'bureaucratic' judiciary should not obscure the importance of the freedom of individual judges to shape their own career. The German conception of judicial independence provides for individual freedom, and, within the established structures, individual judges can create their own career pattern. Judges can enter ministries, teach, serve as collaborators in federal courts, and so on. The activity of judicial unions shows scope for collective and individual opinion. The system is also less bureaucratic than it might appear. At a variety of levels and in a variety of areas, lay judges are used as part of the panel. These participate to ensure that justice is 'near to the citizen'. Judges have to justify themselves to members of the public and, increasingly, have to conduct oral hearings to make the legal outcome understood and, if possible, accepted. In these low-profile ways, the judges can develop their own practice as professionals. It is this individual sense of professionalism and of a professional responsibility for justice that is fostering debates on whether judges should take more responsibility for the administration of justice. Stimulated by budget cuts and competing priorities to which those politically responsible for justice are responding, the judges collectively are developing their ideas of independence to put their practical and operational situation more in line with the independent responsibility they perceive for justice.

4 The Spanish judiciary

The Spanish judiciary is a national body, but widely scattered across some 9,000 municipalities and the provinces. Although the law is typically national, the various Autonomous Communities increasingly have distinctive rules of public and private law. In addition, some provinces have traditionally had distinct aspects of private law (the *ley foral*). The unity of the case-law is secured at the level of both the Autonomous Communities and the nation, depending on the character of the law involved. There is also scope for courts to deal with matters that might otherwise fall through this matrix, especially those of more general importance, at Autonomous Community or national level. The judicial career and the court structures have to negotiate this complexity. At a basic level, there are different official languages in the several Autonomous Communities. A national judge or prosecutor is not required to speak the local language and may use an interpreter, just like one of the parties.[1] In certain areas, such as the Basque Country, the judiciary may be seen as part of the Madrid-based domination. In more recent years, the Spanish judiciary has had to cope with the transition to democracy and the development of a more legally active society. In addition, the rise in the number of women in the legal professions has had a major impact on the demography of the judiciary. As a result, the character of the judiciary has changed.

Spain has developed rapidly since the death of Franco. The advent of democracy was matched by rapid economic and social growth, which included membership of the European Union. Thus both the economic and political structures and the legal norms which govern them have changed very significantly within a period of thirty years. This has had a

[1] See TC 29/415, *El Pais*, 29 April 2005.

major impact on the role of law in society. An indicator of this is the rise in the caseload, particularly in civil and administrative courts. In 1975, the lowest civil courts heard 290,007 cases, but in 1998 this figure had risen to 515,698.[2] Martín had already noted that the number of cases filed with the lower civil courts in Madrid had doubled between 1982 and 1986, with a similar pattern in the Madrid criminal courts.[3] Martin suggested that this increase was due to the demand for justice which is now found in democratic society.[4] Certainly, the advent of democracy did give rise to an increase in complaints against the administration, the courts and in litigation. New institutions such as the *Defensor del Pueblo* (ombudsman) and the *amparo* (constitutional complaint) have provided structured opportunities for complaint, notably about the administration of justice. Toharia also notes the greater propensity to complain in modern Spain, which also applies in relations between individuals. In the 1970s, 68 per cent of Spaniards declared themselves unwilling to start a row, but in 1996 66 per cent stated that they would complain.[5] However, Toharia plausibly argues that this is merely a reflection of the growth in economic activity, rather than a significant increase in the propensity of Spaniards to engage in civil litigation. He parallels the growth in civil caseload with the rise in the number of notarised acts, a proxy for the number of legal transactions. Both have risen, but the proportion of the former in relation to the latter has remained fairly constant (9.9 per cent in 1975 and 9.1 per cent in 1998).[6] Toharia reinforces his economic explanation by noting that 82 per cent of Spanish companies see a rise in litigation as a natural consequence of the growth in the economy. An alternative explanation might lie in the number of lawyers. In 1980, there were 27,983 abogados (75 per 100,000 inhabitants). In 1998, there were 96,000 abogados (240 per 100,000 inhabitants).[7] In 2002, the number had risen to 104,162, with a further 37,485 not in practice.[8] There are thus more lawyers who are chasing work. In some branches of administrative law a further incentive exists. Since litigation has an automatic suspensive effect, this is seen as an advantage in areas such as taxation, where it may take three to five years to resolve a case.

[2] J.-J. Toharia, *Opinión pública y justicia. La imagen de la justicia en la sociedad española* (CGPJ, Madrid 2001) (hereafter 'Toharia'), table 1.3, 24.

[3] V. H. Martín, *Independencia del Juez y desorganización judicial* (Madrid 1991), 28.

[4] Ibid., 30. [5] Toharia, 26. [6] Ibid. [7] Ibid., 23.

[8] Census of abogados on the website of the Consejo General de la Abogacia Española: http://www2.cgae.es.

Whatever the analysis, and even if the Toharia view is the most plausible, the overall result is that the courts play an increasing part in social life, and this has some impact on the social importance of judges. Spain has now developed what Toharia dubs 'a culture of participation' in the legal system.[9] In a 2000 survey, 41 per cent of those questioned said that they had consulted an abogado on at least one occasion, compared with a figure of nearer 20 per cent twenty years before. In addition, 56 per cent had consulted a notary. In a society of greater economic prosperity and numbers of transactions, far more people are drawn into the use of the law, and so the judicial role has greater significance in civil as well as criminal matters.

Obviously the attacks on judges by ETA (the Basque separatist movement) over many years since the 1980s have had a significant impact on security in courts and in the lives of judges who have occupied particularly sensitive positions, not least in the Basque Country itself. At the same time, such attacks have had a limited impact on the ordinary operation of the courts and the lives of most judges. For the most part, the existence of an external threat has merely served to reinforce commitment to the constitutional democratic structures. Although this chapter does not pay much attention to the implications of Basque terrorism, it forms one of the background factors reinforcing loyalty to the post-Franco constitutional order.

Organisational setting and the judicial career

Court structures

The Spanish court system is a national system, but with strong regional and local organisation, and this has significant implications for the judicial career. Under 5 per cent of judicial posts are located at national level. Strong regional centres in the Autonomous Communities provide an alternative attraction for promotion to Madrid. In particular, the importance of regional languages helps those from a particular region to remain in their home area, if they wish. Courts are organised at one of four levels: municipality, province, Autonomous Community and nation. In addition, there are a number of specialist areas (social, constitutional and administrative), as well as generalist courts. Increasing awareness of fundamental rights since 1978, not least in the field of criminal procedure, has led to changes in the long-established structures of courts.

[9] Toharia, 21.

Most civil and criminal litigation is organised within the Autonomous Community, and there is a very limited review of decisions conducted at national level through the Tribunal Supremo in Madrid. The basic civil and criminal unit is a single-judge court, the *Juzgado de Primera Instancia e Instrucción*, located in municipalities. These courts may be split into civil and criminal courts depending on the municipality. In 1988, the Tribunal Constitucional held that the same court could not be responsible for both investigating criminal cases before trial (*instrucción*) and then trying them. As a result, the trial functions for serious cases were assigned to the new *Juzgados de lo penal* at provincial level in 1989.[10] The Juzgado de Primera Instancia e Instrucción continues to try lesser crimes for which no *instrucción* is required, and to carry out the instruction of the more serious offences. Furthermore, as we shall see, many teritorial areas will only have courts presided over by non-professional judges, the *juez de paz*.[11] These courts are maintained by the local municipality. Appeal from their decisions lies to the local Juzgado de Primera Instancia e Instrucción. In some areas, the family law work of the Juzgado de Primera Instancia has been hived off to a special *Juzgado de Familia*.

In one or more centres in a province, there will be specialist courts, staffed by ordinary judges who have passed a test in their specialism. Thus there are the *Juzgados de lo Contentioso-Administrativo* (administrative), *de lo Social* (labour), *de Vigilancia Penitenciaria* (post-conviction criminal matters) and *de Menores* (youth justice). More serious criminal and civil matters go to the *Audiencias Provinciales*. These courts also hear appeals from decisions of the Juzgado de Primera Instancia e Instrucción. These various regional courts are maintained by the local provinces.

At the level of the Autonomous Communities, the supreme court dealing with appeals on points of law (*recursos de casación*) is the *Tribunal Superior de Justicia*. It has jurisdiction over questions of general civil law, local (*foral*) law[12] and the modern special law of the relevant Autonomous Community. The court sits in three divisions, civil and criminal, administrative and social.[13] It has criminal jurisdiction as provided by the Statute of Autonomy.

[10] E. Merino-Blanco, *The Spanish Legal System* (London 1996) (hereafter 'Merino-Blanco'), 92–3.

[11] Below p. 207.

[12] The Tribunal Supremo has competence only where there is no provision of *foral* law applicable. Otherwise, it defers to the competence of the local court in relation to its local law.

[13] Merino-Blanco, 90.

An exception to this organisation of litigation within the Autonomous Community is made for criminal matters with a national extent. The regionally located *Juzgados Centrales de lo Penal* deal with preliminary matters, and the *Audiencia Nacional* conducts trials. The Audiencia Nacional has three sections and deals at first instance with criminal, administrative and social matters. Stimulated by comparison with international standards of criminal procedure, reforms in 2004 have ensured that there is always an appeal in criminal matters.[14] At a national level, there is also a system of military courts. These are of long standing (dating back to the beginning of the eighteenth century under Philip V). Unlike under Franco and before, these courts have no jurisdiction over civilians.

At national level, appeal on points of law lies from the regional Tribunales Superiores de Justicia and from the Audiencia Nacional to the Tribunal Supremo in Madrid, which sits in five divisions: civil, criminal, administrative, social and military. Within the Tribunal Supremo, some efforts are made to avoid differences between the different sections. There are provisions[15] under which a special chamber of the Tribunal Supremo deals both with errors made by single Sala and the resolution of conflicts between the different sections of the administrative Sala. In this way, the regional nature of Spain is respected, especially the increasing differences in the laws between the different Autonomous Communities, whilst maintaining the idea that it is essentially a national public service.

Governance of judiciary and courts: the Consejo General del Poder Judicial

Spain has a very distinctive form of governing the judiciary, which provides significant insulation of the judicial system from politics and an element of judicial self-government. In part this reflects a distinctive ideal of judicial independence, but in part it also provides a way of handling the competing spheres of competence of the governments of the nation and of the Autonomous Communities. The Consejo General del Poder Judicial (CGPJ) is a distinctive feature of the 1978 Constitution in that it tries to insulate the judiciary from the kind of subordination to the executive from which it suffered during the Franco era and before.

[14] CGPJ, *Informe sobre el anteproyecto de ley orgánica de reforma de la ley orgánica 6/1985, del Poder Judicial* (23 April 2003), 51–2.

[15] Art. 61 LOPJ.

Like France in 1946, Italy in 1948 and Portugal in 1976, Spain sought to place the judiciary under an independent council. As a historical antecedent, an advisory body on judicial appointments and promotions had been created in 1917, but the 1978 Consejo is a substantially different body.[16] The membership reflects the need for both judicial and independent voices, but the process of selection does not represent a process of 'self-government' in an Italian sense.[17] Rather it involves a substantial judicial input into the government of the judiciary, and creates an effective organ for negotiating with governments over resources. The extent of the self-government can be seen in the composition of the Consejo, its role in selection and in management, as well as in representation of the judicial service in negotiations with national and Autonomous governments.

Composition

The composition of the Consejo General del Poder Judicial reflects a governance structure for the judiciary in which professionals and political nominees share a direct and continuing responsibility for the performance of the judicial system and for the careers of judges. Its twenty members are chosen by the Cortes (Parliament), twelve from within the judiciary and eight from other lawyers with at least fifteen years' standing in the profession. In 1980, the judicial members were chosen on the nomination of professional associations, but this practice was altered by constitutional amendment in 1985, when the Socialists wanted to exercise more control. The Tribunal Constitucional refused to rule against this reform.[18] A further change was introduced in 2001[19] following an agreement between the parties. This principally affected the twelve places elected from the judiciary. Under the new scheme, thirty-six candidates are put forward to the Cortes. Eighteen are nominated by judicial associations in proportion to their membership.[20] A further

[16] See L. Lopez Guerra, 'Genèse et rôle du pouvoir judiciaire' in T. Renoux, *Les Conseils supérieurs de la magistrature en Europe* (hereafter '*Les Conseils supérieurs*') (Paris 1999), 184.

[17] Cf. C. Guarnieri and P. Pederzoli, *The Power of Judges. A Comparative Study of Courts and Democracy* (Oxford 2001), 41–2.

[18] STC 46/1985 and 118/1986. For an account of this reform introduced by Ledesma, a judge who was Minister of Justice at the time, see J. Sinova and J. Tusell, *La crisis de la democracia en España* (Madrid 1997), 108–9.

[19] Ley orgánica 2/2001 of 28 June, Boletín Oficial del Estado (BOE) no. 155, 12535.

[20] See the instruction of the President of the Consejo General del Poder Judicial, 29 June 2001, giving the Asociación Profesional de la Magistratura the right to nominate ten candidates, the Asociación Jueces para la Democracia four, the Asociación Francisco de Vitoria four, and the Unión Judicial Independiente none.

eighteen are nominated from individual judges who obtain at least seventy-three nominators among the judges. This assists those judges who do not belong to associations. Although the members are chosen by the Cortes, the nominations are agreed by the political parties in advance on a sort of quota basis.[21]

Judges appointed to this function cannot take part in judicial activities during their service. The 'lay' members in 2001 were a former Defensor del Pueblo, a practising abogado, a military judge and a number of law professors. There were two women.

Although the appointing process has a clear political character, the judicial members are still bound by the general prohibition on judges being members of political parties. All the same, their past political activity may be influential in their career. For example, Belloch was a member of the Consejo at the time of his appointment as Minister of Justice in 1993.[22] It has been alleged that political favouritism has led to inappropriate appointments. For example, in April 1992, Eligio Hernandez was appointed Fiscal General del Estato, even though he would only have qualified for the requisite fifteen years of judicial service if his seven years as civil governor and member of the Consejo General del Poder Judicial were taken into account. He felt obliged to resign a few days before the Tribunal Supremo was to rule on the validity of his appointment.[23]

The Consejo has a number of lawyers as assistants (*letrados*). Many of these are taken from the judiciary, and this provides them with a useful platform for their future career.[24]

Governance

The Consejo General del Poder Judicial is responsible for the judiciary and for the general functioning of the courts. But the budget for equipment and buildings, as well as for administrative support staff, lies with the relevant public administration. With devolution, these administrative roles have typically been transferred to the Autonomous Communities. In 2001, the Consejo spent €45,971,000 on the administration of justice, whilst the Ministry of Justice spent €927,247,000 and the

[21] See J. Casqueiro and A. Díez, *El País*, 2 July 2001.

[22] See P. Heywood, *The Government and Politics of Spain* (London 1995), 115–16. Indeed, almost half of the 1990 Consejo left before the end of their period of office to take up political or other appointments: see Sinova and Tusell, *La crisis*, above n. 18, 118.

[23] Sinova and Tusell, *La crisis*, above n. 18, 114–15.

[24] See below p. 194.

Autonomous Communities a further €866,203,000. There was an agreement in 1992 with some Communities, but the Consejo indicated in the *Libro Blanco* that it would like further uniformity of treatment. In general, appropriate levels of support have to be negotiated by the Consejo.

It is in this context that the 2003 reforms created an *Oficina Judicial*, which comes into effect from 2006. Its function is to leave the running of courts to court secretaries who are linked together within a national court service. The Oficina was created to professionalise and modernise the administration of justice. It will attempt to give greater coherence to the planning and equipping of the courts. Its structure allows adaptation to the needs of particular Autonomous Communities, to whom the budget for the administration of justice is increasingly being devolved. The current secretary-generals of the courts (clerks to the court) are to be given greater responsibilities, so as to relieve judges from many administrative tasks, and there is to be a much better use of information technology. The Consejo was able to secure a clear demarcation of functions, so that the legislation states that the Oficina is responsible for facilitating the provision of the public service of justice. This leaves the Consejo responsible for securing that justice is done within the material resources placed at its disposal. But both institutions are responsible essentially for different aspects of the operational side of justice. Both operate within a policy agreed by the executive and Parliament.

Parliament controls the budget and can change the basic rules on matters such as civil or criminal procedure. It is within this framework that the Consejo and the Oficina then can operate with a reasonable degree of discretion. Below them, the local judge *gerente* and increasingly the secretary of the court have some degree of responsibility. The success of this division of responsibility in achieving justice depends significantly on the original brief given to the court service. Since the Spanish system has not come to terms with the radical reshaping of the number and location of courts, a major structural problem remains. There are insufficient judges to deal with the number of court centres and the changing patterns of social life. The importance of the local court as a registry for legal transactions, such as registration of birth or land transfers, also creates a range of work that requires different structures in the information age than are required for the settlement of civil disputes and dealing with crime. Neither the national institutions such as the Consejo and the Oficina nor the local management of courts can offer more than a palliative to the deep structural issues about the operation of the justice system. At this level, the Consejo has the political responsibility to engage with other constitutional actors, the executive and Parliament, in order to promote change. The cross-party pact of 2001 followed the identification of issues by the Consejo and lobbying. The creation of the Oficina with a mission to use information technology to reduce the burden on courts, especially in registrary activities, will be one of the more important outcomes, as well as the substantial increase in judicial numbers the agreement secured.

The function of the Consejo is to develop the agenda of judicial and court reform. For instance, particularly in its *Libro Blanco* of 1997, it has been responsible for identifying the numbers of judges needed. Its president (also president of the Tribunal Supremo) argued before the parliamentary committee on justice that there was a need for some 954 extra judges to bring Spain into line with France and Italy and to have a judge for every 9,000 citizens.[25] (In 2001, there was roughly one judge for every 10,000 citizens.) The existing deficit of judges to fill posts was also noted by judges and lawyers, and became one of the key elements of a cross-party pact on justice of 28 May 2001.[26] In this instance, the Consejo's concern for resources matched the concern of politicians for both law and order and reducing the slowness of the justice system. Rather than a debate occurring internally within the Ministry of Justice, or between the ministries of the nation and the Autonomous Communities, the place of the Consejo as an independent constitutional authority generates a public debate. To some extent, it has yielded fruit in recent years, though many deep structural issues about the number of court centres remain to be grasped.

Promotions

The Consejo General del Poder Judicial is responsible for judicial appointments, but there is far less discretion than this might imply. Most appointments are based on applications and seniority. Until reforms of 2003, there were only about 165 posts (under 5 per cent) where there was genuine discretion. Most of these appointments are for the presiding judges of courts – the Audiencia Nacional, the fifty Audiencias

[25] See *El País*, 28 June 2000.

[26] Ministry of Justice, 'Principios del Pacto de Estado para la Reforma de la Justicia' (http://www.mju.es/g270501.htm). This planned an increase of 1,365 judicial posts over the following decade.

Provinciales, the seventeen Tribunales Superiores de Justicia, and the members of the Tribunal Supremo and the presidents of its Salas. Even here, the Tribunales Superiores may suggest three names from which the Consejo can choose one.[27] In 2002, there were fourteen such appointments made.[28] The 2003 reforms have encouraged the use of evaluations as a basis for judicial promotions.[29] But to balance the increase in discretion, the reforms also increased the required majority to three-fifths for senior appointments. In this way, the political character of appointments is reduced, since there will have to be an agreement between those of different political persuasions and also between the generalist lawyers (often politicians) and judges.

Although Madrid is expensive, the premium for promotion to be magistrado of the Tribunal Supremo is such that there is no difficulty in attracting candidates. Indeed, the supplements to salary which specific posts attract are a major way of securing recruits.

The careers of judges may be managed in other ways. The Consejo publishes the *modulos*, a workload model which serves as a benchmark to judge the effectiveness of a judge. The Consejo conceives it as a technique incorporating its values of efficiency and quality of justice, so as to achieve its mission.[30] For example, for a Juzgado de Primera Instancia (a first instance civil court), there is an assumed caseload of 720 cases and the judge is assumed to work 1,760 hours a year, of which 1,650 are dedicated to judicial work. Having deducted time spent on enforcing decisions, conciliation and other such activities which do not have formal outcomes, a total of 1,250 hours remains. There is then a scoring system for different activities. For example, a trial of a substantial civil case carries twelve points or hours, whereas registration of a mortgage carries one point. If a judge requests permission to undertake external tasks, e.g. teaching in a university on a regular basis, this will be measured against the workload model. Each different court has its own targets.[31] If the judge is within 10 per cent of the expected workload set out in the model, then permission is likely to be granted. But if the judge falls below this work-rate, then permission is not likely to be granted. The modulos serve, however, principally to

[27] This respects the need for some expertise in local law.

[28] CGPJ, *Memoria Anual 2003* (Madrid 2003) (hereafter '*Memoria 2003*'), 12.

[29] Ley orgánica 19/2003 of 23 December 2003, BOE 309/2003.

[30] See *Modulos 2000*, approved 31 May 2000, p. 2: the *modulos* can be found on the website of the Consejo General del Poder Judicial, http://www.cgpj.es.

[31] Ibid.

identify the need for extra judges, and to argue for monies from the Government.[32]

Supervision

Much of the workload of the Consejo, up to a third of its time, is taken up in ensuring that courts are adequately staffed. Where illness, maternity leave or other causes reduce the number of judges, then the Consejo has to rectify this by transferring judges on a temporary basis or by using substitute judges (often retired judges). There is a limited form of discretion here, but predominantly it is a matter of troubleshooting. In 2002, the Consejo drew up with local courts some twenty plans to deal with urgent backlogs that had developed.[33] In order to deal with such problems, the Consejo has power to make subordinate legislation on the management of judges and to produce 'soft law' guidance. For example, it has produced regulations on the juez de paz,[34] and in 2001 it issued an instruction on the use of judicial assistance in certain judicial acts in order to manage the workload in many understaffed Juzgados de Paz.[35] By laying down such rules, the Consejo is able to ensure consistent practice, as well as to guide behaviour. Such guidelines are developed through working groups. These can be both proactive and reactive. For example, a working group has operated for a number of years to review the handling of cases of domestic violence. It is in this area of managing specific generic issues or the problems of specific courts that the Consejo is most effective. In such areas, it will operate particularly through its secretariat.

The Consejo is also responsible for judicial training and can make regulations concerning the *Escuela Judicial* and its programme. It also determines the staffing levels. Through these different powers, the Consejo establishes the basic framework for the judicial career, the competences of its judges, and the working life which will be adopted.

Inspection and complaints

The Consejo General del Poder Judicial has its own inspection service, which is staffed by letrados. It looks at the operation of the court in

32 See Consejo General del Poder Judicial, *Libro Blanco* (Madrid 1997) (hereafter '*Libro Blanco*'), 28–30.

33 *Memoria 2003*, 50.

34 E. Arnaldo Alcubilla, 'Le fonctionnement du pouvoir judiciaire' in *Les Conseils supérieurs*, 191 at 193.

35 CGPJ, *Instrucción n°4/2001, Sobre el Alcance y los Limites del Deber de Auxilio Judicial*, BOE 162 (7 July 2001).

aspects such as time taken for proceedings, number of cases decided and number of cases outstanding. It aims to verify the information that is provided to the Consejo by the court, to check that the court is complying with standards set, and to offer a diagnosis of problems and recommendations for responding to them.[36] The court is judged against the modulos, which serve as benchmarks for efficiency in performance rather than as targets. The Consejo recognises that its basis of statistics on courts and individual judges needs improvement, especially in integrating local and central data.[37] All the same, there are statistics on many major issues, such as staffing, caseload and throughput, which make visits rare events. A number of important matters, such as the staffing, building and operation of the court, fall outside the province of the Consejo. Unannounced visits were very unpopular and have been tried only occasionally. For the most part, visits serve to enable communication of information between the local courts and the central management. Given that court management is separate, then the Consejo has to work by negotiation with local government to improve the situation of a particular court.

The organisation of inspection has been the subject of greater regulation and reform in line with general policies on the public sector. The Consejo General del Poder Judicial issued guidance in December 1999, setting out the framework for inspection. The idea has been to concentrate the process on checking information provided, ensuring that standards are being achieved, and diagnosing organisational weaknesses with a view to proposing recommendations.[38]

In line with general developments in the public sector, there has been an attempt to foster a culture of attention to the citizen within the judiciary, and a special unit has been set up within the Consejo General del Poder Judicial with this remit.[39] Complaints can be seen as diagnostic

[36] Servicio de Inspección, *Balance de la Ejecución del Libro Blanco en el ámbito de la inspección* (16 April 2001, CGPJ website), 6. See also guidelines on inspection of 15 December 1997: Ibid., 17.

[37] *Libro Blanco*, 19. A new database of information on courts and judges has been created, and this has led to substantial benchmarking of different courts in relation to performance measures, called 'norms of good practice': CGPJ, *Memoria Anual 2004* (Madrid 2004) (hereafter '*Memoria 2004*'), 306–9.

[38] See *Balance de la Ejecución*, above n. 36, 17. On the general scope of inspection, see ibid., 5ff.

[39] Ibid., 29: the unidad central de atención al cuidadano to be found on the CGPJ website. Regolamento 1/1998 governs the complaints procedure and forms can be accessed from the same website.

in this situation, and inspection will focus on how complaints have been handled.

Judicial discipline

Judicial discipline is handled by the Consejo, although criminal prosecutions will be dealt with by the Tribunal Supremo, which also hears applications for the review of disciplinary decisions of the Consejo. The number of complaints made each year is substantial, but few lead to full investigations or disciplinary hearings. In 1996, there were 1,413 complaints against individual judges to the Consejo, but only twenty led to disciplinary proceedings being instituted.[40] The number in 2002 was much smaller – 643 leading to forty-eight cases before the Disciplinary Committee of the Consejo and a further thirteen for the governing councils of the Tribunales Superiores de Justicia. The outcomes were that eleven very serious faults, eleven serious faults and fifteen lesser offences were punished.[41] A similar number of disciplinary proceedings is taken against prosecutors each year. Even when action is taken, the Tribunal Supremo may intervene. For example, in 1998, the Consejo considered a judge to have committed a serious fault in failing to write a judgment for any of the 584 cases which he had heard as a single judge. The decision was quashed by the Tribunal Supremo on the ground that the Consejo should have taken more notice of the medical evidence that the judge suffered from depression and did not have the mental element for the disciplinary offence.[42] Sanctions can be significant, e.g. suspension without pay for over a year. But these are only a handful of cases a year.[43] There is no code of judicial ethics nor is there a code of conduct for judges. Therefore standards are set by the case-law of the Consejo and the Tribunal Supremo. This ensures a respect for judicial autonomy, but requires the judiciary to be vigilant in self-government. Because the Consejo is a constitutional authority, it is accountable to other constitutional authorities for its general functioning, e.g. through its annual report. It is in that public debate about its functioning that any control would be exercised, rather than in relation to individual cases. So far, this has not given rise to serious problems, and it is certainly seen as preferable to giving the executive a direct role in judicial discipline.

[40] See F. Badie, 'La responsabilité des magistrats' in *Les Conseil supérieurs*, 169 at 178.
[41] *Memoria 2003*, 16–17. [42] Badie, 'La responsabilité', above n. 40, 180–1.
[43] For statistics, see Arnaldo Alcubilla, 'Le fonctionnement', above n. 34, 199.

Consultation

The Consejo is consulted on laws affecting the status of judges or of members of the personnel of the administration of justice. Its *Comisión de Estudios e Informes* receives such proposed legislation and comments on it at some length. In 2002, it gave opinions on six organic laws (including one on political parties), six major ordinary laws and over ninety other legislative measures, both national and from Autonomous Communities. For example, the Consejo commented on the proposed introduction of the Oficina Judicial in 2003, and suggested that 'the authorities competent in relation to the provision of resources for the administration of justice should consider this competence not as the running of a public service but only as making it possible for the third power of the state to exercise its constitutional role',[44] a phrase that was included in the final legislation. This role is important but limited, because it cannot cover the law which judges apply in general. It is reinforced, however, by regular meetings between the Consejo and the Ministry of Justice to examine a range of issues of common concern and to delineate the responsibilities of each body. The Consejo also undertakes research, e.g. on the implementation of important legislation, such as 'rapid decision-making'[45] in criminal matters, introduced in 2003.

Judges as managers

Senior judges will play limited management roles. The local *gerente* will perform the role of administering the court. There is no local budgeting, so the main function of a presiding judge will be to assign judges to their tasks and undertake other personnel tasks in relation to judges. There is no specific training for these management roles. Much of the day-to-day management of the court operations falls on the secretary of the court, who is now linked into the Oficina Judicial, a kind of court service. This low-level, operational discretion does allow some degree of adaptation of the needs of the service to the very varied needs of the different local situations, which are more diverse in Spain than in other countries studied in this book.

Most senior judges do not have major management tasks, other than in relation to the deployment and careers of other judges. On the other hand, there are a few judges who do, both very senior judges and letrados in the CGPJ, who are engaged in policy-making of a high order. The judicial career therefore contains significant opportunities to shine not

[44] *Informe*, above n. 14, 37. [45] *Memoria 2003*, 43–4.

only on the Bench, but also in making policy in relation to the justice system as a whole.

Judicial self-government?

The Consejo General del Poder Judicial is an independent agency running the judicial service, and it is now being joined by a further administrative agency, the Oficina Judicial, in running the wider court service. To a large extent, this structure provides a guarantee of judicial and court independence. But, in the increasingly devolved structure of the Autonomous Communities, it offers a framework for running a national service that is not simply under the control of the national government. A single agency is able to negotiate at arm's length from the politics of increasing federalism. The control exercised over judicial appointments and education, as well as setting benchmarks for judicial and court workload, ensures that the Consejo is able to set the tone with limited political interference.

There is always a concern that judicial self-government serves the interests of judges and not of justice. The Spanish system has always had a strong emphasis on seniority as a criterion for career advancement. Even the recent criteria for merit appointment for lateral entry are very formulaic, giving points for qualifications, rather than an evaluation of potential to perform in the role. This does tend to serve judges more than the interests of justice. This unwillingness to evaluate effectiveness in the role is reinforced by the limited competition – there are not enough judges to fill all the vacant jobs. The focus is predominantly on the effectiveness of institutions, rather than individuals, in achieving justice, and even this is more a matter of limiting the deleterious effects of lack of resources.

Judicial career of ordinary judges

The ordinary judiciary covers civil, criminal, social and administrative law. There are three grades of judge.[46] Once training in the judicial college has been completed, a person will start as a *juez*. Normally, after seven or eight years, a juez, will have sufficient seniority to obtain a post carrying the status of *magistrado*. Beyond that, a person could aspire to become a member of the Tribunal Supremo. The magistrados of the Tribunal Supremo form a distinct category of judge. At the end of 2003,

[46] The rules on the career are contained in Regolamento 1/1995 of 7 June 1995 on the Judicial Career.

there were 4,194 judges, made up of 679 jueces, 3,426 magistrados and 89 magistrados del Tribunal Supremo.[47] Of these, 58 per cent were men and 42 per cent were women.

Selection

Law has traditionally been a major university subject in Spain.[48] Nearly half the university graduates study law or social sciences. In 2001–2, there were 104,292 students graduating in the first or second cycle of degrees in these subjects.[49] The largest university, Complutense de Madrid, offered some 2,040 places for the 2001 entry into the Licenciado en Derecho. Although statistics are not available on women law graduates, it is likely that the proportion is high. Of all Spanish graduates in 1998–9, 58.08 per cent were women. Whilst the number of applications for law places was high in the 1990s, a number of private universities were founded with law schools. A significant demographic decline in the number of young people of university entrance age has led to a significant decline in the number of enrolments on law courses. As a result, the judiciary will be in an increasingly strong competition with other legal professions for entrants.

Becoming a judge is a career which begins with the *oposición*, the competitive examination for which one prepares (and is privately trained) after leaving university.[50] This entry route was created in 1870 to replace the system of applications and interviews of those already experienced as abogados and fiscales. Such a system was criticised for favouring those with social connections and for leading to political prejudices prevailing in selection.[51] It introduced both professionalism and recruitment on merit, as well as distancing the judges from politics.[52] There are about

47 *Memoria 2004*, 268–70.

48 See J.-M. Scholz, *Gerechtigkeit verwalten. Die spanische Justiz im Ubergang zur Moderne* (Frankfurt am Main, 2003) (hereafter 'Scholz'), 291–2 who notes that of 10,725 students registered at Spanish universities in 1838–9, 5,375 were studying law and a further 131 were studying canon law.

49 See statistics at http://www.mec.es (Ministry of Education).

50 For the most part, the preparation for this entrance examination is privately funded. The two-to-three-year preparation period carries few bursaries and the tutoring also has to be arranged and paid for privately. For a general account, see I. de Otto, *Estudios sobre el Poder Judicial* (Madrid 1989), ch. 6.

51 Scholz, 247, 269, 482–4. Under the decree of 29 December 1838, it was necessary to have at least two years' experience as an abogado to become a fiscal and a similar period as fiscal before becoming a judge.

52 Ibid., 518–21, 1078–9. He notes that this became almost the exclusive route to recruitment to the post of juez by the end of the nineteenth century.

5,000 candidates for the 150–200 places as judge or fiscal (prosecutor) each year.[53] The status conferred by having passed these examinations is significant and so attracts good applicants. There are geographical patterns to recruitment. Many judges come from the less prosperous parts of Spain (Galicia, Andalusia, Castile) or from around Madrid. In interviews of judges in 1986, the principal reasons judges gave for choosing the profession were that they had a sense of vocation (67.2 per cent) and gained enjoyment from intellectual activity and hard work (76.8 per cent).[54] This would match the aspirations of the middle class from which 94 per cent of judges are drawn.[55] In the 1980s, the Catalan government was so concerned about the small number of Catalan recruits that it provided some scholarships for the preparatory years before sitting the competition.

The age profile of judges has dropped as the number of judges has expanded. Thus in 1975, 86 per cent of judges were over forty, but in 2000 the proportion had dropped to 46 per cent.[56] The career of judge is popular with women. In 1986, they constituted about 11 per cent of the corps, but they accounted for 42 per cent in 2003.[57] But among the younger categories, the profile is very different from the more senior judges. Thus whilst there were only two women out of eighty-nine in the Tribunal Supremo in 2003, 38.6 per cent of the magistrados were women. Among the lowest rank of juez, two-thirds were women, and women made up 65 per cent of the most recent recruits.[58] The reasons seem similar to those of career judges in other parts of Europe. A civil service career offers maternity and parental leave arrangements that are generous and reliable. A judge will be able to return to her old grade after a career break.[59] The work is fairly flexible in that the number of court sitting hours is limited and predictable, and much work can be prepared out of the office. The irremovability of a judge means that she cannot be moved without her consent. All the same, the judicial career is a broad national career and promotion may require relocation from one part of the country to

[53] For the figures for 2002 and 2003, see *Memoria 2004*, 24, 26–7. In 2002, there were 5,122 applicants for 180 places (115 as juez and 65 as fiscal).

[54] J. J. Ruiz-Rico (ed.), *Monográfico dedicado al studio sobre la 'Elite juridical española'* (1987) 53 *Documentacion Juridica* (hereafter 'Elites'), 53–4.

[55] Ibid., 41. Only 24 per cent came from the upper middle class.

[56] Toharia, 39. [57] *Memoria 2004*, 268.

[58] Ibid., 269: women constituted 1,323 of the 3,426 magistrados, 453 of the 679 jueces, and 195 of the 298 recent recruits to the jueces.

[59] In 2004, there were twenty-four judges on unpaid leave in order to look after children, in addition to those on maternity leave: *Memoria 2004*, 271.

another. For that reason the career of prosecutor may be more desirable, and so the proportion of women fiscales is higher than that of women judges.

Since it is not possible to fill all the judicial posts from the initial recruitment, it is necessary to have recourse to external recruitment. Lateral entry is an important part of judicial recruitment. In 2003, there were eight promotions to the Tribunal Supremo and two new entrants into the judicial career at this level. The new magistrados were made up from sixty-seven promotions from the rank of juez and four initial entrants at this level. Until 2004, a quarter of posts as juez were reserved for lawyers with at least six years of practical experience (about fifty a year). The profile of those appointed from 1996 to 2001 was that 34.6 per cent were judicial secretaries (court clerks), 28.5 per cent abogados and 24.4 per cent already occupied temporary judicial positions (as juez or magistrado).[60] They enter the Escuela Judicial by means of a special examination, based principally on a file of experience. The experience is graded according to a points system.[61] In addition, a quarter of the posts as magistrado have been reserved for lawyers of ten years' experience. They enter based on file and an interview. Many of the lateral entrants will be fiscales. For example, in the criminal chamber of the Tribunal Supremo (Segunda Sala), of fourteen members, only two had been fiscales and, of seven associate judges, three had been fiscales. The figures show that the judiciary is not generally an attractive option for successful abogados.

Recent trends suggest that entry by established lawyers into the lower rank of juez is becoming unattractive. In the six competitions from 1996 to 2001, for 344 places on offer, only 54 were filled (15.7 per cent). By contrast, in the competition for entry into the rank of magistrado there were 248 applicants for 85 places.[62] As a result, the 2003 reform of the organic law on the judiciary merged the competitions, recognising that there was little demand for entry to the lower grade.[63] Although, as has been said, entry by abogados to the full-time judiciary is low, they are often appointed to part-time judicial posts. Growing esteem and remuneration in private practice now provide incentives for Spanish lawyers to seek a career as an abogado.

The inability of the Spanish selection system to recruit sufficient judges creates significant problems. As we will see, there is a heavy

[60] *Informe*, above n. 14, 15.
[61] See the 'Baremo de méritos' published in BOE no. 260, 30 October 2003.
[62] *Informe*, above n. 14, 13.
[63] Ley orgánica 19/2003 of 23 December 2003, BOE 309/2003.

reliance on part-time and non-professional judges, or judges who have been retired. The growth of the economy and the greater opportunities for work as an abogado has put pressure on the judicial system's ability to deliver justice.

Training and continuing education

There has been a longstanding concern in Spain that university education and preparation for the oposiciónes is too theoretical. Furthermore, the oposiciónes involve presenting answers to questions from a very small number of themes selected from a wide syllabus. To succeed most candidates engage in rote learning of the essential points from notes prepared by their tutor or from books.[64] The more practical side of university education has been limited, not least because of large student numbers and limited resources. In the nineteenth century, practical judicial training essentially involved 'learning by doing'.[65] Particularly in contrast to the German system, this pattern of education and training was perceived as inadequate. A Franco law of 26 May 1944 created the Escuela Judicial in Barcelona, which started work in 1950.[66] The course has undergone various improvements over the years and has a good reputation. The very theoretical education of university study and for the oposiciónes has then to be matched by more practical activities for those who will often be allocated as single judges. The training programme of the Escuela in 2004–5 had an induction course lasting for a full academic year. Its purpose was to focus on the practical application of the law learnt in university study and for the entrance competition. It is case-based, focusing on concrete issues, coming to a sensible decision and the writing of a judgment. In addition, the course aims to give the judges an understanding of the social context in which legal problems arise, e.g. domestic violence or drug addiction. Compared with the longer periods of study in France and Germany, the Spanish training for a long time involved less placement activity and was less practical. Although the 1944 plan was for a programme of eighteen months of courses followed by a year of placement, the course has been reduced in length several times in order to have more judges out in the courts. Until the early 2000s, the need to get judges into court to reduce backlogs caused the Government to reduce the period of academic study to six months. The current placement year aims to provide a longer period of study, a full academic year, followed by a year with a wide range

[64] Scholz, 363, 370, 372–3, 531–2. [65] Ibid., 386. [66] Ibid., 414–15.

of experience.[67] The competitive atmosphere is sustained by the importance of the terminal examination for the allocation of judicial posts. Training for those becoming judges through lateral entry is different, but is also provided by the Escuela.

Continuing education is not obligatory, but a majority of judges see it as important.[68] It is organised by the Escuela Judicial through an education committee, which involves the judicial unions. To be eligible for posts in certain kinds of court, it will be necessary for a judge to pass a specialist examination. There will be the need to recognise special subject competence, for example administrative law. Members of the administrative sections of courts will be chosen from those who have passed the relevant test. The most common specialisations tested are either linguistic or on the *foral* law of a particular province. In 2004, among 4,194 judges, 90 had obtained recognition of their ability to speak one of the languages of an Autonomous Community, mainly Catalan or Valencian. In addition, 141 had passed tests on the *ley foral* or specialist law of a particular area, again mainly for Catalonia or Valencia.[69]

Given that most first postings will be as single judges, many in remote areas, the quality of the practical training is crucial. Although there are no specific studies of the performance of early career judges, as have been undertaken in Germany,[70] public opinion studies do suggest that there are deficiencies in the performance of lower judges,[71] to which the brevity of practical training and limited subsequent supervision in a first post have contributed.

Career

The career of the judge is both bureaucratic and varied. It is bureaucratic in that there are positions for which one has to apply and, as has been seen, appointment depends largely on seniority and formal qualifications. As a national service, it presumes that individuals are free to be sent around the country to match needs in particular areas as they arise. But within that structure, personal preferences can lead individuals into a varied pattern of posts. The path chosen by an individual will reflect both ambition and family circumstances. Roles may be chosen for their geographical location, e.g. close to a family home, rather than

67 Programme of School 2004–6: *Escuela Memoria 2004* (Madrid 2004).

68 *Memoria 2004*, 44–6 shows that applications for places on courses nearly matched the number of judges in each category, whilst two-thirds of all categories of judge actually turned up at training sessions in 2003.

69 Ibid., 271. 70 See above p. 115. 71 See below p. 228.

simply because they represent a 'promotion'. Indeed, personal concerns may be hard to match with the needs of the service as a whole, which explains in part why many less populated centres have no permanent judge.

On leaving the Escuela, posts are allocated formally on the basis of success in the terminal examination. In practice, there may be informal arrangements among the graduands to ensure that their different preferences as to location, proximity to spouses and type of work are satisfied. For example, a higher-placed graduate may prefer to take a posting nearer her lower-placed husband. Many of the posts for the new graduates will be in remote rural juzgados to which it is difficult to recruit volunteers. For the first three years, a young judge will have to serve in such a posting until she becomes sufficiently senior to qualify for a more congenial posting nearer a major urban centre and, frequently, within her preferred region of the country. The judicial career does allow a significant possibility for advancement within a region. Promotion will depend on seniority and experience, e.g. to become a magistrado the judge will need to be appointed to a post which is designated for a judge at this level, such as a major first instance court in a large urban centre. The 2003 reforms have put greater emphasis on specialist experience for promotion to collegial courts.

Apart from seeking promotion through a series of 'frontline' postings in lower courts, many of the more ambitious judges will seek 'back office' posts as letrados (court clerks) in the higher courts. For example, in both the Tribunal Constitucional and the Tribunal Supremo, letrados have a major role in decisions on inadmissibility (*inadmición*) and in preparing other cases for hearing. In the Tribunal Supremo, the *gabinete* of letrados and others with legal experience will prepare the files for decisions on admissibility – summarising the issues, obtaining precedents and rules of law. The decision will be taken in different ways in different Salas, but the pattern is that a small number of judges (three or four) will produce a decision, usually with limited reasoning. In other cases, they will work with reporter judges (*ponentes*) to prepare a case for decision. Being a letrado has a number of advantages. First, the post will be based in a major urban centre. Secondly, the individual's work comes to the attention of senior members of the profession, which may help in any appointment that is not allocated just on the basis of seniority. Thirdly, the work is both collegial and more intellectually interesting than much of the routine work in courts at the lowest level. The role of letrado is one which many able young judges would take, although the posts are also available to academics. Some posts will be for more senior judges, e.g. in more administrative roles within the highest courts. Compared with the role of letrado, nomination as a référendaire in Luxembourg is rare, and there is not yet a clear pattern of career progression following such a posting. All the same, this is likely to lead to a more senior post eventually.

Unlike in France and a number of other countries, judges do not typically serve in the Ministry of Justice but as letrados in the administration of the courts through the Consejo General del Poder Judicial.[72] Given the division of competence between the state and the Autonomous Communities, a ministry posting would carry little prestige, and, in any case, the Spanish conception of judicial independence and the separation of powers would preclude this as a major strand of a judicial career. Such service will give them insights into policy-making on justice as a whole rather than greater understanding of substantive legal principles and policies. It will provide a basis for a different form of career direction, even if the letrado returns initially to a court. Indeed, in order to keep such people in contact with the practical law, reforms of 2003 have limited the period of service as a letrado in the Consejo to ten years.

Judicial corporate life

In the drive to create a new democracy, judicial professional associations have played an important role. Article 127 of the 1978 Constitution permitted judicial associations. The initial approach was to create a single professional association, the *Asociación Profesional de la Magistratura*, which was joined by about 70 per cent of the judiciary.[73] Its role was to propose names for membership of the CGPJ and the Tribunal Constitucional. But the roles of participating in the governance of the judicial system and more generally in raising the issues for the administration of justice in a newly democratic country gave rise to tensions. Currents of political opinion shaped themselves into new associations, which eventually broke away from the main association in 1984. The *Juces para la Democracia* occupied a left-wing role, whilst the *Asociación Francisco de Vitoria* represents a more centre-right tendency. The more

[72] See below pp. 203–4. In 2003, there were 112 judges on 'special service'.

[73] The union of prosecutors, the *Asociación de Fiscales*, is also linked to it and they all form part of a confederation of legal professionals.

right-wing *Foro Judicial Independiente* was formed later. Each has the right to nominate candidates to Parliament to be considered for membership of the CGPJ. Their role is thus very important. The associations are consulted on legal education and on careers, and will campaign on issues concerning the administration of justice. They will make representations on particular legislation, like any professional association. The unions are not the only representatives of the judges. The 2001 reforms of nomination to the CGPJ do give a place to non-unionised judges. But the ability of the unions to organise members to support particular candidates for membership of the governing body of the administration of justice, and their ability to campaign on issues relating to the decisions which it takes, gives the unions an important role in the life of the judicial profession. Judges serve on the local managing body (*junta*), which represents the interests of the judges. But it is only in lobbying at a political level through associations or the CGPJ that professionals can influence the decisions on staffing and resources that affect their ability to function effectively.

Judges have a strong sense of corporate solidarity. In a 1987 survey, judges identified most with their profession (63.3 per cent), their region (34.8 per cent), political ideas (36 per cent) and with their people (28 per cent).[74] Although judges declared themselves more left of centre than right-wing (58 per cent), the perception they have of their colleagues is that they are more conservative. This suggests that political opinion is not actually discussed a lot in a work context.[75]

Links between higher courts and lower courts rely predominantly on informal interaction. The presidents of the Tribunal Supremo and the Tribunal Constitucional will tend to have formal engagements in other courts. This will allow opportunities to find out what is going on in those courts. But there is no formal meeting between the president of either court and the presidents of the lower courts. Other members of these courts will also participate in meetings at which general issues (rather than individual cases) are discussed, but these are not specially convened.

More formally, decisions of the higher courts will be published in law reports, databases and law reviews. In the past there was no specific arrangement to communicate decisions to the lower courts either by a judicial intranet[76] or by more traditional means. Improvements in

[74] Elites, 49–52. [75] Ibid., 46–7.

[76] The judicial centre in San Sebastian is, however, actively looking into the possibility of a judicial intranet.

information technology have been addressing this. With only voluntary continuing education, there would appear to be only limited efforts made to ensure a common approach to problems among the judiciary. Geographical spread, a strong attachment to judicial independence, and underdeveloped infrastructure for communications among the judges have all contributed to a system which can give rise to much misunderstanding among the lower judges of the views of the higher courts, except possibly in a regional context.

Thus the cohesiveness of the judiciary depends in part on unionisation and information technology, as well as on the activity of the Escuela Judicial and the Consejo General del Poder Judicial. But to a great extent, these institutions only create structures for cohesion and the actual experience of judges on the job is also essential to a collective sense of common purpose and values.

History and values

Coming to terms with dictatorship

The starting point for the understanding of the contemporary judiciary in Spain has to be its history during the Franco period. There is a much longer history which has shaped the development of the judiciary, particularly in civil and criminal law, and this remains significant. Indeed, the framework for judicial recruitment and independence was set out in 1870, but the operation of the judiciary was particularly closely supervised by the Franco regime. Thus Heywood remarks, 'the judiciary under Franco operated as an arm of the State, masking its essentially arbitrary nature behind the façade of due legal process'.[77] All the same, it would be true to say that Franco often bypassed the normal judicial process.[78] For this reason, there is now a deliberate attempt to ensure that there are no special courts.[79] The legal values of fascism were developed particularly in the early period of the dictatorship up until the early 1950s,[80] and these focused on the authority of the Caudillo, Franco himself, and the nation as an organic community organised around certain conservative and collective values. In the later period, these had already begun

[77] Heywood, *Government*, above n. 22, 104.
[78] M. T. Newton with P. J. Donaghy, *Institutions of Modern Spain* (Cambridge 1997), ch. 14.
[79] See L. M. Díez-Picazo, *Régimen constituccional del Poder Judicial* (Madrid 1991), 35.
[80] See A. J. Menéndez, 'From Republicanism to Fascist Ideology under the Early *Franquismo*' in C. Joerges and N. Ghaleigh (eds.), *Darker Legacies of Law in Europe* (Oxford 2003), ch. 18.

to decline as a result of the social change that accompanied economic modernisation, but the authoritarian special courts remained.

The values on legal procedure proclaimed in the 1978 Constitution relate to the monopoly of the ordinary courts.[81] There are to be no special courts with their own judiciary and procedure, as occurred under Franco with bodies such as the Tribunal de Represíon de la Masoneria y el Comunismo and the Tribunal de Orden Público.[82] Even administrative courts are integrated. Although they started as separate bodies within the administration in 1845, they were judicialised in 1888 as a distinct court and, from 1904, they were integrated into the ordinary courts, a pattern which was re-established after the civil war in 1956.[83] Many of the structures of the ordinary courts have evolved gradually since the early nineteenth century, but the philosophy underlying their current operation relates especially to ideas of democracy developed in reaction to Franco and to international standards of justice and economic efficiency, as opposed to the rather closed domestic concerns under the dictatorship. The 1978 constitutional values of individual rights and pluralism provide a significant departure in the way the legal system has to operate.

The concept of the 'judicial power' is longstanding in democratic thought in Spain.[84] The essential features are set out in art. 117(1) CE – the judicial power comes from the people and individual judges are appointed by the King as head of state; judges are to be independent, irremovable and responsible only to the law. Formal legitimacy comes in principle from the people, but in practice from applying the law as enacted by popular representatives.[85] Judges really have an institutional legitimacy arising from their organic participation in the bureaucratic judiciary and belonging to the organisation, the judicial power. There is, therefore, a tension between ascribing the legitimacy of judges to notions of democracy and the more practical legitimacy arising from their place in the institutions of the Constitution. The original legitimacy of the judiciary in Spain leads to a distinctive understanding of judicial independence and to structures of governance under the Consejo General del Poder Judicial.

[81] Single person courts are called 'juzgados' and collegial courts are called 'tribunales'.

[82] See de Otto, *Estudios*, above n. 50, ch. 4, esp. p. 90. [83] Ibid., 93.

[84] See M. J. Terol Becarra, *El Consejo General del Poder Judicial* (Madrid 1990), ch. 1.

[85] See J. F. López Aguilar, 'Poder Judicial' in G. Trujillo, L. López Guerra and P. González-Trevijano (eds.), *La experiencia constitucional (1978–2000)* (Madrid 2000), 389 at 397–8.

Judicial independence

Like most legal systems, the role of the judge as supervisor of the legal system and ultimate decision-maker in many disputes requires an important character of independence. As de Otto puts it, 'in so far as concerned the legitimation of the act of applying the law irrevocably, it is precisely the organ which has been disconnected from all other interests and in practice which is independent of those other organs of the State from which particular interests might be pursued'.[86]

In the nineteenth century, there was criticism that judicial appointments were made on the basis of political and social connections, with the implication that these had an influence on judicial decisions.[87] This was obviously a greater concern during the periods of dictatorship in the twentieth century. The Spanish Constitution of 1978 has a particular conception of judicial independence. The judges are to be exclusively dedicated to the roles which are defined by law and are concerned with the guarantee of rights.[88] This is understood broadly to include ancillary administrative roles, such as acting as a registry for property and civil rights. Essentially, the idea is to separate the judiciary from legislative and political roles. Under art. 117 CE, 'judges and magistrados are not subject in the exercise of their functions to orders from anyone'. Independence is conceived both as external and internal. Externally, the judge is irremovable, i.e. cannot be removed against his will. He is subject to a series of incompatibilities to ensure no conflict of interest, and art. 127 CE insists that the judge cannot belong to a political party nor can he take on public functions.[89] In addition, the whole management of the judicial career is under the control of an independent constitutional authority, not a Ministry of Justice headed by a party politician. In the internal handling of particular cases, the judge is subject to a number of protections from ordinary suits against him for his judicial activities. Thus, he can only be detained for a flagrant delict, any criminal action against a judge for actions in the performance of his duties requires the prior approval of the Ministero Fiscal, and he has a privilege of forum in that certain crimes can only be instructed and judged by the Tribunal Supremo or the Tribunales Superiores de Justicia.[90] As has been seen in relation to discipline, control over the performance of judges is exercised by judges themselves, either at the management

[86] De Otto, *Estudios*, above n. 50, 33. [87] Scholz, 1078–9.
[88] Díez-Picazo, *Régimen*, above n. 79, ch. 4, esp. p. 49.
[89] Ibid., 100–1. [90] Ibid., 109: LOPJ, arts. 57 and 73.

level of the local court and its *gerente* or by the disciplinary and criminal systems. The internal freedom is further illustrated by the fact that judges are allowed to give individual judgments, unlike many continental judges.[91] There are duties to give public reasons for decisions, and, as will be seen later, this applies to the *jurado*, the jury in criminal cases. In this sense, all involved in the judicial process may exercise their own judgement and be seen to do so.[92] Both the external and the internal independence of judges is accentuated in the Spanish system in order to generate confidence that the system and its decisions are impartial and not subject to improper influence. But, of course, impartial administration of justice does not, of itself, prevent partisan substantive law. In this area, the consultative roles of the Consejo del Poder Judicial and the Consejo del Estado are meant to identify breaches of fundamental principles, and the Tribunal Constitucional has the role of reviewing enacted legislation to the same effect.

The judicial role

Judicial creativity

The Spanish judiciary engages in judicial creativity in much the same way as most continental European judges by making practically important judicial decisions dealing with old codes and by interpreting new statutes.

Precedent

Spain belongs to the Latin tradition in which precedents are not a source of law.[93] Article 1(1) of the 1889 Civil Code states that the sources of law are statute (*ley*), custom and general principles of law. Article 1(6) states that: 'Case-law will complement the legal system with the doctrine which the Tribunal Supremo establishes in a repeated manner in order to interpret and apply statute, custom, and the general principles of law.'[94] In this way, the status of the decisions of the highest court is recognised, because it has to ensure the unity of the case-law.

[91] Ibid., 104–5: LOPJ art. 260. [92] See de Otto, *Estudios*, above n. 50, esp. 57–9.

[93] A. Ruiz Miguel and F. J. Laporta, 'Precedent in Spain' in D. N. MacCormick and R. S. Summers (eds.), *Interpreting Precedents* (Aldershot 1997) (hereafter 'Ruiz Miguel and Laporta'), ch. 8.

[94] See Merino-Blanco, 45–6.

By contrast, the decisions of the lower courts carry little formal authority. That said, the increasing importance of local legislation makes the Tribunal Superior of the Community an important point of reference. In addition, the Law on Civil Procedure from 1855 and 1881 established that failure to conform to the 'doctrina legal' of the Tribunal Supremo constituted a ground for cassation. The *ley* of 6 August 1984 has amended the terminology of art. 1692(5) and used the term 'jurisprudencia' instead of the old-fashioned 'doctrina legal'. In this way there is a clear recognition that judges are called upon to make law, albeit through interpretation.

In formal terms, 'the judge is bound by (statutory) law and not by precedent'.[95] Furthermore, art. 12(3) LOPJ provides that judges and courts cannot dictate solutions of a general or specific character directed to the lower courts concerning the interpretation or application of the law.[96] The style of judgments does not make it easy to appreciate that judges are making the law and the reasons for which they are doing this. As Ruiz Miguel and Laporta comment, 'The prevailing legalistic and magisterial style does not always leave much space for a deep elaboration of the reasons that justify the interpretations adopted by the court, which usually are asserted rather than argued.'[97] The traditional Latin terse argumentation, found in France and Italy, is deductive rather than discursive, and does not cite precedents. The court adopts legalistic argument, rather than seeking to justify a decision by reference to policy reasons. Unlike the French system, there is no *avocat général* whose published opinions can give the legal community insight into the debates within the court, nor is there any publication of the views of the reporter judge. The one concession is the ability of judges to give individual opinions.[98] Whereas the ordinary courts continue this tradition, the Tribunal Constitucional has adopted a more open and less technically legal style. This is in keeping with its function of being the reference point for constitutional interpretation and explicitly offering guidance to the legislators and the courts by a didactic style.[99] It has been prepared to distinguish between the legal ruling in a case and *obiter dicta*.[100]

[95] STC 49/1985, cited in Ruiz Miguel and Laporta, 270.
[96] De Otto, *Estudios*, above n. 50, 45–6.
[97] Ruiz Miguel and Laporta, 268. [98] See Ibid., 264.
[99] Ibid., 264–5; also de Otto, *Estudios*, above n. 50, 46–9.
[100] STC 6/1991, cited in Ruiz Miguel and Laporta, 280–1.

The sheer number of decisions handed down by the courts does limit the scope for discussion. The lower, single-judge courts handed down 1,002,102 *sentencias* in 2001 out of a total of 1,309,704 handed down by all courts. But even the Tribunal Supremo handed down some 10,178 sentencias, in addition to a further 16,498 summary decisions (*autos*).

That said, in terms of court procedure it is clear that the highest courts are aware of the authority that attaches to their decisions. In the Tribunal Supremo, art. 264 LOPJ provides that judges of the different *secciones* should meet in the *pleno* of the Sala in order to unify the case-law. Similarly, art. 13 of the Organic Law on the Tribunal Constitucional provides that the pleno should meet to resolve departures from previous doctrine.[101] In this way, the courts prepare themselves internally to make decisions having a significant precedential effect. The role of the Tribunal Constitucional in responding to *cuestiones* is deliberately to formulate rulings which will bind for the future.[102]

The status of the Tribunal Supremo as a body which has to resolve difficult questions of law in an authoritative manner for the nation as a whole has always given some recognition to the place of case-law among the practical sources of law. This was found in art. 13 of the 1812 Constitution and firmly settled since the Constitution of 1834. Indeed, the need to ensure consistent case-law is one of the grounds on which the Ministero Fiscal may bring a case to that court.[103]

The justification of the authority of precedent is principally to ensure the unity of the case-law and thus equal treatment of citizens. It also provides for legal certainty. But, while these values are well recognised, the status which lawmaking gives is not recognised. In part, the pressure for unity in the case-law, rather than the judges' own perception of what is right, varies between branches of the law, with civil, and more recently criminal judges in the Tribunal Supremo being more willing to ensure uniformity. The deference to formal sources of law leads the judges to argue that they do not lay down a norm, but rather they articulate the 'criteria of applicability' of norms. In playing this role, the decision has a certain transcendence in relation to the norm.[104] This difficulty leads the ordinary courts not to acknowledge explicitly their law-creating role.[105]

[101] Ruiz Miguel and Laporta, 262 and 275. [102] Below p. 217.
[103] De Otto, *Estudios*, above n. 50, 43–5.
[104] Ruiz Miguel and Laporta, 278–9, citing STS of 18 April 1995.
[105] Ibid., 288–9.

Statutes

In terms of substance, the courts have long recognised the need to go beyond a purely literal approach to texts and to interpret the law to meet changed social conditions. For example, legislation of 1888 had set out very limited circumstances under which paternity could be investigated, but a decision of the Tribunal Supremo in 1934 permitted this in a broader range of cases. The case relied on an article of the 1931 Constitution which had empowered the legislator to enact legislation on the investigation of paternity in unspecified ways. This was taken as a change in climate, encouraging a less restrictive approach.[106] This kind of approach was influenced by opinion of Spanish doctrinal writers who, in their turn, were influenced by authors such as Saleilles and Gény in France.[107]

García de Enterría argues that the primacy of *ley* has been broken by the development of other sources of law – general principles developed by the courts, and the Constitution interpreted by the Tribunal Constitucional.[108] He also describes the process of 'decodification' under which classical codes are amended by a large number of fragmentary rules. It then falls to the judge to restore the coherence of the law. But, in his view, this does not mean that the judge is freed from his subordination to statute. Rather, he has the role of interpreting it so as to facilitate its operation.[109]

Extrajudicial roles

As is made clear in the *Libro Blanco*, the judge is not only a court official, but also a member of the wider legal community. As such, judges are involved in teaching and other activities, provided that these do not interfere with their work. In terms of secondment, in 2004 some 2.6 per cent of judges were on leave or secondment from the judicial service.

The role of letrados with the CGPJ and the bodies which depend on it is important. In 2002, twelve appointments were made to posts as letrados within that body, eight as inspector and four as professors in the Escuela Judicial. Such non-judicial roles are important and enable talented individuals to be attracted into judicial administration. All the

[106] See M. A. Pérez Alvarez, *Interpretación y Jurisprudencia* (Pamplona 1994), 47–50.
[107] Ibid., 36.
[108] E. García de Enterría and A. Mendéndez Mendéndez, *El Derecho, la Ley y el Juez* (Madrid 1997), 51.
[109] Ibid., 53–7.

same, secondment does reduce the body of qualified judges and, after a time, they cease to have experience of court life, and a limit of ten years has been placed on it.[110] Secondment may also be permitted for service as assessor for the Defensor del Pueblo or the equivalent post in the Autonomous Communities.

Although judges are constitutionally prohibited from belonging to political parties,[111] this rather rigid conception of political independence is attenuated in practice. Judges who campaign for political office are given leave without pay (*servicios especiales*). In the past, they used to be allowed to return immediately to judicial duties when their political office finished. This enabled leading judges like Garzón to be persuaded to join the Socialist Party list for the Cortes, to have a ministerial career, then to return to the role of investigating judge, and soon to be investigating his former government colleagues. Now judges have to wait for three years (with only basic pay) before returning to active judicial functions.

Professional judges and the legal community

Judges and abogados

Traditionally judges have been seen as the elite of the legal profession. Whilst they were recruited through the highly demanding and competitive oposiciónes, any law graduate could become an abogado without any further training or examination. Since the 1870 reforms, entry to the judiciary has been a rival and prestigious career in relation to that of abogado. In practice, anyone who now wants to practise as an abogado will need to have undertaken a traineeship with an established member of the profession before he or she is able to begin a successful practice. In addition, the local Bars will often establish training courses. Of course, this depends on the size of the Bar, which is organised around the main regional courts. Some Bars are really too small to establish much by way of training.[112] The creation of nationwide law firms, some of which have international links, has also enhanced training

[110] Above p. 195.

[111] This restriction is supported by the judiciary: 59.6 per cent in the opinion survey of 1987: Elites, 63.

[112] The size of practising bars varied in 2004 from 34 (Tafalla) to 27,993 (Madrid): Censo de abogados, above n. 8.

opportunities. These changes in the structure of firms and increased economic activity have increased the incomes of private practice lawyers, and this has a significant impact on the judiciary. It has already been seen that there are few lateral recruits into the judiciary from established abogados. There are many abogados in rural areas who serve as part-time judges, especially juces de paz.[113] Such part-time judges are seen as second-best and this does not enhance the status of abogados as a whole. Overall, the role of the abogado still has a lower status than that of the judge. But the increasing attractiveness of the successful firms in major urban areas, their increased professionalism and economic wealth is raising their status rapidly. By contrast, the civil service salaries and the geographical mobility often required for promotion reduce the relative attractiveness of the judicial role. In 2004, there were 108,500 practising abogados, which is very substantially greater than the 4,194 judges, and this demonstrates the pattern of demand for good lawyers.

With their increased role in economic life and with their relative independence to speak out on political matters, the Bars also have a lobbying role in relation to legislation which can be at least as strong as the judges' own professional associations. The rapid rise in numbers and the increased professionalism of the abogados will make them increasingly powerful in the future, particularly in local Bars such as Madrid.

Judges and professors

Spain has had a long tradition of high-level legal scholarship in its universities. Spain provided some of the great founders of canon law and international law, as well as of civilian law scholarship. In the nineteenth century, there were already very substantial numbers of law students – as many as 5,375 in 1838.[114] This was set back by the closure of the universities run by religious orders in the 1840s, and academics were also particularly suspected by governments under the various dictatorships. Universities were the focus of purges in the 1930s. But, nonetheless, the Franco regime sought to develop its own legitimacy through legal and political scholarship.[115] This involved a blend of longstanding Spanish scholarship, such as the work of the nineteenth-century scholar

[113] See below pp. 209–10.

[114] Scholz, 291. These constituted 50 per cent of all university students. Even in 1878, lawyers constituted 38 per cent of all students.

[115] See Menéndez, 'From Republicanism', above n. 80.

Donoso, with contemporary fascist writing, notably from Carl Schmitt in Germany, who spoke and wrote in Spanish. This development affected public law in particular, but it illustrates the international character of influences on Spanish legal scholarship, a feature which was repeated in the formation of the 1978 Constitution.

Private law scholarship had flourished since the nineteenth century despite various changes of political regime.[116] It was easier for professors to teach, research and practise in these areas than to engage much in politically controversial scholarship. Many of the structural reforms introduced by Franco had been discussed for many years beforehand, but political instability had prevented them from being adopted. The relative stability of the Franco era provided an environment within which private law scholarship could develop, and many of the leading works of the modern era have previous editions published within the fascist period. Many of the leading professors were involved in reforms.

In the restoration, particularly in creating the Constitution, professors who had been educated outside Spain took a leading role, often assisted by judges from those jurisdictions. Certainly, there are leading professors whose views will be considered by the judges, but the infrastructure of scholarship has taken much time to rebuild, and with it the status of the scholarly output as an important source of law. Professors were involved in the new constitutional court, the Tribunal Constitucional, in part as a check on the judges, who might have been too close to the Franco regime. In addition, the judges and abogados, who are mainly generalists, will necessarily take note of what is published. On the whole, it will be in private law that this is most prevalent. In constitutional law, it is the Tribunal Constitucional that is leading the way, and its own internal seminars between judges and letrados provide as much doctrinal work as is found in textbooks.

Whereas some professors are typically appointed to the highest courts, there have been few instances of career judges producing doctrinal legal writing. Since judgments are brief and typically anonymous and there is no equivalent of the French *avocat général*, there is little scope for serving judges to have a public role in the development of the law. As a result, systematisation and the development of new ideas are presented through academic writings.

[116] See Scholz, 354–84.

Lay judges

Juez de paz

Spain has a long tradition of lay judges, but their place has long been controversial. The medieval *alacaldes* were appointed by the King or the local lord to be defenders of the peace.[117] The liberal constitutionalists of 1812 and 1834 had wanted a professional judiciary, but this was not practical. This balance between history, constitutional theory and pragmatism has characterised the role of lay judges ever since. At root, the problem is that the map of courts has not been reformed. There has not been a radical rationalisation of court centres to reflect the modern demands on the legal system. As a result, there are court centres in many centres of small population. There has been some regrouping, but the local courts serve many administrative purposes, and so still need some form of staffing. This then creates a need for judicial posts in excess of the numbers that could possibly be delivered through the various recruitment processes for professional judges.

For reasons similar to the English justices of the peace, the *alacaldes* had both judicial and administrative functions, although their role extended to civil disputes (both conciliation and decision) as well as criminal cases. The Decree of 22 October 1855 established a new basic law for the lay judge, creating the 'juez de paz' ('justice of the peace') with limited administrative and criminal functions.[118] They were to be chosen for two-year periods without remuneration from people in the local population who fulfilled basic criteria, namely nationality, age over twenty-five and residence in the area. The LOPJ of 1870 included the juez de paz (then called *juez municipal*) within the judicial order. Although there continued to be pressure from liberal politicians and lawyers in favour of a more professionalised judiciary, the lay element was recognised as necessary. A local professional lawyer judge was appointed as the juez municipal in some larger towns, and these were given priority in the allocation of work, as well as a chance of career progression into the ranks of the national judiciary as *juez de primera instancia*.[119] But the number of those available to fill such professional posts was limited. Under the 1907 reforms, only 330 candidates fitted the priority categories for appointment to the 491 major urban courts, leaving a further 8,370 municipalities with lay judges.[120] Franco's law of 19 July 1944 on

[117] See R. C. Gavala, *El Juez de Paz en la Ordenación Jurisdiccional Española* (Madrid 1989).
[118] Ibid., 82. [119] Ibid., 92, discussing legislation of 1893.
[120] Ibid., 107; J. D. Moreno, *Los Jueces de Paz* (Madrid 1987) (hereafter 'Moreno'), 117–32.

the judiciary really consolidated and systematised the pattern of 1907. Under this, in some 8,100 municipalities jueces de paz were appointed, with a preference for legally qualified candidates.[121] Such a system was pragmatic and established stability. The LOPJ of 1985 rationalised the system of first instance courts, and provided that professional judges would staff the Juzgado de Primera Instancia. But in municipalities where it was not possible to have a professional judge, there was to be a juez de paz.[122]

It would be fair to say that historical tradition and practical necessity were not the only concerns which justified the retention of the juez de paz. The most important argument was the idea of popular participation in the courts, a principle enshrined in art. 125 CE and for which the Socialists argued in the drafting of the 1978 Constitution.[123] The lay element contrasted with the professional judge and was seen as particularly important by many in limiting the power of a central government to influence judicial decisions, particularly against those it disliked. In addition, the 1907 reforms by Prime Minister Maura reflected an idea that the municipality was the natural social unit from which the resolution of disputes should come, particularly the efforts at conciliation, which were the main function of the juez de paz. The arguments of convenience and locality continued to be pressed in the debates on the LOPJ 1985, even though many argued that modern communications made urban centres more accessible than many small rural municipalities.[124]

Those arguing against the role of the juez de paz claimed that the system treated similar cases unequally. In urban areas, the litigants had a professional judge, whereas in the small rural communities, they received a decision from a lay judge, albeit aided by a legal clerk (*secretario*).[125] This objection obviously does not apply to the major function of deciding in equity as a form of conciliation, but both judicial decisions and conciliation are allowed by art. 100 LOPJ. Under art. 102 LOPJ, the nominees for being a juez need to satisfy all the conditions necessary for being a judge, except having a licenciado in law. The formal preference for qualified lawyers has gone.[126] The idea that there should

[121] Gavala, *El Juez de Paz*, above n. 117, 108ff. The name 'juez de paz' was restored by this legislation to describe the lay judges.

[122] Ibid., 68.

[123] Ibid., 46–8, 181–6, 201, and Moreno, 226.

[124] Gavala, *El Juez de Paz*, above n. 117, 196–7 and 201.

[125] Ibid., 140–1, 193–4.

[126] For previous requirements see ibid., 227–32, note 94.

be a single body of judges is held strongly by many, who consider that the very existence of lay judges breaches the requirements of art. 117(3) CE under which judicial power is conferred on 'los Juzgados y Tribunales determinados por las leyes'.[127] By contrast, others consider that the requirements of this provision are satisfied if the courts have been created by law, and this does not have direct implications for which kinds of people (judicial, law or military) are appointed as judges.[128]

If the appropriateness of retaining a juez de paz was controversial even in the past, the method of appointment was even more controversial. Appointment by the local municipality brought local knowledge and local popular involvement, but it also brought politicisation and the danger of 'caucuses' (*cacquismo*). There were many changes in the procedure for appointment by the local municipalities between 1812 and 1985.[129] In much of the nineteenth century, the president of the local court, the Audiencias Territoriales, made the appointment, with nominations coming from the governor or the local juez de primera instancia, depending on the rules in force, and based on lists of people eligible in the territory. This led to allegations that the governing party was able to influence nominations.[130] The 1907 reforms moved the decision to the collegial executive, the Salas de Gobierno of the Audiencias, afforced by the presidents of the local abogados and notarios, with the preparatory work undertaken by the local juez de primera instancia.[131] If the basic qualification was being of the right age and living in the territory, there were various attempts to set out some criteria for appointment. A clear preference was set out for lawyers in 1893. In 1934, a disastrous attempt was made for direct election of candidates, which was hastily abandoned.[132] Under the present art. 101 LOPJ from 1985, the juez de paz is appointed by the judiciary – the executive of the Tribunal Superior de Justicia – from among the list submitted after a vote of the full council of the local municipality.[133] There is thus an attempt to balance the idea of popular election with some form of vetting by judicial experts, who have the final say.

It is clear that different qualities of justice are delivered in different parts of Spain. On the one hand, among courts designated for

[127] See in particular the arguments of Moreno, 230–9.
[128] See de Otto, *Estudios*, above n. 50, 55–6.
[129] For a summary see Gavala, *El Juez de Paz*, above n. 117, 223–5, notes 90 and 92.
[130] Moreno, 99–103. [131] Ibid., 103–5.
[132] Gavala, *El Juez de Paz*, above n. 117; Moreno, 155–7.
[133] Gavala, *El Juez de Paz*, above n. 117, 217ff.

the professional judges, there are the full jueces (or in some, more important, courts, a magistrado) in many locations, but a large body of substitute judges – in 2001 there were 498 supplementary magistrados and 1,533 supplementary jueces compared with nearly 4,000 full-time judges.[134] Many are retired judges, but there is clearly a problem of filling judicial vacancies in some places which almost permanently have a substitute judge – even someone who was not able enough to pass the judicial examinations. The number is supposed to decline with the appointment of more full-time judges, but this would still leave 1,350 such appointments. On the other hand, there are many places where no professional judge is expected and the Juzgado de paz is in place. At first instance, there are many unviable court areas with fewer than 7,000 inhabitants. On 30 May 2000, there were 7,680 Juzgados de paz, which are equipped and located by the local government.[135] There are large numbers of jueces to staff these – 2,000 alone in Castile and León. Many of the jueces have a law degree, but some do not. Administrative regrouping has meant that some 2,831 courts are served by 297 groups of secretaries, but rationalisation is far from complete.

The juez de paz is involved in three kinds of activity as a single judge. He or she determines matters where there is no professional-judge court, the Juzgado de Primera Instancia e Instrucción. In civil matters, jueces de paz decide cases up to €90. They then mainly deal with the conciliation of non-matrimonial civil disputes, or provide assistance to other courts in taking statements or other acts of procedure. Judicial statistics show that decisions in disputes are not very significant and have been declining as Spain became more urbanised in the 1960s, and as communications improved. In 1959, there were 8,545 jueces de paz who held a total of 1,777 judicial hearings and were involved in 76,923 other matters (including the conciliation of parties). By 1968, the then 8,382 jueces de paz only held 429 oral hearings and dealt with 19,311 matters.[136] By 1992 some 1,893 cases were begun before all the Juzgados de paz in Spain, of which only 176 resulted in judgments. By 2001, only 406 cases were begun, resulting in 64 decisions.[137] In 2001, there were 14,866 conciliation decisions and 1,270,366 legal acts registered by the Juzgados de paz. Their principal civil function is as a local registry for

[134] *Memoria 2003*, 13.
[135] Ministry of Justice website: http://www.mju.es.
[136] Moreno, 179.
[137] Instituto Nacional de Estadística, *Estadísticas judiciales 2001*: see http://www.ine.es.

legal acts (births, marriages, etc.) and providing certificates. In criminal cases, they deal with minor cases concerning offences against the person or property, or against public order. In 2001, there were 12,142 criminal cases brought before the Juzgados de paz in all of Spain, but there were also 544,206 cautions and 86,612 other actions. In total 653,612 criminal matters were handled by them. In many ways, they deal with matters which are too petty to take up the time of a professional judge, especially in a locality which does not have enough work to keep a professional judge occupied.

There is no formal training for the jueces de paz, but they have formed their own regional associations where they can meet and exchange information. This voluntary activity is supported by the CGPJ, which has organised annual conferences for them since 1998 at which current issues can be debated.[138]

Jurado

There is a limited culture of real lay (non-lawyer) participation in the legal system. It remains predominantly an ideal, rather than a significant reality. The jury has two origins in Spain, both external and dating from the end of the eighteenth century. The jury was part of a politicised and short-lived progressive period.[139] One tradition is the French criminal jury, which was incorporated in the Estatuto de Bayona in 1808 and the Constitution of Cadiz of 1812, but was abolished with the restoration in 1814. The second source is the English libel jury. Fox's Libel Act 1792 became a reference point for liberal opinion in that the jury was to judge the freedom of the press.[140] The *ley* of 22 October 1820 created a jury to deal with criminal libel cases against the press. This jury applied only in a number of short interludes of liberal government. With the liberal era from 1869 to 1874, the jury was given a role in all political offences through the law on criminal procedure of 1872. Although suspended by the restoration of 1874, it continued to be studied by the Ministry of Justice and was reintroduced in 1888. The jury of twelve jurors, drawn from the electoral roll, and three judges was given jurisdiction over all serious criminal offences, including terrorist and economic crimes. It was frequently alleged that juries acquitted

[138] See CGPJ, *Memoria Anual 2002* (Madrid 2002), 244.

[139] See generally Carmen Gleadow, *History of Trial by Jury in the Spanish Legal System* (Lampeter 2000).

[140] On these two origins, see J. A. Alejandre, 'Introduccion historica al jurado español' in *Jornados comnmemorativas de Centenario de la Ley del Jurado* (Madrid 1988), 3.

in violent political or terrorist trials, and this pretext was used by the dictatorship of Primo de Rivera to suspend the jury on grounds of efficiency in 1923. The jury was restored in a more limited form in 1931, sitting together with the judges and deliberating on all aspects of the case.

The inspiration of the 1888 jury was predominantly French, with reference also to other European countries.[141] The idea of judgment by peers was seen as a freedom from persecution by the state, of which judges were traditionally the instruments. In this sense, the jury was a symbol of modernisation. But the ability of the jury to understand legal issues remained a concern. The preamble to the 1931 decrees restoring the jury expressed concern about people being unaware of the seriousness of offences or unable to distinguish law and fact.[142]

Lacking a consistent tradition of the jury, but retaining a sense that jury trial is both modern and liberal, the authors of the 1978 Constitution committed Spain to having jury trial, but without any specific view of its purposes and scope. The institution was the subject of much debate after the Constitution was enacted and it was only finally implemented by the *ley organica* of 1995.[143] This came into force on 1 April 1997 and an official report was produced for the CGPJ in May 1999, covering the first year of operation.[144] Its preliminary conclusion, not surprisingly, was that there will need to be a change in mentality to make the jury work.[145] The report notes that in the first year there was a noticeable 'flight from the jury' by prosecutors and investigating judges, the juez de instrucción. This may simply be a matter of the novelty of the institution, but there is also the sense that the difficulty of the process may make them prefer a purely judicial hearing. Opinions about the jury have fluctuated since 1978. In 1987, a survey reported that 47.6 per cent of judges favoured the jury and 30.4 per cent were against it.[146] By contrast, only 30.7 per cent of prosecutors accepted the idea and 58.7 per cent were against it, and most preferred a system of lay assessors as in

[141] See L. Prieto-Castro y Ferrandiz, 'Aspectos procesales de la ley del Jurado' in ibid., 31; also J. A. Martín Pallín, 'El Fiscal y el Jurado' in ibid., 54 and 56, noting comments made in a report by the Fiscalia of the Tribunal Supremo in 1902.

[142] See the report of the Ministero Fiscal of 1904, reported in ibid. 63.

[143] On this see Merino-Blanco, 180–6.

[144] Report of J. R. Sáez Valcárcel, *Informe sobre la Aplicación de la Ley Orgánica de Tribunal del Jurado desde el 1 de Abril de 1997 al 31 de Marzo de 1998* (CGPJ, 5 May 1999).

[145] Ibid., 6. For example, it appears to take at least half a day to empanel a jury because of objections by the parties and excuses offered by the jury.

[146] Elites, 62.

Germany.[147] Among the ordinary population, in 2000, 49 per cent said they would prefer trial by the jurado, rather than by judges, a figure that has been fairly constant since 1987.[148] For all this, the jury influences the conduct of few criminal trials.

In ordinary cases, the prosecutor prepares the case and the judge merely receives the evidence of both sides with limited prior preparation, particularly in the recently developed *juicios rápidos* (rapid decisions). In serious cases, the criminal process remains strongly judge-controlled and file-centred in this preliminary period, with the file serving as the open basis on which the decision to go to trial is made. There are preliminary hearings (*diligencias previas*) before the juez de instrucción, who will review the file and decide the issues on which a trial will be based. The judge must interview the accused.[149] The existence of the written file enables quite effective use of preliminary issues by the defence before trial commences, e.g. on breaches of fundamental rights and the admission of evidence.[150] The influence of the French model of the investigating judge is clearly visible.

At trial, the procedure is predominantly oral, but with the file playing an important part. Witnesses have to give oral testimony and this leads, as in common-law trials, to discussion of conflicts between witnesses.[151] Jurors may also be active in asking questions. The procedure of decision-making is different from the primary models in the French and common-law systems. Unlike in France, the judges do not decide with the jury. The jury receives a written direction (*objeto del veredicto*), which is far longer than the French questions for decision. Article 52(1) LOTJ requires that the objeto has separate paragraphs on each offence, identifying the issues to be resolved. The 1999 report complains that judges have not developed an appropriate style for these directions.[152] These specific directions are then complemented by a generic oral direction to the jury on coming to their decision. The jury goes off to make its decision on guilt with the written objeto from the judges. The nine jurors have to come to a decision on guilt by at least a majority of seven members when the issue goes against the accused and by a majority of five where the issue is favourable. For example, to accept attenuating circumstances, a majority of five to four is needed. Unlike in most

[147] Ibid., 91 and 116. [148] Toharia, 124.
[149] Report of Sáez Valcárcel, above n. 144, 25–30.
[150] Ibid., 32–4. [151] Ibid., 41–2. [152] Ibid., 51.

countries, the jury has to produce a written justification of its decision. Some juries give very detailed reasons in relation to facts and their legal classification,[153] but not all find this easy. Formally, the judges formulate their decision in the light of the verdict of the jury. Where the judges disagree, this will have to be dealt with on appeal. There is thus a strong effort made to structure the decision-making of the jury, to see that it properly understands its role and that its decisions are defensible. The Report suggests that the experiment has trouble in developing a routine in which lawyers and judges, as well as jurors, are familiar with their role. With only 288 decisions in the first year, there is only a small sample to go on. The story shows also how far external role models are important for the Spanish legal system in its early period of democracy. Those external models have relevance also in times of reform. But there is a tension between judicial conceptions of legality and democratic ideas of participation.

Professional judges and the wider community

Judges and politics: constitutional adjudication

Constitutional adjudication is one of the most obvious ways in which some Spanish judges interact with politics. In relation to the present Spanish constitutional settlement, one needs to distinguish three issues: the existence of a written constitution, the explicit recognition of fundamental principles of law, and the existence of a constitutional court. Each of these gives a role to judges in the creation of the constitutional order.

Spain has had a number of written constitutions since 1812 (the Constitution of Cadiz). The Constitutions of 1836, 1869, 1931 and 1978 were made at turning points in the development of Spanish government, typically at points of radical change from authoritarian to democratic government. Spanish constitutions have concentrated principally on institutions of government, rather than fundamental values. Fundamental principles have not been confined to statements in the Constitutions, but have been enunciated in other major legal texts, e.g. the Civil Code of 1889, the Law on Criminal Procedure (*Ley de Enjuicamiento Criminal*) of 1882, and the Law on Judicial Review of the Administration (*Ley de la*

[153] See the Barcelona jury decision on p. 62 of the Report.

Jurisdicción Contencios y Administrativa) of 1957.[154] The 1978 Constitution contains principles that are superior to the laws voted by the Cortes. This patchwork of sources has led lawyers, as in France, to talk of the 'bloque de constitucionalidad' to embrace both the norms set out in the Constitution and those set out in other documents.[155] On the whole, the 'bloque' has been used mainly to identify norms contained in documents of constitutional value, but not in the 1978 Constitution. These include norms limiting the state or the Autonomous Communities, as contained in the different Statutes of Autonomy that have been enacted since 1978, and parliamentary standing orders, which regulate the enactment of legislation.[156] If enacted texts provide the framework, then the role of the judge lies in interpretation. Unlike in France, the Spanish judge does not have the role of constructing constitutional values through ideas such as 'fundamental principles of law'.

The Constitutional Court, the *Tribunal Constitucional* (TC), is the novelty of the 1978 Constitution. The Constitution of the Second Republic created the Tribunal de Garantias Constitucionales which began work in 1933,[157] but it did not operate for more than a few years. The real models for the TC were the Italian Constitutional Court of 1947 and the German Constitutional Court of 1949. Spain has followed the 'European model' of concentrated constitutional adjudication. In this, there is a distinct court to deal with constitutional matters. Unlike in the United States, that court does not also act as the supreme court in civil, criminal or administrative law matters. But, unlike the Kelsenian model and German and Italian models, the Tribunal Constitucional is not hierarchically integrated with other courts. It is not part of the 'poder judicial'.[158] It stands apart as the guardian of the Constitution. It does not have the monopoly of applying the Constitution, since ordinary courts can also base decisions on it, including annulling subordinate legislation. It only has a monopoly in relation to declaring laws unconstitutional.[159]

[154] Under Franco, there was never an attempt to produce a constitution, but a series of fundamental laws was passed, covering rules both on institutions (e.g. the Law on succession to the Head of State of 1947) and on fundamental values (e.g. the Law on the fundamental principles of the National Movement of 1958): see F. R. Llorente, *La Forma del Poder* (Madrid 1993), 5–6.

[155] Ibid., 99ff, citing STC 10/1982 as the first case to make use of this term.

[156] Ibid., 103–5. [157] *Ley* 14 June 1933.

[158] See E. García de Enterría, *La Constitución como norma y el Tribunal Constitucional* (Madrid 1985), 60–1; Llorente, *La Forma del Poder*, above n. 154, 475–7.

[159] García de Enterría, *La Constitución*, above n. 158, 64–6.

The Constitution of 1978 was based on a broad political consensus between right- and left-wing parties in the period 1976 to 1978. There was a will to make a new start, but not to be too radical for fear of upsetting the army. As Magone identifies,[160] there are a number of phases in building a new constitution. In the transition phase, there needs to be a will to remake a constitutional structure and to negotiate about it. After this come a preparatory and a decision phase. In Spain, these were first managed by the political parties, but with reinforcement from the public by way of referenda in 1976 (on the framework for developing a new constitution) and in 1978 (on the final text). The constitutional settlement of 1978 represents an attempt to subject public authority to the rule of law in the sense of subordination to law. The framework gives rise to rulings of the TC on two broad categories of issue: the separation of powers and the protection of fundamental rights, as well as on the potential compatibility of treaties with the Constitution. The TC has had a major role in the final phase of constitution-building, consolidation. The Tribunal has played an important part in embedding constitutional principles into the routines of the new systems of government and of institutionalisation. Magone argues that in this period, 'A functioning political–systemic culture will only be possible when there is a continuous and consistent intention by the state actors to structure the political field after a generally accepted political design.'[161] A constitutional court cannot make up for a lack of such commitment, but it can reinforce and consolidate the common agreement. It is predominantly in consolidating governmental institutions that the TC has been able to support the basic political will to make the Constitution work. Its role has been to help institutions evolve, once the immediate political consensus on constitution-making dissolved into the ordinary political antagonism which characterises normal political debate.

Given that the decisions of the TC are authoritative interpretations of the Constitution, it is inevitable that they become sources of law in at least a practical sense.[162]

Separation of powers

The TC examines the constitutionality of legislation passed by the Cortes at the instance of a number of public bodies. These actions are divided

[160] See J. M. Magone, *The Changing Architecture of Iberian Politics (1974–1992)* (Leviston, New York 1996), 299–302.

[161] Ibid., 302.

[162] Llorente, *La Forma del Poder*, above n. 154, 482.

into (a) actions for constitutional review (*recurso de inconstitucionalidad*), (b) questions of constitutionality referred by the courts (*cuestión de inconstitucionalidad*), (c) conflicts of competence (*conflictos de competencia*) raised by the Autonomous Communities, and (d) conflicts between constitutional organs. The last two can also be raised against legislation or decisions of the Autonomous Communities by the state (the Prime Minister). By becoming involved in such conflicts between political institutions, the judges have a delicate role in establishing the framework of the constitutional order. The Tribunal has a large number of applications (7,878 in 2003),[163] but as will be seen, most of these are amparos. Among the applications only thirty-six were *recursos*, ninety-five *cuestiones* and twenty-five fell into categories (c) and (d).

Imposing limitations on the legislature has its justification in the notion of the rule of law. Its importance is seen in the structure of both abstract constitutional review (the *recurso*) and concrete constitutional review (the *cuestiones*). As Espín puts it:

> the application (*recurso*) and the reference (the *cuestión*) on constitutionality have as their object to ensure the primacy of the Constitution in the system of sources, opening the possibility of submitting to constitutional control provisions which rank immediately below the Constitution, which are, in their turn, the framework for controlling subordinate norms, and which constitute the scope of action both of public authorities and of citizens.[164]

These issues are direct questions about the compatibility of specific legislative norms (including those having the same force as a *ley*) with the Constitution. Naturally, in interpreting these often very general norms, the TC is shaping the scope for the exercise of political power. The number of cases in these areas is small, but significant. In 2003, the Prime Minister raised thirteen *recursos* against the legislation of Autonomous Communities, and they raised eighteen against national legislation, with only five references being made by Members of the Parliament (two against national legislation and three against that of an Autonomous Community).[165] Ten *autos* suspended legislation pending a decision of the TC.

Conflicts between organs of the state, or between the state and the Autonomous Communities, represent an important further and often

[163] See *Memoria 2003 del Tribunal Constitucional* (Madrid 2004), annex III. For the amparos see below p. 221.

[164] E. Espín, 'Los recursos constitutcionales' in Trujillo et al. *La experiencia Constitucional*, above n. 85, 459 at 463.

[165] *Memoria 2003 del Tribunal Constitucional*, above n. 163, table 7.

more politically charged aspect of constitutionality. It was in this area that the TC handed down its most important decision. The national government passed a law in 1981 setting out a uniform framework for the devolution of power to regional governments. This was challenged by the Basques and Catalans, who argued that there should be different arrangements to reflect the special position of different regions, especially their own, and that they could be given more power than some other regions. The Tribunal held that equality before the law did not require uniformity of treatment and that the law had failed to respect the requirement that different situations should be treated differently.[166] The result was that individual autonomy agreements were negotiated by each region, leading to distinct Statutes of Autonomy. In this way, by interpreting a very general constitutional value, the court facilitated a more ambitious (and ultimately more stable) form of political devolution. But this method of institutionalising the basic constitutional structure has generated a whole host of problems of its own. As Stone Sweet notes, there is insufficient clarity in the constitutional rules governing Spanish devolution of power. In consequence, 'the Tribunal has become a kind of permanently constituted forum for the clarification and revision of the constitutional rules governing Spanish federalism'.[167]

In 2003, there were twenty-five conflicts of competence – twenty-one against the state and one by the state against the Autonomous Communities, with only two conflicts between two Autonomous Communities.[168] Law is used as a mechanism to defend the political autonomy of the regional communities. It is noticeable that, in the period 1980–8, 83.19 per cent of conflict cases were brought by three regions with a strong nationalist spirit – the Basque Country, Catalonia and Galicia.[169] Conflicts between the state and Autonomous Communities have reflected concerns about both protectionism and nationalism, and such issues often divide the judges. A classic area of conflict is language. When Catalonia made it obligatory for school pupils to learn Catalan, this was challenged by the father of a Castilian-speaking child. The Tribunal

[166] See J. Gibbons, *Spanish Politics Today* (Manchester 1999), 20–1.

[167] A. Stone Sweet, *Governing with Judges* (Oxford 2000) (hereafter 'Stone Sweet'), 107.

[168] *Memoria 2003 del Tribunal Constitucional*, above n. 163, table 7. More generally J. García Roca, 'El Tribunal Constitucional como tribunal de conflictos. Los conflictos constitucionales' in Trujillo et al., *La experiencia constitucional*, above n. 85, 489 at 515–16.

[169] García Roca, 'El Tribunal Constitucional', 492.

Supremo decided that the requirement was unconstitutional because art. 3 of the Constitution obliges every Spaniard to know Castilian, art. 27 proclaims the right to free education, and art. 149.1.30 confers on the national government the exclusive power to award diplomas. By contrast, the TC declared in favour of Catalonia based on art. 148.1.18, the power to promote instruction in the language of the Autonomous Community. A balance had to be struck between the various constitutional rights, and this task was for the Catalonian government, subject only to limited constitutional review.[170] More commonly, the conflict is between governments. For example, in STC 147/1996 the Catalan government complained about the state exercising powers on consumer protection to insist on labelling in Castilian. This was held not to preclude additional exercise of competence in consumer protection by the Catalan government.[171] Complaints between the different organs of state are infrequent.[172] In 1999, a new procedure was introduced, the *conflicto en garantía de la autonomía local*, which enables local authorities to complain about the interference by the state or by an Autonomous Community in the freedoms of local authorities, and this led to two cases in 2003. García Roca describes the role of the TC as a 'pacifying function' in sorting out the powers of local bodies.[173] This function depends on the TC's reputation among politicians for impartiality, even where they disagree with its decisions.

These sets of disputes involve the TC in political issues. In the first place, those empowered to bring a *recurso* or to raise a *conflicto* are politicians or political institutions for the most part. Article 162(1) CE restricts the *recurso* to fifty deputies, fifty senators, the President of the Government, the Defensor del Pueblo, and the government or the legislative assemblies of the Autonomous Communities. Apart from the Defensor del Pueblo, the rest are active politicians. The time-limit for

[170] See Stone Sweet, 107–9.

[171] See generally *La sentencia en los conflictos constitucionales de competencia. Actas de las III Jornadas de la Asociación de Letrados del Tribunal Constitucional* (Madrid 1998), part II.

[172] See García Roca, 'El Tribunal Constitucional', above n 168, 497, citing as one of the cases the 1985 conflict between the Consejo General del Poder Judicial and the Chambers over who should have the right to nominate members to the Consejo. Reform introduced by the *ley orgánica* 1/2000 of 7 January 2000 encouraged settlement of disputes by imposing a six-month delay in the proceedings where two administrations do not have a prior agreement on procedures for dealing with conflicts.

[173] Ibid., 517.

bringing the *recurso* is three months from the date of publication of the legislation, and so it has to be commenced while political passions are still high. This is a contrast with the *cuestiones* which are referred by courts in the course of ordinary litigation, and which may have commenced many years after the enactment of the legislation in question. The *conflicto* will have to be brought within two months of the decision of the state or of the Autonomous Community (or one month after an unsuccessful request to the state to change its decision). As a result, the challenge is part of a live political debate,[174] especially since the challenge is restricted to the governments of the state or the Autonomous Communities. The *conflictos de atribuciones* between the organs of central government (the government, the legislative chambers and the Consejo General del Poder Judicial) will also be political in that there will usually be an attempt to restrict the policies of the Government or the ruling parties in the Cortes. It is thus impossible to avoid a degree of politicisation of the TC, even if the court does not enter into questions about the political desirability of decisions.[175] Its success has been to make controversial decisions, but to avoid becoming considered partisan.

Barreiro[176] argues that constitutional courts can often help make issues manageable that are, for some political actors, non-negotiable. Her example is abortion in Spain. The Socialists had this issue in their manifesto in 1982 and passed legislation to allow abortions in limited circumstances. The TC took sixteen months to come to a decision. It struck down the first version of the legislation on the ground that the limitations were not explicit enough to protect the foetus. This forced the majority party to be more explicit in its limitations and the opposition to be more constructive when the legislation returned to the Cortes. As Barreiro points out,[177] the approach of the TC allowed the conservative opposition to alter its position when the law returned for debate in the Cortes and to use the court's decision permitting some form of abortion as a new point of reference, rather than its previous view of outright opposition. Similarly, the Government could justify the limitations on abortions to its supporters. She

[174] Merino-Blanco, 103–4.

[175] See F. Fernández Segado, 'La estructura orgánica del Tribunal Constitucional' in Trujillo et al., *La experiencia constitucional*, above n. 85, 429 at 431–2.

[176] B. Barreiro, 'Judicial Review and Political Empowerment: Abortion in Spain' (1998) 21(4) *West European Politics* 147.

[177] Ibid.; Stone Sweet, 68–70.

concludes that the rational argument adopted by the court to justify its decision may provide a more stable outcome than a decision by a legislature.[178]

The importance of decisions under these different headings is reflected in the procedure adopted. The members of the TC spend three days a week on work in the Pleno to deal with this category of work, even though it constitutes 2 per cent of the caseload. Equally, there is a significant effort made to resolve the separation of powers issues within a year. The timetable responds to the political timescales in which legislatures need to act. The result is that everything else waits. Even *cuestiones* may have to wait for a number of years. The workload is managed by making decisions at three levels. Full judgments (*sentencias*) are few (230 in 2003), but of these most annul in whole or in part laws or administrative and judicial decisions (74 per cent in 2003). Less reasoned decisions (*autos*) will produce positive outcomes in fewer cases (33 per cent of 429 decisions in 2003) and most are resolved rapidly by orders (*providencias*: 6,600 in 2003, of which 89 per cent led to a rejection of the claim).

Protecting fundamental freedoms: the *amparo*

Borrowed from Germany, the *recurso de amparo* is a distinctive feature of the Spanish constitutional system. It is designed to provide a final resort for the protection of fundamental liberties infringed by any organ of government. But, in practice, it has become much more like a fourth level of hearing within the court system. The ambition of the amparo was set out in the early decision of the TC, STC 1/1981 of 26 January 1981, in which it said that: 'The essential objective of amparo review is the protection, by a constitutional body, of rights and liberties . . . when the ordinary means of protection have turned out unsatisfactory.' This ambition is primarily to be the objective guardian of the Constitution, to judge the way in which the courts (and, in theory, other public bodies) exercise their power, rather than to decide individual cases. Its function is essentially pedagogic.[179] But, given the specific cases which trigger its intervention, the court is inevitably deciding individual cases, not least because it has to respond to individual claims of breach of the Constitution. It has limited scope for restating the law, and, to this extent, it has been

[178] Barreiro, 'Judicial Review', above n. 176, 157.

[179] See J. A. Xiol Rios, in *La sentencia de amparo constitucional. Actas de la I Jornadas de la Asociación de Letrados del Tribunal Constitucional* (Madrid 1996), 110.

characterised as an institution engaged in quashing decisions by making rulings on law (*cassacion*), rather than a body concerned with the pure application of the Constitution.[180]

In 2003, 98 per cent of all cases filed with the TC were, recurso de amparo, amounting to some 7,721 cases. Of these, 81.5 per cent were rejected as inadmissible. The Tribunal Constitucional meets in *secciones* of three to deal with such cases. But with only twelve members and one day a week assigned for this work, the rate of progress is slow. Even allowing for the work done by the letrados who work as assistants to the Tribunal and who prepare the case for consideration by the *secciones*, the speed of decision-making has to be high. All but thirty-two applications in 2003 concerned decisions of the ordinary courts, including 2,461 against the Tribunal Supremo. Over 98 per cent of the amparos were brought by individuals, with none brought by the Ministero Fiscal or the Defensor del Pueblo. The TC is typically being asked to overturn the decisions of an ordinary court.

In the field of amparo, the TC is not really the champion of the people against abuses of fundamental rights by public authorities. Rather it has come to occupy a kind of review role in relation to the ordinary courts. Only 140 judicial decisions were annulled in 2003, a success rate of 1.8 per cent. Whereas through *cuestiones* (ninety-five in 2003) the ordinary courts choose to bring the TC into their legal process, the amparo brings them in at the behest of litigants. The rigour of the inadmición process limits the extent to which there is real interference with the courts and discourages further litigation.

All the same, there is a sense in which constitutional law, interpreted by the TC, has served to reshape private law. Stone Sweet gives the example of privacy, where the TC has given a greater priority to freedom of speech compared with the more traditional views of the ordinary judges who favour the protection of honour and reputation.[181] Despite its limited practical importance, some important principles are laid down through the amparo procedure. For example, in STC 49/1999, a review was granted of a criminal conviction based on evidence obtained through telephone tapping in which appropriate safeguards had not been respected.[182] The case followed the decision of the European Court

[180] See I. Díez-Picazo Giménez, in ibid., 37.

[181] Stone Sweet, 119–20.

[182] *Memoria 2003 del Tribunal Constitucional*, above n. 163, 62–3.

of Human Rights in the *Valenzuela* decision.[183] The case concerned telephone calls in 1985 and 1986 that were judicially monitored. The admission of this evidence was not seen as prejudicing the presumption of innocence by the Tribunal Supremo on 19 March 1994, since other evidence had also justified the decision, and a similar view was taken by the TC on 16 November 1994 in rejecting an amparo. On the basis of judicial decisions of the Tribunal Supremo and the TC concerning the legislative reform of the topic in 1988, the European Court of Human Rights was able to argue that the grounds of judicial authorisation of telephone tapping had not been set out with sufficient precision in the law when the telephone tapping in this case occurred. The TC in the 1999 case was able to develop the requirements of legal protection further, especially on the reasons which must be given. The case illustrates the way that the European Convention and European Union law have reinforced the progress towards a rights culture in Spain.[184]

In a more political case (STC 136/1999), the amparo was allowed of members of the extreme Basque separatist party, Herri Batasuna, who had been convicted of collaboration with an armed group (ETA), because of their political propaganda. The TC held that the offence in the Criminal Code (dating from 1973, but amended in 1989) was disproportionate. It laid down a minimum sentence of six years and one day for actions of a legal political party in the course of an electoral campaign.[185] This is an unusual case of an amparo with political implications. But both cases discussed demonstrate the way in which the TC is called upon to update the law. In the telephone tapping case, the reform of 1988 had been criticised as providing inadequate guarantees by the Tribunal Supremo in 1991 and 1992,[186] but no further legislation had resulted. The political context of the Basque Country had changed since 1989, but the legislature had not modified the legislation on political parties linked to terrorist groups.

183 *Valenzuela Contreras v. Spain* (1999) 28 EHRR 483. No damages were awarded in that case as the breach of art. 8 of the Convention did not have a causal link with any injury claimed.

184 P. Pérez Tremps, 'Derecho Constitucional y Derecho Comunitario' in Trujillo et al., *La experiencia constitucional*, above n. 85, 614–17.

185 *Memoria 2003 del Tribunal Constitucional*, above n. 163, 63–6. On the role of proportionality as a ground for review of legislation, see S. Huerta Tocildo, 'Principio de legalidad y normas sancionadoras' in *El principio de legalidad. Actas de la V Jornadas de la Asociación de Letrados del Tribunal Constitucional* (Madrid 2000), 11 at 58ff and 283.

186 *Valenzuela*, above n. 183, paras. 33 and 34.

Composition of the court

Three characteristics are identified as necessary for the constitutional judge: an effort to be open to critical reason, based on the Constitution, a capacity to decide between divergent arguments, and an aptitude for responsible weighing of the consequences of decisions.[187] Given the context of the immediate post-Franco situation in which many of the judiciary were considered to be too close to the old regime, it is not surprising that the guardianship of the democratic Constitution was not entrusted to a body made up, as in Germany and Italy, of members of the judiciary. The Tribunal is made up of twelve members who are appointed for a non-renewable term of nine years. Appointments are made on a three-year rotation. Four are appointed by the Senate, four by the Congress, two by the Government and two by the Consejo General del Poder Judicial. In 2004, two of the members, including the President, were women.

The majority of the members have been university professors. The Consejo General del Poder Judicial will always appoint judges, and the chambers of the Cortes will sometimes do so. Links with the judiciary are informal and semi-formal. There are no formal meetings between the supreme courts or with the courts of the various Autonomous Communities. Protocol visits will give an opportunity to meet and talk, and there may be joint seminars arranged between judges of different courts. Equally, the TC does not have formal links with the Government's legal adviser, the Consejo de Estado, and it does not receive its opinions, unless they have been published. (But under the protection of local competences introduced by LO 1/2000, the opinion of the Consejo del Estado has to be sought before the *recurso* is introduced and this opinion is included in the papers filed for the case.) All the same, informal links exist, not least because two former presidents of the TC have become members of the Consejo de Estado, after finishing in the court.

We thus have a picture of an institutionally distinct organ of government, located in a part of Madrid away from the centre of the judiciary, and not directly linked to courts or to the Government's legal adviser. This initial will to be separate has given way to informal links, which continue to respect the distinctiveness of the institutions, but recognise

[187] Alvaro Rodriguez Berijo, President of the TC, in Xiol Rios in *La sentencia*, above n. 179, 9.

the practical importance of mutual understanding and of co-operation. All the same, both the TC and the Tribunal Supremo have their own pride and sense of status. In a system where there is no formal hierarchical subordination between the courts, there is a need to respect the proper competence of each.

The public image of judges

The judicial role in society

The increase in the involvement of Spaniards with the legal system has increased concern about the system. The number expressing 'no opinion' in surveys on public attitudes to the administration of justice has declined markedly over twenty-five years. This has not led to any increase in favourable attitudes.

Hernandez Martín argues that the supremacy of the judge in Spain results from a number of features.[188] First, the enactment of a constitution and the concentration on the individual as citizen focus attention on the liberal citizen's interest in controlling public power, and not just on private law or criminal law. Secondly, the consensus among all parties and social groups that judges should be impartial and irremovable leads to reduced pressure on them. Thirdly, the legal order has changed through the proliferation of norms over the period. Change is introduced through powers conferred by law, rather than by autonomous actions of the executive. As a result, there is much more scope for judicial interpretation and for litigation. The concentration of power in political parties and the executive increases the role of judges as a counter-weight. In the view of Hernandez Martín, the judges offer the only available protection against statute law passed by the Cortes at the behest of a strong political power.[189] One might add that, in a situation of devolved government, supporters of the Basque and other regions have more confidence in the courts than in other state organs. As has been discussed, constitutional adjudication provides a specifically controversial role for some judges.

The Defensor del Pueblo (ombudsman) offers alternative avenues of complaint. In 2004, he received 28,990 complaints.[190] In many individual cases, complaints were made against a whole range of ministries,

[188] Martín, *Independencia del Juez*, above n. 3, 55ff.
[189] Ibid., 69.
[190] See Defensor del Pueblo, *Informe annual 2004* (Madrid 2005), 27.

and this provided a significant alternative to adjudication. Some 2,394 complaints (8.25 per cent) concerned the administration of justice, but there were only seventy-four decisions requiring corrective action found in that year.[191] Nearly 57 per cent of the individual complaints and 70 per cent of the collective complaints were held to be inadmissible. With 2,422 instances in 2004 of corrective action taken or criticism of the administration, the Defensor offers a significant route for solving complaints generally, even though his role is rather limited in relation to the administration of justice.

Public reputation

The seventh Barometro survey of September 2000 conducted for the Consejo General del Poder Judicial found that only 19 per cent thought the legal system was performing well, while 46 per cent thought it was performing badly.[192] In comparison with other public institutions, the courts are the only institution to have lost standing in public opinion. In surveys from 1984 to 2000, the Cortes rose from 3.0 to 3.6 out of 5 in public esteem, while the courts fell from 3.0 to 2.7.[193]

When one examines opinion about the judges, it is necessary to identify a number of attributes which the public expect. *Impartiality* can be understood in a number of ways. It can mean simply that they have no personal interest in the outcome of a case, but often means that they treat different categories of people equally well. In relation to this second sense, the Spanish judiciary, like many Latin judiciaries, is considered to be biased. Only 46 per cent of the population considered them to be impartial. Compared with the US, there were marked differences in how the Spanish public thought that lower classes, minorities and women would be treated in the legal system. In Spain, 63 per cent thought lower classes would be treated worse, compared with only 19 per cent in the US. A similar percentage of Spaniards (61 per cent) thought that minorities would be treated differently, compared with 47 per cent in the US. Both men and women expected that the system would treat women less favourably (38 per cent compared with 19 per cent in the US).[194]

Independence from the government was meant to be a major feature of the post-Franco reforms. Public opinion has become more cynical in recent years: 60 per cent of the population believe that pressures from the government succeed at least some of the time, 57 per cent believe

[191] Ibid., 28 and 36. [192] Toharia, 81. [193] Ibid., 88–9. [194] Ibid., 11–15.

the same of powerful socio-economic interests and 52 per cent of the media.[195] Interestingly, the percentage of the population who think that the Government tries to influence justice rose from 14 per cent in 1985 to 34 per cent in 2000, and the percentage thinking that it never happened declined from 28 per cent to 18 per cent.[196] Although Toharia points out that people associate the courts with government, this helps to explain the different distribution over time between voters of particular parties, but it does not fully account for the decline in confidence in the judiciary, despite the many safeguards which the 1978 Constitution introduced. All the same, the judges themselves scored 8.5 out of 10 for independence from politics and 8.4 out of 10 for independence from powerful elements in society. They thus score higher than the system of justice, principally because people consider that improper pressure is more likely to be placed on court officials and prosecutors.

Freedom from corruption ought to be a major attribute, but a majority of the population think that there is some corruption. In the survey, 48 per cent thought it was plausible that they could escape criminal conviction by some form of bribe. But among all those connected with justice, the judges were seen as least likely to be corrupt, with 57 per cent of the population thinking that they could not be corrupted at all.[197] Only 49 per cent of Spaniards thought that judges were honest, a percentage similar to France but lower than in common-law countries. In 1975, honesty was placed as one of the major requirements of the system.[198]

The major cause of low confidence in the legal system is delay. Of those surveyed in the 2000 Barometro, 86 per cent identified delay as a major problem and 94 per cent thought it needed to be addressed urgently.[199] The concern of people has moved from legitimacy to the efficiency of the legal system. In this area, the lawyers most blame the Ministry of Justice for providing inadequate resources (scoring between 6.7 and 7.6 out of 10 as blameworthy), compared with the Tribunal Supremo (between 5.95 and 6.4) and the judges (between 5.7 and 6.26). On the whole, the judges and the Tribunal Supremo are most blamed for slowness in civil cases and least in criminal cases.[200]

[195] Ibid., 102. [196] Ibid., 103. [197] Ibid., 119. [198] Elites, 2.

[199] Toharia, 139–40.

[200] J. J. García de la Cruz, *Encuesta a usarios de la administración de justicia* (CGPJ, December 2001), 80, table 63.

Some 46 per cent of Spaniards thought that judges are out of touch, but this is much lower than in the UK (82 per cent).[201] In part this view is reinforced by the perception that the language of justice and its way of doing things is excessively complicated (identified by 84 per cent of respondents).[202] A study of judicial opinions also suggests that, in a number of areas, their views are unrepresentative of the population as a whole. For example, and no doubt relying on their own experience, 76.8 per cent of judges believed outcomes in life depended on intelligence and hard work, whereas only 40 per cent of the population believed this and 31 per cent attributed success to inheritance. Judges also believed more strongly that the state should protect private initiative (62.8 per cent compared with 31 per cent).[203] These are but illustrations of ways in which judges may not be in step with the rest of the community. A study of users of the justice service in 2001 identified a decline relative to 1997 in the belief among litigants that the court or judge understood the reality of the problem that was affecting them. In 2001, 52 per cent of those expressing an opinion felt judges did not understand, compared with 42 per cent taking this view in 1997.[204] On closer inspection, this affects particularly the perception of first instance judges, rather than of administrative law judges. This assessment of the lower civil and criminal judges is mirrored in the low rating they received in the same study from lawyers. They gave the Juzgados de primera instancia 4.85 out of 10 and the Juzgados de Instrucción 4.88, compared with a score of 6.28 for the administrative courts.[205] There is a sense that the younger generalist judges do not command the same respect from litigants and lawyers as specialist or collegial (and thus higher) courts.

Judges and media

Public opinion is increasingly influenced not only by experience of the legal system, but also by the media. Judicial relations with the media are rather haphazard. The Tribunal Supremo has a press office, whose head was himself a journalist. When journalists need further explanation of decisions, he or the Secretary-General will provide a briefing. The official decision will be released by the Gabinete Tecnico of the court. The President may also brief journalists on the work of the court. These

[201] Ibid., 105.

[202] Ibid., 135. [203] Elites, 52–3.

[204] *Encuesta*, above n. 200, 34 and table 15.

[205] Ibid., 66 and table 42. The abogados rate the court clerks (secretaries) much higher: see table 57.

formal channels are supplemented by informal contacts between individual journalists and members of the court known to them.

It is not unknown for judges to appear in the media. Some judges have their favoured channels or journalists and consider that the publicity will advance their career. Judges are meant to comment on the law in general, rather than on individual cases. Certainly, any breach of the secrecy of deliberations will give rise to disciplinary sanctions, provided that the sources of a leak are traced. The profile of individual judges is reinforced by the availability of individual opinions. All the same, the media interest will mainly be focused on high-profile criminal cases, usually with reports of the actions of the juez de instrucción or the fiscal. But it probably takes a person with a political career to have a very high profile, as is seen by the attention focused on Baltazar Garzón.[206]

The Tribunal Constitucional and the Consejo General del Poder Judicial also have their own press offices. In addition, there will be a spokesperson for the institution to deal with journalists. The pattern of individual judges having their own press links and appearing to talk on television is found also in these institutions. All the same, the general impression is that most judges are not willing to talk to the press, both to preserve the image of impartiality and neutrality, as well as to engage in a measure of self-restraint to preserve the standing of justice.

Press coverage of cases will tend to emphasise some judges, such as Garzón, who have courted the media.[207] As has been noted, the publicity given to prosecution enhances the public perception of the judicial role.

Political corruption

The fight against political corruption became important in most Latin countries in the 1980s. The inspiration came from the Italian prosecutors, but there were also issues in Spain and France. The Spanish judiciary was seen as under-resourced and subject to political manipulation. There was also criticism of the Socialists for political appointments, especially as they sought to redress the traditional conservatism of the judiciary. A series of abuses of power were identified, ranging

[206] See, for example, the authorised biography by P. Urbano, *Garzón: El hombre que veía amanecer* (3rd edn, Barcelona 2002).

[207] E.g. *El País*, 11 May 2001: 'Garzón ilegaliza la organización Haika por considerarla "apéndice" y "cantera" de ETA.'

from the Prime Minister's brother using official Socialist party premises for private business meetings, illegal party funding through invoices for fictitious services rendered (the Filesa affair) and fraud by the Governor of the Bank of Spain.[208] The investigations of the culture of sleaze (*cultura del pelotazo*) continued after the Socialists lost power, and were led by investigating judges such as Baltazar Garzón, a former Socialist junior minister. The high profile which he and other judges gained emphasised the importance of the rule of law, but also made the judiciary look more political.[209] This 'hyperactivity' of some judges attracted the media. A good example is the investigation of the Minister of Foreign Affairs, Josep Piqué, for his involvement in the Ecros financial scandal.[210]A similar attention was drawn to the attempt to extradite General Pinochet to Spain, again by Judge Garzón.[211]

All the same, it is often the media themselves who have been the principal investigators of government scandals.[212] Indeed, this issue of political corruption needs to be set in a longer-term perspective. Spain originally followed the European pattern of impeaching ministers before Parliament. But the 1876 Constitution transferred the trial of ministers to the Tribunal Supremo, a jurisdiction which is still found in the 1978 Constitution.[213] Scandals in 1969, at the end of the Franco era, concerned ministers from Opus Dei. These were brought to light in the press and never came to trial due to an amnesty granted by Franco. But the weakness of non-judicial means has reinforced the importance of the judicial means under the democratic government and has strengthened the hand of fiscales and investigating judges to bring ministers to trial.[214]

[208] Heywood, *Government*, above n. 22, 117–19; also V. Pujas and M. Rhodes, 'Party Finance and Political Scandal in Italy, Spain and France' (1999) 22 *West European Politics* 41 at 51–2, 57–8; Sinova and Tusell, *La crisis*, above n. 18, 128–30.

[209] Newton, *Institutions*, above n. 78, 303ff; Gibbons, *Spanish Politics*, above n. 166, 81–3. All the same, Heywood suggests that, 'For all the criticisms to which it has been subjected, Spain's judiciary may prove one of the only effective means by which popular trust in the "state of law" can be restored and maintained' (*Government*, above n. 22, 120).

[210] See *El País*, 22 June 2001, 2 and 6 July 2001.

[211] See Gibbons, *Spanish Politics*, above n. 166, 81.

[212] See Pujas and Rhodes, 'Party Finance', above n. 208, 57–8.

[213] See generally, L. M. Díez-Picazo, *La criminalidad de los gobernantes* (Barcelona 1996), ch. 9.

[214] See debates between the financial prosecutors and those of the Tribunal Supremo noted in *El País*, 6 July 2001: 'El jefe de la inspección fiscal también censura a Cardenal por el "caso Piqué".'

Rising judicial power?

An important stimulus to judicial power has been Europe. The power of the ordinary courts to apply European law rather than national law has given them a new authority and has set them, in some sense, as an antidote to the democratic political system.[215]

The authority coming from Europe and from criminal investigations of corruption by politicians has to be set against the experience of ordinary citizens of the judicial system. The slowness of justice contrasts with the increasing speed of transactions in ordinary life. People experience a dissonance between what López Aguilar labels the 'tempos judiciales' and the 'tempos informativos', the conflict between time as a guarantee of due process and the demand for instant satisfaction.[216] As Newton remarks, 'democracy may have cleansed the institutions of justice but in large measure has so far failed to make them more efficient'.[217] As a result, a public opinion survey of November 1995 found that the Spanish people held the judiciary in lowest esteem among public institutions, even behind the armed forces and the Church.[218] The *Libro Blanco* identifies an increasing sense that justice is performing badly – in 1987 only 28 per cent of the population had this view, but by 1995 this had risen to 46 per cent and to 51 per cent in 1997. The Tribunal Supremo had a backlog of nineteen months. The *Libro Blanco* itself remarks that 'the decisions of the courts are so slow that it is better to avoid litigation'.[219]

The image of the judiciary also suffers as a result of the new public inquisitorial process conducted by the media. The media will hound individuals and it may be difficult for them to have their views heard. Thus the use made by the judiciary of the media may return to haunt it later. On the other hand, the investigation of terrorists and their accomplices, or the pursuit of politicians, gains them popularity.

Conclusion: what shapes Spanish judicial culture?

In one sense, the judges have made a good transition from Franco to modern democracy. They have managed to cope with the new regime without a purge and to gain reasonable confidence of the public in their

[215] López Aguilar, 'Poder Judicial', above n. 85, 416.
[216] Ibid., 417–18. [217] Newton, *Institutions*, above n. 78, 303. [218] Ibid.
[219] *Libro Blanco*, 3.

competence. New judicial tasks, such as constitutional review and the prosecution of corruption, have been carried out without much fuss and certainly without great purges. This has been managed in part by the expansion of many parts of Spanish society. Political scientists suggest that economic and social change was affecting Spain profoundly in the 1960s, before the end of Franco's regime.[220] Spain's transition was consensual, rather than conflictual in character, based on many multi-party agreements. Lawyers played a substantial role in all governments.[221] The growth of judicial numbers and political appointments from outside the judiciary to the Tribunal Constitucional and the Consejo General del Poder Judicial ensured that institutions were able to change. A large number of new appointments from among younger people also helped to effect a change in mentality. But the forces for change were not only external, but internal. Attitudes of judges also revealed a willingness to work the new system. Already in the 1985 study of judicial elites, 86 per cent of judges supported democracy as the best regime, and 89.2 per cent thought that their colleagues were upholding democracy.[222]

This adaptability, which Spanish judges have had to show over the past two centuries as regimes have come and gone, fits naturally with a more bureaucratic system. It is not surprising that civil servants and lawyers should feature so highly among the ministers and politicians of both Franco and of modern democracy. They are best at establishing routines which will bed down a new political and administrative system, and which is considered necessary for a successful transition. The bureaucratic system has also enabled the judiciary to keep pace with social change, particularly the increasing place of women in the workforce. But the bureaucratic system leads to limited creativity and a significant burden in dealing with the increasing demands from a growing economy and consumer society.

The judiciary has been able to rise to the challenges of constitutionalism, partly through the creation of an independent court drawn substantially from outside the judiciary, but also through a willingness

[220] See J. Tusell and A. Soto (eds.), *Historia de la transición (1975–1986)* (Madrid 1996), ch. 5, which suggests that changes in the economy, in the Church, the universities and the press had all led to delegitimating the Franco regime by the early 1970s; also Magone, *Changing Architecture*, above n. 160, 342ff.

[221] According to Magone, 33.6 per cent of Franco's ministers were drawn from jurists, administrators and civil servants; and 21 per cent of the Cortes of 1982–6 and 1986–9 were lawyers: Magone, *Changing Architecture*, above n. 160, 265 and 423.

[222] Elites, 59.

of judges to take on this role. The European Union and the European Convention have more direct bearing on the Spanish judges. The other challenge has been to defend the governmental system against political corruption, in which some judges have played a prominent part. Equally, many have lost their lives in the fight against ETA terrorism.

As democracy has become embedded, the focus has moved to achieving justice. Despite the judicial involvement in the administration of justice, especially through the Consejo General del Poder Judicial, there are structural features which the judges themselves cannot alter. The map of courts, with the inability to reform the location of courts, wastes personnel which is scarce. The civil service wages are not high compared with the increasing income of the Bar in a commercially developing country. Thus judicial performance and judicial status are not high for reasons that predominantly lie outside judicial control. As a result, there is an apparent contradiction between public opinion on the merits of judges and of the system as a whole, a view that the judges themselves share.[223] The lack of initial selection and training for the profession of abogado gives an educational premium to those who pass the oposiciónes to become a judge, and thus, as in countries such as Sweden and Germany, the judicial selection process provides an indicator of high-quality students. But the increased opportunities and income of the Bars has made the judicial profession less attractive in the longer term.

[223] See above p. 228.

5 The Swedish judiciary

The important feature of the Swedish system is its long continuity. Although there have been significant moments of constitutional and legal change, there is a great deal of institutional continuity and evolution, rather than revolution. Such a climate naturally leads to a pragmatic and piecemeal approach, rather than a major re-ordering, as in France in 1789 and 1958, or Germany in 1949. The interesting feature is the capacity for change that the Swedish system exhibits. In many ways, it is more modern than either the French or German systems. To a great extent, although outwardly the structures of courts and judicial careers have remained very similar, their character has slowly changed very significantly.

The lack of revolution has perhaps strengthened the process of developing indigenous models of the judicial and legal process. There has not been a marked crisis of confidence in the way in which the domestic system operates since 1809, and even then that crisis was predominantly constitutional, rather than affecting the legal system as a whole. A country with a small population, Sweden has traditionally looked outwards for ideas and has assimilated them as it considered appropriate. Though engaged with the outside world, there has been an autonomous pace of development, enabling Sweden to 'cherry-pick' ideas from outside. External influences within Scandinavia have been important, and constitute a constant point of reference, but Sweden has been prepared to develop in its own ways.

Sweden has a distinctive governmental culture of co-operation and a privileging of consensus and compromise, which affects the role that the judiciary is called upon to play. Radical social conflict is not presented to the courts for resolution, since the political process largely succeeds in deflating it. The political and administrative processes enjoy a higher degree of confidence than in many Latin countries,[1] and problems of the corruption of politicians have not been as intense. The judiciary has not felt it necessary to stand apart as the clean-handed scourge of a corrupt political and administrative system. Rather it exercises influence in a more low-key way.

There are signs that these national dynamics are changing. Europeanisation has imposed external models of judicial action, for example in administrative law, requiring a more distinct process of judicial review and a more individualistic conception of the rights of the individual. Debates on judicial independence have intensified, with the prospect that the judiciary may adopt a more confrontational role within governmental institutions. The protection of fundamental rights in the Strasbourg sense brings forward the possibility of constitutional review by the judiciary. Economic liberalisation, through the EU and more global trends, has lessened the capacity of the national government to impose distinctive policies, while opening up the possibility of greater Swedish influence in Europe. More generally, the importance of individualism in a consumer society has heightened the place of individual rights and the decline in the importance of collective processes. Many of these processes lead to an enhanced role for the judge and make the Swedish position more like other European countries. These trends will recur pervasively through the presentation of the Swedish judiciary in terms of its internal culture and its relationships with other legal actors and the wider community.

Internal organisational structures and character

Geographical factors as a context

Sweden is a large and sparsely populated country. Communications in the past were difficult and there was a lot of local diversity. This was reflected, as we shall see, in the role of the lay judges, the *nämnd*, in ensuring that the law kept abreast of local conditions. All the same, since the seventeenth century, there has been a gradual centralisation of the country. Reforms in the 1970s have reduced markedly the number of local courts, so that there is not the same problem of out-of-date court structures as exists in France and Spain. The courts are regional

[1] *Eurobarometer* No. 59 (Brussels 2003), table 1.1c, p. B3 shows a 66 per cent confidence rate in the legal system, compared with 43 per cent in France and Spain and 47 per cent in the United Kingdom.

until the very highest level. Judicial mobility is encouraged in the early stages of a career, such that the different areas of the country can be properly staffed by judges. The use of modern communications, such as telephone- and video-conferencing, has enabled justice to be delivered in a spread-out country with less travelling than used to be the case, creating the possibility of reducing the number of court centres. Thus, although geography marks the activity and career of the judges, in a number of ways, there is perhaps less difference between the justice in different regions compared with some of the Latin countries.

Court structures

Sweden has courts of general jurisdiction covering civil and criminal law (*allamäna rätt*) and special courts dealing with administrative law (*förvaltningsrätt*). Following reforms in the 1970s, each of the two branches of courts operates at three levels. There are regional first instance and appeal courts, with a national supreme court. Although there are distinctive structures of courts, there is not the same radical distinction between public and private law that is found in France, in part because there is a common cadre of judges who service both courts, and who may move between them in the course of a career.

The workload and staffing of courts

The first instance general court is the *tingsrätt*, which deals with criminal, civil and land cases. In 2004, these district courts decided 133,610 cases (including 65,917 general civil cases and 65,070 criminal cases) and had 640 judges and 492 *notarie* (trainees).[2] In civil cases judges will typically sit alone, but in criminal cases they will sit with a nämnd.[3] The *hövrätt* is the regional appeal court. In 2004, it decided 23,294 cases and had 421 judges sitting in collegial courts and, in criminal cases, with a nämnd.[4] The *Högsta Domstol* (HD) is the national supreme court which

[2] The statistics used here are compiled from two annual reports produced by Domstolsverket: *Domstolsstatistik 2004* (Jönköping 2005), tables 1.1, 1.8, 1.12, 2.1, 2.4 and 2.7, and *Årsredovisning 2004* (Jönköping 2005), 91. Domstolsverket also produces a short English-language set of statistics, *Facts about the Swedish Judiciary 2004* (Jönköping 2004).

[3] In 2004, judges sat in a collegial court in the tingsrätt in only 2.1 per cent of civil cases and with a nämnd in 1.4 per cent of cases, but sat with a nämnd in 78.3 per cent of criminal cases: *Domstolsstatistik 2004*, tables 1.6, 1.7.

[4] In 2004, judges sat in the hövrätt with a nämnd in 9.8 per cent of civil cases and in 66.6 per cent of criminal cases: ibid., table 1.10.

dealt with 5,205 cases in 2004 and had fifty judges, of whom eighteen were full members of the court.[5] This is also a collegial court.

The administrative courts are more recent. At first instance, there is the local *länsrätt* which decided 97,889 cases in 2004 and had 237 judges. Most cases are decided on paper, with normally only about 17 per cent decided after an oral hearing. Cases are almost evenly divided between routine matters where there is a single judge and more contentious cases where the judge sits with a nämnd.[6] On appeal, cases are heard by the collegial *Kammarrätt*, which decided 24,067 cases in 2004 and had 214 judges. The national appeal court is the *Regeringsrätt* (RR), which heard 7,940 cases in 2004 and had fifty-six judges of whom eighteen were full members of the court. This is a collegial court.

There are a number of other courts, for example the *hyresnämnder*, dealing with rent cases, and the *arrendennämnder*, dealing with tenancy cases. These deal with substantial numbers of cases (29,945 and 1,284 cases respectively in 2004) and have their own judges, but lie outside the main courts system.

The growth of administrative justice

The creation of these administrative courts has followed a slow process of evolution. The basic principle established in the eighteenth century was that 'decisions, reached after an appropriate procedure – as in the central administrative agencies, the county governments, and the special tribunals – should have legal validity and that the ordinary courts should be prevented from taking up the same matters'.[7] The Swedish tradition had two means for providing redress. First, many matters of social regulation were given to local councils, with administrative appeal to the county governor. From 1909, appeal from the governor lay to the RR.[8] No equivalent systematic control was established over the actions of administrative boards and ministries. Within each of the administrative boards (or activities run by local government) there were procedures for dealing with complaints, sometimes set up as committees or panels. Hierarchical review was thus an integral part of the administration. To this was added in appropriate cases some form of specialist tribunal

5 The rest would be judges on secondment, often working as assistants.

6 In 2004, judges sat in the länsrätt with a nämnd in 54 per cent of cases and on their own in 45.2 per cent of cases : *Domstolsstatistik 2004*, table 2.3.

7 S. Jägerskiöld, 'Administrative Law' in S. Strömholm (ed.), *An Introduction to Swedish Law* (Stockholm 1981), 75.

8 Originally appeal lay to the King-in-Council (*statsråd*). See generally ibid., 85–6.

connected to the relevant board or ministry. Secondly, as is explained later, the existence of the Ombudsman provided an alternative line of redress.

The tradition was thus not of judicial review by courts, but of independent redress within the administrative structures, a tradition not dissimilar to the Netherlands and Britain. Following the Second World War and the signature of the European Convention, questions were raised about the limited role of the Swedish courts. In particular, the question arose about the practice of letting decisions on personal freedoms be taken by administrative authorities without redress in the courts. In 1982, the European Court of Human Rights in Strasbourg[9] held that the very limited scope of judicial review and the reliance on hierarchical review of the merits of cases breached the right under art. 6(1) of the European Convention to a determination of civil rights and obligations by an independent and impartial tribunal. In that case, a landowner complained about long-term planning blight caused by the issue of permits for expropriation which were withdrawn only after many years. A decision was reached by the administration, but this could not be challenged in the courts unless the administration had acted ultra vires. Traditional Swedish views that such administrative regulation was an administrative matter were rejected. Likewise the availability of a remedy on the merits through the *Justitieombudsman* was not sufficient. Similar cases extended the notion of 'civil right' quite far. For example, in *Zander v. Sweden*[10] neighbours complained against the grant of a licence to run a waste tip first to the local council and then to the central administration. Their complaints were rejected, but they brought a successful action in Strasbourg on the ground that the absence of judicial review (at the time) deprived them of their right under art. 6(1).

This systematic external challenge to Swedish conceptions of how to provide redress to those affected by administrative decisions led to a reform of the administrative courts. The structure of tribunals had grown up as a set of exceptions on an *ad hoc* basis to the general principles of hierarchical and ombudsman review. But a more systematic system was established in the 1970s and 1980s. The general administrative courts (länsrätt), established at county level in 1965, were

[9] *Sporrong and Lönnroth v. Sweden* (1982) 5 EHRR 35; also *Pudas v. Sweden* (1988) 10 EHRR 380, para. 31. The latter case concerned the revocation of a licence to run a taxi.

[10] (1993) 18 EHRR 175; see generally A. W. Bradley, 'Administrative Justice: A Developing Human Right?' (1995) 1 EPL 347.

given expanded jurisdiction in the 1970s. The old national fiscal court (Kammarrätt) was expanded in 1971 into a regional set of appeal courts, with expanded jurisdiction. A more systematic attempt to create independent administrative courts was undertaken in 1971 by widening the jurisdiction of the RR and making it independent of ministries, a process completed under the Constitution of 1974. But it was only in 1998 that the right of appeal to administrative courts, as opposed to a hierarchical authority, was introduced, giving the courts competence broadly on both procedure and merits and making the distinction between appeal to the courts and appeal to a hierarchical superior less clear. This is seen as a feature that distinguishes Sweden now from its neighbours and was criticised by the 1999 Democratic Audit,[11] because it retains the close connection between administration and the courts and blurs the distinct functions of each.

Dispute resolution

The courts have traditionally been collegial. This tends to reduce the number of cases that can be handled by the court, even if the court works by way of a *referent*.[12] Courts are now delegating more tasks to a single member in order to speed up decisions. The Government sees a sense of urgency and speed as a mark of efficiency.[13] Apart from ordinary judicial proceedings, the courts have a limited role in dispute resolution. In commercial cases, there is a long tradition of arbitration. The private nature of these proceedings makes it difficult to ascertain the number of cases involved, but it is generally agreed that this is significant.[14] In relation to consumer cases, a state-funded board for consumer complaints – *Allmänna reklamationsnämnden* – was established in 1968. Members are made up from representatives both of business and consumers, with a legally qualified chairperson.[15] It has a written procedure and its decisions are not binding, but are typically complied with. This manages to keep down the number of consumer cases in the ordinary courts to around 15,000 a year, of which about three-quarters are brought by businesses.[16] Unlike a number of other countries in Scandinavia and

[11] See O. Petersson et al., *Report from the Democratic Audit of Sweden 1999. Democracy, the Swedish Way* (Stockholm 1999), 58–68.

[12] A *referent* is a kind of reporting judge charged with preparing a draft decision for consideration by the whole court.

[13] Regeringens skrivelse 1999/2000:106, *Reformeringen av domstolsväsendet – en handlingsplan*, 21.

[14] See M. Bogdan (ed.), *Swedish Law in the New Millennium* (Stockholm 2000), 221 and 510.

[15] See ibid., 206–7. [16] Ibid., 219.

elsewhere, judges have not been given the obligation to conciliate the parties. The existence of other bodies at communal or social level which deal with such matters continues to limit the need for judges to take an active role in this regard.[17]

Governance of the judiciary and of the courts

In keeping with the Swedish tradition of administration through boards and not ministries, the government of courts is divided between *Domstolsverket* (DV) for personnel and equipment and judges as managers in charge of their own operations. The Ministry of Justice retains a major defining role for the system as a whole. The result is a limited form of judicial self-government. The Democratic Audit of 1999 argued that the use of administrative agencies in general has considerable democratic advantages in maintaining a clear link between power and responsibility.[18] The agency allows judges to participate in power over the legal system, but it does not require them to be responsible directly to politicians for the outcome, since only the DV is accountable in that way. On the other hand, there are ways in which the agency can ensure the accountability of judges themselves.

Domstolsverket

DV was established in 1975 as an independent judicial administration. Although fears had been expressed by the Skåne Hovrätt that this would lead to centralised control, it has largely brought independence, in that it is an administration into which judges have an input.

DV is directed by a board (*Domstolsverket styrelsen*) which consists of no more than ten members appointed by the Government, including the chief executive. Its membership represents judges, politicians and the legal professions. In 2005, it had equal numbers of men and women members. Its members included four judges (including a leader of Domareförbundet, the judicial union), two members of the Riksdag and one from local government, a union representative of the administrative personnel, and a representative of Advokatsamfundet (the advokat association). Its chief executive Thomas Rolén, appointed in 2005, is a judge who also worked for some time in an advokat firm and in Stockholm University before joining the Ministry of Justice as an administrator in

[17] See SOU 1994:99, *Domaren i Sverige inför framtiden – utgångspunkter för fortsatt utredningsarbete* (hereafter 'SOU 1994:99'), 52–3.

[18] Petersson et al., *Report from the Democratic Audit*, above n. 11, 80.

1993.[19] He worked as legal secretary to the privatisation commission from 1992 to 1994. He thus epitomises the mix of administrative and judicial roles which leading judges can undertake.

DV is responsible for the overall management of the courts, its staffing levels and equipment. The chief judge of a court has only limited budgetary control. There is an annual round of local meetings to discuss the budget for each court. Apart from recurrent expenditure, there is money for special initiatives. The annual report comments on the improving competences of judges and collaboration between courts in order to enhance efficiency of courts.[20] DV is also concerned to improve the competences of judges and more generally the working conditions of all employees, e.g. in the management of stress.[21] DV is charged by the Ministry of Justice not only to distribute the budget, but also to monitor the efficiency of the courts. It produces statistics on the efficiency of courts that look at the number of cases resolved, the time to judgment in different types of case, and the throughput of different courts (described in some sections of the report as 'productivity').[22] This monitoring, combined with control of the budget, enables DV to encourage improvements in performance that are proposed by the courts themselves. It also takes the initiative to set up working groups to suggest new ways of working more efficiently in the courts. These efforts to change practices inevitably give rise to conflicts with the judges themselves who consider that DV is interfering with judicial independence.[23] In 1999, there was a particularly severe round of budget cuts (over 10 per cent) that the DV had to administer and that obviously clashed with the judiciary's perception of its appropriate role and ways of working.[24]

There are also conflicts concerning the extent to which DV should be engaged in direction of the court system and how far it should focus on the education of judges and court infrastructure. The Government has been keen to consolidate courts and to use new technology methods to provide justice in the locality. Such changes require changes in

[19] Ministry of Justice press release, 25 November 2004.

[20] See *DV, Årsredovisning 2004*, 20–1.

[21] Ibid., 28. The report (p. 107) sets out plans to create individual training development programmes for all chief judges.

[22] See ibid., ch. 2.

[23] See, for example, the article by Judge T. Gregow, 'Domstolsverket lägger sig i vårt arbete', *Brännpunkt, Svenska Dagbladet*, 4 September 2000.

[24] See the debate between the Minister of Justice and representatives of judges in 'Domstolen i framtiden' (1999) 4 *Tidskrift för Sveriges Domareförbund* 13.

working patterns and education for judges.[25] If much of this agenda is not controversial, leading judges are still concerned that DV is being used to direct the administration of justice in ways that conflict with judicial responsibilities and independence. Thus the establishment of a 'criminal law group' to draw up sentencing guidelines had to be withdrawn when the judges union, Sveriges Domarförebund, protested that this was outside the competence of DV. Some judges are concerned that using DV to spearhead change will compromise their professional judgement and they demand that judges remain in charge of the direction which DV is taking.[26]

In more recent years, there have been moves to devolve more administration to the courts themselves, with the resultant need to improve the administrative abilities of judges as managers.[27]

Judges as managers

The traditional role of the presiding judge of a court was leadership in decision-making and in approach to work. He was to guide the development of the law and the way colleagues came to decisions. He would also recruit and train younger judges (notarie and fiskaler). He would lead the court in activities such as producing *remisser* (responses) to committee reports. He was often involved in new developments in the court, but was not responsible for the management of the court, nor for the career development of individuals.

The court system is now managed in a more specific way. Performance targets are set by the Ministry of Justice for the resolution of different categories of case. The job of the president is to monitor performance and to see how his court can achieve the target. In particular, there are targets for the timescales within which cases are to be decided. The idea of measuring performance is not new. Comparing the performance of judges in the hovrätt in terms of time taken and number of cases decided was an internal tool in the 1940s.[28] Nevertheless, the main tool of management is encouragement, rather than orders. Performance is also enhanced by bidding for projects. These are supplements to the budget of the court for activities which the administration

[25] See Minister of Justice, T. Bodström, *Brännpunkt*, *Svenska Dagbladet*, 28 March 2001.

[26] See O. Ekstedt, *Brännpunkt*, *Svenska Dagbladet*, 3 April 2001.

[27] See documents produced by working groups of DV: *Praktiska Ledningsfrågor* and *Lederskap och Chefskap* (Jönköping, April 2000).

[28] See H. Elliot, *Ur en domares liv* (Stockholm 1958), 244 for the use of the coefficient system in Umeå.

approves. Thus the Svea hovrätt obtained a rebuilding project and the Göta hovrätt obtained some additional posts to undertake an experimental reorganisation. The elaboration of such proposals is part of the role of the president. This involves networking to discover the kinds of project likely to be supported.

The other aspect of management is that of personnel. The presiding judge has a responsibility to develop the careers of judges within his court. He has to produce reports on the progress of judges undergoing training (notarie and fiskaler). Promotions procedures also require him to provide references on members of his court (which the affected person can see).[29]

DV has been responsible for developing training courses for managers and these are to be developed further under recent proposals. The Hirschfeldt committee suggested that it is necessary to keep together both the management and the leadership aspects of the role of the chief judge in a court.[30] As a manager, the judge is responsible to external authorities, such as DV, for meeting performance targets and for personnel and financial matters. He is also responsible for overseeing developments. Among colleagues, the judge is internally responsible for providing leadership within the court, but as *primus inter pares*. He must, however, respect the independence of judges in coming to their decisions. The manager's concern is to avoid maladministration, but he cannot dictate how decisions should be reached. The contrast is made between the Swedish DV, which is part of the administration and is linked to the Government, and the Danish *Domstolsstyrelsen*, which is a more independent body directed by the judges themselves.[31] The Danish administration was separated from the Ministry of Justice on 1 July 1999, and has thus become a potent model for the freedom many Swedish judges wish to have in the government of their own courts.

Courts are of very unequal size and so the management workload is very different. Whereas in the Svea hovrätt management is a full-time role, in a small tingsrätt this might occupy only 20 per cent of a chief judge's time.

[29] See below on promotions, p. 248.

[30] SOU 2000:99, *Domarutnämningar och domstolsledning – frågor om utnämning av högre domare och domstolschefens roll*, 398.

[31] See, for instance, P. Eriksson, 'Domstolsverket (S) och Domstolsstyrelsen (DK) – Olika sätt att reglera domstolsadministration' (2000) 1 *Tidskrift för Sveriges Domareförbund* 23.

Ministry of Justice

The Ministry of Justice has a broad remit covering law reform, the administration of justice (including the police and prosecution authorities), and (since 1999) general issues of democracy and public administration. It has divisions for dealing with different branches of the law, as well as for the other areas of its activity. Legislative proposals are considered by the Division for Legal and Linguistic Draft Revision which is the central point of contact with *Lagrådet*.[32] The Ministry operates through thirty agencies. The basic division is between policy and budget issues, and operational issues. The Ministry is responsible for setting policies, including the legal rules, but agencies, including DV, *Åklagarväsendet* (prosecution authority) and *Polisväsendet* (police authority), are responsible for carrying out the main policies.[33] The Minister of Justice is thus responsible for setting the agenda. This can be in terms of budget cuts, as in 1999, requiring new ways of working, but also presenting the agenda of expectations from the community which require changes in the way courts work, e.g. to cut delays.[34] Given that Swedish ministries are not as large as ministries in other countries, it is this steering role which is the most important part of its work.

Overall, there is a significant level of judicial independence within a framework of performance targets set by DV in the light of general directions by the Ministry of Justice. In broader areas of policy, there has to be negotiation and here the judicial unions have a significant role.

Judicial career

Selection

The Swedish selection system is based on a meritocratic competition, which is open and transparent, and which is based on prior experience, predominantly university achievement in law. It is managed by independent bodies.

Since 1749, the tradition in Sweden has been that students undertake basic university studies in law before applying to become judges. Law is only taught in a small number of universities – originally Lund

[32] See below p. 270.
[33] See Ministry of Justice, 'Ministry of Justice – Organisation and Duties', Fact Sheet Ju99.03e (Stockholm 1999).
[34] See L. Freivals, Minister of Justice, 'Domstolen i framtiden' (1999) 4 *Tidskrift för Sveriges Domareförbund* 13.

(1668) and Uppsala (1477), but now also Stockholm (1907), Göteborg and Umeå.[35] The law faculties have a traditional role in educating generally for the public service – not just the legal professions of judge and advokat, but also the police, prosecutors and other civil servants.[36] A significant number of students will also become legal advisers in private firms.

At the end of the law degree (*juris kandidatexamen*), a candidate applies to become a notarie (trainee) in one of the lower courts. The applications are handled by the judicial administration, Domstolsverket. The application is judged according to a points system, which favours high academic achievement, but is flexible enough to take account of alternative prior experience. Only about 30 per cent of applicants are successful,[37] so entry to this programme is an indicator of esteem. In 2004, there were 654 notarie (492 in the general courts and 162 in the administrative courts). There have traditionally been on average nearly 250 trainees recruited each year. The numbers for 2004 show a sharp decline since 2002 when there were 751 notarie.[38] Budget cuts have led to a reduction in the number of available places.

The three-year programme involves periods in the lower courts as tingsnotarie and then a year as överrättsnotarie (formerly called a *fiskalaspirant*). This is a practical training period in which trainees will learn on the job how decisions are prepared, how decisions are written, and other aspects of the judicial role. In the lower courts, one learns the way of handling common types of case, and in the upper court one deals with different issues of law. The notarie period also offers an opportunity to see different kinds of work and to form a view as to one's ultimate desired specialism. There will also be a number of formal short training courses. It has been recognised that the present situation leads to training which is uneven between locations, and a more structured and systematic organisation of the notarie period is under consideration.[39] As in Germany, this is seen as a general legal education,

[35] There are a number of law courses in other universities and colleges, but these are part of business and other degrees, rather than programmes of a law faculty.

[36] See below p. 274.

[37] See generally DV, *Vägen till domaryrket* (Jönköping, 1999) and *Det svenska domstolsväsendet – En kort introduction* (Jönköping 1999), 8; N. J. Baas, *Onderzoeksnotities 2000/8: Rekrutering en (permanente) educatie van de rechtsprekende macht in vijf landen* (Ministry of Justice, Netherlands 2000) (hereafter 'Baas'), 102. In 2002, 935 students passed the juris kandidatsexamen: see the statistics from the Högskoleverket (http://nu.hsv.se), table 5.

[38] DV, *Årsredovisning 2004*, 91.

[39] Regeringens skrivelse 1999/2000:106, above n. 13, section 6.3.

and even advokaten will wish their recruits to have been through the process. (But this is now changing as law firms try to attract law graduates directly and have their own training programmes.) After this initial training period, a number of candidates are recruited as fiskal for about nine months in the lower or upper courts. The individual will not be allowed to be judge on her or his own, but may take part in collegial decisions.

The next long phase is as an assessor (*icke ordinarie domare*), usually starting as an *adjungerad* for one to two years. There is an average of about 90–100 posts a year. (This gives some idea of the continuity rate of about 40 per cent between trainee and final phases.) During this period, an individual is not a permanent judge with a secure position in a particular court. Instead, the assessor has a series of fixed-term positions, as they fall vacant. The objective (according to interviews conducted for this research) is to ensure a broader experience, both within and outside the judiciary. The period as assessor may last eight years. At the end of it (aged about forty-three), an individual may be able to obtain one of the limited number of posts as a permanent (*ordinarie*) judge.[40] In 2004, there were 955 such ordinarie judges, a reduction of fifty posts since 2002.

The basic process of initial selection of notarier is controlled by DV. But further recruitment is governed by the *Tjänsteförslagsnämnden för domstolsväsendet* (TFN), an independent recruitment body discussed later. Particularly since the 1970s, there has been scope for individuals to be recruited from outside the career judiciary to more senior posts. The advertising of posts makes this possible. In part this was introduced to have a greater range of experience, but it was also motivated by government concerns that the career judiciary was too conservative and out of tune with current legislation.[41]

The position of women

The first woman judge was appointed in 1923, but it took until the 1960s for the first woman chief judge to be appointed. The position has changed rapidly since then. An interesting feature of Swedish legal professions is the gender distribution. Table 5.1 shows that women are

[40] Fewer than 8 per cent of permanent judges were under forty in 2004: see DV, *Årsredovisning 2004*, 93.

[41] K. Å. Modéer, *Den svenska domarkulturen – europeiska och nationelle förebilder* (Lund 1994) (hereafter 'Modéer, *Domarkulturen*'), 58.

Table 5.1 *The gender of lawyers in Sweden*[42]

	Advokaten (2002)	Åklagare (2002)	Judges (2002)	Juris kandidat graduates (2002)
New entrants (a year)	249	22	approx. 250 (notarier)	935
men	157 (63.1%)	8 (36.4%)	38%	355 (38%)
women	92 (36.9%)	14 (63.6%)	62%	580 (62%)
Active members (total)	3,505	706	2,409	
men	2,889 (82.4%)	376 (53.3%)	70%	
women	616 (17.6%)	330 (46.7%)	30%	

found more frequently in public sector employment (as judges and prosecutors) than in private practice (as advokat). In most countries, work predictability and flexibility, especially in relation to career breaks, are seen as advantages of the public sector. There is a clear difference between those over forty and those under forty in all professions, reflecting the greater number of women going into legal professions since the 1960s. Thus, 60 per cent of prosecutors under forty are women, but 73 per cent of those over fifty-five are men. Among judges, 65 per cent of the *icke ordinarie* judges are women, but 72 per cent of the *ordinarie* judges and 89 per cent of the chief judges (average age fifty-eight) are men.[43]

Given the proportions of women in the different age groups, there is a time-lag before women achieve equal representation in the senior echelons of the profession. All the same, DV is being encouraged to use techniques such as mentoring to encourage women to feel able to apply for the most senior positions.[44] But, as has been mentioned, geographical mobility is an essential part of progression in the Swedish judiciary. Someone who is willing to take a senior position at a young age in a

[42] Sources: SOU 1999:31, *Advokatväsendet i Sverige* for advokaten; Riksåklagaren, *Årsredovisning 2002* (Stockholm 2003), 62 on prosecutors; DV, *Årsredovisning 2002* (Jönköping 2003) for judges; Högskoleverket (http://nu.hsv.se) for students.

[43] DV, *Årsredovisning 2004*, 94.

[44] Regeringens skrivelse 1999/2000:106, above n. 13, 29–30, and DV, *Årsredovisning 2003* (Jönköping 2003), 94.

less favoured location, e.g. in northern Sweden, is likely to appear more experienced and better qualified than someone who has remained in a lower-rank post in a more populous area. This structural feature of the system also helps to explain the lower number of women applying for senior positions. In the five years from 2000 to 2004, women constituted just under 25 per cent of applicants for senior positions (head of court and the like), and just over 27.5 per cent of appointees, a figure which is very similar to the 27 per cent of women among the eligible class of ordinarie domare.[45] But the numbers in very recent years have been rising. In 2003 and 2004, women constituted 34 per cent of applicants for senior positions in courts and were 41 per cent of those appointed.[46] With a particular focus on mentoring and encouragement of eligible candidates, the Swedish are doing more than simply relying on the 'trickle up' approach to achieve greater representation of women within the senior judiciary.

Promotion

Since 1975, the process of promotion has become relatively open, though there remains a distinction between lower and higher posts.[47]

Lower posts are advertised (now on the website of DV) and there is an application form. Candidates are required to provide information about their experience to date and the names of referees who can attest to the qualities of the person. The application is then examined by TFN, which will make a decision. The candidates are not interviewed. The committee of TFN is made up of senior judges with two employee representatives. As a result, one can say that it constitutes a degree of self-government at this stage.

Senior posts remain within the control of the Ministry of Justice, as in the past. Traditionally, these have not gone only to career judges. A number of famous instances have occurred where places on the HD have been allocated to leading practitioners, not just to judges.[48] Lateral movement is important to bring in not only advokater, but also prosecutors. In a 2000 committee report on the appointment of the higher

[45] See DV, *Årsredovisning 2003*, 90, 94–5; DV, *Årsredovisning 2004*, 94.
[46] DV, *Årsredovisning 2004*, 106 and 107.
[47] See generally DV, 'Appointment of Permanent Judges and the Position of the Appointments Review Committee for the Judiciary and its Method of Working' (leaflet, Jönköping 1997).
[48] See K. Å. Modéer, *Lemän och Lagerlöfvar* (Lund 1999), 84 on Gunnar Bomgren appointed in 1955; 119–20 on Marianne Lundius appointed in 1998.

judiciary,[49] it was suggested that the power of the Government to appoint the highest judges should be modified by the introduction of a committee which would propose a number of suitable candidates from which the Government's choice would be made. But the Government's role would be maintained, as would the selection based on an assessment of the merits of candidates. The system is not based simply on seniority. Although there was talk in the mid-1980s that recruitment to the Kammarrätt and HD would be divided equally between those who had experience of government offices, those who had other external experience, and those who had purely judicial experience, the reality is that nearer 80 per cent are drawn from those who have governmental experience. The reason is that working in government provides detailed knowledge of particular fields (and expertise is desirable in an appeal court) and there is an understanding of legislative procedure and thus the weight to be attached to preparatory materials and other legislative documents. The idea of openness to various non-judicial professions is quite important. The appointments will typically be to the higher courts, especially from among academics.

Interviews also suggested that being known in government circles, e.g. through committee work, is relevant to promotion. If a person is known to be good by those who make the appointments, she is likely to be preferred over those who are not known. Vacancies are not advertised and, although it is difficult to identify individual 'political' appointments, there is still a sense that other, equally meritorious, candidates may have been overlooked.

Review of the Swedish system of appointments was triggered in particular by the creation in 1999 of *Domstolsstyrelsen* in Denmark and by the adoption of the European Charter on the Status of the Judge. (This neatly illustrates the major influences on Swedish legal development.)

Training and continuing education

Since the seventeenth century, initial training has followed essentially an apprenticeship model. Modéer writes that 'Swedish judicial culture in the 19th century was formed by legal education and training, by law professors at the Faculties of Law and by senior judges in the Courts

[49] SOU 2000:99, above n. 30, ch. 3. The Report was inspired in part by the need to bring Swedish practice into line with the European Convention on Human Rights.

of Appeal [*hovrätter*].'[50] A number of short courses are organised by DV in a number of stages spread over the training, but there is no general judicial college course as in France.[51] There are ideas to have a more systematic traineeship programme for notarier.[52] There are special courses for new assessors (three weeks for the *icke ordinarie domare*) spread over the year, and five-week courses for new permanent judges. In addition, there are courses in leaderships for chief judges. In principle, notarier and fiskaler take part in courses on a voluntary basis, but nearly all will do so.[53] There are individuals responsible in each court for oversight of training. As a result, the subjects provided by DV meet the interests of the judges, e.g. in 2002 on EU law or the UN Convention on the Rights of the Child. Training events may also be attended by advokater and åklageren.[54] In addition, there are some bursaries for judges who propose their own subjects of work, and in 2002 five judges spent a six-month period in the ECJ.

Unlike the French, there is a limited theoretical aspect to training and also a limited national programme. There is no sense that trainees should be given placements in a number of different administrative functions. It is very much a judicial activity. All the same, there are placements in the tax administration (*Riksskatteverket*), in the debts office (*Kronofogdemyndighet*), in the consumer court (*Allmänna reklamationsnämnden*) as well as in the prosecution (*Justitiekanslern*). These institutions are closely connected to the judicial process. Unlike the French and Germans, there is no attempt to expose the recruits to private practice and the problems which lawyers face.

Continuing education does exist, both in a general and in a specific way. On the whole it is voluntary, unlike in many parts of the public sector. The administrative staff of courts have well-developed continuing training programmes. There is a *Domar akedemi* run on an unofficial basis by the University of Lund, which puts on some events. Although there is a growing public sector culture of continuing education, this has yet to be embedded in the judiciary, which is an individualistic

50 K. Å. Modéer, 'From "Rechtstaat" to "Welfare State": The Swedish Judicial Culture in Transition 1870–1970' in W. Wesley Pue and D. Sugarman (eds.), *Lawyers and Vampires. Cultural Histories of Legal Professions* (Oxford 2003), 151 at 155.

51 See O. Ekstedt, *Domarakademi i Sverige* (http://www.algonet.se/domarefb/tidskr/tfsd200034.htm).

52 See DV, *Idéskiss till Notarietjänstgöringens* (DV-rapport 2003:5, Jönköping 2003).

53 Baas, 106.

54 See DV, *Årsredovisning 2002*, 25–6.

profession. Programmes are put on by DV in response to demand. The pace of change, and the need to develop expertise in a range of new fields, has encouraged government to press for greater judicial continuing education, not only at the initial stages.[55] Given the geographical distances between judges, a number of courses are provided on a distance-learning basis.

Socialisation

Given the geographical spread of postings, it is important that judges remain in contact. The traditional method of the notarie period as training involved a posting often to fairly remote centres. The trainee would often be put up in the house of the president of the country court (*häradshöv*).[56] In urban centres, the relatively small size of the court secures ease of contact. It is possible for judges in different courts to know each other. The traditional structure was very patriarchal – a kind of family structure with the head of court as head of household. The collegial nature of courts and their relatively modest size continues to make some corporate identity possible. In 1999, of ninety-five tingsrätter, only three had over fifteen judges (Malmö with thirty-five, Göteborg with forty-five, and Stockholm with 100), and eighty-four had fewer than ten judges. A similar picture exists in the administrative courts, with twenty länsrätter having ten judges or fewer, and the same three areas having more (twenty in Göteborg, thirty in Skåne, and fifty in Stockholm).[57]

The process of induction brings the younger judges into the life of the appeal courts and provides a framework for some homogeneity. Movement outside one's region for promotion or the next posting in an early career ensures a degree of mixing between judges. Being a judge is very much a national function. Administrative postings, such as a committee secretary or working as a non-permanent judge in one of the supreme courts, will provide an opportunity to work in Stockholm. Among the judges interviewed, geographical mobility is a common feature in their career history.

[55] Regeringens skrivelse 1999/2000:106, above n. 13, 28.

[56] See Elliot, *Ur en domares liv*, above n. 28, 112–15 describing a period in the early 1910s; Modéer, *Domarkulturen*, 35–8. Modéer, 'From "Rechtstaat" to "Welfare State"', above n. 50, 159 explains how trainees lived without salary as members of the family.

[57] DV, *Årsredovisning 1999* (Jönköping 2000), 8–9.

Discipline

At present the Swedish judiciary is subject to controls within the civil service as a whole on matters of discipline. The State Disciplinary Board is responsible for appeals from judges who have been disciplined by superiors, or where discipline of a serious kind is involved. The Justitiekansliet is also involved in issues of the malfunctioning of the court system. The Hirschfeldt committee suggested that this might pass into the hands of an internal judiciary committee.[58]

Judicial corporate life

In the nineteenth century, judges worked very much in an individual fashion.[59] Collective action has come as the result of the decline in the patrician status of the judge and the more bureaucratic role which is now performed. As a result, professional civil service associations have formed. The main trade union for lawyers is JUSEK (*Förbundet för jurister, samhällsvetare och ekonomer* – the Federation of Lawyers, Social Scientists and Economists). Created in 1969 by a merger between unions founded in the 1940s, it is part of one of the main public sector confederations. JUSEK is responsible for classical trade union activities in negotiating over wages and working conditions, mainly with the *Statens arbetsgivarverk* (the Civil Service Collective Bargaining Agency). It is a regular *remissinstans*.[60]

The *Sveriges Domareförebund* is part of JUSEK, with a particular focus on the judicial career. Its objectives include the representation of Swedish judges in issues of lawmaking and the administration of the law, as well as protecting judicial independence. It is thus a remissinstans, but also has regular meetings with DV. It also represents Sweden in international meetings of judges. The union works like a professional association and encourages debates on questions of general interest. As well as performing its representative functions, it has standing in connection with the development of the law and the interests of judges. Its candidates are frequently elected to the various bodies responsible for judicial appointments and representing judges in the planning activities of DV.

58 SOU 2000:99, above n. 30, section 4.10.
59 Modéer, 'From "Rechtstaat" to "Welfare State"', above n. 50, 162.
60 On remissen, see below p. 270.

History and values

History of the judiciary

Up until the eighteenth century, the judicial function was predominantly performed by the nobility. Following the reforms of the early nineteenth century, the judges were officials appointed by the King, rather like the church bureaucracy. The lower court structure remained divided between town and country. The country courts followed the division of thane (*ting*) and hundred (*härad*) that had existed for a thousand years. In these rural courts, the judge would sit with the nämnd, a group of twelve local farmers. The court was thus part of the local community. In towns, the courts (*rådhus*) were developed by the mayor, who was often judge as well. The appeal courts were the King's power of intervention into local justice, either in the King's (Privy) Council or through the *Sveahovrätt*, a collegial court established in 1614. As Modéer points out, this diversity of tradition between rural, urban and collegial demonstrates the way in which Swedish legal culture is impregnated with *continuity* from the past.[61] Although there have been important moments of reform, there has not been the same kind of radical discontinuity represented by the French Revolution or the Second World War. All the same, in recent times one can detect a number of distinct tendencies or periods, marking a change in direction for the operation of the courts.

The model of judiciary introduced in the nineteenth century was that of the public servant, applying the law in an impartial manner. It has been described as the model of the 'office-holder' (*ämbetsmannastaten*).[62] The role involved a combination of knowledge (of the law) and administrative drive.[63] The function was one to which the best of the social elite could be appointed by the King. This strongly nationalist and conservative nineteenth-century tradition could be described as the model of *traditional authority*, carrying a distinctive folk-legitimacy.[64] The judge was the representative of the state, but especially in the häradshov or the rådhus the judge's decisions represented local traditional standards. The authority was inherent in the office, structured in a hierarchical manner. Strömholm describes Sweden in the second half of the nineteenth century as 'agrarian, peripheral, intellectually conservative, economically weak, socially and politically a little old-fashioned

[61] Modéer, *Domarkulturen*, 17.
[62] SOU 1994:99, Del A, 55.
[63] Modéer, *Domarkulturen*, 22.
[64] Ibid., 56.

in comparison with surrounding countries, to a great extent altogether marked by mercantilism and a strong administrative-state structure and government'.[65]

If the institutional structures were very much homegrown, the legal culture was broader. As in other parts of Swedish life, French influence had been strong in the eighteenth and early nineteenth centuries, with transmission of the ideas of Montesquieu[66] and the governmental ideas through the French Marshal Bernadotte (who became the Swedish King Charles XIV, 1818–43). English political and economic ideas were equally followed, including the introduction of the jury for press cases. Later in the century, German legal ideas were picked up in legal studies.[67] Judges, like other Swedish lawyers, undertook visits abroad, within Europe initially, but after the First World War to the United States, to which a large number of Swedes had emigrated in the middle of the nineteenth century. The picture is thus of institutional specificity, with a strong continuity with the past, but an eclectic engagement with external ideas.

Institutional specificity was reinforced by two national features. The first was the development of an indigenous and influential tradition of legal theory, the school of Scandinavian Realism at Uppsala. By challenging received wisdom, a climate was created in which action through law was seen as possible, even desirable. In this approach, judges had an instrumental role in the achievement of the welfare state, rather than a distinct or independent social function. The second was the rise of the Social Democrats as a political party – they have formed the largest party in Parliament almost continuously since 1914, and were in government continuously from 1932 to 1976. The party challenged the inherited traditions of a conservative society and introduced substantial democratic reform. Its idea of a new society in Sweden, *folkshemet*, involving social co-operation, was the key feature of this agenda. Strömholm notes the impact on the law of this movement. Whereas legislation before 1850 occupies only eleven volumes, that from 1850 to 1920 occupies a further forty, and that from 1921 to 1989 occupies some 2,000 volumes.[68] Judicial

[65] S. Strömholm, 'Efterklang, kris och genombrott – Det intellektuella klimatet i Sverige 1850–1920' in R. Nygren (ed.), *Högsta domsmakten i Sverige under 200 år* (Lund 1990), vol. I, 131 at 132 (my translation).

[66] See T. Vallinder, 'Who is Included in Sweden's Judicial and Legal Elite?', unpublished conference paper, Bellagio Conference Centre, 1985 (hereafter 'Judicial Elite').

[67] Modéer, *Domarkulturen*, 45.

[68] Strömholm, 'Efterklang', above n. 65, 135.

recruitment, like that of the public sector in general, became broader, both socially and in terms of experience. Judges were appointed from outside the narrow cadre of career judges to provide a broader range of experience.[69]

Under these two influences, the favoured model of judiciary was that of *instrumentalism* – the judge as implementer of the reforms approved by the legislator. In particular, this applied to the role of the law in social control, e.g. of anti-social elements such as criminals and alcoholics. But the judges were seen as old-fashioned and conservative. New court structures, such as the Labour Courts created in 1928 and the social insurance appeals bodies, were created outside the judicial hierarchy and with other staff, typically with lay elements. The role of judges was altered significantly by changes to criminal procedure. A change in the authoritarian tradition of Swedish courts was brought about by the changes in court procedure (*rättegångsbalkan*) of 1948. In criminal cases, the inquisitorial function of the judge pre-trial was transferred to a newly created profession of *åklagar* (prosecutor). The layout of the court was changed to make proceedings more informal and the dress code was also changed, away from the traditional dark clothes. The majesty of the judge and his powerful role were replaced by a more passive role. The court arrangement where all parties and lawyers were seated conveyed a different image of the law, and provoked different kinds of intervention. The Social Democrats were concerned to use the law as an instrument of reform, a role to which the more naturally conservative judges were less suited. They were much more in favour of evolutionary and gradual development. (For instance, the rättegångsbalkan was the result of debate from 1928 to 1948.) Until 1974, the Riksdag could remove a judge from office without giving reasons. But this power was removed by art. 11.5 of the Constitution.

The modern period, beginning in the 1970s, emphasised the *democratic judiciary*. The post-1968 critique of established social institutions made its mark during the premiership of Olof Palme (1969–76). As in Finland, there was criticism that judges were neither independent nor representative of society.[70] The Palme government was keen to push through major change in society, rather than to promote gradual change. The idea of instrumentalism was emphasised by the 1974 Constitution in

[69] This was, in part, a consequence of narrowing the range of experience of judges by removing their role in criminal investigations through the 1948 procedural reforms.

[70] Modéer, *Domarkulturen*, 56.

which there is no separate chapter on the judicial power; rather, it is subsumed under a general heading of 'the judiciary and general administration'. The judicial power is said to come from the people (and, by implication, from Parliament as the representative of the people). This equation of the judiciary with the administration in a single chapter provoked some outrage among judges.[71] The democratisation of government and the administration was part of this change of social mood. Service of the people and openness were features of the new agenda.

A number of reforms illustrate the tone of the period. In 1977, the lay judges were given individual votes, rather than one block vote, and so were more able to outvote the professional judges. Lay participation was extended to the appeal courts. In addition, oral argument was introduced in the appeal courts, rather than the traditional bureaucratic approach of a decision on written submissions. The creation of Domstolsverket in 1975 was designed to modernise the operation of the legal system.

The constitutional and European movement of the 1990s has gradually changed the climate. Sweden joined the EU in 1995 and brought the European Convention into domestic law. This has begun to introduce a *European model* into the Swedish judiciary. The emphasis is on values and policies which stand above those of the national legislator. In particular, the judge is the guardian of progressive values coming from beyond Sweden. This enhances the status of the judicial role. Already, the 1970s had seen a gradual judicialisation of administrative courts.[72] As has been shown, under pressure from the European Court of Human Rights, administrative courts independent of the administration were created. The social insurance courts were abolished and their activity transferred to the administrative courts. These actions caused changes in domestic law, but also gave the domestic judge a status in certain respects as superior to national government. The judge became increasingly an instance of control, rather than an instrument for achieving government policy. There was also a movement in Nordic countries for constitutional review[73] which exercised some influence on Swedish thinking. As yet the

[71] See G. Petrén, 'Domstolsverket och domstolsväsendet – en studie i regeringsteknik' (1975) *Svensk Juristtidning* 651.

[72] B. Holmström, 'The Judicialization of Politics in Sweden' (1994) 15 *International Political Science Review* 153 at 156 argues that this also dejudicialised the administration by clearly separating administrative and judicial matters.

[73] See R. Slagstad, 'The Breakthrough of Judicial Review in the Norwegian System' in E. Smith (ed.), *Constitutional Justice under Old Constitutions* (The Hague 1995), 81; C. Smith,

Swedish courts have not been keen to set aside legislation, and there is a divergence of opinion about whether this would be a good step for the Swedish judiciary to take. All the same, the European Convention's concept of a hearing by an impartial tribunal has been an important legal argument, and the EU and the Convention are setting the agenda for legal debate in competition with the national legislator.[74] The novelty of the European agendas means that the small number of judges who have experience in these fields (either arising from studies or from work in the European courts) have an important role in education. Judges are concerned to implement European law. Like the British, the Swedes are serious in wishing to carry out commitments, and they like to know where they stand in terms of what European law requires. The somewhat vague, compromise and under-articulated decisions of European courts clash with their more direct and clear approach. That said, there is a broad welcome for the new status that judges enjoy within society.

It would be fair to say that the emerging *European* model is not fully developed. The three elements of constitutional review, the European Union and the European Convention are discernible as the new shape of legal debate. The tendencies are more pronounced in other parts of Scandinavia and Europe. As yet the Swedish courts have been mainly recipients of arguments from decisions of the courts in Strasbourg and Luxembourg in this area, rather than generating new interpretations.[75] There remains concern about the extent to which judicial review of legislation will bring about a preventive effect of caution among the legislators.[76] Indeed the protection of fundamental rights was a strongly debated subject in the 1970s prior to the adoption of the 1974 Constitution, as well as later, because of the concern that these rights would be used as a brake upon social reform. There continues to be a close link between the standards of performance expected of the judiciary and those of general administration. In a 2000 government report, public

'Judicial Review of Parliamentary Legislation: Norway as a European Pioneer' [2000] PL 595, both emphasising a watershed decision of 1976.

[74] On the European Convention see E. Holmberg and N. Stjernquist, *Vår författning* (Stockholm 2000) (hereafter '*Vår författning*'), 50ff, and on the European Union see ibid., 184. Of the first fourteen cases in which Sweden was condemned before 1990, nine were in respect of failure to provide redress before an independent and impartial tribunal as required by art. 6 of the Convention: Holmström, 'Judicialization', above n. 72, 156.

[75] See J. Nergelius, 'Domstolarnas självständighet i ett komparativt oct EU-perspektiv' in T. Håstad and L. Lewin (eds.), *Politik och Juridik. Grundlagen inför 2000-talet* (Uppsala 1999), ch. 2.

[76] *Vår författning*, 192.

expectations of efficiency and effectiveness of the public administration are applied directly to the judiciary.[77] At the same time, it recognises the importance of fundamental rights.[78]

Dominant ideas

Swedish law has a number of distinctive influences. Among the most important in the twentieth century were the legal theory of Scandinavian Realism and the political theory of Social Democracy. Both have shaped Swedish law in similar directions. A further dominant idea has been that of social consensus. In the contemporary world, these dominant features are coming under challenge.

Scandinavian realism

Twentieth-century Swedish law was strongly influenced by an indigenous theory of law, Scandinavian Realism, developed at Uppsala University.[79] The leading writer was Axel Hägerström (professor 1911–33),[80] together with his disciples Vilhelm Lundstedt (professor 1914–48) in Uppsala and Karl Olivecrona (professor 1933–64) in Lund. They encouraged a critical analysis of received traditions. The realists challenged metaphysical ideas and emphasised the human creation of moral ideas. This encouraged a debate about moral ideals and values, and gave law an important place in the creation of a social climate of ideas.

Their writings are based on two ideas. First, metaphysical notions of 'ought' and 'right' have no existence in the world of fact and are essentially superstitious notions. The only reality to which they correspond is in the minds of citizens. In other words, there is no objective moral order that requires certain actions to be performed. My sense of obligation to perform such actions lies in my own belief that I have such an obligation. The task of legal theory is not to determine what an objective moral order demands, as natural lawyers suggest, but to explain how people come to acquire a sense of obligation. Secondly, legal utterances are in the form of commands to the citizen and this form of words encourages them to adopt an attitude of willingness to comply with what is required. Rules of law are designed to change people's attitudes,

[77] Regeringens skrivelse 1999/2000:106, above n. 13, 28. [78] Ibid., 5.

[79] See F. Schmidt, 'The Uppsala School of Legal Thinking' (1976) 22 *Scandinavian Studies in Law* 149.

[80] See generally J. Bjarup, 'Epistemology and Law according to Axel Hägerström' (1985) 29 *Scandinavian Studies in Law* 11.

rather than to predict what courts will do (as American Realists would believe). The emphasis is on what J. L. Austin[81] calls the 'illocutionary' force of law, rather than the performative character: 'The word "ought" and the like are imperative expressions . . . Their sole function is to work on the minds of people, directing them to do this or that or to refrain from something else – not to communicate knowledge about the state of things.'[82] This approach of demythologising the normative aspects of law leads to a strong positivism. Law reflects the will of the legislator, not some higher standard. Law is also an important mechanism for changing the climate of ideas in society. According to Olivecrona, 'the use of force [by the law] is one of the chief factors in moulding our moral standards, and not the other way round'.[83] For Lundstedt, legal theory is required to study these psychological processes and to see how, for example, the criminal law can change behaviour.[84] For example, there might be controls on alcohol and attempts to deal with those who are alcoholics. Such an instrumentalist view of law provides scope for the legislator to define and achieve social change, and gives the judge no independent role to challenge this. The judge is there to carry out what the legislator has willed.

Social democracy

The Social Democratic Party (SAP) governed Sweden for most of the twentieth century, including a continuous period of forty-four years from 1932 to 1976 (with a very short interregnum for some weeks in 1936). The result was that it shaped the political agenda and also the law and the administration in Sweden. As Anton points out, the administration (which includes the judiciary) was an unrepresentative and conservative elite. All the same, it was able not merely to adapt to the Social Democrats in power, but also to play a constructive role in creating the kind of more equal and progressive society which that party wished to achieve. For him, the traditional high status of the civil service, its loyalty to the system, the clarity of roles which politicians and administrators were expected to perform, and the consultative policy-making style

[81] J. L. Austin, *How to do Things with Words* (Oxford 1962), ch. 1.

[82] K. Olivecrona, *Law as Fact* (1st edn, London 1939), 21; also A. Hägerström, *Enquiries into the Nature of Law and Morals* (English edn, London 1952), 192–6.

[83] Olivecrona, *Law as Fact*, above n. 82, 156.

[84] A. V. Lundstedt, *Superstition or Rationality in Action for Peace* (London 1925).

of Swedish government all contributed to a relatively uncontentious change of direction among the administration.[85]

The Social Democrats themselves identified three phases in their activity in the twentieth century. The period up to 1918 was the struggle for *political democracy*; the 1930s and 1940s involved the creation of *social democracy* through a universal social welfare system and employment rights, a sense of solidarity in creating security (*trygghet*) for all; the third period of the 1970s involved the creation of *economic democracy*, ensuring a sharing of the benefits of economic change.[86] The ideology involved a set of core values about what constituted the basis for a decent society, rather than a blueprint or vision for a new society. The five central themes identified by Tilton are integrative democracy, *folkhemmet*, equal consideration of all citizens, social control of the economy, and the idea that a proper expansion of the public sector expands freedom of choice.[87] The central tenet is *folkshemmet* ('the people's home'). As described by a prime minister in the 1930s,

> The basis of the home is togetherness and common feeling . . . Applied to the great people's and citizen's home this would mean the breaking down of all social and economic barriers that now divide citizens into the privileged and the unfortunate, into rulers and subjects, into rich and poor, the glutted and the destitute, the plunderers and the plundered.[88]

As Tilton suggests, 'Solidarity and equality of consideration characterize the good home; there consensus is the objective and democratic persuasion the method of governance.'[89] There was an obvious clash with property rights. But the approach taken was not nationalisation, but a combination of social control over some of the exercise of property rights, and a system of economic planning. In this context, property was conceived as a bundle of rights, some of which might be restricted or reduced in the interests of social solidarity.[90] The process was gradual and partial, such that it clashed in only limited ways with constitutional requirements. All the same, Social Democracy represents a different path to liberalism, and it is not surprising that many of the cases brought before the European Court of Human Rights have been in the field of the regulation of property rights, as were some of the Social Democrat Party's early clashes with Lagrådet.

[85] T. J. Anton, *Administered Politics: Elite Political Culture in Sweden* (Boston 1980), 181–3.
[86] T. Tilton, *The Political Theory of Swedish Social Democracy* (Oxford 1990), 4–5.
[87] Ibid., 257–69. [88] Per Albin Hansson, cited ibid., 259.
[89] Ibid., 259. [90] Ibid., 266.

The consequence of a clash between traditional judicial values and the new social democracy was a view that the judges should reduce their role to being faithful appliers of the law as enacted, rather than upholding traditional values. In the words of one cabinet secretary interviewed by Anton in the 1970s, 'Legislation is nothing more than a means for achieving desired social purposes . . . In my view a good lawyer is one who understands that he is nothing more than a technician, who knows how to structure law to achieve social ends.'[91]

Consensus-building

One of the longstanding traditions in Swedish government is the building of consensus. This does not deny that there are significant differences in views between sections of the community. Rather, the process of decision-making tries to include opponents in the decision-making process and possibly reconcile them to the outcomes. To begin with, ever since the thirteenth century, the legislative process has had a strong consultative dimension. The formal pre-legislative consultation or *remiss* process and the use of committees help to involve various sections of society (and not just politicians) in the law-making process. As Anton suggests, it can serve as a way of co-opting or neutralising opponents. But he also reports from his interviews with administrators and politicians that there is a very strong tradition of being willing to compromise, even when they know that they will win a political debate.[92] This approach has been reinforced by the absence of significant social upheavals in the past 200 years. Change, though very significant, has been gradual, and opponents have learnt to reconcile themselves to the changed condition of society. The presence of a relatively small and ethnically homogeneous society in the nineteenth and early twentieth centuries has made easier this sense of consensus-building.

This has an impact on the law in a number of ways. The existence of political procedures for developing consensus has not led to the need for the courts to intervene to establish social peace or to adjudicate on major contentious issues. The establishing of civil liberties has not been the function of judges, but the political process. There has not been the need for the judge to act as impartial social arbiter. The role of judges has been in dealing with more individual situations. Equally, the existence

91 Anton, *Administered Politics*, above n. 85, 59.
92 Ibid., table 5.6.

of alternative ways of resolving differences has reduced the conflict resolution role of the courts. Even where there was substantial social conflict in the development of the industrial revolution, the Swedes found mechanisms to bring the social partners together, including by creating the labour courts in 1928.

Contemporary challenges

Situations are changing. Sweden not only has an indigenous ethnic minority, the Sami, in the north, it now has a large number of inhabitants who have immigrated from elsewhere, who live mainly in the south. The individualistic, modern culture also emphasises individual rights, rather than collaboration in social solidarity. Norms emerge from outside the consensus-building process within Sweden, especially from the European Union. There has also been a long tradition of developing legal rules in collaboration with other Nordic countries. As Bernitz puts it,

> Nordic Legal Unity is not only a practically determined phenomenon and a question of the technique of legal cooperation. It is based, in principle, on a common legal tradition which forms part of the larger community of culture and social life of the North. It will be a challenge for the future to promote and cultivate this common Nordic legal culture and heritage within the more extensive framework of European cooperation.[93]

Since some of these Nordic countries are outside the EU, there is a tension between different sources of legal development. The natural cultural affinity, as well as the regular meetings at all levels, between representatives of these different legal systems serves to maintain this distinctive feature of the Swedish legal culture. As a result, Nordic countries continue to provide points of reference.

The 1980s and 1990s were characterised by significant social and political changes.[94] Economically, the deregulation and globalisation of markets has limited the scope for social control of the economy operated in a single country. Entry into the European Union in 1995 was a recognition of this and the consequent need to pool aspects of sovereignty over economic and social issues. Politically and administratively, the rise

[93] U. Bernitz, *European Law in Sweden* (Stockholm 2002), 111.

[94] See J. Pierre, 'Legitimacy, Institutional Change, and the Politics of Public Administration in Sweden' (1993) 14 *International Political Science Review* 387; S. Strömholm, 'General Features of Swedish Law' in Bogdan, *Swedish Law*, above n. 14, 38; Petersson et al., *Report from the Democratic Audit*, above n. 11, ch. 4.

of the new right-wing party (*Ny Demokrati*) pushed political debate away from the need to use the public sector to deliver social improvement. The Public Administration Act 1985 departed from previous legislation in the field by introducing the idea of the citizen as client of the administration. The involvement of the private sector in a number of activities, e.g. railways and the post, has softened the boundaries between the state and civil society.[95] Many remaining parts of the public sector are governed by objectives set centrally. Rather than ministries directing what is done, agencies or franchisees are expected to meet agreed targets (*målstyrning*). This has changed the character of the public administration and the way in which social reform is achieved. At the same time, it helps to introduce a new role for law. The citizen as client, rather than beneficiary, is more likely to make claims. Target-setting is more likely to lead to conflicts which are not resolved by hierarchical orders. The European Convention merely adds to the change in pattern. The judiciary becomes more of the arbiter between agencies or between citizens and the administration which is meant to serve them. All the same, in terms of values, legality is a subordinate goal, and often values such as legal certainty and equality before the law matter less than efficiency in the achievement of established goals. Once again, individual rights and liberties matter less than other values which the public administration has to respect.[96] But it has been noted that, in recognition of the more individualistic tendencies of modern culture, the Social Democrats have been turning many of their social goals and aspirations into individual 'rights': the right to health care, the right to a decent dwelling, and so on.[97] This may be a change in form, but it does, as we shall see, give potential for greater involvement of the courts in relation to legislation.[98]

Judicial independence

The Swedish conception of judicial independence has to be understood in relation to its history. There have been no radical purges. The judges act as good officials of the state who contribute to the government of the country, rather than as some separated check on the executive or Parliament. The importance of administrative and public service tasks

[95] Pierre, 'Legitimacy', above n. 94, 393–4 and 397.
[96] Ibid., 398.
[97] Holmström, 'Judicialization', above n. 72, 162.
[98] Below p. 270.

within the judicial career is testimony to this. On the other hand, the Swedish system operates by way of checks and balances between organs of government and agencies.[99] The independent role of the judiciary is part of this sharing of power. All the same, judicial review of the administration and of legislation does not have the same high status as in other legal systems. The Swedish judicial system has been traditionally respectful of the prerogatives of the administration and of Parliament. Control over the administration is exercised by a number of bodies, not just the judiciary. The King's Council, the Kammarrätt and then the Regeringsrätt have been bodies which have exercised independent judicial supervision over the administration. But, until recently, the administrative court system was not systematic in the range of institutions it covered. This reflected a more pragmatic and piecemeal approach of tackling problems as they occur, rather than a formalist and doctrinaire attachment to principles of independent judicial review of the administration. Constitutional review must also be placed in its institutional setting. With the strength of judicial *preview* through remisser and Lagrådet has diminished the need for post-enactment judicial *review*.[100] There is not a stand-off between the judiciary and the elected representatives, but a sense of collaboration. Indeed, the initial presentation of judicial review of legislation as a check on the legislator appeared antidemocratic, rather than as progress.[101] In Holmström's view, the growth of constitutional review is linked to different ways in which organisations are undertaking politics in the era of decline in the corporatist state.[102]

The character of judicial independence is well illustrated by the governance arrangements. The governing organ, DV, is not an institution of judicial self-regulation, much as many judges would now like it to be. On the other hand, DV acts as a buffer between the Ministry of Justice and the judges as managers at court level. Central government seeks to exercise a strong influence over the direction of all branches of government, and this Swedish tradition of integrating judicial activity within social reform perhaps explains an absence of will to translate

99 This is not to suggest that the separation of powers ideas of Montesquieu had no influence on the Constitution-making of 1809 or later: see T. Vallinder, 'Montesquieu and Constitution-making in Sweden, 1809–1815', *Vetenskapssocietetens i Lund, Årsbok 1989*, 112. I merely suggest that the rigid separation of powers seen in some other countries did not take place.

100 See below p. 270.

101 See Holmström, 'Judicialization', above n. 72, 157.

102 Ibid., 161–2.

judicial independence in the application of the law into a strong version of judicial autonomy to decide how it should organise itself as a separate branch of government. Sweden is not unique in this regard, but its way of accommodating the tensions between steering judicial activity as a whole and respecting judicial independence is distinctive. On the whole, the model adopted has been that of other independent agencies of government, of which there are many in Sweden.

As has been seen,[103] the judicial unions are much more like professional associations than political actors. There is not the same rivalry between political tendencies which is seen in the different judicial unions in other, especially Latin, countries. Their participation in judicial governance is a further illustration of the participatory style of government in Sweden, and of the low-key approach to judicial independence both within and beyond the judiciary.

Judicial roles

The concept of the judge as office-holder connects her or him to the governmental process in the widest sense. The judges contribute to the processes of giving direction to society both in their judicial role, through their interpretation of statutes and making precedents, and in their extrajudicial roles. In Sweden, there is a very distinctive role for the judiciary to participate actively in the pre-legislative review of proposals, often in draft bill stage, or even in the formulation of policy. This is more active than is seen in many countries and in some way is similar to the Conseil d'Etat in France. The underlying culture of the judiciary is close to that of administrators. In substantial part, this is because the Swedish conception of administration is more removed from politics than in many other countries. There is not the same antagonism between courts and administration as is seen elsewhere, and the value of consensus building permeates many of the processes in which the judges become involved.

Judicial creativity

Lawmaking is part of the function of the judiciary, both within the parliamentary process and in court. It is not surprising that, traditionally, Swedish judges have given priority to statutes as a source of law. In this way, they have remained in their role as subordinates to the

[103] Above p. 252.

will of the legislator in whose pre-legislative process judges participate, as will be seen in the next section. As early as 1916, Sjögren J argued: 'Even a bad statute is preferable to the insecurity which is inseparably connected with the discretion of the judge. If necessary, the individual may in private law matters – and only these are referred to here – adjust his relations to a bad statute, but against the power of the judge the individual is defenceless.'[104] In his view, the judge should adopt a teleological interpretation of statutes.[105] This kind of subordination involves active co-operation with the legislative objective. As Ekelöf describes, the judge does not confine himself to a narrow linguistic approach to the words of a provision, but has to decide upon the 'sphere of application' of the provision, which may be wider or narrower than the apparent and literal meaning.[106] The judge is not confined to the intentions of the historical legislator, even those expressed in the preparatory works, but has to work out the best way to implement the provisions within the sphere of application which is appropriate today. While others have argued that Ekelöf's advocacy of a full-blooded teleological approach has not been followed by the courts, it remains true that a strongly purposive approach is adopted in Sweden.[107] Graver calls the approach adopted 'evaluative' in that the norm is not a given, but has to be reasoned out of the statute – the provisions of the statutes are not to be applied formalistically, but serve as reasons which justify the decision to be reached.[108] Others would lay stress on the importance attached to preparatory works, which are frequently cited and almost universally consulted by the courts. Certainly, these are consulted more frequently and more explicitly than in other legal systems, no doubt because the judges were often involved in the law-creation process, but also out of

[104] Cited by Folke Schmidt, 'Construction of Statutes' (1957) 1 *Scandinavian Studies in Law* 155 (hereafter 'Schmidt').

[105] See ibid., and O. Ekelöf, 'Teleological Construction of Statutes' (1958) 2 *Scandinavian Studies in Law* 75 (hereafter 'Ekelöf').

[106] Ekelöf, 85–9.

[107] See A. Peczenik and G. Bergholz, 'Statutory Interpretation in Sweden' in D. N. MacCormick and R. S. Summers (eds.), *Interpreting Statutes* (Aldershot 1991) (hereafter 'Peczenik and Bergholz'), ch. 9, esp. p. 317; Schmidt, 196–7. The approach is described by some as a historical interpretation approach because of the emphasis on preparatory materials, but there is also a purposive direction: SOU 1994:99, 63.

[108] H. P. Graver, 'Norms and Decisions' (1988) 32 *Scandinavian Studies in Law* 47. See also S. Strömholm, 'Criteria of Relevance in Legal Reasoning' (1975) 19 *Scandinavian Studies in Law* 227, 240, who considers that the text of the law provides 'a rough network of criteria of relevance' in reaching the decision applying the text.

deference to the superiority of the legislature.[109] Peczenik and Bergholz suggest that the distinctive approach to statutory interpretation in Sweden is that interpretational issues are regarded as being about the *harmonisation of the statute and other materials*, rather than using the materials in order to interpret the statute.[110] Certainly, the historical purpose will be contained in the preparatory materials. Peczenik and Bergholz therefore argue that the judge is able to evade responsibility for an interpretation by suggesting that it is already contained in the materials that have to be harmonised. A broader approach to the interpretation of statutes that pays less attention to the views of the original legislator will be more in line with the need to enforce fundamental rights.[111] Certainly, an excessive reliance on preparatory materials can be seen as a throwback to the idea that the judge is really part of the administration.

Apart from applying provisions according to the best view of what the legislative policy means in the contemporary context, Folke Schmidt argued that there were two other areas of judicial development of statutes. In the first place, there is development by analogy. He cites the example of *Marian v. Jan*, where a statute provided that the father had to pay for a mother's expenses during pregnancy, even if the child were stillborn. A court required the father to pay the mother's expenses where she had terminated the pregnancy through an abortion.[112] This practice follows from the assumption that the legislator is rational, though some have argued that this form of expansion of the law has to be limited to situations where one is sure that the legislator would have wished to extend the scope of the provision as the court proposes.[113] In the second place, there is a duty to make the legal system as a whole up-to-date. As a result, 'the judge should make it his constant aim to rejuvenate the old laws on the model of the new'.[114] This follows from the priority given to coherence of the legal system. For Peczenik and Bergholz, 'Mutual adaptation of interpretation of statutes and other sources of law, such as legislative history and precedents . . . is commonly regarded as the core of statutory interpretation.'[115] This importance given to coherence also involves the weighing and balancing of general maxims of

[109] Peczenik and Bergholz, 324–7. [110] Ibid., 320–1.
[111] Holmström, 'Judicialization', above n. 72, 161.
[112] Schmidt, 190.
[113] Peczenik and Bergholz, 339–41 and 318–21. [114] Schmidt, 196.
[115] Peczenik and Bergholz, 312.

law, moral norms and even logical propositions. Clearly, the commitment to this kind of contemporary coherence requires the judge to engage in evaluation of the priority to be given to different aspects of the law by means of a weighing and balancing of reasons.[116] The style of judgment reflects this in that there is a strong emphasis on a rational analysis of the legislative text in the context of the preparatory materials.

The judge in court is not engaged in a wide-ranging process of law reform. The judge is not able to call on sociological and other data to provide the basis for an independent evaluation of social needs.[117] It is clearly anticipated that the application of European Union and European Convention law will push statutory interpretation further in the direction of teleological interpretation.

Judge-made rules have played an important role in Swedish law. In its formative period, during the sixteenth and seventeenth centuries, judicial decisions built up a common law. From the Code of 1734 until the early part of the twentieth century, the role of judges in making rules, rather than just applying them, was stressed. In the twentieth century, the authoritative importance of precedents became more openly acknowledged and debated.[118] If the traditional judicial style involved the bald statement of a rule applied to facts by way of subsumption, the modern trend of decision-writing is not only more discursive, but also openly refers to precedents in appropriate cases.[119] Precedents will be cited, and the court will enter into dialogue in setting out the reasons for and against its decision. Precedents are frequently cited by way of reference in judgments, but some are discussed at more length.[120] Some judicial decisions are treated as leading cases that have significant standing as statements of the law.[121] Given that the 1734 Code is old, and although it has been reformed substantially, there is significant scope for judicial decisions.

Furthermore, explicit acknowledgement of the right of the HD to make precedents was given in the reform of procedural law in 1971, under which HD is allowed to give leave for hearing cases in which it is important to give a general ruling by way of a precedent, or where a serious error of law has been made by the lower court.[122] The

[116] Ibid., 317. [117] Ibid., 354, 331.

[118] See SOU 1994:99, Del A, pp. 54–5.

[119] See G. Bergholz and A. Peczenik, 'Precedent in Sweden' in D. N. MacCormick and R. S. Summers (eds.), *Interpreting Precedents* (Aldershot 1997), ch. 9 at pp. 295–6.

[120] Ibid., 297. [121] Ibid., 306. [122] Ibid., 294.

Justitieombudsman (JO) criticised courts for failing to follow precedents, most notably in 1947. Although the legislative committee of the Riksdag responded by stating that judicial decisions only had weight in relation to the reasons given, a more general academic and judicial opinion has acknowledged that decisions of the higher courts have a greater weight.[123] In modern times, it is recognised that the function of the higher courts is to establish precedents which lower courts can follow. Thus, in a recent government report, it was stated that 'the highest courts should chiefly have a precedent-creating function'.[124] This was the culmination of developments during the past century. Originally, the HD heard appeals on law and fact. But delays were long, as much as two-and-a-half years in 1913. As a result, a leave stage was introduced. All the same, issues of fact continued to be tried, especially in criminal cases. After the 1971 reforms, this became less defensible and there was an increasing focus on points of law (*prejudikat*).[125] Nevertheless, the issue is whether the role of the HD is to produce the best rule, or merely to correct defects in decisions made by the lower courts. The suggestion is that this leads to different kinds of personnel and authority: 'Does one want to have an HD dominated by deep-thinking theoreticians in place of sensible practitioners?'[126] Although it may be going too far to say that lower courts are *bound* to follow decisions of the higher courts, they carry substantial weight.

Justification used to be in a brief, magisterial style which did not engage with the arguments for and against. As it has become more accepted that judges can engage in lawmaking, so judgments have become more discursive.[127] This more developed style is facilitated by the opportunity judges have to deliver individual opinions.[128] All the same, the judgment is typically quite brief. As Peczenik and Bergholz remark, 'Swedish courts do not overdetermine their judgments by giving more than sufficient reasons for decision.'[129] As a result, the style of decision-making is described by them as the 'sophisticated subsumption method'. It includes the basic arguments for a solution and supporting references, but not even as discursively as in a German judgment.

[123] Ibid., 300.
[124] Regeringens skrivelse 1999/2000:106, above n. 13, 9.
[125] See B. Bengtsson, 'Ändringsdispens och prejudikatdispens' in Nygren, *Högsta domsmakten*, above n. 65, 267.
[126] Ibid., 289.
[127] Bergholz and Peczenik, 'Precedent in Sweden', above n. 119, 294–5.
[128] Ibid., 297. [129] Ibid., 343.

Judicial involvement in lawmaking

Remissen

The process of remissen is a long-established part of the consultative process by which legislation is made in Sweden. Anton calls it a process to domesticate disagreement and to resolve conflicts before proposals go public. In his view, 'Royal Commission reports and government bills indicate considerable disagreement on major proposals, but the *remiss* process usually keeps such disagreement confined behind closed doors or along the metallic strands of telephone wire that link various members of the involved elite.'[130] Remisser can be given publicity in the media by their authors, but are frequently made simply as contributions to the formulation of policy by interest groups.

The courts are a remissinstans (a body invited expressly to respond to a remiss) not so much because they are an interest group (except in certain issues of institutional reform), but because they have a view of how the law might be implemented. Practical administration issues are a frequent concern in consultation processes. As Vallinder remarks, if the Svea Hovrätt, the JO and JUSEK criticise a proposal, this will weigh heavily against it.[131] Within the different courts, remisser are handled in a variety of ways. In a large court, one of the junior judges, an *adjungerad*, will draft a reply which is discussed by the president and chairs of relevant sections of the court (*lagmän*), or even by all chairs. In smaller courts, the president may do this himself. Thus, participation in the pre-legislative process is an integral part of judicial activity and helps the judges to feel part of the governing process in the widest sense.

Lagrådet

The *Lagråd* (LR) was created in 1909. The Constitution of 1809 had given the function of pre-legislative advice on legislation to the HD, but the work was already becoming too substantial by the turn of the century. The LR is composed of members of the HD and the RR, a minimum of three sitting in relation to each opinion, though they can also call on experts to assist them. Rather like the Conseil d'Etat in France, its role is to advise on the legal soundness of legislative proposals and their compatibility with the Constitution.[132] The LR does not have a competence to judge the merits of proposals. From 1909, consultation of

[130] Anton, *Administered Politics*, above n. 85, 164.
[131] Judicial Elite, 22.
[132] See generally *Vår författning*, 144–7.

the LR was compulsory in relation to civil and criminal laws. The Social Democrats saw this institution as conservative. For example, it expressed reservations in 1919 on the proposal for an eight-hour working day, and in 1938 about the proposal to require paid holidays for workers. It also commented that the expropriation law ought to have regard to the impact on the housing market.[133] The LR's concern for established contractual and property rights clashed with the welfare-state philosophy of the Social Democrats' reforms. Algotsson thinks that the conflict was exaggerated.[134]

In 1971, the Social Democrats passed a law that made consultation of the LR by the Government voluntary. Their concern was to speed up the legislative process and reduce the obstacles, such as consultative procedures. The opposition wanted compulsory reference on tax and fundamental rights matters. A widely accepted compromise of voluntary reference emerged in the 1971 legislation and was confirmed in the Constitution (RF). This was modified by the conservative/liberal coalition in 1979 to the extent that, if the Government decides not to ask the advice of the LR, it has to provide reasons for this decision to Parliament. A moral pressure, rather than legal pressure, is thus established. At the same time, the potential scope of references to the LR was widened. In its post-1979 version, RF art. 8-18 states that the LR shall give an opinion on laws which affect the Constitution, press freedom and a number of fundamental rights, or where the law is important from a private or a public viewpoint. The Constitution specifies that the LR shall give an opinion on (1) how the proposal relates to the Constitution or legal order in general, (2) how its provisions relate to each other, (3) how the provisions affect legal certainty, (4) whether the proposal is so drafted that it can achieve the objectives for which it is being passed, and (5) whether problems might arise in interpreting it. The LR must avoid general policy grounds. Increasingly, the role of the LR will be to identify conflicts with European norms. There were sixty-three references of bills to the LR in 2002.[135] The number of times the LR is called upon to give an opinion varies significantly from year to year.

The LR will give its opinion just before the bill is presented to Parliament. Since the courts will typically have responded by way of remiss to

[133] See K.-G. Algotsson, 'Lagrådet, rättstaten och demokratin' in Håstad and Lewin, *Politik och Juridik*, above n. 75, 37 at 43 (hereafter 'Algotsson').
[134] Ibid., 42.
[135] Lagrådet website (http://www.lagradet.se); also *Vår författning*, 146.

the consultation paper, many of the issues will have been raised at an early stage. The LR primarily deals with the final text and with the drafting of what is put forward. Its commentary is then taken into account by the Government. For example, in the case of the courts reform, the bill was sent to the LR on 21 October 1999, the LR deliberated on 1 November and the bill, with substantial commentary from the Government, was published on 18 November, including the opinion of the LR in Appendix 8.[136]

Algotsson suggests that the rather legal–technical approach of the LR to the Constitution will not transfer well to the issue of compatibility with European norms.[137] His view is that the LR focuses on a formal sense of legality through its technical approach. It does not have competence to discuss the merits of proposals to the same extent that the French Conseil d'Etat does. All the same, the LR does make use of European norms as part of its concept of legality. For example, in relation to a proposal to reform court procedure, the LR specifically discussed the European Convention in relation to the retrospective effect of the law.[138] According to Vallinder, a comment on constitutionality by the LR would have an important influence on the view of a later court on whether a legal provision was *manifestly* unconstitutional, as is required for judicial review under RF art. 11-14.[139]

Elisabeth Palm, Vice-President of the European Court of Human Rights and a judge of the HD, chose to spend most of a contribution to a volume on the rule of law in talking about the LR and its work.[140] In her analysis, the work of the LR provides an important contribution to constitutionality in Sweden. Indeed, the LR was described by Andrén as 'the main constitutional bulwark of judicial influence on public legislation'.[141] Although it is less direct than the remiss procedure, the LR has greater influence and allows senior judges to shape the legislation that they and their colleagues may have to implement in their judicial capacity.

136 Regeringenskansliet, Proposition 1999/2000:26, *Effektivisering av förfarendet i allmän domstol.*

137 Algotsson, 52.

138 See Proposition 1999/2000:26, above n. 136, 239.

139 Judicial Elite, 30.

140 E. Palm, 'Le contrôle préliminaire et *a posteriori* des lois en Suède' in *Mélanges Braibant* (Paris 1996), 569ff.

141 N. Andrén, *Modern Swedish Government* (2nd edn, Stockholm 1968), 206.

Extrajudicial activities

Judges and administrators

There are longstanding connections between the career of judge and that of administrator in Sweden. It is not a total accident that Chapter 11 of the RF brings 'The Judiciary and General Administration' together. One of the most distinctive features of Swedish public administration is the widespread use of independent agencies or boards. A system of administrative boards with regional sub-units, staffed by professional civil servants, was in place by 1634. The system was improved by the addition of a tier of ministries in 1840, but political control by the Riksdag only became a reality in the twentieth century. Under this system, policy-making by the King or Riksdag and administration by the boards were clearly separated. But the boards combined administrative and judicial tasks, a pattern which has some similarity with the activities of English justices of the peace in the same period. In Anton's view,

> Administrative power was . . . a function of Swedish insistence that 'policy' and 'administrative' decisions were clearly distinct and that the latter could be made simply by applying the law to the facts of a particular case. The administrative boards initiated in the 17th century were designed to provide such legal judgments, free from 'political' interference.[142]

They took decisions on disputes affecting individuals within their remit, with eventual appeal to the Kammarrätt in Stockholm, established in 1695. The independence and high status of the civil service paralleled the position of the judiciary much more than in many other European countries. The authority of the office-holder attached both to civil servants and to judges. The independence of the administrative boards continues to be safeguarded under RF art. 11-7: 'No public authority . . . may determine how an administrative authority may make its decision in a particular case concerning the exercise of public authority against a private subject or against a municipality, or concerning the application of law.' This establishes a status and a spirit of working which is similar to that of the judiciary. The system of government keeps administration and judicial activity conceptually distinct from politics, and reduces conflict by an attempt to clarify each specialised role.[143] At the same time,

[142] Anton, *Administered Politics*, above n. 85, 5.
[143] Andrén, *Modern Swedish Government*, above n. 141, 161; Judicial Elite, 16.

informal contacts between the formally distinct organs is essential to make the system work, while each retains its distinct responsibilities.[144]

This traditional similarity between much of the administration and the judiciary is reflected in a number of ways. In the first place, university education in law was the traditional preparation for entry into the civil service. To quote Anton, 'in the past, middle and upper-class individuals interested in a government career went to university, studied law, and moved into civil service posts that required use of their legal training'.[145] He notes that the proportion of law graduates among new entrants to the civil service fell from more than 60 per cent in 1917 to 52 per cent in 1947 and by the 1960s it had fallen to 25 per cent as recruitment diversified to include more social scientists. Nevertheless, among his civil service interviewees in the 1970s, 55 per cent of those working in ministries and 40 per cent of director-generals of boards aged over forty were lawyers.[146] The requirement of legal training for many administrative positions declined over the early twentieth century, but was only formally abolished in 1964. As Holmström suggests, legal education went alongside a particular conception of the role of the administration: 'The Swedish state apparatus before the democratic – and Social Democratic – era looked like a machine staffed by legally-trained people dealing with public matters in a formal, rule-applying manner.'[147]

A second feature, already noted, is the way in which Sweden was late in developing a clearly distinct administrative court structure. The combination of independent boards combining administrative and judicial tasks, and supervision by the JO, provided a system of redress for individuals that was more robust than in the politically dominated administrations of other countries.

The third feature is a shared culture. The tradition of the boards and the courts emphasised independence, political neutrality, expert competence and loyalty to the system. Indeed, one characterisation of the traditional model of the Swedish administrator is that of a judge, applying legal rules.[148] There is also a strong emphasis on clarity about

144 See Pierre, 'Legitimacy', above n. 94, 390.

145 Anton, *Administered Politics*, above n. 85, 27–8.

146 Ibid., 28.

147 Holmström, 'Judicialization', above n. 72, 153.

148 Anton, *Administered Politics*, above n. 85, 57: 'Knowledge of administrative law together with personal qualities of objectivity and impartiality define the "classic" Swedish view of administrators as judges, whose chief responsibility was to select and apply legal rules to problems presented to them.'

the permitted boundaries of one's action.[149] These values are shared more strongly than in some other countries between judges and the administration. Both traditionally shared the elite conservative background and a common training in the university law faculties. Both have adapted socially and politically to accommodate the change in society brought about by the years of Social Democrat rule. In the case of the administrator, this has required what Anton describes as the 'soft activist' model, taking the initiative to achieve changes which will further policy goals established by the politicians. This takes him away from the more passive approach of the administrator as a 'judge', applying predetermined rules to situations that arise. In the case of the judge, the role is to collaborate in lawmaking by a teleological interpretation designed to achieve the new objectives set by the legislator, rather than clinging to a conservative status quo. In this setting, both administrators and judges are loyal and independent experts, but the administrator will focus on achieving results by compromise and pragmatism, whereas the judge in court has to declare entitlements under the rules. But, of course, the judge out of court, particularly in legislative reform committees, has to adopt the similar 'soft activist' approach to the administrator, achieving results through pragmatism and compromise.

Thus, judicial and administrative hierarchies and careers are distinct. Each has its own place in the constitutional system. Judges are not there simply to do as they are told, but share with the JO a role as independent checks on the administration, the police and other organs of government in the defence of the interests of citizens. The Swedish tradition of independent administration does not set the judiciary apart as much as in countries with a more integrated or politicised public administration. There are important shared values in the ways in which the administration and the judiciary operate in relation to the political process. Both are drawn in through consultation into the process of formulating legislative proposals. Judicial career development encourages the building of bridges between the administration and judges.

Judges as committee secretaries

The tradition in Sweden is that law reform is prepared by a committee established by the sponsoring ministry. Participation in legislative reform committees is an important part of the career of many judges.

[149] Ibid., 162–3.

This participation usually occurs at two stages in a judge's life. As an assessor, a judge may be seconded (full- or part-time) to be the legal secretary to a committee. Such a body will consist of ten to twenty persons. If the matter has significant political implications, the committee will typically consist of members of different political parties and interest groups. In other cases, the composition may be more technical.[150] The role of the legal secretary is to draft the report, especially any recommendations for a draft bill.[151] An *ordinarie* judge (especially a chief judge) may be asked to chair a committee, especially where the matter is a technical law reform. The typical chair is a head of division within the HD or KR, who has some specialist knowledge of the area. Being chair will be a burdensome task for a judge, though it is manageable if there is a judge as referent and another as secretary. The role is rather delicate. If the minister's initial ideas turn out to be unacceptable, the chair of the committee has to find a way of helping the minister to save face, e.g. by withdrawing the brief from the committee. Accordingly, some expertise in leading committees of this kind will be helpful. Political affiliation may also be a relevant consideration.

The advantages of committee work are that it provides broader knowledge and understanding of particular fields for judges, and helps them to develop or extend their expertise. It also provides judges with an understanding of the administration and how it works.

Other administrative roles

There is no established government legal service. Ministries may, however, have legal-trained officials working for them as part of the secretariat, giving legal advice. In this situation, it is often thought useful to bring in a judge into a ministry or other administration to perform legal advice or administrative roles.[152] Frequently, a judge will serve as a legal secretary in a ministry, where she or he may help in the development of particular proposals, which may subsequently be sent for consideration by a law reform committee. Alternatively, a judge might accept a posting in an administration. For example, as in France, a judge might

[150] Where law reform is more urgent, officials within the ministry will typically undertake the preparations for a legislative proposal. Committee reports are published in the *Statens offentliga utredningar* (SOU).

[151] Some judges interviewed for this research actually delayed appointment as *ordinarie* to be able to carry on such activities.

[152] Judicial Elite, 29 and 32.

be called upon to head a particular administration with a limited legal element, e.g. in relation to estate services for the army.[153] With increasing importance in recent years, a judge may accept an administrative posting within DV, undertaking both policy and legal roles.

Although there may be personal contacts between individual members of the administration and individual judges, there is no tradition, as in France, of requesting judges to provide informal legal advice. The view was expressed in interview that, when a judge acts as a committee secretary, he is the employee of the commissioning department, and so should not ask for informal opinions from colleagues who are still active judges. This suggests an attitude of wishing to keep the different roles of judges and administrators separate, even when colleagues may be performing both roles.

External commitments

A major area of concern is whether judges can undertake arbitrations.[154] Until recently, judges were allowed to be arbitrators (and to retain the honorarium for this work), but it was decided that this should not be allowed. One judge, Ulf Nielsson, resigned from the HD in order to continue with his arbitration work. Political commitments are now rare. Lawyers are not a large group in the Riksdsag and, of these, perhaps one or two are judges. In the past, more judges and lawyers were involved in politics.[155]

Professional judges and the legal community

Justitieombudsman

The origin of the ombudsman role goes back to 1766, as an investigatory and controlling role in relation to government. The JO was seen as an essential feature in the separation of powers set out in the 1809 Constitution, and was created as 'a general national power', appointed by Parliament. The role of this parliamentary official was to exercise control over

[153] Elliot, *Ur en domares liv*, above n. 28, 138ff.

[154] See, for example, E. Holmberg, 'Om domarkarriären' (1999) 3 *Tidskrift för Sveriges Domareförbund* 15.

[155] For example, the leader of the conservatives in the First Chamber during the constitutional crisis of 1914 was a judge of HD: see L. Lewin, *Ideology and Strategy: A Century of Swedish Politics* (Cambridge 1988), 94–5. Holmström, 'Judicialization', above n. 72, 154, suggests that, at that time, about a third of the upper chamber and 10–15 per cent of the lower chamber of the Riksdag had legal qualifications, and about 10 per cent and 6–8 per cent respectively were judges.

the executive power of administrative boards. His duty was to conduct inspections and to initiate prosecutions of wrongdoers. As 'special prosecutor', he obtained his information from the public, the newspapers and inspections. But the role developed essentially into a complaints system.[156] (In relation to central government, a similar role was already performed by the *Justitiekanslern*, an equivalent of the Attorney General.) As the role has developed, his focus remains the control of the administration, which includes the courts but excludes elected local government, who have their own organs for redressing grievances. The function of the JO is to investigate the correctness of administrative decisions and the impartiality of officials, as well as, in more recent years, the protection of rights.

The law of 1986 establishes four individuals as the JO. They are elected for five years by the Riksdag.[157] They conduct investigations and may attend meetings of administrative boards, agencies and courts at their choice. Although established as a tool of the Riksdag, especially in the twentieth century, the JO has become an instrument of popular control of the administration. The JO receives a substantial number of written complaints – 5,051 in 2002–3. This role of making findings and recommendations in relation to individual complaints has made it an important institution. By contrast, the original role of prosecuting officials has declined significantly. Whereas 5–10 per cent of investigations resulted in prosecutions in 1900, there have only been between two and four prosecutions in each of the past few years.[158] For the most part, this has been because prosecution has not been seen as appropriate. In addition, reforms of 1976 reduced the role of the JO to the prosecution of criminal actions within the official duties of an individual, leaving these to disciplinary proceedings. The JO limits his prosecutions to the commission of ordinary criminal offences.[159] Over the years, a number of such ombudsman functions were created, e.g. into other aspects of government, such as the army. In addition, a number of new ombudsmen, covering children, disabled people, homosexuals and consumers, have been created.

The role of ombudsman provides an alternative to judicial redress. As has been seen, this has been an important aspect in shaping the scope of

[156] Judicial Elite, 32–3.
[157] See *Vår författning*, 205–6; T. Bull, 'The Original Ombudsman: Blueprint in Need of Revision or a Concept with More to Offer?' (2000) 6 EPL 334.
[158] Bull, 'Original Ombndsman', above n. 157, 337.
[159] Strömholm, 'General Features', above n. 94, 45.

review by the administrative courts. But the JO also has a role in being the recipient of complaints against the courts. In 2002–3, there were 670 complaints against the ordinary courts, which led to 141 investigations and 14 adverse reports.[160] There were also 104 complaints against the administrative courts, leading to 57 investigations and 6 adverse findings. Complaints relate to matters such as delay in proceedings or lack of clarity in reasoning.

Åklagarna

The *åklagar* (prosecutor) is responsible for leading the investigation in some serious cases, reaching the decision to prosecute and presenting the case in court. He is involved in the investigation less than the French examining magistrate, but more than the English crown prosecutor. The position thus offers the opportunity for individual work and responsibility. Although a distinct profession since 1948, the prosecutor occupies a role that is closely associated with the judiciary. Indeed, judges may spend some of their assessor period as prosecutors. One possible attraction is that being a prosecutor enables a person to stay in the same town, rather than moving around the country from one temporary post to another. It is also well paid. Rather like the English Crown Prosecution Service, the prosecution service in Sweden found it difficult initially to obtain recruits. But it has gradually succeeded in developing a high and attractive profile. On 31 December 2002, there were 758 åklagare in post. There were twenty-one new trainees during the year, thirteen women and eight men, proportions similar to the entrants to the judiciary.[161] Ten came through the placements in the åklagare organisation, four from the judiciary, two from other organisations, and three from the economic crime agency. Women now predominate among applicants as well as among successful candidates. They form 60 per cent of those under forty, and the majority of those between forty and fifty, but they only form 27 per cent of those over fifty-five, most of whom occupy the senior posts.

Although not part of the judiciary, there is a close professional relationship between the public service of prosecutors and the public service of judges, which may be reflected in both the similarity of career structure and participation by some individuals in both careers over a working life. All the same, the judicial career retains the higher profile.

160 Justitieombudsman, *Åmbetsberätelser* (Stockholm 2003), 18.
161 See Åklagarorganisationen, *Årsredovisning 2002* (Stockholm 2003), 60–1.

Advokaterna

It is less common for a judge to become an *advokat* (private lawyer). The profession was traditionally not highly regarded, and it was not well structured. A private association of lawyers (the *Sveriges Advokatsamfund*) was created in 1887 with thirty-eight members,[162] but it really only came to occupy a significant position after the reforms of procedure in 1948. As has been noted, the inquisitorial system left little space for them to achieve successes through defence or to obtain remedies.[163] As a result, the role of the advokat was not well known. Since then, the roles of criminal defence, civil litigation and commercial advice have increased the status and wealth of the advokaten. In 2002, there were 3,505 practising advokaten, compared with 2,568 in 1992.[164] There is clear reluctance on the part of some older members of the profession to appoint women.[165] In order to apply to become an advokat, it has recently been necessary to apply to Advokatsamfunden after training. The normal qualifying period is five years of practical experience, though it is reduced to two to three years in recognition of other prior experience. In 2002, the association decided to introduce an entrance examination from 2004.[166] Law graduates may also work as legal advisers in firms, for which they do not need the same qualifications, but they then do not have rights of audience in the courts.

Transfers between the advokat and judicial professions are rare. For a judge to become an advokat would take a number of years. A judge would normally get only one year's leave of absence to begin training as an advokat, but this might be enough to launch a change of career, leading initially to a position as an associate lawyer. All the same, there are instances of judges becoming an advokat and even of them returning to a higher post in the judiciary at a later stage.[167] Although the larger firms developed training programmes for their new recruits in the 1990s,[168] service as a notarie is still a mark of distinction and a

162 SOU 1999:31, *Advokatväsendet i Sverige*, 63; Modéer, *Lemän och Lagerlöfvar*, above n. 48, 29–30, 85–7; K. Å. Modéer, 'Samhället behöver advokater med ideal och samhällsengagemang' (1996) 62 *Advokaten* 9/96, 7.

163 *Advokatväsendet i Sverige*, 63.

164 Ibid., 68.

165 See Modéer, *Lemän och Lagerlöfvar*, above n. 48, 119–21.

166 Åklagarorganisationen, *Årsredovisning 2002*, 8.

167 For example, Susanne Knöös was an assessor in the KR before joining the law firm Lagerlöf and then became Justitieombudsman: Modéer, *Lemän och Lagerlöfvar*, above n. 48, 120.

168 See ibid., 121 and 160.

training route preferred by the law firms. Those who have undertaken this notarie training can expect to receive a higher initial salary.[169] Nevertheless, the standing of law firms is on the increase, especially with international work and links, as well as higher salaries compared with the judiciary.

The traditional status of the judge relative to the advokat and the åklagar is changing. A meeting of the *Sveriges Domareförbund* in October 2000 heard a number of papers from younger judges arguing that three factors are affecting the status of judges. First, there is security. One does not have job security until one reaches the status of *ordinarie domare*, which is ten to twelve years after completing the basic training. Secondly, there is the lack of predictability in terms of what posts will be available and in what locations. Thirdly, there is the issue of salaries. In a commercial practice in a large city, an advokat would earn 45,000 kr a month after three years, compared with an assessor (who has three more years of experience) who earned only 35,000 kr.[170] As a result, relatively few members of the other professions apply to be judges. While judges have a long education, they remain generalists in a legal system which is becoming more complex, particularly with the addition of EU and European Convention laws. But the broadening of the legal career to include increasing international dimensions is more marked in the careers of advokaterna than in the public sector. It would be fair to say that the traditional elite status of judges is declining as the advokat career becomes both more attractive and more lucrative. Indeed, the recent reductions in judicial appointments can only accelerate this loss of the best candidates to the law firms.

Academic lawyers

The law faculties of the universities have a collective influence in a number of ways. As has been seen, they teach all the prospective lawyers, including judges. The faculties are also influential in the remiss procedure. In addition, there may be some individual connections between law faculties and the judiciary. Some judges give lectures at the university as an extra activity in their career. More commonly, they will lecture in law in the Hogskol (more equivalent to further education).

[169] See the guide to starting salaries on the JUSEK website (http://www.jusek.se). In March 2001, the starting salary for a lawyer was 21,000 kr a month, whereas that for a *notariemeriterade* was 23,500 kr.

[170] See R. Nordh, 'Den framtida domarrekyteringen och domarkarriären' (2000) 4 *Tidskrift för Sveriges Domareförbund* 9.

Although judicial procedure requires the parties to be active in shaping the issues and presenting them, the judge is still responsible for legal researches. A referent will be appointed from among the judges and he has to prepare the draft judgment. This role involves the conducting of research. Research will include relevant theses and legal writings. A judge will look at these where they exist. The precedents of the higher courts will, however, be a significant influence. Doctrinal writing will not be discussed very much in judicial debates, though the HD has taken to quoting academics in judgments since the mid-1990s.[171] All the same, the opinions of leading authors, e.g. Ekelöf and Olivecrona on procedure, will carry weight. Authors may have a particularly high status because of a number of factors – for example, they may sit as *ad hoc* judges (for which no additional qualification is required).

Some academic lawyers are appointed to the Bench and yet continue to have some link with their law schools and continue writing. For example, at the time of writing, Professor Bertil Bengtsson still writes in Stockholm as well as sitting in the HD. (Academics also give opinions to lawyers, rather than work as members of law firms, though some are part-time members of faculty and occupy such positions.)

Relationships between academics and judges have been varied. There has been the long-held view that academics are too theoretical and not of much real use to the life of the practitioner. This stems from a basic mistrust of the academic lawyer. But, in more recent years, there has been a greater self-confidence among the judges, and some of them are undertaking work in the universities, even doctorates.

Lay judges

History

Lay judges (*nämndemän*) are an important and distinctive feature of the Swedish legal system.[172] As Modéer remarks, 'The nämnd are the most

[171] There are no systematic studies of the role of doctrinal writers, but interviews with academics and lawyers confirm this development. An illustration can be found in a decision of the Högsta Domstol (Case T 3040–03, 10 November 2003, pp. 4–5), which cites academic work and judicial decisions to justify an interpretation of the European Convention on Human Rights.

[172] Diesen defines the lay judge as someone who performs a judicial role without the requirement of prior legal education: C. Diesen, *Lekmän som Domare* (Stockholm 1996) (hereafter 'Diesen'), 14.

distinctive feature of the Swedish legal culture.'[173] The earliest judges in Sweden were laymen, either the nämnd or the local lord. Professionalisation came with requirements of writing in the upper courts and the teaching of Swedish law in the universities, beginning at Uppsala in 1620. The growth in importance of the King's judges was designed to eclipse the power of the local nobles and culminated in the Code of 1734, which gave many tasks to the professional judges appointed by the King.[174]

The nämnd has its origins in decision-making in rural communities in the early Middle Ages, where it was a way of the tribe resolving problems within its community through a judgment of the community itself. The nämnd became the general form of proof in criminal cases by the time of Magnus Ericksson's general law of the realm in 1347.[175] This form of decision-making in the häradshov covered the large, rural part of the country. At this point, the nämnd could be conceived as essentially a decision-maker (*rådgivare*). The nämnd decided questions of law as well as fact, and a majority of seven could impose itself on the judge.[176] Only with the professionalisation of judges and legal education did the nämnd come to be reduced effectively to the role of assessor (*bisittare*) in the 1734 Code.[177]

The role of the nämnd was to give a single decision, albeit by a majority vote, so there was pressure to reduce its size. The committee on procedural reform of 1948 upheld the importance of nämnd participation, but reduced its size from twelve to nine for serious cases and to three for less serious cases. The main reasons for retaining the nämnd were that the lay judges had a broader experience of life and understanding of people, which complemented the legal knowledge of the (typically younger) professional judges. They also offered a perspective appropriate to deciding how to apply the law to individual cases and to decisions based on general issues of fairness, rather than technical law.[178]

Function

The 2002 review committee report on the nämnd[179] identified three contributions of lay judges:

[173] Modéer, *Domarkulturen*, 41.
[174] Ibid., 114–15. [175] Ibid., 111. [176] SOU 1994:99, 173.
[177] Diesen, 115, 119. [178] Ibid., 125.
[179] SOU 2002:61, *Framtidens nämndemän* (Betänkande från Nämndemannakommittén) (June 2002), 53.

1. to guarantee effectiveness by keeping judicial decisions in line with social values;
2. to maintain confidence of citizens in the effectiveness of courts;
3. to keep the interest of the public in the effectiveness of justice by collaboration of lay people.

The nämnd have traditionally come from the local community, though obviously they originally represented only those who could vote, the propertied classes. During the twentieth century, the importance of the nämnd in offering a democratic dimension to the legal process was stressed by the Social Democrats. The broadening function for the nämnd in reforms of the 1970s had as its objective to offer an element of popular control over this branch of the public service. In 1971, the nämnd was extended from the rural häradshov to the newly created tingsrätt, predominantly located in urban centres. Lay judges were introduced into family and civil cases, and also into the appeal courts and administrative courts. In the tingsrätt, there is normally one judge and (since 1983) three nämndemän, but any case involving a possible sentence of more than two years in jail has four or five nämndemän. In family cases, there are three judges and two nämndemän, and in the länsrätt, there is one judge and three nämndemän. Since 1977,[180] on appeals to the hovrätt relating to criminal and family cases, two nämndemän sit with three judges. The Kammarrätt has a similar composition for appeals from the länsrätt. The justification was expressed largely in terms of the difference of experience and expertise which lay judges bring to their task: 'laymen with mature judgment and general life experience . . . have a good background for judging questions of evidence. But, through habit and greater expert consideration, professional judges in general have greater possibilities than lay judges to come to an objectively right assessment of evidence.'[181] These arguments emphasise the need for the court to contain a blend of expertise when it handles socially complex situations, such as crime and sentencing and domestic matters. Technical legal expertise is not the only quality required of the decision-maker, particularly when lower court judges may be quite young, with limited social experience. This remains the predominant justification offered for the role of the nämnd.[182]

[180] Participation by nämndemän in the appeal courts was originally proposed in 1931 and was debated several times thereafter before the 1977 reforms: see SOU 1994:99, 180–4.

[181] Justifications of the 1971 reforms, cited in Diesen, 129.

[182] See, for example, an article by the president of an administrative appeal court, A. Bondestam, 'Nämndemännen tillför juristerna klokskap' *Nämndemän*, no. 2/2000, p. 9.

The extension of the role of lay judges was also supported by arguments about the need to increase public confidence in judicial decisions. Further democratisation came in the 1983 reform that gave an individual vote to the nämndemän. Thus, rather than coming to a collective decision before they can outvote the judge, individual nämndemän can vote according to their own views and may form coalitions with one of the judges to prevail. The nämnd has always been a mechanism for popular involvement in justice. Unlike the Justice of the Peace in England, it was not simply the mechanism for the local gentry to govern the rural community. In its modern guise, the nämnd has been given the role of representing the community in the administration of justice, and thereby calling the judges to account within the decision-making process itself. As Diesen puts it,

> Through the participation of the nämndemän the perspective of the general public comes into the operation of the courts and can exercise a democratic control, which promotes confidence in the administration of justice. A further objective of this participation is that it guarantees that legal decisions are in line with the public's sense of justice and that, through the broader life experiences, conditions are established for a rounded solution to matters.[183]

The nämnd was selected from among those entitled to vote. The choice by the local community is now reflected in the appointment of the nämnd by the local authority. Since 1863, members have been chosen by the commune, and since 1975 on a proportional basis. Nämndemän are usually chosen from members of the authority in proportion to the political representation at the last local elections. As one interviewee put it, the nämnd is one of a range of committees on which a local councillor may choose to sit. The Riksdag has made it clear that being a member of the nämnd is a special role, which is not a political task, despite the method of appointment. Certainly, nämndemän interviewed suggested that political affiliation is not a major determinant in how people carry out their task. Individuals have their own views on criminal justice, the upbringing of children and so on, and these are political positions in a broad sense, rather than ones that are confined to a particular political party.

[183] Diesen, 255. Similar words were used by the Government in Regeringens skrivelse 1999/2000:106, above n. 13, 32. The importance of public confidence in the legal system and of democratic principles was also stated by the committee on judges in 1994: SOU 1994:99, 302.

Membership and training

There are now some 6,000 nämndemän – 5,500 in the lower courts and 500 in the appeal courts. Although there have been suggestions for training to be provided centrally, training is predominantly provided through a voluntary association of lay judges, the *Nämndemannaförening*, with some funding from DV for events such as visits to other courts. The local association may also obtain funding for its activities from the local commune.

The importance of popular participation in justice gives rise to concerns about the representative character of the nämnd. In a 1992 report by DV, 58 per cent of nämndemän were found to be men, 94 per cent were over forty years of age, with 63 per cent from the oldest age groups – 23 per cent were pensioners. Moreover, 27 per cent worked in the administration, compared with only 1 per cent of the population as a whole, and 65 per cent had an income of at least 160,000 kr a year, compared with 17 per cent of the population as a whole.[184] In 2000, 45 per cent of nämndemän were over sixty and only 8 per cent under forty.[185] The present system effectively hands over nominations to the political parties, and a review in 1994 suggested that a more open system of recruitment was desirable.[186] The 2002 Committee recognised a particular problem in ensuring representation of ethnic minorities within the nämnd.[187] Previously only Swedish nationals could serve as lay judges, and it was not possible for people to hold Swedish nationality with any other nationality. The 2001 reform of nationality law has enabled people to hold dual citizenship, and this may be attractive to those who have come to Sweden since the mid-1970s, and who have retained the nationality of their country of origin.

The role of the nämnd is complex and pulls in a number of different directions. In the lower courts, they are fellow judges with individual votes. In the appeal courts, they are more assessors exercising a controlling or accountability function. Certainly, by their very presence,

184 Diesen, 140–1.

185 Ministry of Justice press release, 'Utredning för att breda rekryteringen av nämndemän till landets domstolar', 30 November 2000.

186 See Regeringens skrivelse 1999/2000:106, above n. 13, 32–3, requesting a broader social base than at present.

187 In general, the issue of ethnicity within the Swedish legal system is approached as a problem of how judges relate to litigants and participants in a trial, rather than as a matter affecting the composition of the judiciary itself. Thus, the emphasis is on training judges to be aware of ethnicity issues: see DV, *Årsredovisning 2003*, 100.

they are able to inject both different knowledge and an element of social accountability into the professional judges' decision-making process. Because they are politicians, they have a way of offering feedback to the legislator about the operation of the legal system. Only to a limited extent do they represent the population (as *folksdomar*).[188] It is inevitable that they will be drawn from the older and more experienced members of society, and their work commitments will make it difficult for many employed members of society to participate. That said, there are arguments for greater social representativeness or perhaps more attention to specialist knowledge.

Operation

In her study of the work of nämndemän in over 4,000 cases in the Svea hovrätt, Landolf[189] found that the lay judges disagreed with the professional judges in only 2 per cent of cases and made a reservation in a further 7 per cent (a similar percentage to disagreements among professional judges). In 18 per cent of criminal appeals, there were divergent opinions among the judges, but in only 2.6 per cent was the majority made up of a single professional judge and two lay judges. Dissent is much higher in the difficult appeal cases compared with the lower courts. Dissent was six times more frequent in the Svea hovrätt than in the Stockholm tingsrätt. Now dissents show only one aspect of where lay judges make a difference, but their low number perhaps colours the perception among judges that lay participation makes little difference to the outcome. But, as Bankowski's study of lay judges in Scotland shows,[190] conceptions of legal justice among professional and lay judges may not be all that different. My own limited interviews with nämndemän suggest that there is some attitude of deference shown by the lay judges to the professionals, as well as a respect for authority and expertise. The rules of the court also limit the influence of the lay judges. Under the Code of Criminal Procedure, deliberations of the court start with the youngest professional judge or the reporter expressing a view, followed by professional judges in order of seniority before giving the lay judges a chance to express their opinions. This does give rise to a 'snowball' effect in many decisions, whereby there is little

[188] Diesen, 337–8. 'The Swedish nämndemän can therefore be characterised as a jointly responsible co-judge without legal knowledge' (ibid., 331).

[189] Cited in Diesen, 315–16. On the work of lay judges in the appeal courts, see SOU 1994:99, 310–11.

[190] Below p. 333.

point in the lay judges making much of a contribution to discussions unless they disagree with what the professional judges have already proposed.

The justifications for the contemporary role of the nämnd mainly involve some criticism of the competence of professional judges to decide alone. A study of Swedish appeal court judges suggested that 60 per cent of respondents thought that lay judges had no place in the appeal courts because the issues are predominantly legal questions. Of the respondents, 70 per cent claimed to have good working relationships with the nämnd, but only 36 per cent were positive about the value of the contribution that they made to decision-making.[191] A different survey also found strong objections to lay judges in the appeal courts, but a division of opinion about their role at first instance between the ordinary courts, where only 10 per cent were against having lay judges, and the administrative courts, where 40 per cent were against. Since the lay judges only came into administrative courts in 1971 and into the appeal courts in 1977, but have been traditional in the ordinary courts at first instance, one can detect a certain reluctance among judges in those courts to accept 'recent' changes, particularly as they were introduced by a particularly radical Social Democrat government under Olof Palme. Efficiency and effectiveness are perhaps stronger-weighted arguments among judges than a particular version of democratic representativeness.

The jury exists only in press cases (widened in 1991 to include other branches of the media). It was introduced in 1815 following constitutional reform at the beginning of the nineteenth century along the model of the English jury.[192] The nine-man jury is chosen from a list of jurors proposed by the political parties.[193] It determines criminal liability by at least six of its members in a relatively small number of cases. Its job is essentially to protect political speech against government interference. Jury independence was reinforced by legislation in 1999, whereby proportional representation was introduced.[194]

[191] Diesen, 316–17. Good working relationships are traditional – in the nineteenth century there was often overnight accommodation provided in the courts for the nämndemän if they had come from a distance and there would be convivial relations between them and the professional judges out of court: see Modéer, *Domarkulturen*, 41.

[192] See T. Vallinder, 'The Swedish Jury System in Press Cases: An Offspring of the English Jury Trial?' (1987) 8 *Journal of Legal History* 190.

[193] This fell foul of the ECHR in Strasbourg in *Holm v. Sweden* (1993) 18 EHRR 79.

[194] See generally T. Vallinder, *Nio edsvurna män. Jury och tryckfrihet i Sverige 1815–2000* (Stockholm 2000), ch. 15.

Judges and the wider community

We have already seen that judges have an important public role in pre-legislative procedure, either within the policy-making committees as chairs or secretaries, or as respondents to consultation in the remiss procedure, or as members of Lagrådet, scrutinising the bill before it goes to Parliament. Relationships with the lay judges are also an important way in which the professional judges engage with the wider community. Constitutional review, such as it exists in Sweden, and the general public perception of the judiciary and the legal process show further the relationships and standing of judges in the wider community.

Judges and politics: constitutional adjudication

The Swedish Constitution does not favour judicial review of legislation. Elisabeth Palm notes that it is usually said that there are two important institutions in relation to Swedish constitutional protection, the Ombudsman and Lagrådet.[195] The point is that constitutional rights and procedures are safeguarded predominantly by non-judicial means, rather than by a constitutional court as in Germany or the US.[196] As Cameron suggests, the Swedish approach essentially is that 'where there is a specific statutory right, there is no practical need to resort to interpreting a more abstract constitutional norm'.[197] LR carefully ensures that the statutes are properly drafted with due respect for fundamental rights and existing entitlements, and the Ombudsman provides cheap and effective redress for administrative failures to respect rights. Constitutional review has never been a major part of the rule of law or of ensuring constitutionality.

This position on constitutional review is reinforced by the conception of liberty that has dominated Sweden in the past half century. As Tilton points out,[198] 'liberty is not the central Social Democratic value that colours all others; for liberals it is, but for Social Democrats equality and solidarity possess at least equal importance'. The individualism characteristic of much American constitutional review has not been the primary characteristic of the Swedish legal order. Even more recent

[195] Palm, 'Le contrôle preliminaire', above n. 140, 571; Petersson et al., *Report from the Democratic Audit*, above n. 11, 55–8.

[196] Writing in 1968, Andrén (*Modern Swedish Government*, above n. 141, 207–8) noted that constitutional review was merely theoretical and marginal.

[197] I. Cameron, 'The Protection of Constitutional Rights in Sweden' [1997] PL 488, 502.

[198] Tilton, *Political Theory*, above n. 86, 253.

changes have predominantly looked at the objectives and expectations met by public services, rather than new rights susceptible of judicial protection.[199]

Judicial review of legislation was not formally contained in the Constitution of 1809 and was rejected by the Riksdag and most political parties in the 1930s.[200] It was only late in the process of constitutional revision in the early 1970s that a consensus emerged on a very limited form of constitutional review. Under RF art. 11-14, a court or an administrative agency can refuse to apply a provision only where it is manifestly contrary to the Constitution. The Swedish tradition has been to rely on preview of legislation to prevent undue interference with rights. In the structure established by the 1974 Constitution, some (absolute) rights can only be restricted by way of constitutional amendment, while other (relative) rights can be restricted by legislation only by special procedures in Parliament.[201] For example, the procedure can be delayed by a minority of ten MPs, unless a five-sixths majority in the Riksdag permits the ordinary legislative procedure to continue. This protection by way of parliamentary procedure is supplemented by the legislative preview work of the LR. The constitution committee (*Konstitutionsutskottet*) serves as a major guardian of constitutionality in this regard. In addition, the JO also serves as a cheap and inexpensive protector of fundamental rights. Cameron argues that developed theories of constitutional interpretation arise where there is either an old constitution or one that is difficult to change.[202] Neither of these applies in the case of the 1974 Swedish Constitution, which can be amended by a simple majority in Parliament, albeit expressed on two occasions with a general election intervening between the two votes. There is also a strong tradition of deference to Parliament and the democratic will expressed through it. This view was strongly held by the Social Democratic majority, which was suspicious of any potential obstacles to its reforming agenda, and it was also held by the judiciary. The rights tradition has not been based on natural rights, but on a view of rights as political decisions.[203] As a result, constitutional review by judges is not seen as a major way of protecting rights. Given that the Constitution was not enacted to produce

[199] See above p. 263.
[200] See B. Holmström, in C. N. Tate and T. Vallinder (eds.), *The Global Expansion of Judicial Power* (New York 1995), ch. 19, at 354–6.
[201] See above p. 257.
[202] Cameron, 'Protection', above n. 197, 506.
[203] Ibid., 503.

major change, the enactment of a list of fundamental rights was not seen as introducing the need for a change in practices by the judiciary.

The incorporation of the European Convention and the entry into the European Union in 1995 have produced a change in approach among the courts, and a greater willingness to engage in constitutional review. An example is the decision of the HD for Västra Sverige which struck down a ban on the wearing of uniforms connected with a political party as manifestly contrary to the freedom of expression.[204] In *Klippan AB*, influenced by EC law, the Kammarrätt decided that a law which introduced retrospective liability for clearing up pollution violated basic principles of administrative law. A firm which had created pollution and then sold on its activity in the 1970s could not be made liable by a law of 1988.[205] In a third case, *Laasagård AB*, art. 6(1) of the European Convention was relied upon to evade a limitation on the jurisdiction of the courts. The administrative courts have jurisdiction only in matters specifically mentioned by legislation. In this case, a company applied for a grant to the country administration, but was told it was out of time, and its appeal was rejected by the Swedish Agricultural Administration. The Kammarrätt of Jönköping held that the prohibition on bringing an action in the courts could be set aside as manifestly contrary to the Constitution.[206] But, to date, the number of cases has been limited.[207] The European Convention was not given priority over national law, and so the established approach by which the courts only question the constitutionality of legislative provisions that are 'manifestly unconstitutional' is retained, and with it a strong deference towards the legislature.[208] With the European dimension to Swedish law, there is clear evidence that this will increasingly be challenged.[209]

Holmström notes that there has been a change in the way politics is conducted which may extend the role of judicial review. In the past, the consensual character of decision-making led to decisions being made by the involvement of interest groups with the Government in decision-making. But thereafter, the compromises reached would be respected. The use of individual rights actions in the courts reflects a different way

204 Decision of 9 April 1996: see *Vår författning*, 194.

205 See Bull, 'Original Ombudsman', above n. 157, 212.

206 See H. H. Vogel, 'Swedish Administrative Law in a State of Change' (1997) 3 EPL 26 at 28–9.

207 See Holmström, above n. 200, 358–61.

208 Bernitz, *European Law*, above n. 93, 49 and 93.

209 See ibid., 213, talking of a 'boom' in constitutional law; also Cameron, 'Protection', above n. 197.

of achieving ends by interest groups. The first leading case in Strasbourg, *Sporrong and Lönnroth*,[210] was selected and backed by Swedish building and housing interests, who picked the lawyers. In the first successful case of review against a statute, the plaintiff used a lawyer provided by the Federation of Swedish Farmers.[211] In his view, 'it may be the case that "the corporatist state" is mouldering but the organized interests are not. They have found new ways of doing politics and promoting their interests. One of these is the court option, or the American way: if you cannot win by negotiation or pressure group politics, sue them!'[212] On the other hand, the Democratic Audit of Sweden concluded in 1999 that there was no pressing need for constitutional reform in Sweden, apart from the issue found in the rest of Europe – the absence of a public space in which to debate the increasingly important decisions coming out of the European Union.[213]

Public image of justice

Public opinion

There are no recent studies of public opinion in relation to the judiciary. Interviews for this research detected a difference between the expectations of judges and those of the public. Judges are concerned to resolve disputes, while the public wants justice to be achieved. Its standards are not necessarily those of the legislator. Therefore there is a clash between popular sentiment and justice according to law. The clash can be illustrated by the need to revise the RF in 1996 to deal with child pornography. The legislator had to fill gaps in the law which did not make the possession of child pornography unlawful. In order to amend the law on press freedom, it had to accelerate revision to the Constitution, avoiding the nine-month period between votes in the Riksdag.[214] The normal legal procedures were bent in order to achieve a political outcome in line with popular sentiment.

An important source of influence has been co-operation with other Nordic states. Co-operation began with Scandinavia in a formal way in 1872 to cover areas such as family law, contract, torts, company law and intellectual property. During the 1960s, the Swedes went their own way in order to achieve faster progress on social reform, but since the

[210] *Sporrong and Lönnroth v. Sweden* (1982) SEHRR 35.
[211] Holmström, 'Judicialization', above n. 72, 162.
[212] Ibid.
[213] Petersson et al., *Report from the Democratic Audit*, above n. 11, 148.
[214] See Cameron, 'Protection', above n. 197, 497.

1970s co-operation has been renewed. There are also many informal contacts. The argument that a reform would achieve Scandinavian harmony remains strong, even if Norway and Iceland remain outside the EU.[215]

Judges and the media

Relations with the media are not specifically structured. There are situations when the court will inform the media about cases which have been decided. But formal press releases are rare. (In the Göta hovrätt, there might be ten press releases a year.) The tingsrätt may have contacts with journalists who regularly attend its hearings, but this is less likely with the higher courts. DV does organise some courses on how judges should present themselves to the media, but these are at an early stage. This aspect forms part of the induction course for new chief judges.

Advokaterna or Åklagerna are the more usual sources of information on individual cases for the media, and they will be the ones to provide interviews. Judges will not give interviews on individual cases in which they have been involved, though they may pass specific, public information. In an interview for this research, one senior judge suggested that the 'modern view', shared by himself and his colleagues (and some of his immediate predecessors), requires the judge to respond to press inquiries. Older judges would have refused to talk to the press at all. This change involves a recognition that the media have become an important channel of information to the people and that it is important that people understand what is being done in the courts. The reporting of leading cases in the press can include photographs of all the judges, nämndemän, prosecutors, lawyers and parties, but there is no televising of court proceedings.[216]

The chair or secretary of a committee is a public figure who would be expected to talk to the media about its work. Of course, there will be differing levels of media interest according to the subject-matter. There is no specific guidance on the issue, nor any particular training. Judges are freer to talk in this context, subject to the obvious requirements of discretion about the internal proceedings of a committee.

There may also be spin-offs, e.g. invitations to take part in debates on a topic connected with the subject-matter of the committee. Here judges

[215] Strömholm, 'General Features', above n. 94, 41.

[216] A good example is the trial of Mijailovic for the murder of the Foreign Minister, Anna Lindh: see *Dagens Nyheter*, 16 and 20 January 2004 and *Svenska Dagbladet*, 23 March 2004.

may well accept an invitation to take part, but this is not very common. Judges are in demand to answer questions or to take part in debates on justice, but they are reluctant to receive publicity. This self-effacing approach is reflected in the fact that judges give few public lectures and rarely write books. Some judges may, however, write columns in the newspapers. They may be involved in university teaching, but this is in a more confined environment. Certainly some judges cited in this chapter are writing articles in newspapers about the administration of justice.

Conclusion: what shapes Swedish judicial culture?

Modéer argues that there are five dimensions to the judicial culture: the ideological (philosophical and professional, as well as political), professional and ethical rules; the legal dimension (the Constitution and the procedural codes affecting ways of working); the local environment (such as architecture); legal education and training (especially its public sector focus); and the judicial career.[217]

The Swedish judiciary shares a number of characteristics with other career judiciaries. Its gender profile and base in university legal education are found commonly in other systems. It is perhaps more open to external recruitment than some judiciaries, though this mainly leads to the recruitment of prosecutors in mid-career. The lack of a judicial college and the reliance on a combination of apprenticeship and short courses is not uncommon, especially in Germany and England. In terms of task, Sweden shares with many systems a common judicial body to deal with administrative, constitutional, criminal and civil matters, although it has distinct court hierarchies.

The distinctiveness of the Swedish internal culture is marked by sets of relationships. In the sphere of *governance*, the Swedish judiciary is very much under an independent central administration in which it exercises a partial autonomy. Geography and organisation encourage some limited autonomy in administration, but within clear performance targets and budgets which are set by a government agency in which judges participate but do not have a dominant role. In terms of *activity*, the judiciary is closely involved in active administration and policy-making. Institutionally, the Swedish tradition of consultative government has associated the judiciary (among others) in the process of developing

[217] Modéer, 'From "Rechtstaat" to "Welfare State"', above n. 50, 163.

policy through remissen. Judges are also chosen as senior, independent figures to chair committees developing policy, a role which is much more like that of English senior judges or members of the French Conseil d'Etat than that of career judges in most countries. The regularity of this involvement is distinctive. The structure of individual judicial careers is almost designed to encourage involvement in the administration. The lack of tenure until their early forties leaves judges searching for postings every few years, many of which will be in the administration. The role of committee secretary is particularly common and a 'royal route' to further advancement, but there are also postings in the more active administration, not just the Ministry of Justice. The dispersed character of the administration, with a multiplicity of independent agencies, enables judges to undertake administrative tasks which are not overtly politicised. Judges are thus involved in making policy and in the active administration on a frequent basis. There are clearly recognised judicial tasks, performed by the courts in their ordinary judicial functions, and these involve the normal development of the law in which any judiciary engages. But the Swedish involvement is more extensive. The self-image of the judge is of a member of the administration, and judicial independence has to be understood in this context. The absence of a major power of constitutional review is substantially mitigated by the involvement of judges in the way legislation is made.

Judicial tasks in Sweden reflect those performed by judiciaries anywhere in Western Europe. But there are four distinctive features which arise from the institutional position which the judiciary occupies. In terms of dispute resolution, the judges occupy a very classical 'judicial' role of deciding disputes presented to them by making rulings. There is less emphasis on conciliation because there are a number of other bodies which can perform this task. The existence of public bodies such as the Justitieombudsman (and the many newer ombudsmen) and the bodies to deal with debts and consumer complaints make it unnecessary that the courts take a central role in conciliation and arbitration. Well-developed and specialist bodies perform that role effectively. The existence of other routes to resolve complaints was also a reason for the slow development of a distinctive administrative court. The organisation of the administration provided ways in which individuals could have their grievances resolved, often by an independent panel, without the expense of a judicial process. The sense that each body within government has its place and that the control against dictatorship lies in the dispersion of power can partly explain the slow growth of both judicial review of the administration and constitutional review.

Judicial lawmaking has long existed. Its importance is acknowledged. At the same time, the spirit of deference to the legislator persists, especially in the use of a form of purposive interpretation and attention to the preparatory materials as guides. Within its proper sphere, the judiciary can perform a distinctive role which does not trespass on the prerogatives of the legislature. The particular methods of interpretation and the co-operative role in lawmaking are distinctive features of the Swedish system, which is not as doctrinaire as the French or German systems about the proper place of the judiciary.

In relation to other legal professions, the judges are an academic elite in terms of their selection. The traditional low standing of the advokat profession is rapidly changing, not least because there are many multinational law firms in Sweden, and European law has made a big difference to the kind of work undertaken by lawyers. The privileged position of the judges within the administration has made them dominant in lawmaking initiatives compared with academics, but the consensual nature of Swedish government brings the academics into the pre-legislative process. As universities expand, then the privileged status of the judge is diminishing in relative terms.

The Swedish professional judges have a very distinctive *relationship with lay judges*. The involvement of lay judges is long-standing and traditionally represents a moderating influence of local opinion on the administration of justice. Today, the need to respect local diversity has largely disappeared as society has become more homogeneous. But this has been replaced by a concern to democratise the judicial process and introduce both a diversity of expertise and experience, as well as some form of popular control. The extent of involvement with lay judges is distinctive – not only in criminal cases, but in administrative and family law, as well as appeals. It is a moot point whether this does actually increase public confidence in the judiciary, but there is certainly no sign that there is a lack of confidence in the judges, whatever criticisms may have been made in the early 1970s by politicians that they were out of touch with contemporary developments. It may be that this structural dimension of the administration of justice enables professional judges to be aware of broader social concerns and relate their justifications for decisions to them.

Overall, the Swedish judicial culture reflects the best of the Swedish public administration tradition. There is a loyalty to the system and a willingness to carry out tasks they are given independently and effectively. Like other administrations, there is a sense of the judiciary's proper place in the dispersed system of power in government. Its job is to respect its place and the place of other institutions. Like the rest of the administration, it operates in a co-operative fashion with other parts of government, especially the legislature, both in preparing legislation and in enacting it. There has not been the need to adopt a confrontational approach to the executive or the legislature, even though the judiciary is prepared to give remedies for mistakes that have been made. It is this fidelity to duty which has gained the judiciary its social respect.

6 The English judiciary in comparative perspective

Introduction: can continental Europe offer any useful lessons?

Despite the current willingness to refer to European standards, there are traditionally some concerns about using European systems as a useful reference point for the English judiciary. An obvious objection to European experiences might be that their judges are typically recruited immediately after university study and have a career. This is less an objection than it might seem at first. To begin with, we have seen that not all continental judges are recruited straight from university. Many are recruited laterally at a later stage in their professional lives. But, more importantly, as Stevens noted in 1993, over the past thirty years the English system has been gradually developing a career.[1] If we look at the way the path to the Bench is now shaped, England has embarked down the road of a career judiciary. Being a recorder is a typical prerequisite to the Circuit or High Court Bench. Being a deputy district judge is a path to the District Bench, which may lead to the Circuit Bench. From the period of starting as a recorder to retirement, a typical judge may spend twenty-five years of their professional career involved in judicial work, moving from post to post and often gaining promotion. Being a judge is not an end of career position, but a career in its own right. So the ideas of judging as a job and of career management are increasingly important features.

It has not been the English tradition to consider that there is a 'judicial career'. In the first place, there has not been a developed conception of promotion – being a High Court judge has been an achievement in its own right, as is shown by the conferment of a

[1] R. B. Stevens, *The Independence of the Judiciary. The View from the Lord Chancellor's Office* (Oxford 1993) (hereafter 'Stevens, *Independence*'), 169.

knighthood. In the second place, the existence of a career is masked by the division of the judiciary into a number of different corps: members of the House of Lords (now to become 'the Supreme Court'), the High Court and Court of Appeal, the circuit judges, and the district judges, as well as a host of lay magistrates and tribunal members. A coherent picture of the 'judiciary' as a whole is only emerging gradually. In a comparative perspective, it is necessary to look at these different groups together to see how the judicial function is performed, even if the particularity of local perceptions must be retained as an important dimension. The division into distinct groups is more radical even than in Spain.

The judicial career

The most prominent feature of the last forty years is the rapid increase in the size of both the judiciary and the legal profession in general. Table 6.1a, b offers a picture of a substantial rise in the lower judiciary, the legal professions and the student population, and notes how the gender balance among these different groups has changed, with the judiciary changing at the slowest pace. The 2005 figures show that still only 8 per cent of the senior full-time judiciary and 18 per cent of the lower full-time judiciary are women. The statistics do show a large rise in the numbers in the legal professions and in the lower judiciary, which has become a significantly larger proportion of the judiciary as a whole. Part-time posts have also increased in importance over the period. The figures do not include the numbers of tribunal members, most of whom are part-time, but who constitute another significant body of judicial appointments. There is no consolidated picture of the tribunals, whose number is estimated at about 137. The number of members involved is about 20,000. The Department of Constitutional Affairs records the appointment of 1,927 full-time chairmen, 390 fee-paid legal members and 3,724 fee-paid lay expert members,[2] but there are other appointments. The arrangements will be made more coherent as a result of the implementation of the Leggatt reforms, scheduled for 2007.[3]

[2] Department of Constitutional Affairs, *Judicial Appointments Annual Report 2003–4* (London 2004), part II.

[3] Sir Andrew Leggatt, *Tribunals for Users. One System, One Service. A Review of Tribunals* (London 2001) (http://www.tribunals-review.org.uk/index.htm).

Table 6.1a *Profile of the judiciary in England and Wales*

	1970			1993			2005		
	Total	M	F	Total	M	F	Total	M	F
Senior Judges									
House of Lords	10	10	0	10	10	0	12	11	1
Court of Appeal and Heads of Division	17	17	0	29	28	1	42	40	2
High Court	73	72	1	93	89	4	108	98	10
Lower Judges									
Circuit Judges	103	102	1	490	465	25	636	569	67
District Judges/Registrars	108	Not known		269	250	19	430	346	84
Stipendiary Magistrates/District Judges (Magistrates' Court)	45	43	2	79	70	9	128	101	27
Total number of full-time judicial posts[4]	356			970			1,356		
Ratio of senior to lower full-time judges	2:5			2:13			2:15		
Part-time Judges									
Recorders and Assistant Recorders	112	111	1	1,242	1,153	89	1,391	1,196	195
Recorders in Training	–	–	–	52	41	11	45	38	7
Deputy District Judges	20	Not Known		747	658	89	811	611	200
Deputy District Judges (Magistrates' Court)				Not known			167	129	38
Total number of part-time judicial posts[5]	132			2,041			2,414		
Ratio of full-time to part-time judicial posts	2.7:1			1:2			1:1.8		

[4] Members of the House of Lords, Court of Appeal and High Court, plus circuit and district judges and district judges (Magistrates' Court).
[5] This figure excludes chairs of tribunals.

Table 6.1b

	Wider Legal Community		
Solicitors	(1970) 24,407 (3% female)	(1993) 61,329 (29% female)	(2004) 96,757 (40.5% female)
Barristers	(1970) 2,584 (5.7% female)	(1992) 7,271 (19% female)	(2004) 14,364 (32.3% female)
Undergraduate law students	(1971) 6,934[6]	(1994) 34,500 (54% female)	(2003) 44,435 (60% female)
Acceptances to universities to read law[7]	(1970) 2,096 (23% female)	(1993) 9,172 (55% female)	(2003) 16,261 (65% female)

[6] Figures from R. L. Abel, *The Legal Profession in England and Wales* (London 1988) (hereafter 'Abel, *Legal Profession*'), table 3.3. His table 3.2 produces a lower figure of 5,998 undergraduates. No percentage for women is given.

[7] The percentages of all law students entering Oxford and Cambridge in these years are 19 per cent (1970), 5.3 per cent (1993) and 3.1 per cent (2003).

The House of Lords/Supreme Court

The Law Lords are a distinct group of judges, not least because the House of Lords and now the Supreme Court is a United Kingdom institution, rather than just an English court. Since its members also serve as members of the Privy Council, which serves as a supreme court for a diminishing number of members of the Commonwealth,[8] the experience required is not limited to England, and a separate recruitment is necessary.

The history of the House of Lords as a judicial body is well presented by Robert Stevens.[9] It is only necessary here to highlight some significant features of that history. In the first place, the status of 'Lord of Appeal in Ordinary' was only created in 1876, when the House of Lords was reinstated as the highest court. It had been abolished in the English judicial reforms of 1873,[10] and had lacked a systematic membership beforehand. Having jurisdiction for appeals from England and Wales, as well as Ireland (now only Northern Ireland) and Scots civil matters, the composition needed to reflect the distinctive range of expertise required. There are typically two Scottish Law Lords and sometimes a Northern Irish Law Lord. Since 1876, there has been a 'committee' of the House of Lords staffed by permanent Law Lords, afforced at various times by retired Law Lords and former Lords Chancellor. The Lord Chancellor sat until the resignation of Lord Irvine in 2003.

The function of the House of Lords is to deal with difficult points of law and interpretation. Its workload is light by comparison with other supreme courts in this book. In 2004, it delivered sixty-seven judgments and decided a further ten cases without a hearing. It received 111 applications, but refused leave in a significant number of them. The appeal courts in the various jurisdictions may give leave to appeal, so there is a major filter exercised either by them or by the House of Lords itself over the cases with which it deals. The fields of law in which cases typically arise are taxation, commercial contracts, human rights and public law, as well as tort. In 2004, among forty-five appeals from England and Wales, there were six administrative law, thirteen human rights and two planning cases, as well as four tax, four intellectual property and four commercial and company cases. There were no cases on criminal law

[8] In 2004, the Privy Council gave sixty-eight decisions, eight of which were without a hearing: Department of Constitutional Affairs, *Judicial Statistics, Annual Report 2004* (Cm 6565; 2005), table 1.1.

[9] R. Stevens, *Law and Politics* (London 1979).

[10] Supreme Court of Judicature Act 1873.

or family law, so the focus of the House of Lords does not mirror the predominant branches of law in the lower courts.

The concentration of work in specific branches of law encourages a focus on appointments from those judges who have had significant commercial practice. The appointment of the first woman as a Law Lord came in 2003. Her appointment also increased the number of former academics among the membership to two. In recent years, a number of members have previously had an academic career or, like Lord Woolf, have published significant scholarly works. Indeed, from the appointment of Lord Blackburn in 1876, there have been a number of Law Lords distinguished for their scholarship.[11] It is in the appointment of former academics or writers of scholarly texts that a parallel can be found to the appointment of professors to supreme courts in other jurisdictions. As will be commented on below,[12] these academics or scholars do not enter directly, but pass through a period of practice as a barrister.

The new Supreme Court created under the Constitutional Reform Act 2005 will retain most of the distinctive features of the House of Lords, except that it will no longer be part of the legislative chamber and its members will lose all connection with this non-judicial side. As Kate Malleson documents, the saga of the creation of the Supreme Court results from a more intense consideration of the notion of formal judicial independence, following the Human Rights Act 1998 and a number of decisions of the European Court of Human Rights.[13] The judges of the Supreme Court will be appointed by the Lord Chancellor upon recommendation of a selection panel. The panel will represent the different jurisdictions and will have to consult with appropriate judges in the relevant jurisdiction before coming to a decision. The panel will then present the Lord Chancellor with a name which he can accept or reject or invite the panel to reconsider. The Supreme Court will be an autonomous administration with a President and Chief Executive, and its own administration. The provisions on the Supreme Court can only come into force when a building is ready (s. 148(4) and (5)). The process

[11] Lord Blackburn wrote a number of major works, notably *Benjamin on Sale of Goods*: see A. W. B. Simpson, 'Innovation in Nineteenth Century Contract Law' (1975) 91 LQR 235, 271. Lord Woolf is the joint author of a leading textbook on administrative law: S. A. De Smith, H. Woolf and J. Jowell, *Judicial Review of Administrative Action* (5th edn, London 1995).

[12] Below pp. 317–18 and 329.

[13] K. Malleson, 'Modernising the Constitution: Completing the Unfinished Business' (2004) 24 *Legal Studies* 119.

of creating this body has come after many years of prompting, even if the actual impetus for the creation itself came rather hastily after a Cabinet reshuffle.

The Court will have jurisdiction over devolution matters (which most countries would consider to be about the relative powers of a federal government and its constituent states) and over human rights. The former set of powers were given to the Privy Council by the 1998 devolution legislation, while the latter went to the House of Lords. Clearly this was not a sustainable solution. Like other common law supreme courts, there is also to be jurisdiction over civil, criminal and administrative law matters. But it is unlikely to lead to a marked increase in caseload. As a result, the new Supreme Court could be expected to hand down after full hearings seventy to eighty judgments a year, a not dissimilar number to the US Supreme Court (although the latter deals with far more applications which are turned down by summary procedure). It will not be similar to any of the supreme courts discussed in other chapters of this book.

The High Court and Court of Appeal

The superior judges of the English and Welsh system are typically appointed direct into the High Court and are then promoted according to need to the Court of Appeal. It has been normal for well over a century that those appointed to the High Court have served as recorders for a number of years beforehand. This period as a part-time judge has provided individuals with an opportunity to try out the judicial task and see if they like it. Likewise, it was possible for the Lord Chancellor and his permanent secretary to have some assessment of individuals.[14] The qualification for appointment as a recorder is the same as that for being a High Court or circuit judge, namely that a person has been qualified for at least ten years with rights of audience.

The processes of appointment were based on an ability of key individuals to know more or less the entire field of eligible candidates. Since being a High Court judge required the person to be a QC, this reduced the field of candidates to barristers working in London and appearing in the superior courts. The small number of judges could be consulted and could be expected to know the individual's performance

[14] Formal appraisal was only introduced on a pilot basis in 2005: below p. 313. For a discussion of the process of informal assessment of performance, see Stevens, *Independence*, 88–92.

quite well. The permanent secretary was able to make a trawl of the field, have files on each person and produce recommendations to the Lord Chancellor. Stevens documents the powerful role of the permanent secretary in the process, as well as its complete lack of transparency. In more recent years, there has been a more transparent process with interviews.[15]

Unlike most European jurisdictions, the High Court and the Court of Appeal are generalist courts. High Court judges are appointed to one of the three divisions: Queen's Bench, Chancery or Family. Judges may also be appointed to more specialist lists, notably the 'administrative court', the 'commercial court', the 'technology and construction court' and the 'admiralty court' in the Queen's Bench and the 'companies court' and the 'patent court' in the Chancery Division.[16] The result is that many judges spend at least a significant part of their time on specialist work, even if they may also have to undertake some more general civil or criminal work, according to the needs of their Division. Chancery business is concentrated in London, although there are eight provincial centres. In the case of the Family and Queen's Bench Divisions, work is divided between the High Court in London and a number of first-tier Crown Court centres in the provinces. The result of this allocation of work is that many judges of the High Court have to spend some time in the year 'on circuit' in a provincial centre, living and working away from home.[17]

Criminal work has always been conducted on a regional basis. Since 1971, serious criminal cases have been tried in the Crown Court. Within the Crown Court, there are a number of centres organised on the basis of regional circuits. Centres are designated as falling within one of three tiers.[18] First-tier centres deal with the full range of criminal and civil business, and are visited by High Court and circuit judges, and by recorders. Second-tier centres are similar, but without civil jurisdiction, and third-tier centres deal with all but the most serious business and are visited by circuit judges. The word 'visited' is appropriate as High Court judges and recorders in particular are likely to be serving away from their home base. In 2004, the Crown Court disposed of 81,750 cases, 51.6

15 Ibid.

16 On the work of the different divisions of the High Court, see S. H. Bailey, J. P. L. Ching, M. J. Gunn and D. C. Ormerod, *Smith, Bailey and Gunn on the Modern English Legal System* (4th edn, London 2002) (hereafter 'Smith, Bailey and Gunn'), 105–14.

17 For the impact of this on diversity, see below p. 318.

18 Smith, Bailey and Gunn, 98–104.

per cent of which were guilty pleas. It also dealt with 31,156 committals for sentence from the magistrates and 12,882 appeals against their decisions. These figures are substantially lower than the over 100,000 trials which were held in the early 1990s, though much of this decrease is balanced by a substantial increase in committals for sentence. It does, however, mean that there are substantially fewer jury trials, since they are confined to not-guilty pleas at trial in the Crown Court. Many acquittals at trial resulted from a direction by the judge (58 per cent), as opposed to a not-guilty verdict from the jury (31 per cent). High Court judges heard only 1,635 criminal cases in the Crown Court in 2004. Whereas circuit judges sat for 74 per cent of the sitting days in the Crown Court, High Court and deputy High Court judges sat for only 5 per cent, leaving 21 per cent of sitting days to recorders.[19]

Since 1999, the civil procedure has similarly been unified. Work between the High Court (often sitting in the provincial Crown Court) and the county court has been organised along 'tracks'.[20] The *small claims track* deals with cases under £5,000 and is allocated to the district judges in the county court, who undertake arbitration. In 2004, there were 46,100 such cases, some 68.8 per cent of which were debt claims.[21] The *fast track* deals with most other defended cases up to £15,000, most of which are dealt with in the county court. Other cases are allocated to *multi-track*. Typically, these cases are either complex or need to be managed in a flexible way, or are for a significant value. Most multi-track cases will be dealt with in the Queen's Bench Division of the High Court. In 2004, 14,670 cases were disposed of after trial in the county court and 750 in the High Court. This represents a significant change from the pre-1999 period. The High Court judges are thus allocated the most complex work. However, because of inadequate numbers, circuit judges or recorders may be appointed to sit as deputy High Court judges. The 1999 reforms, named after Lord Woolf who produced the reports leading to the Civil Procedure Act 1997,[22] introduced greater pre-trial 'case management', which involves both setting a timetable for the pre-trial exchanges of pleadings and documents between the parties and setting a date for trial and arranging for experts to be appointed and their evidence clarified. The result is a greater focus

[19] Department of Constitutional Affairs, *Judicial Statistics*, above n. 8, 132.
[20] Smith, Bailey and Gunn, 698–9, 704–6, 736–9.
[21] Department of Constitutional Affairs, *Judicial Statistics*, above n. 8, 51.
[22] Lord Woolf, *Access to Justice: An Interim Report* (1995) and *Final Report on Access to Justice* (1996).

on contested issues at trial and an increasing amount for the judge to read pre-trial. The processes of case management and an increase in written, rather than oral, evidence and argument has changed the work of the judge from the neutral umpire who came with a blank mind to listen to the evidence and arguments from each side to much more the focused interrogator whose attention is concentrated by the pre-trial process and by the trial advocates on the specifically difficult parts of the litigation.

Judicial review and the hearing of appeals by way of case stated from tribunals and magistrates' courts constitute the bulk of the work of the 'Administrative Court', as it has been called since 2000.[23] In 2004, 4,207 applications were received by the Court, over half of which related to immigration and asylum.[24] Leave to bring review was refused in 65 per cent of cases. Only 334 substantive decisions were reached, over 80 per cent by a single judge. There were 130 cases stated from magistrates' courts, most of which were criminal (which shows the loose nature of 'administrative' law in England). In addition, there were 2,282 other applications, most of which were appeals in relation to national insurance. Since few judges hearing these cases are specialists in either immigration or national insurance, this collection of 'administrative law' cases in the loose sense represents an activity of generalist expertise in statutory interpretation and analysis of administrative action. Beyond the courts, there are the large number of tribunals which deal with about 1 million cases a year, staffed typically by lay judges with a legally qualified chairman, who is not a judge.

Family work is still allocated between the magistrates' courts, the county court and the High Court. Public law cases involve applications mainly by local authorities dealing with the care or supervision of children or emergency proceedings. Private law cases involve issues brought by individuals, such as custody and adoption of children. In 2004, 22,051 public law applications and 107,349 private applications were made to all the family courts. Of these, 65.7 per cent of public law applications and 16.3 per cent of private law applications were brought in the magistrates' courts (family proceedings court). The respective percentages for the county courts were 33.3 per cent of public and 83.4 per cent of private law applications, leaving the High Court with 1 per cent and 0.3 per cent of the respective categories. Most of the work in relation to

[23] *Practice Direction (Administrative Court: Establishment)* [2000] 4 All ER 1071.

[24] Department of Constitutional Affairs, *Judicial Statistics*, above n. 8, tables 1.13 to 1.15.

children is conducted in chambers, so the skills required of the judges are very different from those needed to hear and probe advocacy in open court. High Court judges are given the more difficult matters, such as contested divorces, wardship and the adoption of children, and major proceedings under the Children Act 1989. Divorces are judicial proceedings – there were 166,042 in 2004, as well as 123,434 maintenance and other ancillary orders.

The work of the Chancery Division involves more pre-prepared documentation and analysis of technical law in fields of property, trusts, insolvency, taxation and probate. Judges of this Division are unlikely to be used to try criminal cases. In 2004, there were 2,918 cases disposed of after trial or hearing, as well as some 30,966 bankruptcy or company winding-up proceedings.

The Court of Appeal sits in two divisions. The Criminal Division is usually composed of one Lord Justice of Appeal and one or two High Court judges. Much of its work deals with appeals against sentences imposed by the Crown Court (7,591 cases in 2004), and the rest of the work deals with appeals against conviction (1,782 cases in 2004). The Civil Division disposed of 1,059 final appeals and 316 interlocutory appeals in 2004, but also dealt with a significant number of applications for permission to bring an appeal. Because counsel are required to provide skeleton arguments, summarising the points that they will wish to make, the oral hearing on appeal is now very focused and substantially written in character.

The Circuit Bench

As will appear from the figures given above in relation to civil and family work, the county court is the workhorse of the civil justice system. In 2004, over 1.5 million claims were brought for the recovery of debts or the recovery of property (rented or mortgaged). With over 30,000 bankruptcy petitions and 166,042 divorce petitions, there is a large proportion of routine uncontested cases.

The County Court judiciary was established in 1846. This created a route for local judges and small claims. Initially sixty judges were appointed, which was substantially more than in the superior courts of common law and Chancery. The selection process was necessarily more formalised with applications and references, even if the Lord Chancellor was not limited to applicants.[25] Some applied because of lack of success

[25] P. Polden, *A History of the County Court 1846–1971* (Cambridge 1999), 242.

at the Bar, others for a different pace of life. The first woman county court judge was appointed in 1962.[26] Promotion to the High Court was rare in the past, with only eleven instances in the 125 years from 1846 to 1971,[27] but this is now increasing. In 1971, the county court judge was renamed a circuit judge and was given criminal jurisdiction as a judge of the new Crown Court. A circuit judge must have at least ten years' experience of advocacy rights (a general right of audience) or three years as a district judge.

The registrar was originally an administrative officer of the court, but has now become a lower tier of judge, the district judge. The original judicial jurisdiction in Chancery and small claims matters grew during the nineteenth century,[28] and especially with the creation of a small claims arbitration in 1971 for matters under £1,000, but a party could always refuse to accept the arbitration and to have the matter tried by the county court judge. The Courts and Legal Services Act 1990 expanded this jurisdiction and conferred the title of district judge on the registrars. The Woolf reforms have now entrenched this process by making this level of decision compulsory. A district judge must have at least seven years' experience of advocacy rights.

The other judge given the title of district judge (Magistrates' Court) is the stipendiary magistrate, a fully qualified lawyer with at least seven years' experience of advocacy rights. The work of the stipendiary has been studied by Seago, Walker and Wall. They found that the stipendiary shared the culture of the lay magistrates with its concern for common sense and localness, rather than a culture produced by training and professionalism.[29] The district judge (Magistrates' Court) performs a very important task in being more speedy with business and able to perform the same work as thirty-two magistrates, and coping with administrative business.[30] But there remains an important place for the lay magistrate as part of the local culture of justice.

The increasing responsibility of the circuit judges and district judges has made the role a lower judiciary, though not simply an entry-level judicial position. As with the recent reforms in Spain, high-fliers appointed from the legal professions have to be enticed with a higher post. The important feature of this career is its ability to bring in both women and solicitors. The position as registrar, now district judge, was

[26] Ibid., 249. [27] Ibid., 259–60. [28] Ibid., 276–80.

[29] P. Seago, C. Walker and D. Wall, 'The Development of the Professional Magistracy in England and Wales' [2000] Crim. LR 631, 645.

[30] Ibid., 638.

always a potential post for solicitors. Many solicitors are now appointed as circuit judges, though they are still only a minority.

The attractiveness of the judiciary lies in the predictable and less strenuous workload compared with private practice.[31] But it is also the change of work that provides the attraction of a mid-career move. Such reasons are similar to those found in the other jurisdictions discussed in this book.

Reforms of 2005

The Constitutional Reform Act 2005 has introduced a number of changes to the ways in which judges are appointed, managed and disciplined. In terms of judicial selection, it has finally created a Judicial Appointments Commission, whose job is to recommend names for the Lord Chancellor to appoint to any judicial post in England and Wales, excluding lay magistrates.

The Commission is an independent body, chaired by a lay member and composed of five judges (taken from the different levels of court), a solicitor and a barrister, as well as a lay justice, a tribunal member and five lay members. Since the lay members must never have been practising lawyers, this will give a non-judge majority. The Commission will have to nominate special panels to appoint heads of division and the members of the Court of Appeal, since the Act creates a special composition for these panels. In other cases, the Commission can decide how it works. As with the members of the Supreme Court, the Lord Chancellor receives a report and a single recommendation, which he can accept, reject or invite reconsideration. The forms of application and the need for interviews will be settled by the Commission itself.

The Lord Chief Justice is to be the President of the Courts of England and Wales and this will be a substantial administrative task. Within the budget conferred by the Lord Chancellor, he will have to ensure appropriate arrangements for the welfare, training, guidance and deployment of judges. He will also be responsible for appointing judges to various committees (a task currently performed by the Lord Chancellor). He will be the person through whom discussions with ministries on public expenditure will take place.[32] Like the heads of the Scottish and Northern Irish judiciaries, he will have the right to make written representations on behalf of the judiciary to Parliament, the Lord

[31] See A. Clarke, 'Soliciting Justice' (1999) 96 *Law Society Gazette* 28.
[32] Below p. 321.

Chancellor and ministers in general. These powers under ss. 5 and 7 formalise the practices of recent times, most notably illustrated by the Concordat of 2004.

In terms of discipline, the powers to remove senior judges remain with Parliament, upon an Address of both Houses. The powers of the Lord Chancellor in relation to other judges are transferred to the Lord Chief Justice. Under s. 115, in consultation with the Lord Chancellor, the Lord Chief Justice may make rules for the procedure to be followed in disciplinary matters, though the Act does not specify much about the content of such rules. A greater formality will be an essential improvement on the arrangements hitherto, which have lacked the formality expected in other countries.

Overall, the changes introduce a greater formality and professionalism into the processes of appointing, disciplining and managing judges. As the judiciary has grown in size and complexity, the existing informality of procedures has become inappropriate. The large size of a career judiciary cannot be managed on the procedures for the barristers appointed late in their professional lives.

Part-time judges

A distinctive feature of the English system is its reliance on members of the legal profession acting as part-time judges. As can be seen from table 6.1b, the number of these judges is now very significant. Nearly 60 per cent of judicial posts are part-time. The function of the part-time post is both to fill a need and to provide a training ground for potential full-time judges. It is this latter aspect that makes it appropriate to consider the part-time posts as part of a continuum with the full-time judiciary and to see this as part of a career. This 'fee-paid' work, as it is termed, has problems. Individuals need to serve a minimum number of days a year, which can be difficult to fit into another full-time career. It is noted that solicitors' firms often find it difficult to release their members for such long periods where there is no obvious benefit to the firm. (After all, it only qualifies the person taking on the work to leave the firm for a different employment.) Because of the case-law of the European Court of Human Rights, the part-time judges were given fixed-term appointments of at least five years in 2000, rather than the previous precarious system of not renewing an appointment for the following year.[33]

[33] See Smith, Bailey and Gunn, 242–3.

The internal judicial culture

Recruitment and selection

Compared with the other countries studied in this book, English judicial recruitment has been informal, unstructured and lacking in transparency. The system was designed for a period when there were 1,000 barristers, forty senior judges and sixty county court judges. The Lord Chancellor could become personally involved in appointments and records could be kept on individuals by his office. This became impossible to sustain as both the numbers of judges and the numbers in the professions increased in the 1970s. But it has taken a very long time for a seriously professional approach to be adopted in relation to judicial recruitment and selection.

The procedure for appointing judges until the 1990s was more like the election of members to a club than an appointment to a job. The Lord Chancellor's Department published its explanatory document 'Judicial Appointments: The Lord Chancellor's Policies and Procedures' in 1986. Under that procedure, it used to survey the field of qualified applicants and take soundings among senior judges who could be expected to have encountered the individuals at work. The individual was then invited to become a judge. In the 1960s, Lord Gardiner LC said that he had interviewed every candidate before appointment to the Bench. The process of consultation and soundings applied to the top 150 posts, including those in the High Court, until 1997, when advertisements were made inviting applicants to the High Court. Advertisements for posts below the High Court had been introduced in 1994. This informal procedure attracted criticism in two respects. First, it depended on the visibility of individuals to leading judges. Not all suitable individuals would have a practice that brought them sufficiently to the attention of the consultees to enable sufficient comment to be made.[34] Secondly, there has been consistent evidence that those consulted did not always respond in terms of the criteria for appointment set out by the Department. The questions asked were often insufficiently focused on the range of qualities needed for being a judge, as opposed to being an advocate.[35] The creation of job descriptions did not fully achieve focused responses. In

[34] See *Report on Judicial Appointments and QC Selection, Main Report* (London 1999) (hereafter 'Peach'), 5 and JUSTICE, *The Judiciary in England and Wales* (London 1992) (hereafter 'JUSTICE'), 12.

[35] JUSTICE, 12; Peach, 10; Commission for Judicial Appointments, *Annual Report 2004* (London 2005), § 3.23–4.

part this is because there has been a traditional view that success in the courtroom as an advocate is a good preparation for being a judge, a view that has been criticised.[36]

The most obvious evidence for suitability for appointments to the full-time judicial posts would include performance as part-time judges, e.g. as recorders or deputy district judges. But, until the pilots in 2005, there was no formal system of appraisal of part-time office-holders.[37] Indeed, Lord Taylor rejected performance appraisal for judges in general as incompatible with judicial independence.[38] Although this was claimed by judges to be a good testing ground for suitability for the Bench and individuals have been refused a renewal of appointment because of their performance, it did not generate directly usable evidence. A pilot scheme of appraisal for fee-paid judges (recorders) was begun in 2005, but this is an area in which the practices of the English judiciary lag behind continental judiciaries.

The 1990s saw the introduction of formal interviews by selection panels for the lower judicial posts, and this was eventually extended to the High Court. The Peach Report recommended the civil service practice of using assessment centres[39] and this was subsequently introduced for the competition for deputy district judges.

Progress in creating a formalised appointments process that reflected good public sector practice was hampered by the judges themselves. They clung to soundings and Lord Taylor rejected a Judicial Appointments Commission in 1996. But the procedures adopted in the past did not fit either the Nolan Principles on Appointments to public offices adopted generally in the mid-1990s or normal private sector practices, including those used within the legal professions. Many of the proposals of JUSTICE in 1992[40] have found their way into the Constitutional Reform Act 2005. As has been noted, this introduces a Judicial Appointments Commission composed of lay and judicial members, with a lay Chair. Its appointment process is likely to build on the most recent reforms: advertisements, job descriptions, interviews and formal references, rather than unstructured soundings. The process will resemble the external application routes in other systems, but it marks a significant extension of professionalism in judicial appointments, and a greater recognition of a career.

[36] See D. Pannick, *Judges* (Oxford 1987), 52. [37] Peach, 16; JUSTICE, 12.
[38] K. Malleson, *The New Judiciary* (Aldershot 1999), 64.
[39] Peach, 11. [40] See Peach, 5; JUSTICE, 12.

Diversity

The issue of diversity has been a much greater concern in England compared with other countries studied in this book. There are three converging reasons. The first is that the legal professions and the judiciary have been criticised as a narrow social elite for very many years. The judges were identified as white, male and upper middle class, drawn from those educated at public schools and Oxbridge.[41] In 1967, 76 per cent of barristers came from Oxbridge.[42] That was not wholly surprising, since in 1953, 49 per cent of law students studied at Oxford and Cambridge. More surprisingly, the Sutton Trust reported that in 2004, 82 per cent of barristers in leading chambers were from those two universities and this was down from 89 per cent in 1989, and there was no difference between those aged forty and below and older barristers.[43] The percentages among partners in 'magic circle' solicitors firms had declined in the same period from 65 per cent to 53 per cent, with a marked difference between those over forty and those under forty.[44] But given that Oxford and Cambridge have barely increased undergraduate numbers at a time when the numbers in the professions have been rising rapidly, some decline in their share of the pool of leading barristers and solicitors is inevitable. In an increasingly meritocratic and socially diverse society, this was the subject of concern and criticism, particularly where obtaining pupillage and tenancy depended on social connections, rather than any objective assessment. Abel argued that the increased competition for places at leading universities created a more exclusive system, even if the social backgrounds were becoming less elite.[45] The visibility of public schools and a narrow number of elite universities contrasts with a less obvious way in which similar social backgrounds are manifested in other judiciaries.

The second reason was the small number of women on the Bench and in the senior ranks of the professions. Abel identifies 1965 as the point from which women began to enter the legal professions in significantly

[41] See H. Cecil, *The English Judge* (London 1970), ch. 1; J. A. G. Griffith, *The Politics of the Judiciary* (4th edn, London 1991), 30–6.

[42] Abel, *Legal Profession*, 48. He notes that among barristers going on to the Bench between 1727 and 1875, 70 per cent had been to university and in the main this would have been Oxford or Cambridge.

[43] Sutton Trust Briefing Note, 'The Educational Backgrounds of the UK's Top Solicitors, Barristers and Judges' (June 2005) (http://www.suttontrust.com/reports/Comparison_educational_backgrounds.pdf), 5–6.

[44] Ibid., 8–9. [45] Abel, *Legal Profession*, 48.

larger numbers.[46] England was so far out of line with other European countries that female participation has been a much more prominent issue.

The third and connected reason was the example of the civil rights and women's rights movements in the United States, which have more influence on an English-language, common-law country than in the rest of Europe. This influence has been significant in raising the profile of ethnic minorities on whose participation statistics have been kept since the 1980s, whereas there are no such statistics kept in any of the other countries studied in this book. The shared Anglo-Saxon perception of society as a collection of social communities contrasts sharply with visions in other countries, notably France. Social events in Britain, such as the Brixton riots and the Stephen Lawrence affair, have convinced decision-makers that unintended bias may occur, and that this needs proactive measures. One sign was the creation of the Ethnic Minorities Advisory Committee of the Judicial Studies Board in 1991.

A significant problem for improvement in the recruitment of women to the judiciary has been the loss of younger women from the profession.[47] The high attrition rates have been noted since 1971. Among those women called to the Bar in 1965, 47 per cent had left ten years later, compared with only 13 per cent of men.[48] A study by the Bar Council in 1999[49] found that among the 459 people called to the Bar in 1988, 40 women (26.5 per cent) had left ten years later compared with 48 men (15.6 per cent). Among those who left the Bar within the years of call 1988–98 46.6 per cent were women, even though the percentage of women called was only 36.4 per cent. Women were leaving at a much higher rate than men, particularly in the period between two and six years from call.[50] The result of these trends is that the pool of those women eligible for appointment to judicial positions is greatly reduced. As a result of both the lower entry rate of women into the Bar and this higher attrition rate among those women called, it would be necessary to make appointments to the judiciary from the pool of

46 Ibid., 79–85.

47 See generally C. McGlynn, *Women in the Law* (London 1998) and C. McGlynn, 'The Status of Women Lawyers in the United Kingdom' in U. Schultz and G. Shaw (eds.), *Women in the World's Legal Professions* (Oxford 2003), ch. 9.

48 Abel, *Legal Profession*, 83.

49 See 'Bar Council Exit Survey' in DCA, *Increasing Diversity in the Judiciary* (CP 25/04, 2004), 113.

50 Ibid., 115.

women barristers at a higher rate compared with appointments from the pool of men in order to achieve equal numbers of judges appointed from each pool. If we take the 1988 cohort of barristers as an example, in order to achieve parity in the numbers of men and women appointed, the rate for the appointment from the pool of women barristers would have to have been 2.34 times higher than that from the pool of men.

Studies of the solicitors' profession show a similar trend.[51] A similar pattern of attrition in the numbers of women in the profession is identified to that of the Bar. As a proportion of those holding practising certificates in 1997–2001, 1.6 per cent of men, but 2.4 per cent of women ceased to renew in 2002. On average, male non-renewers were aged fifty-two, whilst women non-renewers were aged forty, and 60 per cent of these women were aged thirty-one to forty, compared with only 22.7 per cent of men.

Although the entry rate for both barristers and solicitors has reached equality between men and women, there is no indication that attrition rates are becoming more equal, and so greater parity in the numbers of men and women appointed can only be achieved by securing a higher appointment rate for judicial appointments among women than among men. The judicial career has to be more attractive. The Department of Constitutional Affairs has drawn up its own statistics on the gender balance in applications and appointments in four appointment cycles to judicial offices from 1999 to 2002.[52] That found that among 634 applicants for the post of circuit judge, 73 (11.5 per cent) were women; among the 124 persons appointed, 25 (20 per cent) were women. Among the 2,987 applicants for the various posts as district or deputy district judge, 906 (30 per cent) were women, and 30 per cent of those appointed were women. There is no sign that application rates among women are high enough to achieve parity of appointments in the foreseeable future. Malleson[53] questions the validity of the trickle up hypothesis on which ministers and judges have relied, and indeed it does not appear credible. By way of an analogy, the annual statistical report of the Law Society reported that in 1992 79 per cent of men but only 55 per cent of women solicitors with ten to nineteen years of

[51] J. Siems, *Equality and Diversity: Women Solicitors* (Law Society Research Study 48; 2004).
[52] DCA, *Diversity*, above n. 49, 104–7.
[53] K. Malleson, 'Prospects for Parity: The Position of Women in the Judiciary in England and Wales' in Schultz and Shaw, *Women*, above n. 47, 175 at 177–80, and Malleson, *New Judiciary*, above n. 38, 123–4.

experience in private practice were partners. The report for 2004 shows that 73 per cent of men, but only 48.8 per cent of women with that same experience are partners.[54] The hypothesis fails to take account of the greater likelihood that women are in public sector, employed barrister or solicitor positions, and so are less likely to be appointed as judges in a system setting a premium on advocacy experience, but who, on continental experience, are more likely to provide a pool of applicants for the judiciary. Thus among solicitors working in local government in 2004, 57.7 per cent were women, and among the Crown Prosecution Service 53.5 per cent were women.[55] Within the Bar, the variety of practice means that the traditional practice of self-employed professionals providing legal services directly to individual clients amounts to only one-third of those qualifying as a barrister.[56] Since judges are typically drawn from this latter group, there appear to be structural features of the English legal professions that militate against the same gender split within the judiciary as is found in the rest of Europe.

There are also similar concerns about the low number of ethnic minority candidates for judicial appointment. In 2003, 2.6 per cent of the judiciary at circuit judge level and below came from ethnic minorities, as did 5.5 per cent of legal tribunal members. If non-legal members are included, the figure rises to 6.9 per cent. By contrast, 7.9 per cent of solicitors and 10.7 per cent of barristers came from non-ethnic minority backgrounds in that year.[57] Among barristers with ten years' call and over, the figure was 7.7 per cent. Application rates among ethnic minorities are higher for district judges (8.6 per cent in 2001–2) and part-time immigration adjudicators (17.1 per cent) than for circuit judge positions (3 per cent).[58] The legal professions attract an above-average proportion of people from ethnic minorities, but there are concerns about the character of practice into which they go and their relative visibility in the appointments process.

There has been concern for some time that judicial working practices made the task less attractive. In the first place, the need for a judge to have part-time experience was difficult for many juggling family

54 *Trends in the Solicitors' Profession, Annual Statistical Report 1993* (Law Society 1993), 11; *Trends in the Solicitors' Profession, Annual Statistical Report 2005* (Law Society 2005), 13.

55 *Annual Statistical Report 2005*, 16.

56 J. Shapland and A. Sorsby, *The Junior Bar in 2002* (Institute for the Study of the Legal Profession, University of Sheffield 2003), 107.

57 DCA, *Diversity*, above n. 49, 120–1, 128–9.

58 Ibid., 126.

commitments. JUSTICE had recommended in 1992 the creation of part-time permanent appointments.[59] The other concern was the requirement that High Court judges spend three months of the year on circuit.[60] These matters continue to be debated.[61] The Commission for Judicial Appointments argues:

> The judiciary needs to be reflective of the diversity of the society it serves. Increasing the diversity of the bench, so that it better represents society, will increase the confidence of all stakeholders, whether court users, the legal professionals or the general public, in the judicial process and in the end of justice as a whole.[62]

The evidence basis for the assertion is difficult to identify. Abel argues that representativeness has two senses.[63] First, the outsider should have access to positions of power and prestige. Secondly, role occupants from different backgrounds will behave differently. He is concerned about the implication that inborn characteristics, as opposed to socialisation, affect decision-making. On the other hand, Malleson does think that the evidence points to some differences in sensitivity and performance.[64]

The House of Lords Select Committee on the Constitutional Reform Bill in 2004 demonstrated the longstanding reluctance of government and judiciary to examine specific steps to deal with diversity issues. It refused to give any specific interpretation or content to the notion of 'merit' as the criterion for judicial appointments. The Committee agreed that diversity should be promoted, but were unable to agree on whether the Judicial Appointments Commission should have a statutory duty to engage in a programme of action to promote diversity.[65] Its compromise of giving the Commission a duty to have regard to the need to encourage diversity was included in s. 64(1) of the Act. As will be seen, positive efforts were made at an early stage to appoint women magistrates and parity has long been reached. Following the Bill, the Department of Constitutional Affairs produced a Consultation Paper and this has been followed up by the announcement of new measures to try to encourage

[59] JUSTICE, 19–21, followed by Peach, 18–19.

[60] Peach, 18–19. [61] DCA, *Diversity*, above n. 49, ch. 5.

[62] Commission for Judicial Appointments, *Annual Report 2004*, above n. 35, § 2.14.

[63] R. L. Abel, *English Lawyers between Market and State* (London 2003) (hereafter 'Abel, *Market and State*'), 152.

[64] Malleson, *New Judiciary*, above n. 38, 111.

[65] Select Committee on the Constitutional Reform Bill, *Volume 1: Report* (HL 125-I, 2004), §§ 323–46.

diversity, including different ways to gain experience before appointment as judges and a reduction in the length of experience required,[66] but this suggests that there is a long way to go in identifying adequate responses to the issues.

Judicial training

Until the 1960s, the English judicial tradition combined the cult of the amateur and the practice of 'learning on the job'. Barristers who became recorders or judges were expected to have learnt enough by observation of others to know how to conduct themselves as judges. Lord Parker CJ introduced sentencing discussions in 1963, and this turned into a sentencing conference. In 1976, Lord Bridge's committee produced a report recommending a more systematic structure for judicial training – a 'pupillage' sitting alongside a more experienced judge and an induction programme with annual refresher courses. This was carried through by the creation of the Judicial Studies Board in 1979. Initially focused on judges in criminal matters, training extended to civil and family matters in 1985. It then took over the training of magistrates and tribunal members. In 1995, the Clayton Report recommended that training be extended to the High Court and Court of Appeal judges. This gradual emphasis on training was assisted by the experience of training large numbers of judges on major legal changes. The earliest were the Children Act 1989 and the Criminal Justice Act 1991. Perhaps the most significant was the systematic training of all judges in the Human Rights Act 1998, which involved 3,680 judges attending at least one of sixty-four seminars.[67] In 2005, there were seminars for all judges exercising criminal jurisdiction. In addition to training sessions, manuals were produced as support for judges ('benchbooks').

The extent of a change of culture towards a more professional approach to judging has been the result of the leadership given by senior judges and the involvement of judges in both running the Judicial Studies Board and giving many of the sessions.[68] The success of this approach from the Judicial Studies Board was commented upon by the Peach Report in 1999: 'It is a tribute to the Judicial Studies Board and an indication of its success that the judiciary in general recognise the importance of the training and development processes and have

[66] DCA, Diversity, above n. 49, and Summary of responses published March 2005, chs. 3 and 5. Written Statement of the Lord Chancellor, 13 July 2005.

[67] Judicial Studies Board, *The Judicial Studies Board: 25 Years* (2004), 10.

[68] Malleson, *New Judiciary*, above n. 38, 161–3, 179.

come to accept the need for organised programmes.' But it went on to argue that 'The real problem is ensuring that development takes place in the courtroom in the absence of a readily identifiable hierarchy and a management relationship where a mentoring role can be taken for granted.'[69] That sort of management and appraisal structure had been recommended by JUSTICE in 1992, but remains to be acted upon.

Judicial representation

The English judiciary is unusual in Europe in that it lacks any union activity. At the same time, there are powerful mechanisms through which the judges influence the development of the law and of legal institutions.

In the first place, there is a Judges' Council.[70] This has had a variety of forms. From 1873 until 1981, there was a statutory Judges' Council, set up to review the implementation of the Judicature Act of 1873. From 1988 until 2002, there was an informal Judges' Council covering only senior judges. In 2002, this was dissolved and replaced by a body which included all of the judiciary, including some magistrates and tribunal members. It now brings together all the judges, but is dominated by the senior judges. It operates mainly through its executive, which has representatives of all levels of the judiciary. It will nominate the judicial members of the Judicial Appointments Commission.

The informal Councils have been convened to discuss matters of general interest, especially at moments of turmoil. Famously, the courts were shut for half a day while the judges debated the reforms proposed in Lord Mackay's Green Paper of 1988.[71] The judges used this mechanism to make formal representations to the 2003 consultation on judicial appointments. In one sense, it operates as a collective voice of the judiciary, but in another it does not operate like a union in the same way that continental judicial unions work. The continental unions have representatives who sit on the governing body of the judiciary. In other cases, they make representations to government about the needs of the courts and the judicial service, including on judicial salaries. In other words, they are campaigning organisations, and they typically represent different political leanings within the judiciary through different unions. The Judges' Council transmits collective views, but it is

[69] Peach, 16. [70] Lord Justice Thomas, 'The Judges' Council' [2005] PL 608.
[71] Abel, *Market and State*, 57.

traditionally more a deliberative, rather than a campaigning organisation. It makes representations, but, until the Constitutional Reform Act 2005, it had no direct way of having a seat at the table of the decision-makers. In a period during which the level of public expenditure on the courts and judicial service is prominent in political debate, the English judiciary has lacked the same kind of voice that is expressed through continental unions, even by those in Sweden and Germany that are less allied to political parties. Under the recently created arrangements, senior judges will sit as board members of Her Majesty's Court Service, the executive agency in charge of the courts. At circuit level, the presiding judge and the circuit administrator have a close partnership. But at more general levels, judicial input into the national public spending reviews has been more informal.[72]

To a great extent, the judiciary has relied on three voices to speak for them. In the first place, the senior judges, either the major office-holders (Lord Chief Justice, Master of the Rolls, President of the Family Division and Vice-Chancellor, to be joined by the President of the Queen's Bench Division) or the Law Lords, will speak out in an individual capacity as unofficial spokespersons for the judiciary. Under the Constitutional Reform Act, that has become formalised by allowing the Lord Chief Justice, as President of the English and Welsh courts, to present written submissions to Parliament. Secondly, retired senior judges, especially Law Lords and ex-Lords Chancellor, will be free to express views that serving office-holders feel inhibited from expressing.[73] Thirdly, the Bar, in which the judges often occupy senior positions, will ride to the rescue. The debates on Lord Mackay's Green Paper and the changes resulting from the desire to abolish the office of the Lord Chancellor in 2003 illustrate these tendencies clearly.

In relation to the Constitutional Reform Act 2005, the proposals to abolish the office of the Lord Chancellor were sprung on the judiciary (and the wider political community) in June 2003. Judicial criticism of the proposals, including the creation of a supreme court, led to discussions within the Judges' Council and between the Department for Constitutional Affairs (as the Lord Chancellor's Department had become) and senior judges. The result was a 'concordat' between Lord Woolf CJ on behalf of the judges and the Lord Chancellor, in which the responsibilities of the judges and ministers were made clear, before the

[72] Thomas, 'Judges' Council', above n. 70, 623–4, 627–8.

[73] See, for example, the debates on Lord Mackay's Green Papers: ibid., 35–43 and 49.

Constitutional Reform Bill was laid before Parliament.[74] The public image was of a deal brokered between a union leader and a minister to enable the latter to secure the safe passage of legislation. Indeed, when a former Law Lord successfully blocked the legislation by securing that it be referred to a select committee for further scrutiny, Lord Woolf spoke against the delay.[75]

The structure of representation in the past has made significant use of the participation of past and present senior judges in the House of Lords. The second chamber has provided a platform for them to criticise government proposals and to take initiatives, such as Lord Scarman's attempts to introduce a Bill of Rights long before it became a mainstream political issue. The English judiciary has had until 2005 a unique platform for public and informal pressure on parliamentary and governmental decision-makers. This form of representation has long since ceased to be possible in the continental countries discussed in this book. As a result of the greater distance between judges and political decision-makers, more organised and transparent mechanisms exist through which the views of judges are represented to decision-makers. The reforms under the Constitutional Reform Act 2005 have created a much greater distance between the judiciary and governmental and political institutions. As a result, the traditional informal and oligarchical system of influence may well give way to more formal structures. In any case, the increasing numbers of judges and the diversity of activity between judges at different levels may require structures additional to the Judges' Council. The existence of interest groupings such as the Association of District Judges and the Magistrates' Association may presage further groupings. In this, it is unlikely that the English will follow the Spanish and French models of judges associations based on political allegiance.

Judicial independence

The concept of judicial independence is complex and it involves as much the status and ways of working of the judiciary as the formal mechanism by which they are appointed and removed.[76] Stevens has suggested that 'Perhaps the most acceptable way of characterising the role of judicial independence in England is to say that, while the independence of

[74] See the statement of Lord Falconer, *Hansard HL*, 26 January 2004, cols. 13–17.

[75] *The Times*, 9 March 2004.

[76] For a modern judicial restatement of this idea, see T. Bingham, *The Business of Judging* (Oxford 2000), 55.

the judiciary is casual at best, the English have a strong commitment to the independence of individual judges.'[77] I have argued elsewhere that judicial independence involves characteristics such as impartiality and political neutrality far more centrally than ideas such as irremovability.[78] Shetreet demonstrated that the formal guarantee of judicial irremovability contained in the Act of Settlement 1701 was merely intended to make judges independent of the King, not of Parliament, and certainly not to be free actors as a third branch of government.[79] Indeed, it is a guarantee that does not apply to judges below the level of the High Court, who form the majority of judges. Judges also cannot be sued for their judicial acts, but this is an immunity that does not apply to magistrates.[80]

The formal position is that judges of the High Court and Court of Appeal cannot be removed from office except by an Address from both Houses of Parliament. The process has never been successfully invoked against an English judge since it was created in 1701 (although it was successfully invoked in relation to Irish judges in the early part of the nineteenth century). More commonly, public criticism of a judge in Parliament and outside may lead to fellow judges putting pressure on him to resign. A good example was Lord Denning who published criticisms of members of a jury which many read as racist in tone. Although he had been a very good judge, he was over eighty and he was persuaded to step down. Public criticism of Lord Lane, particularly over his handling of miscarriages of justice, was thought to have contributed to his decision to retire early as Lord Chief Justice in 1992. The ethos of 'doing the decent thing' predominates in the system.

Until the Constitutional Reform Act 2005 created a more formal procedure, all other judges were subject to removal by the Lord Chancellor for misconduct. In practice, the Lord Chancellor would give the person in question a hearing. The process was swift, but rarely invoked. An example was when Judge Campbell was found smuggling whisky on his yacht from France to England. In other cases, the Lord Chancellor might issue a reprimand to a judge, sometimes publicly.[81]

[77] Stevens, *Independence*, 5.
[78] J. Bell, 'The Judge as Bureaucrat' in J. Eekelaar and J. Bell, *Oxford Essays in Jurisprudence – Third Series* (1987), 51–3.
[79] S. Shetreet, *Judges on Trial. A Study of the Appointment and Accountability of the English Judiciary* (Amsterdam 1976), 8.
[80] See generally A. A. Olowofoyeku, *Suing Judges: A Study of Judicial Immunity* (Oxford 1993).
[81] For illustrations, see Stevens, *Independence*, 166; Smith, Bailey and Gunn, 242.

The concept of impartiality requires an honest decision, uninfluenced by personal relationships or prejudice, based on general, and not unique considerations, and appealing to standards that are representative, and which the judge would be willing to apply in similar circumstances in the future. The core feature is the appearance of impartiality. In the *Pinochet* case, the House of Lords had to set aside its own decision that had been reached with the participation of Lord Hoffman who was a member of the charitable board of one of the parties to the case. This was a classic common law conception.[82] The European Convention has led to a more formalist position, including the ending of the role of the Lord Chancellor as a sitting judge and of the participation of the Law Lords in the activity of the legislature. Such a formalist position is derived from a conception of the separation of powers in a more expansive form than the more 'casual' attitude, as Stevens put it,[83] that has prevailed hitherto.

The other connected component of judicial independence is political neutrality. This has been understood in different ways. In one sense, it has been understood as a requirement of disengagement from social activitism.[84] Abel-Smith and Stevens argued that the period from the 1890s up until 1955 or 1960 was marked by limited judicial creativity.[85] The narrower judicial role reflected a greater legislative activity, often from left-of-centre governments who did not value judicial interference.

A particularly English view of the independence of the judiciary was stressed by the Judges' Council in its response to the consultation papers of 2003 on the abolition of the office of the Lord Chancellor. The judges were happy to make a clearer break between themselves and the Lord Chancellor as head of the judiciary if he was to become increasingly an ordinary minister. This would fit into a model of the separation of powers, even if that model had not been a major feature of the English tradition, compared with that of other jurisdictions. The Judges' Council argued that 'Judicial independence depends, not just on law or resources, but on the tradition of restraint that the stronger arms

82 *R v. Bow Street Metropolitan Stipendiary Magistrate, ex p. Pinochet Ugarte (No. 2)* [2001] 1 AC 119.

83 Above p. 323.

84 For example, Sir Henry Slesser, a former Labour minister, wrote: 'When I became a judge, naturally I resigned from all political and semi-political associations, and even in church matters, I felt it right not to take part in any work of a markedly polemical nature, so my retirement from the world really took place in 1929. After that date my only public contacts or utterances were in court.' *Judgment Reserved* (London 1941), 1.

85 B. Abel-Smith and R. Stevens, *Lawyers and the Courts* (London 1967), ch. 5.

of the State exercise in their relationship with the judiciary.'[86] In their view, the deployment of judges should be under the judges and adequate resources supplied.

The office of Lord Chancellor was becoming increasingly administrative.[87] Lord Mackay pointed out in 1995 that it had a staff of 11,000 and a budget of £2.3 billion.[88] The need to give directions about the proper administration of the system of justice clashed with the judges' own sense of their right to determine how they conducted cases, especially individual cases. This led to the President of the Employment Appeal Tribunal resigning over a clash with the Lord Chancellor about his court's failure to use sufficiently certain procedures in order to reduce the backlog of unmeritorious cases.[89]

The debates surrounding the Constitutional Reform Act 2005 threw into relief the issue of the relationship between the role of judges as managers of the judicial process and wider responsibilities for resources in a context of judicial independence. Lord Browne-Wilkinson had already complained of the increasing managerialism of the Lord Chancellor's Department and argued that the judges should have greater control over the disposal of the resources made available for the administration of justice.[90] The Judges' Council pointed to examples in the common law world where judges had been given responsibility for resources as a support for judicial independence, but commented: 'It is recognised, however, that it may not at present be possible to adopt a system of that kind.'[91] But it then went on to press for particular measures to give judges an input into the decisions on resources. With the existence of Her Majesty's Courts Service (from 2005 as a unified administration including the magistrates' courts) dealing as a Next Steps Agency with the operation of court facilities and the treatment of court users, the idea of a Judiciary Agency, similar to that in Sweden or Spain, would follow the emerging trend of opinion among English judges.

[86] 'Judges' Council Response to the Consultation Papers on Constitutional Reform' (November 2003), § 20 (http://www.dca.gov.uk/consult/supremecourt/responses.sc081.pdp).

[87] See Lord Mackay, 'The Lord Chancellor's Role within Government' (1995) *New Law Journal* 1650; D. Woodhouse, *The Office of Lord Chancellor* (Oxford 2001).

[88] Mackay, 'Lord Chancellor's Role', above n. 87, 1651.

[89] See F. Purchas, 'Lord Mackay and the Judiciary' (1994) NLJ 527; Smith, Bailey and Gunn, 277–8.

[90] N. Browne-Wilkinson, 'The Independence of the Judiciary in the 1980s' [1988] PL 44, 53–7. Cf. the views of Lord Mackay, *The Administration of Justice* (London 1994), 13–15 and 17–18, who distinguished between judicial decisions and administrative decisions, especially on resources.

[91] Judges' Council, above n. 86, § 43.

Judges and the legal community

Judges and practitioners

A key dimension of the legal community in England has been the close connection between Bench and Bar. Paterson's study of the Law Lords in the 1970s found that the judges primarily influenced the tone and content of the arguments of counsel, rather than the other way round. Counsel adjusted their arguments to what was perceived as persuasive in relation to their judicial audience.[92] Should there be professional criticism of judicial decisions, this is less likely to come directly from the profession. At the same time, the profession, through the Inns, provides a mechanism for informal communication. More often, a key communication found by Paterson was between the Law Lords and members of the Court of Appeal who were Benchers of the same Inn. The informal interaction might also be reflected in the way speeches are written.[93] However, the most important influences were within the Law Lords, and the same would apply to the Court of Appeal. Speeches are written to show due acknowledgement of the views of colleagues in the court.[94] In 1962, Megarry was able to describe the corporate spirit of the Bar with its strong relationship to the judiciary, and he wrote as someone who had been a solicitor.[95]

Interaction with the solicitors' profession has not been so great. Since 1971, solicitors have been able to become circuit judges, but it took until 1993 before the first solicitor circuit judge was appointed to the High Court. The background of judges as court advocates was reinforced by the role of the senior judges in vetting applications from solicitors to have rights of audience under the Courts and Legal Services Act 1990. Although the solicitors' profession has grown in size, importance and esteem in the last fifty years, the links between judges as a group and the solicitors' profession remain somewhat distant.

Judges and academics

The traditional perception was of the academic as a subservient part of the legal community.[96] Judges were invited to give speeches, but few academics were treated as of significant standing. Paterson found that the Law Lords in the 1970s rarely interacted with academic writings, and

[92] A. Paterson, *The Law Lords* (London 1982), 23–4 and 60–1, 65.
[93] Ibid., 86. [94] Ibid., 90, 95, 111–13.
[95] R. Megarry, *Lawyer and Litigant in England* (London 1962), especially 69–72.
[96] See Abel-Smith and Stevens, *Lawyers and the Courts*, above n. 85, 365.

they were mainly used to reinforce, rather than to change, thinking.[97] The exceptions would be individual writers who carried personal authority. Where such authors had created a groundswell of professional opinion, then their views were most influential. The attitudes of academics contributed to this. Paterson argues that they were reticent in criticising incumbent judges, journal editors might censor criticism that was too strong, and barristers were reluctant to cite articles that were too critical of sitting judges.[98]

There are two distinctive features of the English legal culture at play in the relative status and interaction of judges and academics, both of which have been changing significantly. In the first place, the legal academic community was small until the 1960s. Even as late as 1975, there were only 692 full-time academics working in British law schools, though this had grown by 1996 to 2,440.[99] Cownie reports from her research that less than 20 per cent of her sample of academics regarded academia as their first serious career choice.[100] The practitioner focus of career ambitions demonstrates the relative status of the different professions. Unlike many continental countries in which the academic has a high status when engaged as a consultant for legal advice, no such status attached in England. If an academic wants to have some practice activity, then she or he must become professionally qualified, though some limited concessions were made in the 1990s to ease entry to the profession for established academics.[101] So when the number of academics was quite low, their status was low and their output often deferential, the impact of the academics on the judiciary could have been expected to be far less than their continental counterparts'. Increasing numbers of academics and an increasing emphasis on research within universities, not least because it has been a major driver in funding law schools,[102] have increased the quantity and quality of critical commentary on the decisions and policies with which the courts are engaged. There is a greater body of work on which both barristers and judges can rely to provide them with ideas and criticisms, as well as surveys of the existing law.

[97] Paterson, *Law Lords*, above n. 92, 12–13.
[98] Ibid., 20.
[99] A. Bradney and F. Cownie, 'British University Law Schools' in D. Hayton (ed.), *Law's Futures* (Oxford 2000), 2. W. Twining, *Blackstone's Tower* (London 1994), 26–33 notes that there were only about 130 law academics in 1945; see also Abel, *Legal Profession*, 266–8.
[100] F. Cownie, *Legal Academics, Culture and Identities* (Oxford 2004), 79.
[101] Ibid., 75–8.
[102] Ibid., 133–41; A. Bradney, *Conversations, Choice and Chances* (Oxford 2003), ch. 5.

The second feature is the inevitable importance of the judges in leading legal development in a common law system. As Lord Goff wrote in 1983, 'It is therefore important that the dominant element in the development of the law should be professional reaction to individual fact-situations, rather than theoretical development of legal principle. Pragmatism must be the watchword.'[103] All the same, he argued that professional opinion desired and used the work of jurists, and so, in his view, 'the work of the judges has become more and more influenced by the teaching and writing of jurists'.[104] Lord Goff was an Oxford academic who went to the Bar, but continued to publish, notably as joint author of a pathbreaking work on a new area of English law, the law of restitution.[105] His own judicial work enabled the law of restitution to be accepted by the House of Lords as a branch of English law.

Duxbury has charted the increasing influence of academic writing in modern times.[106] He points to an emphasis on the personal contacts and persuasion of individual academics in their dealings with members of the judiciary and the legal profession to a more institutional or professional authority of legal writing as a genre. Whereas he notes that Oxbridge tutors in particular would be sought out to discuss current legal issues,[107] the more modern examples of criminal law or administrative law show the interplay between legal commentators and legal decision-makers in a more generalised way.[108] Birks was able in 1998 to cite a long list of academics who had influenced contemporary legal development.[109]

It would be fair to say that the Law Commission has served as an important intermediary between academics and judges. Its members include both academics and judges, and it uses academics to provide guidance and research for particular projects. It then consults widely among the academic, judicial and professional communities, before producing recommendations. In a number of instances, its recommendations have been implemented not by formal legislation, but by case-law

[103] R. Goff, 'The Search for Principle' (1983) 59 *Proceedings of the British Academy* 169 at 185–6.

[104] Ibid., 182.

[105] R. Goff and G. Jones, *The Law of Restitution* (1st edn, London 1966; 6th edn, 2002).

[106] N. Duxbury, *Judges and Jurists* (Oxford 2003), ch. 5.

[107] See ibid., 105 n. 213 and 84–111 on the influence of Pollock and Goodhart as editors of the *Law Quarterly Review*.

[108] Ibid., 102–13.

[109] P. Birks, 'The Academic and the Practitioner' (1998) 18 *Legal Studies* 397, 398–9; P. Birks, *Reviewing Legal Education* (Oxford 1994), 2–6.

development in the courts. The process of refining and testing ideas within the Commission is more thorough and more reliable than testing simply in the forensic forum of an individual case. It is therefore not surprising that its results have been adopted. But also importantly, it has been a forum in which the qualities of academics have been tested at length in practical policy-making and in legal drafting. This may well explain why the first two practising academics appointed to the Bench had been Law Commissioners – Lady Brenda Hale in 1994 (eventually the first woman member of the House of Lords) and Sir Jack Beatson in 2004. In other jurisdictions, such appointments would not have seemed remarkable, but they marked a significant change in the traditions of the English legal community.

Judges and the wider community

Lay and professional judges

The English legal system has a very long tradition of using lay judges. Morgan and Russell note that there is a 'bewildering variety of models' for decision-making in lower courts used world-wide, with a variety of justifications, but 'the heavy dependence on lay judges in England and Wales appears to be unique'.[110] Any comparison will show that the involvement of lay people is not correlated with the extent to which democracy is embedded.[111] This section does not deal with tribunal members, about which there is little analysis, but these represent a similar kind of voluntary sector of the judiciary.[112]

The Justices of the Peace have existed for a long time. The modern foundation lay in the Justices of the Peace Act 1361 which authorised the commissioning of individuals to maintain public order and to undertake judicial and administrative tasks. The justices developed the practice of dealing with petty offences on a summary basis, as well as dealing with more serious offences at Quarter Sessions.[113] This developed into a more systematic Magistrates' Court (called 'Petty Sessions') in 1849. Apart from the criminal jurisdiction, they had matrimonial jurisdiction (especially on maintenance issues) from 1878 and jurisdiction over juveniles from

110 R. Morgan and D. Russell, *The Judiciary in the Magistrates' Courts* (RDS Occasional Paper No. 66, Home Office 2000) (hereafter 'Morgan and Russell'), 105.

111 Ibid., 116.

112 See generally Smith, Bailey and Gunn, 235–8.

113 T. Skyrme, *The Changing Image of the Magistracy* (London 1979), (hereafter 'Skyrme'), ch. 1.

1908. In the current system, magistrates have jurisdiction over criminal offences carrying a penalty of up to £5,000 or six months' imprisonment.[114] The workload of about 2 million criminal cases dealt with by the magistrates' courts a year has been constant since the 1980s.[115] The magistrates deal with 95 per cent of all criminal cases, and the lay magistrates perform the vast bulk of this work. Their children's court jurisdiction deals with the problems of children whose behaviour would be criminal if adult. In addition, they deal with a number of matrimonial matters, mainly the maintenance of children. Until 2005, they used to have a major function in licensing premises for the consumption of alcohol and gambling, functions which were essentially administrative in character.

Although until 1968 there were a substantial number of ex officio magistrates (initially mayors and ex-mayors, as well as other local dignitaries), the magistrates in modern times have been drawn from ordinary members of the local community. Given the many thousands appointed, the Lord Chancellor could not expect to be involved personally in appointing magistrates. Advisory Committees were set up in 1912 in order to present names, but publicity leaflets encouraging interest only date from 1967. Individuals were usually put forward by associations and groups in the locality, including trade unions and political parties. It is only since 1970 that interviews have been introduced and a more professional appointments process established.[116] Appointments are made through local advisory committees that advertise vacancies and then conduct interviews before making recommendations to the Lord Chancellor. Shadowing schemes exist to encourage applications from under-represented groups, particularly from ethnic minorities.[117] In the annual exercises since 1999, some 1,400 magistrates have been appointed every year in England and Wales.

In 2004, there were 28,029 lay magistrates (50.6 per cent men and 49.4 per cent women).[118] This number of magistrates has remained fairly constant since the 1980s. Most are white (93.5 per cent), though black

[114] Smith, Bailey and Gunn, 64–70.

[115] Home Office, *Criminal Statistics, England and Wales 2003* (2004), table 1.1 gives the figure of 2,001,000 cases in 2003, of which 509,000 were indictable offences. Some 71.6 per cent of defendants were found guilty in the magistrates' courts, compared with 75 per cent of those tried in the Crown Court. For earlier periods see Seago et al., 'Professional Magistracy', above n. 29, at 632.

[116] Skyrme, ch. 4.

[117] Department of Constitutional Affairs, *Judicial Appointments*, above n. 2, 18.

[118] Ibid., 28.

and Asian communities are represented (2.2 per cent and 3.3 per cent respectively). The first 212 women were appointed in 1920, some twenty-five years before the first woman stipendiary magistrate and forty-two years before the first woman county court judge. Women made up 22 per cent of the Bench in 1947 and 37 per cent in 1977.[119] Now there are equal proportions of men and women, and the current concern is much more about the diversity of the magistrates' bench in terms of social and particularly ethnic mix than about political balance, as in the past.[120]

In terms of social background, in 1977, 10 per cent were medical practitioners and 12.5 per cent were from the education professions, whereas trade union officials accounted only for 2.7 per cent and manual workers 8.2 per cent.[121] The Morgan and Russell study suggested that the Lord Chancellor's Department (LCD) figures on social background underestimated the importance of retired and professional groups among the magistrates.[122] The 2004 figures give 35 per cent as over sixty and only 3.5 per cent under forty. Nearly half (47.1 per cent) are between fifty and sixty. The LCD recorded 26 per cent of lay magistrates as retired, whereas interviews suggested this might be as high as 40 per cent. The LCD recorded a further 25 per cent as lecturers/teachers, healthcare professionals or other professionals, whereas 69 per cent in interview gave their present or former occupation as falling in this category. Professional and managerial backgrounds represented 63 per cent of lay magistrates in urban areas, compared with 31 per cent of the population, and the situation was more extreme in deprived areas (79 per cent of magistrates from these backgrounds compared with 20 per cent of the population). Public sector employees (in education, healthcare or central and local government) provided some 29 per cent of lay judges. The figures are comparable to those recorded in Sweden and German for lay judges. Both for Morgan and Russell and for Auld, the main issue is how the voluntary work of being a magistrate can be made compatible with the lives of a wider range of individuals, especially in terms of getting time off.[123] In this the English position is, again, not very different from the position in Sweden and Germany, although the training obligations

[119] Smith, Bailey and Gunn, 47.

[120] Department of Constitutional Affairs, 'National Strategy for the Recruitment of Lay Magistrates' (London 2003), esp. § 28.

[121] Skyrme, 59–60. [122] Morgan and Russell, 16 and Appendix A3.

[123] R. Auld, *Review of the Criminal Courts of England and Wales* (2001) (http://www.criminal-courts-review.org.uk/ccr-00.htm) (hereafter 'Auld'), §§ 72–4.

are more extensive and the proportion of work undertaken by lay magistrates is much larger than that performed by lay judges in the other jurisdictions.[124]

The attitude towards political affiliation as a criterion in judicial appointments is markedly different in relation to the magistracy compared with the professional judiciary. While politics has declined in relation to the latter, it has maintained a prominence in relation to the magistracy. The 1910 Royal Commission stated that 'It is important that persons of every social grade should be appointed as Justices of the Peace'[125] and so political imbalance was to be avoided. Figures have been analysed to show that even in 1977, 34 per cent of justices were Conservative, 31 per cent Labour and 14 per cent Liberal. Political affiliation is one factor which is monitored in order to ensure the representativeness of the magistrates' bench. In 2004, the political affiliations recorded were 32.3 per cent Conservative, 25.7 per cent Labour, 12.7 per cent Liberal Democrat and 23.7 per cent 'unknown'. Although political balance has not ceased to be an issue, the broader question of social diversity has become more acute.[126] In 2003, the Lord Chancellor announced that a wider range of factors would be identified from the Office of National Statistics to provide benchmarks against which to judge the representative character of the Bench.[127]

The lay magistrates are supported by about 1,800 professional advisers, and these have had to be legally qualified since 1999.[128] This provision of legal support is stronger than that available in some French lay courts, and represents a compromise between the need for expertise and the need for social experience in coming to decisions. The magistrates' clerks have increasingly taken on administrative functions in relation to scheduling of cases and initial assessments for case management purposes that have contributed to blurring the line between the respective judicial and administrative roles of lay magistrates and their advisers, a blurring which Auld recommended should not be extended.[129] The magistrates' courts came under a unified courts administration, Her Majesty's Courts Service, in 2005.

The magistracy has had a longer record of a more formal approach to training than other parts of the judiciary. The Magistrates' Association

[124] Above pp. 154 and 284. [125] Auld, § 57.

[126] E. Burney, *JP: Magistrate, Court and Community* (London 1979), ch. 5 on the appointment and characteristics of magistrates.

[127] Department of Constitutional Affairs, *Judicial Appointments*, above n. 2, M8.

[128] Auld, § 52. [129] Ibid., § 58.

was formed in 1920, with one of its objectives being the provision of training for magistrates on a voluntary basis. Provision was made for training by the Justices of the Peace Act 1949, but it took a number of years before local Magistrates' Courts Committees organised events.[130] An obligatory induction course was introduced in 1966 and obligatory refresher courses were introduced in 1979. The move from a voluntary to a compulsory system was gradual, but it compares favourably with the voluntary character of training for lay judges in Germany and Sweden. The effectiveness of the training system has depended not only on active local groups, but on powers given to the Lord Chancellor in 1973 to issue directions on training. The creation of a National Advisory Council on the Training of Magistrates in 1964 provided the first stage in a process of systematically reviewing the needs of the magistrates, and has culminated ultimately in its incorporation into the work of the Judicial Studies Board, through which the magistrates are linked into the general framework of judicial training.

A key question is whether lay senses of justice and legality differ from those of the professionals. The justification for the lay magistrates is that they reproduce a community sense of justice. But studies of the operation of the lay justices in England and in Scotland have not produced any evidence that their decisions in any sense subvert lawyers' notions of legality.[131] Rather, where the law requires interpretation or discretion, they bring to bear their particular experiences of society in the application of the law. Between social workers, the police and lawyers, there is a danger that the lay element shrinks. But, as Burney noted, most of the demand to replace lay magistrates with professionals comes from lawyers, and might miss the importance of the link to public opinion, however imperfect, that the lay system provides.[132] As has been noted in relation to stipendiary magistrates, it is the localness and the character of routine justice that defines the special character of justice in the magistrates' courts, whether it is conducted by lay or professional magistrates.[133]

[130] On training, see Skyrme, ch. 6; T. Skyrme, *History of the Justices of the Peace* (Chichester 1994), 793–9.

[131] See Z. Bankowski, N. R. Hutton and J. J. McManus, *Lay Justice* (Edinburgh 1987), 168–72: 'this "lay acid" does not dissolve the legalness of the system, for it is only allowed in as long as it is contained and constrained by the legal view of things' (181).

[132] Burney, *JP*, above n. 126, 216.

[133] See Seago et al., 'Professional Magistracy', above n. 29.

Judges and politics

The relationship of English judges to politics has to be considered in relation to four areas, all of which affect the senior judiciary, but are of very little relevance when we consider the routine justice delivered by the lower judiciary. The four areas are (a) lawmaking and contentious legal interpretation, (b) the judicial control of the executive and of Parliament, (c) the judicial implementation of sentencing, and (d) the role of the judge as a public figure.

Judicial lawmaking[134]

The distinctive political importance of the senior judiciary as lawmakers in England is summed up by Lord Nolan:[135]

> The powers and responsibility of an individual judge are immeasurably greater than those of an individual member of the executive or of the legislature. The judge may be overruled by three other judges in the Court of Appeal, and in rare cases they in turn may be overruled by five judges in the House of Lords, but the power wielded by the judges over those involved in the cases before them and over the development of the law remains out of all proportion to the number of people exercising it.

The position of the English judiciary as a creative body has varied over time. Stevens argued that until the end of the nineteenth century with an amateur House of Commons and a recently professionalised civil service, the governmental machine was not strong enough to undertake the full range of necessary reforms, and so the courts had to undertake the role, albeit reluctantly.[136] All the same, the judiciary was principally engaged in analytical interpretation, rather than the creation of law.[137] Whilst this more restrictive role was possible to a limited extent until the 1960s, this became impossible with the increased activity of government. Jaffé noted in 1969 that English judges were still less innovative than US judges, but he also noted a recognition in Britain that Parliament was notoriously slow in dealing with many necessary changes,[138] and that judicial lawmaking is not incompatible with a democratic society.

[134] See generally J. Bell, *Policy Arguments in Judicial Decisions* (Oxford 1983).
[135] Lord Nolan and Sir Stephen Sedley, *The Making and Remaking of the British Constitution* (Oxford 1997), 71.
[136] Stevens, *Law and Politics*, above n. 9, 107. [137] Ibid., 69.
[138] L. Jaffé, *English and American Judges as Lawmakers* (Oxford 1969), 29, but cf. p. 19, citing the *Final Report of the Committee on Supreme Court Practice and Procedure* (Cmd 8878; 1953), § 642. R. Stevens, *The English Judge* (Oxford 2002), ch. 2, and Stevens, *Law and Politics*, above n. 9, 335.

All the same, he noted that the underlying policy reasons for decisions would have to be made more explicit.[139]

Modern judicial creativity can fruitfully be analysed in relation to three core areas. In the first, judges have had a traditional role in relation to the common law, equity and crime, where many of the principles have been judge-made and in relation to which there is limited parliamentary interest. In this area, judges have felt happy in developing the law to use basic principles to apply to changing social circumstances. Although Abel-Smith and Stevens consider the first half of the twentieth century to be an 'era of stagnation',[140] it was a major period for developing the torts of negligence and defamation, as well as the law on implied terms in contract. In some fields, there was innovation, but in others, such as privity of contract or the protection of consumers against unfair contract terms, the judges felt the changes would be too great to introduce by way of judicial lawmaking. In these and some other areas, the judges did not keep the law abreast of social change and attitudes. The Law Commission often makes proposals, but it often remains for the judges to implement them.

Secondly, in modern areas of legislative policy, such as social security, most of the law comes from statute and the role of the judges has been as interpreters of texts. In the past, judges were typically reluctant to adopt a creative approach to the interpretation of such social welfare texts. In more recent times, judges have adopted a more purposive approach, which tries to give effect to the social purpose of legislation, even if this involves some creative interpretation of the words.[141] Laws LJ described the movement as one of degree, rather than a radical shift:

> The difference between purposive and literal construction is in truth one of degree only. On received doctrine we spend our professional lives construing legislation purposively, inasmuch as we are enjoined at every turn to ascertain the intention of Parliament. The real distinction lies in the balance to be struck, in the particular case, between the literal meaning of the words on the one hand and the context and purpose of the measure in which they appear on the other. Frequently there will be no opposition between the two, and then no difficulty arises. Where there is a potential clash, the conventional English approach has been to give at least very great and often decisive weight to the literal meaning of the enacting words. This is a tradition which is weakening, in the face of the more purposive approach enjoined for the interpretation of legislative measures

139 Jaffé, *Lawmakers*, above n. 138, 92; A. Denning, *The Changing Law* (London 1953), 45.
140 Abel-Smith and Stevens, *Lawyers and the Courts*, above n. 85, 111.
141 J. Bell and G. Engle, *Cross on Statutory Interpretation* (London 1995), 16–20, 192–7.

of the European Union and in the light of the House of Lords' decision in *Pepper (Inspector of Taxes) v. Hart*.[142]

All the same, the difference over time is a step change.

A third area relates to modern situations of social controversy which is not party-political. Examples might be the provision of contraceptives by doctors to under-age girls without the consent of their parents,[143] the sterilisation of intellectually handicapped adults,[144] and the approval of the separation of conjoined twins, even though one of them would die as a result.[145] A very good example of this area is *Airedale NHS Trust v. Bland*.[146] In this case, a man was in a permanent vegetative state, but his body was still functioning, provided that he was fed through a tube. The House of Lords decided the circumstances in which the doctors could lawfully accede to the wishes of his parents that the feeding stop and that he be allowed to die. Clearly the judges were having to establish policies on medical treatment and the point at which actions of the doctor would amount to murder, which were extremely controversial. These are clear cases of the judges making the law in areas where there was inadequate previous precedent or statute.[147]

A key message has always been the different character of judicial law-making. Sir Wilfred Greene MR said in 1938 that 'insofar as a judge may be said to "make" law he does so in a sense so different from that in which the legislature makes law that the use of the same word for the two operations is highly misleading. I prefer therefore to use the word "interpret".'[148] Sir Kenneth Diplock (as he then was) also made a similar distinction in 1965 that 'the broad organisation of society is for Parliament, the regulation of human relationships within the framework of that organisation for the courts'.[149] It is very clear from both, and particularly from the latter, that they did not think that judges did not change the law, but they asserted that there was a distinct place for the judiciary and its lawmaking. The distinction was expressed by several judges by appealing to the notion of consensus – judges take

[142] *Ashworth (Oliver) (Holdings) Ltd v. Ballard (Kent) Ltd* [1999] 2 All ER 791, 805.

[143] *Gillick v. West Norfolk and Wisbech Health Authority* [1986] AC 112.

[144] *Re F (Mental Patient: Sterilisation)* [1990] 2 AC 173.

[145] *Re A (Conjoined Twins: Surgical Separation)* [2000] 4 All ER 961.

[146] [1993] 1 All ER 821; see also *R (on the application of Pretty) v. DPP* [2001] UKHL 61, dealing with the question of assisted suicide.

[147] For a political analysis, see D. Robertson, *Judicial Discretion in the House of Lords* (Oxford 1998), 381–90.

[148] W. Greene, *The Judicial Office* (Holdsworth Society Address, Birmingham 1938), 11.

[149] K. Diplock, *The Courts as Legislators* (Birmingham 1965).

an idea from the consensus, while the legislator is able to use authority to force a new development.[150] The judges are claiming to work within existing paradigms, rather than shifting paradigms by way of a step change. Robertson[151] rightly criticises this idea that judicial law-making in many of the areas discussed above can simply be based on consensus: 'In the end these assumptions within which the paradigms are developed are dependent on common, shared, professional expectations which are largely inchoate, and which are quite unsuited as the basis of creative law making which shapes our lives.' In his view, the ideological basis for new paradigms needs to be more explicit and justified.

Judicial review

In public law, judges have been asked at various times to exercise control over the discretion of the executive. There have been periods of differing levels of activism. It is well documented that in the period between the 1920s and the 1960s, judicial review of the exercise of executive discretion was very limited. The judges deferred to the authority of the politically elected institutions. But the effectiveness of parliamentary control was called in question by the Crichel Down affair in 1954, and greater access to appeal to the courts as well as greater independence for tribunals followed the Franks Report in 1957 and the Tribunals and Inquiries Act 1958.[152] Most areas of administrative action had tribunals with proper structures for appeal. But, unlike in Germany and the United States, there was no statute on administrative procedure, and a number of sensitive areas remained outside the tribunal system and without formal appeals on a point of law. These became the field for judicial review. Many such areas – prisons, immigration and refugees – fall within the remit of the Home Office, and many of the most heated clashes since the 1990s have been with Home Secretaries of different political persuasions.[153] In this field, leading judges have worked in dialogue and even in collaboration with academics to develop the constitutional

[150] See Lord Radcliffe, *The Law and its Compass* (London 1961), 11, 53 and 63–4, and P. Devlin, 'Judges and Lawmakers' (1976) 39 MLR 1, 5. Lord Bingham seems to endorse this view of limited lawmaking in *The Business of Judging*, above n. 76, ch. 2, especially pp. 33–4.

[151] Robertson, *Judicial Discretion*, above n. 147, 400–1.

[152] For an overview, see J. Jowell, in V. Bogdanor, *The British Constitution in the Twentieth Century* (Oxford 2003), 373 at 384–90, and De Smith, Woolf and Jowell, *Judicial Review*, above n. 11, 1–006 to 1–022.

[153] Stevens, *English Judge*, above n. 138, 71–2 and 129–36.

principles that underlie the new judicial review.[154] There is also some limited evidence that judicial review has an impact on bureaucratic behaviour.[155]

Three types of situation illustrate the potential for conflict between the executive and the courts. Governments with inadequate majorities have been tempted to use the royal prerogative or existing statutory powers in order to carry out policies. The Labour Government of 1974 sought to revoke television licences bought early by astute licence payers in order to avoid a licence fee increase.[156] The same Government sought to use statutory powers of 1944 in order to make it compulsory for local education authorities to adopt a comprehensive school system.[157] A Conservative Government sought to use the prerogative to provide a less costly system for compensating the victims of criminal injuries, despite the fact that Parliament had recently enacted a different scheme, which the Home Secretary was now planning not to bring into force.[158] A second area of conflict would be where the Government wanted to act quickly in order to introduce a new policy, rather than wait to obtain new legislative powers. A third area is where the courts declare that local authorities are unable to implement their views of necessary social change without obtaining new statutory powers (which is impossible because the local authority and Parliament are dominated by different parties). An example would be when the Greater London Council was prevented from introducing a lower fares policy on London Transport because the House of Lords considered controversially that existing statutory powers did not allow London Transport to operate at a loss.[159] Challenges to central government policies on local government finance were, however, rebutted.[160] Critics have often commented unfavourably on many of the positions adopted by the courts,[161] and the scope for political conflict is clear. It may be that judges have traditionally been deferential in the area of national security,[162] but human

[154] See, for example, the contributions to C. Forsyth and I. Hare, *The Golden Metwand and the Crooked Cord* (Oxford 1998), and the bibliography cited by Jowell, above n. 152.

[155] See G. Richardson, in M. Hertogh and S. Halliday, *Judicial Review and Bureaucratic Impact* (Cambridge 2004), ch. 4.

[156] *Congreve v. Home Office* [1976] QB 629.

[157] *Secretary of State for Education v. Tameside MBC* [1977] AC 1014.

[158] *R v. Secretary of State for the Home Department, ex p. Fire Brigades Union* [1995] 2 AC 513.

[159] *Bromley LBC v. Greater London Council* [1983] 1 AC 768.

[160] *Nottinghamshire CC v. Secretary of State for the Environment* [1986] AC 240.

[161] J. A. G. Griffith, *Judicial Politics since 1920* (Oxford 1993), ch. 6.

[162] For example, *R v. Secretary of State for the Home Department, ex p. Brind* [1999] 1 AC 969.

rights considerations are encouraging greater activism even in this area.

The United Kingdom has had a less developed idea of the legal constitution than most of the countries in this book except Sweden. Because of a long continuity of institutions, the constitution has been seen by some lawyers and judges as predominantly a description of institutions and practices, rather than as a legally normative corpus of rules and principles.[163] The development of principles of the judicial review of administrative action had already begun to change this, but the constitutional changes particularly since 1997 have accelerated the process. The courts gained powers under European Union law to disapply domestic statutes where they conflict with EU legislation, which was put into effect in the *Factortame* case in 1989.[164] Here the House of Lords was suspending the application of a statute at the direction of the European Court of Justice, but the precedent was set. The Scotland Act 1998 and the Northern Ireland Act 1998 created legislative assemblies with powers in the courts to annul legislation which exceeded the powers of those bodies. Effectively a federal constitutional jurisdiction was established, though it has mainly had impact in relation to human rights issues, notably by quashing the power to appoint temporary sheriffs.[165]

The Human Rights Act 1998 was, according to Stevens, predominantly psychological in its impact.[166] For many years, judges had already been using the European Convention as a benchmark for the interpretation of English law. The interpretative obligation in s. 3 of the Act did not add anything formally new. But the formal power to give a declaration of incompatibility provided an additional way of altering the Government's agenda. When a declaration is given, then the Government has to decide whether to propose an amendment of the law to bring it into line with the Convention or to take other action to maintain the incompatibility, e.g. by registering a formal derogation from the Convention. This is the nearest that English judges come to a constitutional review.[167] An example was *A (FC) and others v. Secretary of State for the Home Department*[168]

[163] See S. Sedley, in Nolan and Sedley, *British Constitution*, above n. 135, ch. 2. D. Feldman, 'None, One or Several? Perspectives on the UK's Constitution(s)' [2005] CLJ 329 argues helpfully that the UK constitution is a locus of competing visions of the way the country should be governed.

[164] *R v. Secretary of State for Transport, ex p. Factortame (No. 2)* [1989] 1 AC 374; see also *R v. Secretary of State for Employment, ex p. Equal Opportunities Commission* [1995] 1 AC 1.

[165] *Starrs v. Ruxton* 2000 JC 208.

[166] Stevens, *English Judge*, above n. 138, 115.

[167] See C. Gearty and A. Tomkins, in Hayton, *Law's Futures*, above n. 99, ch. 4.

[168] [2004] HL 56.

in which a number of individuals challenged their detention without trial. They were held because they were suspected of being a danger to national security, but they could not be expelled to another country. The House of Lords held that s. 23 of the Anti-terrorism, Crime and Security Act 2001 was incompatible with articles 5 and 14 of the European Convention insofar as it is disproportionate and permits detention of suspected international terrorists in a way that discriminates on the ground of nationality or immigration status, and it quashed the Government's derogation from the Convention. Lord Bingham[169] stated that

> [T]he function of independent judges charged to interpret and apply the law is universally recognised as a cardinal feature of the modern democratic state, a cornerstone of the rule of law itself. The Attorney General is fully entitled to insist on the proper limits of judicial authority, but he is wrong to stigmatise judicial decision-making as in some way undemocratic. It is particularly inappropriate in a case such as the present in which Parliament has expressly legislated in section 6 of the [Human Rights Act] 1998 . . . to render unlawful any act of a public authority, including a court, incompatible with a Convention right, has required courts (in section 2) to take account of relevant Strasbourg jurisprudence, has (in section 3) required courts, so far as possible, to give effect to Convention rights and has conferred a right of appeal on derogation issues. The effect is not, of course, to override the sovereign legislative authority of the Queen in Parliament, since if primary legislation is declared to be incompatible the validity of the legislation is unaffected (section 4(6)) and the remedy lies with the appropriate minister (section 10), who is answerable to Parliament. The 1998 Act gives the courts a very specific, wholly democratic, mandate.

The significance of human rights cases in the recent caseload of the House of Lords suggests that the new Supreme Court will have a significant constitutional function.[170]

Sentencing discretion

Sentencing is an area in which politicians wish to set the framework and judges implement it in relation to individual cases. The difficulty is that politicians, particularly in a media-driven society, wish to react to individual examples of the sentencing policy in order to make general adjustments. The judges, on the other hand, take the view that they have a responsibility to ensure justice in individual cases, and see the directions given by politicians as an interference with judicial independence. This

169 Ibid., para. 42.

170 See Jowell, above n. 152, at 390–5, and D. Feldman, in Bogdanor, *British Constitution*, above n. 152, ch. 11.

has been coupled with extrajudicial clashes between successive Lords Chief Justice and the Home Secretary over the respective roles of judges and the executive in deciding sentencing policy, with the judges openly criticising the more draconian policies of the executive.[171] One particular area of conflict was in relation to the management of life sentences. When the young killers of a child had been sentenced to detention at Her Majesty's pleasure, the Home Secretary sought to impose a minimum period of detention without examining the interests of the child killers in question. The minister was under immense political pressure in this case, but the House of Lords held that he needed to act like a judge and was wrong to be inflexible in the exercise of his discretion.[172] In both these areas of sentencing and dealing with the post-sentencing management of offenders, the judges have been given a greater role, e.g. through the creation of a Sentencing Guidelines Council, but this does not really diminish the political sensitivity of this area of their activity.

Judges as public figures

English senior judges are major public figures. This is symbolised by the knighthood conferred on a High Court judge when he is appointed. (A woman becomes a Dame.) Many members of the Court of Appeal will be Privy Counsellors. The Law Lords, until recently, have sat in the House of Lords in its legislative capacity. They have been expected to stay clear of controversial topics, and to be 'resident technical consultants to the legislature',[173] but some of their interventions have been more than technical, e.g. on the Constitutional Reform Act or the reforms to the legal system proposed by Lord Mackay.[174] Salary levels are also high. One consequence is that senior judges have traditionally been used to chair public inquiries. They are seen as both authoritative and politically neutral figures. Many examples can be cited of judges becoming involved in socially controversial matters in extrajudicial roles. Even in the era of limited judicial creativity, judges were frequently chairing committees on either socially or politically controversial matters. In the former category there were the Scarman Report on the Brixton Riots in 1981 and

171 See Lord Taylor in 1995: Malleson, *New Judiciary*, above n. 38, 58–62; Lord Woolf, 'Making Sense of Sentencing', 12 May 2005 (http://www.dca.gov.uk/judicial/speeches/lcj120505.htm).

172 *R v. Secretary of State for the Home Department, ex p. Venables* [1998] AC 407.

173 L. Blom-Cooper and G. Drewry, *Final Appeal* (Oxford 1972), 203.

174 Above p. 321.

the Macpherson Report on the Stephen Lawrence inquiry. In the latter category, there were the 1959 Devlin Report on Nyasaland, Denning on Profumo, Scott on Arms for Iraq and Hutton on the David Kelly suicide. There have also been inquiries finding the reasons for disasters and making policy recommendations (e.g. the Taylor Report on the Hillsborough football stadium disaster, which led to major changes in the operation of stadia).[175] Drewry criticised this practice as 'harnessing the myth of judicial impartiality' and involving it in political controversy.[176] A more modern version of this concern raises issues about the compatibility of inquiries to the human rights interpretations of judicial impartiality, as well as with the important observation that the authority of a judicial inquiry trades on the authority of the judicial office.[177] Drewry was clear that 'it is wholly misleading to see the political process as something wholly separate from the legal process, there is constant interaction between the two. And "government" is a composite activity which embraces both.'[178] Yet he is unwilling to give the judges too large a role.

The strength of the judicial voice depends on the strength of other voices in public. At various times, particularly when the political opposition in Parliament has been weak, then the voice of the judges has carried greater weight or has at least been more audible.[179]

The public standing of the judiciary

The public standing of the judiciary has been one reason why judges have been given extrajudicial tasks such as chairing inquiries. There is, however, an ambivalence in this notion of public standing. The reputation of judges for impartiality and conscientious application of the law has been reinforced by a notion of judicial independence that keeps them above criticism to the same extent as applies to other organs of government. Blom-Cooper[180] wrote in 1966:

[175] See Stevens, *English Judge*, above n. 138, 29, 43 and 58.

[176] G. Drewry, 'Judges and Political Inquiries: Harnessing a Myth' (1975) 23 *Political Studies* 49; Griffith, *Politics of the Judiciary*, above n. 41, ch. 2; Smith, Bailey and Gunn, 274–6.

[177] J. Beatson, 'Should Judges Conduct Public Inquiries?' (2005) 121 LQR 221; Bingham, *The Business of Judging*, above n. 76, 64.

[178] G. Drewry, *Law, Justice and Politics* (London 1975), 3; Stevens, *English Judge*, above n. 138, 86.

[179] Stevens, *English Judge*, above n. 138, 140, 147; cf. his similar comments on the late nineteenth century before politicians became more professional and the professional civil service became established: Stevens, *Law and Politics*, above n. 9, 107.

[180] L. Blom-Cooper, 'The Judiciary in an Era of Law Reform' (1966) 37 *Political Quarterly* 378.

> Criticism of the judiciary over the last fifty years has been confined to conversation over the coffee cups and to the seclusion of private solicitors' offices and barristers' chambers . . . The English have not only placed their judges on a pedestal; they have also cloaked them with an immunity from public criticism which tends only to diminish the quality of justice administered by those so privileged. Rather the prestige of the judiciary is maintained by virtue of its remoteness from public comment.

This attitude is reflected still in the debate on the way in which judicial independence was to be secured under the Constitutional Reform Act 2005. The Judges' Council was concerned that, should the office of Lord Chancellor be abolished or changed substantially, there would be no one to defend the judges against improper attacks from senior politicians, usually the Home Secretary. The Concordat between the Lord Chancellor and the Lord Chief Justice led to a provision in the Act which made it the duty of the Lord Chancellor to act as guardian of judicial independence. The preoccupation with defending the judges against attack reflects a certain conception of the judges as being on a pedestal. In part it also reflected the Kilmuir rules of 1955 under which serving judges were not supposed to give interviews to the media. Under this system, judges needed someone else to act as their voice, usually the Lord Chancellor. Since Lord Mackay became Lord Chancellor in 1987, this has been relaxed. Lord Taylor introduced a press conference in 1992, when he became Lord Chief Justice, and his successors have also appeared on radio and television to talk about the work of the judiciary. Indeed, the Lord Chief Justice has regularly defended judges against what he perceived to be improper attack, and he orchestrated the judges' concerns about the abolition of the office of Lord Chancellor.

Studies of the perception of the public suggest a large measure of ignorance about the legal system. As Genn put it, 'Expectations of courts, judges and lawyers are not shaped by personal experience, but by televised representations and tabloid atrocity stories. Most people's experience of courts is as a spectator – watching and reading about what goes on in high-profile and generally criminal cases.'[181] Her study of civil cases reported that 66 per cent of those interviewed for a major survey thought that most judges were out of touch with the lives of ordinary people, and only 13 per cent disagreed with this view.[182] Only a bare majority (53 per cent) agreed with the statement that they were confident that

[181] H. Genn, *Paths to Justice* (Oxford 1999), 246.
[182] On this point, see also Abel, *Market and State*, 137ff.

they would get a fair hearing in court.[183] While 79 per cent of those who attended court thought that the judge understood the case well, less than half (47 per cent) felt that the judge favoured neither side.[184] The court process was often seen as alienating and intimidating.

Lord Nolan argued that

> Much of the responsibility for the poor publicity which judges often receive lies with the judges themselves. The legal profession in general and the judges in particular have always been bad at cultivating public relations . . . but in recent years judges have increasingly come to recognise the need to anticipate public reaction to controversial decisions and to cater for it in the judgment – or even, in extreme cases, by holding a press conference.[185]

An example of a more recent willingness to discuss controversial issues was the set of interviews given by Sir Alan Ward on the conjoined twins affair, whether doctors would be permitted to separate conjoined twins, even where one of them was almost certain to die as a result.[186] For Lord Nolan, a telling difference lay in the evidence of the attitudes of jurors towards judges and the legal process in criminal cases in which they had been involved, and the more general, critical views expressed about sentencing and the criminal process in more general surveys of public opinion.[187]

Of course, senior judges have long had a platform of public lectures to present their views on their role, the state of the law and the need for change. Far more than other judiciaries studied in this book, the senior judges have been accorded status and opportunities to take on a lead role in proposing law reform.

A major reason for change has been the impact of the high-profile cases on the miscarriage of justice. Many concerned the conviction of people suspected of involvement in IRA terrorist offences. But there were other cases involving ethnic minority defendants. The principal reasons for the wrongful convictions lay in the evidence produced by the police, either from confessions or from forensic evidence. But another reason was the way in which the judges handled the trials and the appeals. Statements, especially from Lord Lane CJ, gave the impression that the

183 Ibid., 239–41 and 229–32. 184 Ibid., 221–2.

185 Nolan and Sedley, *British Constitution*, above n. 135.

186 *Re A (Conjoined Twins: Surgical Separation)* [2000] 4 All ER 961.

187 Nolan and Sedley, *British Constitution*, above n. 135, 69–70, drawing particularly on M. Zander and P. Henderson, *Crown Court Study* (Royal Commission on Criminal Justice, Research Study No. 19, 1993).

judges were siding with the establishment and were not open to the possibility that the criminal system could have made a mistake. The eventual need for cases to be re-opened after major public campaigns cast the judges in the role of wrongdoers whose professional misdeeds had been exposed. Their unwillingness to be active in uncovering the miscarriages and their apparent hostility to the people wrongly convicted undermined confidence in the impartiality of the judiciary.

A further aspect of the public perception of the judiciary lies in their social composition. The legal profession is necessarily an unrepresentative group, an educational elite. But the problem with the legal profession lies in its character as a social elite. As a social elite, it is perceived as remote from the concerns of ordinary citizens, a matter that affects both its lawmaking and its ability to speak on behalf of the community.

The lay magistrates have a distinct public reputation. As the Auld Committee noted, the various studies of public opinion suggest that the role of the magistrates is not widely visible to the public – the public does not appreciate how many decisions are taken by the magistrates.[188] Among those who are informed, there is a high level of confidence in the magistrates,[189] though among court users there is greater confidence in professionals for managing court business more effectively. The public thinks that professional magistrates (now district judges) are more likely to reach correct decisions on guilt or innocence, but lay magistrates are considered overwhelmingly more likely to represent the views of the community and to be sympathetic to the circumstances of defendants.[190] The value of the lay magistracy may be to provide symbolic legitimacy, even if the social composition of the magistrates is not really that different from that of professional judges.[191] Given that the district judge will also work in a specific area for a long time, it is not clear that lay judges represent a different kind of 'local justice'.[192]

Conclusion

In a speech marking his retirement in 2005, Lord Woolf CJ remarked that in the 1950s 'the justice system was, by comparison with today, a

188 Auld, § 30, citing Morgan and Russell, who found that 75 per cent of a random sample of those questioned did not know about the existence of both professional and lay magistrates.

189 The opinion poll reported by Morgan and Russell gave a 63 per cent confidence in the magistrates, compared with 64 per cent for judges and 68 per cent for juries.

190 See Morgan and Russell, xi and 58–64.

191 Ibid., 9; Auld, ch. 4, § 34.

192 Auld, §§ 35–7.

cottage industry. It is so no longer.'[193] That characterisation of the justice system applies to the organisation and management of the judiciary. In the speech, he recalled how he first became an assistant recorder at short notice with no training and with no formality in the appointment process. The contemporary system is far removed from that, but it is still moving into an era of mass and professionally organised justice.

In the 1950s and 1960s, the organisation of the judiciary was informal and amateurish, based on two pillars. First, the Bench was drawn from a small, mainly generalist Bar and, in particular, a small cohort of QCs. This provided a club of able judges who would know each other quite well and had a general reputation for impartiality, integrity and effectiveness. Appointees were known figures to the judges and the performance of judges could be monitored and even sanctioned informally. Training was undertaken by practice and informally. The second pillar of the system was the lay magistracy. The magistrates represented local justice and dealt with 95 per cent of criminal cases, and many family law matters as well. This way of dealing with the bulk of criminal justice did not require much legal training, and any training was predominantly voluntary. Holding the two together was the Lord Chancellor with a small staff. He was able to be involved in a very personal way with much of the process of appointing and overseeing judicial appointments and performance, not least because he would typically be active in sitting in the House of Lords in its judicial capacity.

The contemporary position has changed. The number of judges, both full-time and part-time, has increased very substantially. The backgrounds of judges have become more heterogeneous. The Bar has become more specialist and solicitors are appointed increasingly to the lower judiciary. There is no longer a single club to which present and aspiring judges belong. There is no single social process, except possibly through the training activities of the Judicial Studies Board, that gives the judiciary a sense of common identity. All the same, the system remains hierarchical and is perhaps becoming increasingly so. There are three distinct groups of judges: the UK-wide members of the House of Lords, the senior English and Welsh judiciary serving in the High Court and the Court of Appeal, and the lower judiciary dealing with the routine civil and criminal cases. The House of Lords and its successor, the Supreme Court, will make important legal policy and lawmaking decisions, and will be drawn from the most senior judges in each of the three domestic

[193] Speech, 14 July 2005 (http://www.dca.gov.uk/judicial/speeches/lcj140705.htm).

jurisdictions who will have been mainly leading practitioners and some of whom will have been academics. The senior judiciary will very largely be drawn laterally from the leading members of the Bar, though there may be one or two leading solicitor advocates appointed, as well as a few promoted from the Circuit Bench and the very occasional academic. This group of judges now deals with the most important civil and criminal work, either because of the gravity of the subject-matter or because of the legal or factual complexity. The lower judiciary is increasingly drawn from the generalist Bar, often regionally based, and from the solicitors. This group is likely to be more female and more likely to look for promotion. It provides the professional judiciary dealing with routine cases, alongside the lay magistrates and tribunal members. The Constitutional Reform Act 2005 has grouped the High Court appointments with those of the lower judiciary, but this is not likely to have a major impact on the character of appointments or on where the judges are drawn from. In comparison with European countries, it will be interesting to see whether the unified appointments and training processes do lead to a sense of an integrated judiciary, or whether the groups will remain distinct. Much of the attention in analysis of the judiciary is given to the senior judiciary, but the importance of the lower judiciary will grow as attention turns to ways of improving the effectiveness of routine justice.

Perhaps the largest growth in the last thirty years has been in the number of part-time judges, and in their increased professionalism. The part-time recorders undertake much routine justice and free up the High Court and senior circuit judges to deal with difficult cases and to undertake administration. Within the English system, the part-time judiciary is a first, but not irrevocable, step on the judicial ladder and replaces the early career judicial posts found in other legal systems. The use of part-time posts at all levels in the system is one of the unique features of the English system, but it is clearly under strain to the extent that individuals work in private practice as solicitors. Continental experience suggests that the public sector may provide a more likely pool of candidates for part-time and full-time judicial functions, a pool that is underexploited in England.

There are three features around which the increasing professionalisation of the judiciary in England is developing. The first is an emphasis on training. Without a judicial college training new recruits, organised induction and occasional retraining has become a necessity. The Judicial Studies Board has come to be accepted as a necessary part of judicial practice and has ensured a greater professionalism in the approach to issues such as sentencing and social diversity, as well as providing major updates in new legal developments. On the whole, the courses are less academic than those provided in Germany and France, but, like other judicial schools, the key to acceptability is that the programme is designed and run by judges for judges. The professionalism is extended in England to the lay magistrates in a way which recognises their importance in the legal system and is more thorough than elsewhere in Europe.

The second feature is judicial appointment. Here the 'cottage industry' approach is slowly breaking down, but the system has still some way to go before it is as transparent and professional as most of the other countries studied in this book. The one distinctive feature is the open way in which diversity issues are being addressed, especially in relation to ethnic minorities. Whereas it could be said that the English have a peculiar problem in the low numbers of women on the Bench, the issue of ethnic minorities is more widespread, but is addressed in a less focused way elsewhere.

The third area of professionalism is administration. Judges have long been involved in aspects of the administration of courts. But a more systematic organisation has been growing over the last thirty years. The reforms of 2005, including the creation of Her Majesty's Court Service to deal with the general administration of the courts, will ensure a more coherent managerial structure for the courts and a clearer division of functions. The result will be a need for greater management training for judges with key administrative roles. The greater professionalisation of appointments will also require greater professionalism in the management of judicial personnel, and the tentative steps towards appraisal systems can be seen as part of this. As we have seen, other systems have much longer experience of appraisal and performance indicators as tools in managing large judiciaries in an organised but fair way. These processes become inevitable when the scale of the judiciary is no longer amenable to informal monitoring and guidance.

A major area that remains to be developed in the emerging professional judiciary is the accountability of judges for their performance. Malleson notes that the judges have been reluctant to be drawn into systems of scrutiny.[194] The system has relied on mechanisms of soft accountability, such as openness and representativity, rather than formal

[194] Malleson, *New Judiciary*, above n. 38, ch. 6.

reporting.[195] Unlike the French Cour de cassation, the Conseil d'Etat, or the German Bundesgerichtshof, to name but three supreme courts, there is no annual report produced by the Court of Appeal or the House of Lords, though s. 54 of the Constitutional Reform Act 2005 now imposes the duty to produce such a report on the Supreme Court. Whether this will include a substantive review of its legal activity is not yet clear. The Lord Chief Justice has sometimes given evidence to parliamentary select committees, but this has not been a direct mechanism of accountability. Malleson is right that transparency of reasoning is an important part of accountability of the judiciary, and the UK judges are very full in giving reasons for their decisions, compared with their continental European counterparts. But this focuses on individual decisions, rather than on trends and priorities. The recognition that resources are a key part of the effectiveness of judges in performing their responsibility for doing justice may well lead to giving them a greater say in how resources are used, but this will bring with it greater accountability, as in Spain and Sweden. It is in this context of New Public Management that the English judiciary really has yet to develop a coherent view and to relate it in a sensible way to the notion of judicial independence.[196] Andrew Le Sueur[197] has described this as an 'emerging debate' and sees in the 2005 reforms potential lines for development, but the mechanisms are still underdeveloped.

195 Ibid., 38.

196 See Seago et al., 'Professional Magistracy', above n. 29, 650–1 and 640; G. Drewry, 'Judicial Independence in Britain' in R. Blackburn (ed.), *Constitutional Studies* (London 1992), 160.

197 A. Le Sueur, 'Developing Mechanisms for Judicial Accountability in the UK' (2004) 24 *Legal Studies* 73.

7 Factors shaping the character of the judiciary

This book has focused on the importance of institutional features in shaping the character of a judiciary and its corporate role. Goodin argues that there is a 'stable, recurring, repetitive, patterned nature of the behaviour that occurs within institutions and because of them'.[1] Such institutional features provide the framework not only for stability, but also for continuity and change. This analysis suggests that institutions have an important role in shaping the development of individuals within their role. It does not imply that individuals are shaped only by their institutions. The multiplicity of the influences on a particular individual makes this inconceivable. Rather, an institutional analysis identifies a regularity of influences that offer both opportunities and constraints to the collection of individual actions. Particular individuals may have their own path within the judiciary and outside it, but the institution itself does offer initial formation and possibilities for activity.

Institutions are formally designed in that there are organisational structures; but they also have informal features. Once established, the institution will operate not simply within the tramlines established by its organisational structure, but will be part of a wider social activity to which it relates. The judiciary is not just a body deciding cases within the formal hierarchy of courts, but it is also a constitutional institution negotiating its place within the separation of powers, a social institution that contributes to the solution of issues such as crime and family breakdown, and a set of legal professionals who have to establish their place both within the legal community and among professionals in general. The multiplicity of dimensions of any social institution and its development can be captured only by examining its formal and

[1] R. E. Goodin (ed.), *The Theory of Institutional Design* (Cambridge 1996), 22.

informal aspects.[2] The specific contribution of this work is to highlight both the formal structures such as careers, training and promotion and informal features such as the network of influences that contribute to the character of particular national judiciaries.

The book has focused particularly on the internal character of the judiciary as an institution, but it has also attended to its place within the legal community and within the wider community, especially in relation to politics. The character of these different relationships can be explained not only by the diversity of tasks assigned to judges, but also by the place of history, organisational structures and values in determining their role. The fact that the judiciary has particular roles and has operated in this way for some time does not just reflect rational or deliberate planning, but also the way in which the judiciary has adapted to events. In this adaptation, there are four important factors that shape the judicial role: history, task, organisational structure and values. Each is interrelated, but has a distinctive contribution.

History

This book shares with Geller the view that historical experience, rather than constitutional theory, has the main impact in shaping the judiciary as a social group. Geller argues that 'History often imposes practices on us for which there never was any theory but that which was invented after the fact.'[3] There is no single universal judicial task, but rather a series of tasks that have become part of the portfolio of specific groups of judges over time. There are similarities between countries, but also significant differences. Past events and experiences have given rise to the design of different institutions. The various chapters in this book have sought to explain the historical factors that have shaped the judicial professions in the different countries.

The comparison between five countries with relatively similar social settings and values demonstrates that judicial tasks are not always the same, and are not always carried on in the same way. In many ways, the most extreme difference is shown by the use of lay judges in the different systems. Popular involvement in justice has been a feature of all the systems, but they have adopted it and expanded it for many different

2 See J. S. Dryzek, 'The Informal Logic of Institutional Design' in ibid., ch. 4.

3 P. E. Geller, 'Staffing the Judiciary and "Tastes in Justice"' (1989) 61 S. Calif. LR 1849, 1854.

reasons in the face of the gradual professionalisation of the judiciary. In France, the forms of lay involvement as judges have depended on the sector of judicial work.[4] Commercial and labour law have had long-standing lay involvement as judges, often deciding without professional involvement. But the use of the jury is limited to a very small set of criminal cases, those tried in the *cour d'assises*, and was never present in the civil or administrative courts.[5] In Germany and Sweden, there has been the tradition of the lay judges as assessors in a wide variety of cases, including in administrative courts. In Germany, the practice of having assessors was more common in certain fields, such as crime and commerce. The lay judges were given a new prominence in the settlement of the Bundesrepublik in 1949. In Sweden, there was an earlier tradition of lay judges going back to the Middle Ages, which continued particularly in the criminal courts. It was given a new life by the reforms of the 1970s, in which popular participation was seen as a social advantage in the modernisation of governmental institutions. The English magistrates and, later, tribunal members offer different versions of popular involvement, but also expertise of non-lawyers. By contrast, the Spanish lay judges have a very different past. They are the continuation of local justices chosen from among the community and, in the last century or so, making up for the lack of sufficient professional judges. But they are now almost always qualified lawyers, rather than lay people. Each system has a different history of why lay judges have a role and where they now fit in. There is no necessity that lay judges should exist or play any particular role. Often for conjunctural reasons, a particular form of lay judiciary has arisen. A good example is the very different structures for lay commercial judges. There has been a long tradition in Europe of involving commercial people in the resolution of disputes on commercial matters, but its form varies. In France, the pattern of the commercial courts pre-dating the Revolution has become embedded, and it has been difficult to change, despite persistent criticism. The German pattern dates from the nineteenth century, and takes the form of lay assessors in a court led by a professional judge.[6] In England, the tradition was for a commercial jury, but this has now lapsed.

History has also influenced the creativity of judges and their involvement in lawmaking. The Swedish experience and that of the Conseil d'Etat in France focus on the contribution of judges as experts on the law and administration in pre-legislative debates. This contribution

[4] Above pp. 91–2. [5] See above ch. 2. [6] Above p. 155.

provides these judges with a strong voice in shaping the law. In the pre-legislative role, the judges act as a politically autonomous body, but with limited power to determine the eventual rules that are enacted. This role also gives them some authority in using pre-legislative materials when they interpret the legislation in post-enactment litigation. By contrast, the Germans and Spaniards have focused attention on post-enactment review, either abstract or concrete, with limited judicial involvement in the pre-legislative process. The English experience of parliamentary sovereignty has given judges a lesser role in creativity in the past. But as Parliament became overburdened, so judges have taken on more creative roles both in court and in pre-legislative institutions such as the Law Commission.

My thesis is that institutions are designed and develop as a response to previous experience. To begin with, the brief for any new development is strongly influenced by what has occurred, especially in the recent past. The French attitude to judicial lawmaking at the time of the creation of the Tribunal de cassation in 1790 and the writing of the Civil Code in 1804 was influenced by the experience of the Parlements as obstructions to reform.[7] The dominance of the model that the judge is merely 'the mouth of the law' has been identified as a persistent, though distorting, image of the judicial role in France and countries influenced by it.[8] The separation of public and private law courts in France results too from experience with the Parlements.[9] These experiences also led to a long resistance to the judicial review of legislation.

Cappelletti suggested that in recent times there was an almost universal appeal of constitutional review. But he recognised that 'differences in approach to judicial review remain as testimony to past divergences'.[10] The importance and structures of constitutional review reflect values which many countries share about the role judges should play in limiting legislative power, but they also reflect an engagement with past experiences that are particular to one jurisdiction, rather than universal phenomena. Even the creation of the Conseil constitutionnel in 1958 reflects a response to past problems, rather than an anticipation of future issues and a desire to meet them.[11] It was given competence

[7] J. P. Dawson, *The Oracles of the Law* (Westport 1968), 305–14, 367–71, 375–86.

[8] J. Merryman 'How Others Do It: The French and German Judiciaries' (1989) 61 S. Calif. LR 1865, 1874.

[9] See *French Legal Cultures*, vii–viii, 66–71, 188–9, 245–6.

[10] M. Cappelletti, *The Judicial Process in Comparative Perspective* (Oxford 1989), 146 and 148.

[11] J. Bell, *French Constitutional Law* (Oxford 1992), 20–9.

over elections in reaction to experiences in the Fourth Republic. There may have been some anticipation in giving the Conseil jurisdiction to rule on the powers of the Government to legislate to modify provisions in *lois* or to challenge attempts in Parliament to legislate in the sphere of governmental legislative competence. But the level of strategic anticipation of future issues, such as fundamental rights, was limited. The German Constitution is very much a response to the past. Its selection of constitutional values is strongly influenced by an assessment of the values breached by the Nazis. Its idea of constitutional review also reflects a consideration of the failings of the Weimar system, as well as some ideas developed as early as the constitutional convention in Frankfurt in 1848. In their different ways, the two illustrate Cappelletti's comment that the constitutional justice of these two countries reflects a desire to learn the lessons, whilst avoiding the pitfalls, of the past.[12]

Spain illustrates the way in which a legal system's own experience can be used in conjunction with the previous experience of other countries. The Spanish, emerging from the Franco era, were concerned to have constitutional systems in place that would meet some of the problems of the past. The German experience seemed to offer a successful model to be copied. Similarly, the jury was copied at times from English and French experiences in order to provide defences in press and criminal cases against oppression (and it was abolished several times because that liberal objective no longer conformed to the values of those in power). To a great extent, this way of working illustrates the model of the reflective practitioner mentioned in chapter 1.[13] Experience leads to reflection and changes. In this case, traumatic experience crystallises the need for institutional change and sets the context for it. The reflection is a problem-solving exercise. In Spain, there was long deliberation about institutions, and so there was more design in the structure of institutions than there was in France. All the same, the Constitution remains to an important degree a dialogue with Spain's past.

The political and social continuity in Sweden provides a different kind of history, and explains different developments. Constitutional review is not really seen as a need. Even though the Constitution is more recent than in Germany or France, the authors did not experience the same need to restrain the legislature or the Government through constitutional review. There are longstanding procedures of legislative preview and complaint against administrative authorities that serve to meet

[12] Cappelletti, *Judicial Process*, above n. 10, 132. [13] Above p. 11.

many of the issues that constitutional review resolves in other countries. There are different Swedish approaches to solving problems. The more gradual adjustment to democracy and the experience of a strong and continuous Social Democrat government from the 1930s suggested the need for a different institutional balance than in other countries. At the same time, the more recent exposure of Sweden to the EU and the European Convention has given greater prominence to judicial mechanisms for dealing with problems, and to a greater emphasis on rights. The English experience also suggests that the history of the role of Parliament in establishing freedoms in the seventeenth-century revolutions long limited a role for judges in constitutional review.

The last point is important in that it cannot be assumed that, because countries have historically developed in distinctive ways, they will always remain distinctive. Common issues and common external pressures will also have an influence on legal development. To stress the importance of history is not to suggest that legal systems are autochthonous. This feature merely stresses the importance of the local context for understanding the way a judiciary operates.

Whilst the judiciary is not a prisoner of its history, the heritage of particular national judicial institutions is a major determinant of its present design and its modes of operation. The design and modes of operation establish routines, into which new members are inducted and which are often perpetuated out of convenience or even inertia.[14] However debatable they may have been initially, such design and modes of operation create an established set of arrangements. As long as they continue to function reasonably effectively, or nothing better can be imagined or afforded, then they will tend to remain in place. A good example is provided by national styles for giving reasons in judicial decisions. There is no particular reason to alter a way of working which provides solutions that are equally valid as alternatives in terms of justice or efficiency. They will be 'good enough' to do the jobs that are expected. These judicial activities will provide a context for other institutions in legal professions, in government and in society more generally, and will thus become embedded in the way in which activities take place in that society. Breaking out of the system that has grown up is not an easy exercise, and is therefore often avoided, even if there are problems with the way in which institutions currently operate.

[14] On the importance of routines, see R. David, 'Introduction' in K. Zweigert and U. Drobnig (eds.), *International Encyclopaedia of Comparative Law* (Tübingen 1971), vol. II, part 5, § 57.

Task

The range and nature of the tasks that a judiciary has to perform will have an influence on the character of the judicial role. Although adjudication will be a major defining task of the judiciary in western legal systems, the portfolio of tasks that are performed by the judiciary may be more varied. On the whole, there are few 'inevitable' features of a judicial role. There may be tasks that are commonly performed, such as presiding over criminal trials, but this is not the workload of many administrative or constitutional judges. There are many tasks, such as those of the investigating magistrate, that are peculiar to only some judiciaries.

Adjudication is a special form both of resolving disputes and of governance, which lies at the core of judicial activity. As Shapiro points out,[15] the triadic relationship between the two disputing parties and a judge who decides the outcome is a distinctive form of dispute resolution. The parties sacrifice a significant amount of control over the outcome in order to reach a decision, but in return they have important procedural rights of participation. As a system of governance, adjudication is the exercise of control through the application, interpretation and refinement of rules. It is not always the optimal solution for dealing with social issues. It is not obvious that the solution to general social problems should privilege the perceptions of certain individuals or sections of society who happen to be parties to particular litigation. Governance through rules may preclude a more flexible and wide-ranging debate. In short, the involvement of judges in the resolution of social problems through their core task of adjudication is only one option among many for handling social problems. The decision to use adjudication represents a social decision, which has significant implications for the judicial role, as well as for society in general.

The reasons for choosing to give particular roles to judges are multiple. First, there is the mission of the legal system. For example, London seeks to be a leading commercial centre and this has an impact on the way in which the judges seek to establish a reputation for professionalism, impartiality and probity.[16] Within administrative judiciaries, there may be differences of emphasis between the resolution of grievances, a major concern in Spain and Germany, and ensuring the efficiency and reputation of the administration, which can be seen as more prominent in France.

[15] M. Shapiro, *Courts. A Comparative and Political Analysis* (Chicago 1981), 1–10.
[16] R. Stevens, *The English Judge* (Oxford 2002), 82.

Secondly, the role of the judiciary depends on the availability of other social and governmental institutions to resolve certain issues. For example, Stevens argues that the modern English judge has a strong voice because of the relative weakness of the voices of the Church and the civil service.[17] The assignment of a task may relate to the expertise and reputation of a particular group of judges and the procedures that its courts adopt. The assignment of tasks is therefore not simply a function of the relative position of the 'judiciary' as a block in relation to other groups, but the merits of giving this task to this particular group of judges. English judges are frequently called upon to perform the task of 'wise man' on issues of social controversy, even outside the formal setting of litigation.[18] On this analysis, the judicial role is not fixed but variable. In other words, the position of the institution among governmental and social institutions is important. This applies to both the judicial and non-judicial tasks. As was seen in chapter 1, Van Caenegem makes a similar point about the relative roles of judges and others within the legal community.[19]

Thirdly, there is the effect of serendipity. A number of things just happen for circumstantial reasons without proper planning. The development of the Spanish *juez de paz* serves as an excellent example.[20] There were a number of rational plans to transfer this role to professional judges, but constraints of finance and personnel prevented this from ever happening. The existence of specific models that can be generalised at a moment of reform is a further example of this. The Napoleonic reforms to create French labour courts and commercial courts were based on models that were in existence in relation to parts of France.[21] There was no attempt to sit down and design an institution from scratch.

The particular tasks of judges will involve them in different relationships with other social actors. Constitutional adjudication will bring to the fore relations with politicians, whilst criminal law will bring close connections with the media. These are related to the intrinsic interest of the task and will have an impact on the character of the role and the qualities of the people who are asked to perform that role. In certain areas, particularly those just mentioned, it will not be sufficient for the judges to satisfy the standards of the legal community, either advocates or academics. The task may regularly involve the wider community. But

[17] Ibid., 140, 147. [18] See above pp. 341–2. [19] Above p. 36.
[20] Above pp. 207–11. [21] Above pp. 91–2.

the extent to which this will happen depends on the circumstances of a particular period or country.

Assigning particular tasks to the judiciary does not have a direct impact on how the judiciary is organised. A good example is the control over the administration. The French use specialist administrative judges who have a different training and career pattern from other judges, but this is not replicated in the other continental systems, even though they have separate administrative courts. Indeed, the judicial character of the Swedish system of control over the administration has only been formalised since the 1970s. The relative importance of the courts and the Ombudsman in France and Sweden shows that a different weight is attached to the judicial role. The English common law demonstrates that one can have judicial review with a common corps of judges and a common set of higher-level institutions, though the system works by having a large number of tribunals staffed by non-professional and lay judges. Guarnieri and Pederzoli see the connection between judges and prosecutors as important in some jurisdictions.[22] But it is less obvious that the potential for performing both judicial and prosecutorial functions within the same career has any marked impact on the performance of the two tasks.

Even in the common task of judging criminal cases, the task is performed in different ways, depending on the procedures adopted in the system. Two obvious factors illustrate this. Where the judge is expected to lead the questioning (typically from a file), the organisation and preparation of the trial is different from where the judge comes to be informed by the prosecution and defence and to arbitrate between them. The judge is also able to direct the hearing more easily than where she has to respond, without much preparation, to the presentation of information and argument by the advocates of the parties. A second factor is whether the professional judges are deciding alone or with lay jurors or assessors. The judge with lay members is making sure that the lay people are aware of what is going on and can play an appropriate role. In such a process, all concerned have to negotiate the lines between the role of legal professionals and popular understandings of fairness and justice in the criminal process. The low level of lay participation in the French criminal justice system gives the professional judges a more dominant role in the culture of the criminal justice system compared, for example, to Sweden where the lay judges have a more frequent role,

22 Guarnieri and Pederzoli, 110–11, 118–20.

and are themselves elected councillors with a strong legitimacy of their own. One might also add that the role of the judiciary and prosecutors in the pre-trial process is also significant in terms of the process, but has no direct consequences for whether these two professions are closely connected or not. At best, it can be said that to describe a task that the judiciary performs, it is necessary to set it in a context of procedure and institutions.

Some tasks are sufficiently distinct that they require special arrangements, often in terms of court institutions and judicial personnel. For example, many countries in this book assign the task of constitutional review to a different group of judges from ordinary matters. The distinctly political character of the task leads to a separate appointments procedure with distinct criteria. This is particularly the case where abstract constitutional review brings judges deeply into the political process. The examples of France and Germany bear this out in different ways, and Spain has modelled its position on Germany. In all three, there are distinct criteria for the appointment of constitutional judges. France has the most distinct criteria because it is willing to appoint as members of the Conseil constitutionnel those who have no legal experience. The Conseil constitutionnel is also institutionally separate in that there is no procedure for the ordinary or administrative courts to refer matters to it. In Germany and Spain, there are connections between the courts, but the criteria for appointment to the constitutional court are distinct, and it is clear that different forms of expertise are required. But in England and Sweden, where there is barely any constitutional review, there is no separate court and no distinct appointments procedure. The result is a more homogeneous judiciary, though this may change as human rights litigation becomes more prominent.

Organisational structure

The organisational structure is an important feature of the character of the judiciary in a particular country. Individuals become judges by becoming part of an organisation that has its own ethos and range of activities and procedures. The organisation will affect not merely the range of work undertaken (whether it is limited to administrative law or is more diverse), but also the standing of the individual and the ethos within which the work is undertaken. The key organisational features are the division of the judiciary into different corps, internal features such as education, training and socialisation, hierarchy and leadership, as well as the situation of the judiciary in the wider context of diversity and relations with other social groups through contacts, influence or even formal representation.

Judicial corps

The most important feature in shaping the character of the judiciary is the nature of the judicial corps. The corps is the socially and institutionally defined group to which a judge belongs and in which she operates. Entry, socialisation, career, mutual support, values and ethics relate to the judge's own particular corps. The corps is the carrier of a tradition, as well as the reference group for the judge as decision-maker.

To begin with, the character of the judiciary in a particular country is shaped by the number of divisions of the judicial corps and their relationship both to each other and to other groups of lawyers.

The existence of radically distinct judicial corps in France has important consequences. Their functions and experiences are distinct, their formation is distinct, and their relationships to the various social and political actors in society are distinct. The very limited transfer between corps maintains their diversity and limits their collective cohesion as 'the judiciary'. The pattern is replicated in relation to lay judges as well. As was seen in chapter 2, each group has to be described distinctly, even with regard to core aspects such as judicial independence. There is dialogue between the judges and also conscious alignment of their positions, but there remains an important aspect of distinctiveness in each group, and there are few formal mechanisms for developing a common position. There are not even common unions or professional bodies representing judges across the sector. The German experience is formally more unified, with only the constitutional judges operating in a distinct realm of appointment and professional circles. But at a practical level, the fragmentation of judges between Länder and across a number of different court systems does create a distinct set of experiences. The English judiciary has different groups, which are national, though the lower judiciary is in practice more regional. There is, as yet, limited movement between ranks, and only recently have the lower judges been included in the work of the Judges' Council. In Spain and Sweden, there is much more of a common judicial corps. In Spain, judges in the main cities will be able to specialise. In Sweden, there are fewer judges and there is no long-term career in simply one particular branch of work, be it administrative, civil or criminal.

The distinctiveness of constitutional judges has been commented upon already. The general picture is that the task of undertaking constitutional review requires a distinct body of judges. In Spain and Germany, they may be drawn from those qualified for judicial office, but this does not necessarily require the individuals to be judges. In France, the appointments can be more diverse. Whatever their background, these judges remain distinct in their appointment and operation from other judges.

The distinctiveness of the judicial corps results not only from initial recruitment, but also from training and continuing education. The processes of socialisation include some form of placement in which the trainee has the chance to learn the job under supervision. This apprenticeship model of learning creates close bonds with a number of members of the profession in a way that being part of a year group at a judicial college could never fully realise. Even though judges will often practise sitting alone in their early years, the training and initial post-qualification placements will often be in collegial courts where senior members of the profession can mentor and support the new recruits. The German model does not use a judicial college to transmit values and ideas. There are training courses, but not a general socialisation. The contrast is with Spain and France that have this structure. Continuing education can also support this kind of socialisation, and the kinds of courses put on in Sweden and France do enable judges to meet each other, as well as to extend their skills.

As has been seen, the English common law has a close connection between the Bench and Bar and this has affected the character of the judiciary and the way it works.[23] The more radical separation of judges and advocates in other systems studied in this book gives a different character to their judicial professions. In Germany and, to a lesser extent, in Sweden, common education provides a basis for mutual understanding. The German model of the unitary legal education gives the judge and advocate a common experience of legal education out of which they later diverge. This educational experience is a mass experience for about 10,000 lawyers a year spread over the sixteen Länder, which cannot hope to provide a strong socialisation process in comparison with the more concentrated English Bar. German judges have little experience of full

[23] See A. Paterson, *The Law Lords* (London 1982), 29–34 on the way in which the judiciary offers a lead to the Bar. Also Guarnieri and Pederzoli, 75 make the point that the organisational character of the judiciary affects its reference groups to whom it looks for approval and inspiration.

professional life in private practice, and there are few mechanisms for networking, except at a purely social level. The Swedish model of an initial common formation for an elite of law graduates provides a closer socialisation, if only because the numbers are much smaller. As in Germany, some of those who undertake the common professional training as a *notarie* will go into private practice, and so this provides a basis for mutual understanding between the professions. There is also a limited movement between the different professions. But, for the most part, the reputation of the judiciary is high and *advokater* have taken some time to establish a high standing for their own profession. The French and Spanish models have created a greater separation between advocates and the professional judiciary. Competitive examinations and a judicial college channel judges into a very different experience of the law, which gives them very limited insight (except by way of training placement) into the work of the advocate's profession. The judges have their own networks and continuing formation, so there are few opportunities, except the purely social, in which judges and advocates can reflect together on the way the law is developing.

A further possible area for connections between judges and advocates is the character of lateral entry to the judicial profession. In France, this has become very important, whilst, in other countries, lateral entry has been less extensive. All the same, it is clear that the initial recruitment competition does not suit all potential candidates and later entry is an important feature in the modern judiciary of most countries. Lateral recruitment increases diversity in the judiciary and poses problems for socialisation within the judiciary. The differences in prior experiences have value for the way in which the judiciary can handle the kinds of cases coming before it. But, if the new recruits have little scope for promotion, then it can create a two-tier system of life-long judges occupying senior posts and the lateral recruits serving as frontline dispensers of routine justice. Given the universality of recruitment from other legal professions, the English are increasingly using judicial training as a mechanism for creating common understandings and approaches. Reliance on this entry route makes it more difficult to make significant advances in the area of diversity, since there is no way of bypassing the problems of diversity that already exist within other professions.

A more common professional connection is between the ordinary judiciary and the prosecutors. In France, they form a common profession. In Spain, Sweden and Germany, they will share a common formation, and the prosecutors provide the largest group of lateral entrants into the judiciary. It may also be possible for judges to take up posts as prosecutors, as in Sweden or some parts of Germany. That bonding between the groups has important effects on how the judges are perceived by the population. By contrast, the lack of a pathway for members of the Crown Prosecution Service to become judges creates very different dynamics. The investigative function is seen in Spain and France as something with which judges are also involved, not least as investigating judges. The judge is not fully detached from the pursuit of criminals.

The distinctiveness of the judicial corps is shaped not only by these structural relations to other judicial or lawyer groups, but also by reference to other groups, particularly within the public sector. For continental judiciaries an important reference group is the civil servants. Judges are civil servants, typically recruited as part of a career. The judge's terms and conditions reflect those of a civil servant. Career protection, procedures for complaint about treatment, and conditions on matters such as parental leave, all typically follow civil service patterns. In Sweden, the judicial union is part of the civil service union, and in other countries there are merely links between judicial professional associations and the mainstream civil service unions. The civil service thus provides the career model and a point of reference. At the same time, judges usually feel the need to differentiate their role from the executive character of the civil service. As one civil service career among many, the judiciary participates in the exercise of governmental power in a variety of ways. On this perspective, it is perfectly normal for the judge to accept secondment to the Ministry of Justice, or to take on other public sector functions. The idea of the judge as the occupant of a public office shapes the performance of the function of judging, rather than the character of the career as a whole.

Lay judges form separate corps of their own. They are usually treated as a group apart from the professional judges. They are not integrated into professional judicial training, and often have difficulties in having training of their own. Because such individuals have their own professional lives and are judges for small parts of their time, the groups often have difficulty in developing a cohesion. It is interesting to note how many of the initiatives for training and discussion among lay judges discussed in this book have come from self-help.

Education, training and socialisation

Mestiz and Pederzoli argue that structures of education have a significant impact on how the judiciary works. They contrast the specialist legal educations of different groups of judges and lawyers in France with the generalist education in Germany:

> The separate training adopted in France pursues the aim of specialization, but it does not allow the development of a common cultural background facilitating relationships between [judges] and lawyers. The unitary model adopted in Germany, though supplying this background, takes too much time to provide the specific skills and abilities needed to perform any professional role.[24]

The analysis of this book would be to confirm the insight of the tension between specialist and unitary legal education, but with the emphasis on its impact on the separation of judges into a number of different corps distinct both from each other and from advocates.

The processes of education and training not only secure the technical competence of judges, but also are mechanisms of socialisation. Through the judicial colleges, where they exist, the group of judges can be formed into a common understanding of their role, and can establish networks of contacts both among themselves and with established members of the profession that will be of use to them in the future. The long training of French ordinary judges achieves this to a greater extent than the shorter Spanish training, especially as the former has a much stronger role in continuing education. The Conseil d'Etat also ensures a degree of commonality of approach by having all recruits come for a placement in it, even if they will be working in the lower administrative courts. The German and Swedish models are more dispersed in that the trainees will include many who do not intend to carry on to be judges. This is especially true of Germany, where such people are the vast majority of trainees. The diversity of courts to which the trainees are sent enhances this diversity. It is only really when the judge becomes a *Richter auf Probe* and is subject to more specific scrutiny in a collegial court that the training and socialisation become more specific and bond the judges together. Size also is important. The corps of constitutional courts, the Conseil d'Etat in France, the superior judges in England and the Swedish judiciary are sufficiently small to enable a common ethos to be developed throughout working activity. The more diffuse judiciaries have less of a common outlook, and this is reflected, in part, by the strength and diversity of the judicial unions.

[24] A. Mestiz and P. Pederzoli, 'Training the Legal Professions in Italy, France and Germany' in C. N. Tate and T. Vallinder (eds.), *The Global Expansion of Judicial Power* (New York 1995), 155 at 171.

Continuing education is of variable quality within the judiciary. Some skills are learnt primarily on the job, such as drafting, though there may be prior exercises at the judicial college or training centre. Subject knowledge may have come from prior education, but will often come from specialisation developed on the task and then supported by further, more formal, education.

Hierarchy and leadership

The judiciary is a body of professionals. As a result, it behaves in radically different ways to the 'command and control' structure of an industrial organisation. As a professional, the judge has her own authority and legitimacy arising from her qualifications and status, her knowledge of the law and experience of applying it. The exercise of professional judgement is critical to her role, and this is not just a matter of following orders. Authority relationships in this kind of culture are importantly distinct from relationships between managers and employees in industrial or office settings. There has to be a combination of the exercise of authority to ensure tasks are performed properly with a significant element of collegiality which respects the independent professional status of those being managed. Different systems negotiate these features in different ways.

It is useful to distinguish hierarchy or management and leadership in this context. Hierarchy depends on the authority of position to confer legitimacy and status on what is being required of another. In some systems, a Minister of Justice can order that a criminal investigation be discontinued, or can issue directions about the management of the court system. In such a setting, the pyramidal structure naturally explains the relationships of judges to other bodies. Leadership operates differently in a professional setting. Leadership may involve taking initiative to start or discontinue discussion of reforms to legal rules or practices, even if it does not necessarily require the leader to come up with the answers. Bensimmon and her colleagues comment that

> While organisational leadership is important, it may be a mistake to believe that all leadership must come from *leaders*. In many organisations – and it would seem particularly true in professional organisations – much of the guidance and support may be provided by the participants, the nature of the task, or the characteristics of the organisation itself.[25]

[25] Cited in R. Middlehurst, *Leading Academics* (Buckingham 1993), 25–6.

This comment applies strongly to the judiciary, which has its sense of vocation to serve justice independently and without fear or favour. Such a sense of personal vocation places clear neutralising limits on the effect of external hierarchical dictation. Persuasion, rather than command, has to be the major tool of leadership. A potent illustration is the way in which, in all the systems discussed, lower courts retain the authority to decide cases contrary to the precedents of higher courts, where they consider the precedent to be wrong. In the higher courts of all the systems that have been discussed in this book, judges sit in collegial panels and, with few exceptions, have to reach a collegial decision. As a result, there is room for much leadership within such collegial groups that escapes the notice of the observer. The dynamics of the group will often depend on an individual person, such as the reporter preparing the draft decision, taking a lead. The plurality of individuals and their backgrounds provides a diversity of inputs into the decision, but it is tempered by the need to reach a common position.

Leadership can be both institutional and individual. Institutional leadership attaches inherently to certain roles. A court institution may well play an important collective leadership role, for example both the German Constitutional Court and the French Conseil d'Etat have an important role in shaping legal development in general, not simply in their own branch of law. This will be performed through formal decisions or advice. In most of the jurisdictions studied here, judicial decisions of superior courts are not binding, but have a strong authority. This is perhaps an obvious example of institutional leadership within the legal community. But this can be seen equally in countries such as Sweden where courts have a formal role as consultee (*remissinstans*) in legislative reform. Inherent authority may attach to an individual's hierarchical position as a result of a person's professional status or standing. In the German system, it is well recognised that a professor has a particularly high professional standing and, even if not a hierarchical superior, will exercise a leadership role, especially if she or he is also a judge. In the English common law, membership of the House of Lords tends to confer a similar authority not only in relation to judgments, but also in relation to legislative debates on legal development. Individuals may also have a personal authority. An advocate general or equivalent may well develop a reputation for particularly good argumentation and ideas, and others will follow this lead. The authority of individual French commissaires du gouvernement as doctrinal writers provides a good example.[26] In Sweden, the role of individual judges in acting as chair or secretary of law reform committees enables them to exercise individual leadership roles.[27] In courts that only give a single collegial judgment, there is little scope for identifying such individuals outside the informal reputation that these people develop. As in the case of any professional bureaucracy, the formal emphasis focuses on authority and on collegiality in the exercise of leadership.

Alongside the potentially diffuse nature of leadership within the judicial community, there are more hierarchical, managerial roles that affect the character of the judiciary as an organisation. Management by hierarchical superiors is an important feature of the organisation of the courts and of the careers of judges within a bureaucratic profession. In some systems, the judges are directly under a ministry. The ministry can determine the career and promotion of the individual, and, in some systems such as France and England, may have power to intervene in individual criminal cases. At the very least, the ministry is likely to have a strong influence on the resources that support the judge in her duties.

In Spain and Sweden, in different ways, judges are subject to an independent agency, rather than a ministry. In the Spanish system, this gives judges more control, since they are strongly represented in the management of the Consejo General del Poder Judicial. In Sweden, Domstolsverket is a more executive agency in which judges are involved at board and administrative levels. Political involvement is less direct than where a ministry is in charge. The ministry and politicians are involved with the overall framework of policy and resources available to the agency, and in nominating politician members of the agency's management board. But within such an agency, there is more judicial participation in settling the organisational priorities of the judiciary. For example, the Consejo General del Poder Judicial in Spain maintains a strong control over the judges and their performance. The *modulos* that it issues provide benchmarks for satisfactory performance, and are used as the basis for decisions on individuals' careers, and Sweden has equivalents.[28] It is noticeable that this area has become more prominent for the involvement of the English judiciary within the Concordat of 2004, without this giving rise to the creation of a judicial agency.[29]

At an individual level, in all systems, senior judges have some management responsibilities in relation to the careers of more junior judges. Procedures of appraisal and references for promotion strengthen the

[26] Above p. 86. [27] Above p. 276. [28] Above pp. 182 and 241. [29] See above pp. 321–2.

importance of the hierarchy within a court and the need for less senior judges to meet the expectations of senior judges. The criteria for judging the performance of judges are often so loose that there is large scope for professional judgement. This hierarchy is particularly important where the politicians play a limited part in promotion decisions and transfers of judges between functions. The German local courts seem to be more self-governing through the Präsidialrat. The English have relied on informal systems in this area, but the transparency required by the reforms of 2005 will inevitably bring in more formal systems of appraisal and references by senior judges for appointment and promotion decisions.

At local court level, it is normal that presiding judges will manage the distribution of work between judges and monitor the overall efficiency of the court. For this France has been developing the role of judicial court managers, handling local resources. In practice, even Spanish courts retain considerable operational independence, and the framework set nationally is not very constraining. The role of the English presiding judge of a circuit is more limited, but is another version of local management of court lists. In Germany, the role of the presiding judge is limited by co-decision processes involving other judges. These different ways of balancing between local professional autonomy in operational matters within centrally set objectives reflect the limits of a purely hierarchical model of managing judicial professionals in the service of the administration of justice.

The extent to which management in relation to judicial activity is contentious depends on the aspect of the judicial role over which it is exercised. There is an important distinction between control over court infrastructure and resources on the one hand and over judicial careers on the other. The latter impinges more directly on the professionalism of the judge and her sense of vocation and legitimacy. Even within that more professional sphere, where the global performance of a judge is assessed, the interference is less than where an assessment is made of individual decisions on cases, where the intimate zone of professional judgement is called in question. The value of judicial independence excludes managerial evaluation of individual decisions and leaves control to the formal appeal process.

Social diversity

The organisational structures have a significant effect on the character of social diversity reflected in the membership of the judiciary. Female participation is the most documented feature of social diversity. It has been noted already that women are far more present in the career judiciary (and in the role of career prosecutor) amongst the countries studied here than in the predominantly self-employed careers as an advocate.[30] The full career judiciary is the most popular with women, because it offers a framework within which family commitments can be managed, either because the civil service offers structured and generous parental leave or because there is flexibility in being able to move when a spouse or partner has a job move. The regular hours, the ability to take files home in many countries (often made necessary because of the lack of office space in courts), and the written character of much of the work enable quite a bit of flexibility in the way judges work. But the institutional structures of career development can also have an impact on the advancement of women within the judiciary. The extent to which mobility is required in order to gain different experience as a condition precedent to advancing to the most senior posts is a structural feature that impacts on the position of women in the highest judicial posts. It is not simply a question of encouraging individuals to aspire to the highest posts; progress on this element of diversity requires attention to structures.

The issue of social diversity is part of a concern about the way judges can speak on behalf of the wider community and are connected to it. Until recently, this issue has been of limited concern in relation to the professional judiciary. There has been deference to professional standing that prevails over concerns about the social representativeness of the judiciary. In countries where there has been concern about the social background of the judiciary, this has typically come as part of a general concern about public sector employment. By contrast, the lay judiciary depends for its legitimacy on its representative character. Its members represent the community in whose name the judicial panel makes decisions. Consequently, the backgrounds of these judges have been of special concern, particularly in England, Germany and Sweden, where appointments are for a number of years. By contrast, in France, the lay judges either are chosen at random from the electoral roll (the jury) or, often, are elected by a constituency (the *juges consulaires*).

Structure of contacts and influence

One of the important features that define an institution is its relationship to leading actors internally and externally. It was noted in

[30] Above pp. 52–3, 82, 118–20, 246–8.

chapter 1 that the influence of the judiciary is difficult to chart.[31] Some links and thus potential for influence occur in the normal or natural way in which a judiciary operates, some are based on formally created structures, and some are more informal. Natural influences can be illustrated by the close links between the English superior judges and the Bar, or the Swedish judges and the administration, or between the French Conseil d'Etat members and the active administration and political sources of power. Such links do not need to be created, but occur in the course of the ordinary way in which a particular judiciary operates. More formal structures exist to give judges a role in influencing legal development beyond the remit of deciding individual cases. The French Conseil d'Etat gives both legal advice and comments on draft legislation, and the Swedish courts and Lagrådet have a pre-legislative role. The creation of constitutional review mechanisms also provides formal opportunities for at least some branches of the judiciary to be involved in influencing the legislative process and in controlling elected politicians. More informally, and more contingently, there are ways in which individual judges can exercise influence. In many systems, judges will often serve as civil servants of the Ministry of Justice, the judicial administration agency or as prosecutors. In such roles, they will have policy and executive experience, but within a limited range of activity that is closely connected to the administration of justice. The English Law Commission may also provide a vehicle for similar policy-making influence. The extent to which these different forms of link are considered appropriate will depend on conceptions of the judicial role, in particular judicial independence. In such a context, judicial independence is understood very differently in France compared with Spain in which there is a separation between judges and the active administration or politics.

By contrast with the common law, in the other systems studied here contacts with the range of legal professions are more limited. Advocates generally fall outside the natural reference groups of judges. There will be professional and informal contacts with individual members of the professions, but they do not provide a source of criticism or reflection in a regular way. On the whole judges find their reference group within their particular judiciary. This is reinforced by the structures of hierarchy, and by the structures of collective action. Academic writers may serve as a reference group of authoritative commentators without themselves being part of the network of formal contacts. Informally, there will

[31] Above p. 36.

be connections between the judges and the local law faculties, and academic commentators may speak at judicial training events. Even within the common law, academics may sometimes be appointed to the Bench.

Collective action

Collective action by the judges represents a typically informal set of links both within and outside the judiciary. The existence and importance of professional associations of judges is exceedingly varied in the countries studied. Where there is an agency or judicial council on which judges have places, this provides an incentive for the creation of judicial unions. The Latin model is for diversity among unions, representing the divergent social and political outlooks among judges. This pattern reflects civil service unionisation. By contrast, the Swedish and German unions are more like professional associations dealing in a unified way with the judicial agencies and ministries of justice.

Professional associations can serve a number of functions. The first role is in socialisation, bringing judges together. On the whole, such a function can be performed effectively only when the majority of judges belong to the same association. The English inns of court have performed this role over the past century and a half, but there are few equivalents. Most continental associations will group together volunteers, typically because they share a political outlook, rather than simply because they share the role of judging. They do not socialise the broad range of judges – that role is most commonly performed, in practice, by the judicial training colleges.

The second role of associations is representation and lobbying, particularly in relation to ministries or agencies responsible for the judiciary. Traditionally, this has not been needed in England in a formal way, but this is now changing with the latest reforms of the Judges' Council. Because of the size and diversity of the judiciary, both ministries and judges feel the need in most systems to have intermediaries with whom the governing body can deal. The structure of public sector collective bargaining is therefore the model adopted. Though the associations typically are involved in discussions on pay and conditions, this does not exhaust their activity. As the collective voice of the judiciary, which has aspiration to serve justice and not merely to be a functionary of the legal system, each association will express aspirations for the future of the legal system and how it may serve justice better. As a lobbying organisation, it will request greater resources for the system. But it will also defend certain characteristics of the legal system against politically inspired changes, e.g. in relation to the rights of those in custody under criminal investigation, and it will promote changes in legal practices, e.g. in the use of non-custodial sentences. Although often allied to political parties, judicial associations, as single-issue pressure groups, may well argue for solutions that are different from those advocated by the parties to which they are often allied. The role of the judicial associations as sources of ideas is often a particularly important, independent contribution to the development of the legal system.

Values

The values that shape the judiciary are drawn not only from external ideas about the appropriate level of creativity in performing tasks and the character of judicial independence, but also from internally conceived ideas about the nature of the judicial role. The dominant values of the judicial role at any one period are actually a compromise between historically received ideas, external views of the political, social and legal communties, and internally generated ideas within the judiciary itself. The main values discussed in earlier chapters have been lawmaking creativity, judicial independence and the conception of the role as a public office or as a bureaucratic job.

Lawmaking creativity

The extent of the variability of the judicial role can be seen in the context of creativity. As Lenoble states, the historically inherited continental model of the judge as uncreative executor of the law has had to be revised in the light of what judges do.[32] Judicial creativity in the interpretation of the law is widely accepted by both judges and the legal community. The English common law has more readily accepted this. But, as Vogenauer argues,[33] within both continental and English systems there has been a 'period style' about the degree of creativity in interpreting legislation that is thought appropriate. External signals encouraging greater creativity in recent times have included the creation of constitutional courts and charters of rights in Spain and Germany, the creation of the Law Commission in England and the Section du Rapport et des Etudes in the French Conseil d'Etat, and the accession of the

[32] J. Lenoble (ed.), *La crise du juge* (Paris 1990), 2.

[33] S. Vogenauer, *Die Auslegung von Gesetzen in England and auf dem Kontinent* (Tübingen 2001), 1295–1305.

different countries to supranational legal orders, which the judges are empowered to enforce. Internally, there may be a sense that the legislature is not able to act effectively to deal with problems, such as liability for road traffic in France.[34]

That said, the interesting question is the degree of creativity involved in a particular area of work. Guarnieri suggests that there are dimensions to lawmaking creativity: high and low normative creativity, and high and low degrees of political autonomy.[35] Where there is little scope to create new norms and little political autonomy, then the judge is essentially the executor of laws. Where the judge creates norms and has high autonomy, then the role is that of a political judge, someone who is a strong political authority in her own right. By contrast, where the normative creativity is less, but there is political autonomy, then the judge can be seen as an independent guardian of what the law lays down. This analysis suggests that one needs to examine not only the creative initiative of judges, but also the limits to political autonomy. Some judges dealing with legally routine matters may be creative in terms of individual solutions. A judge dealing with family matters may be individually creative in the sense of developing a novel way of handling a problem, without that being normatively binding. But for the most part in the lower courts, routine legal questions and routine solutions are the standard fare. The culture of the judge is to deal with the litigants in a fair and proper manner in handling such cases, so people feel that justice has been done to them. That notion of routine justice permeates even the highest courts in many countries, including the German and Spanish constitutional courts dealing with constitutional complaints. For the most part, such roles are as executor of the law. Where lawmaking does occur through judicial decisions, only in the English common law and in rare cases elsewhere is the decision binding on future courts. The freedom of lower courts acts as a check on the autonomous authority of the higher courts. Even in England, the power of Parliament to overrule decisions by legislation also serves to limit the political autonomy of the highest court, and similar actions were taken by the French Parliament in the face of lawmaking by the Cour de cassation that was deemed to have overstepped the mark.[36] High levels of political autonomy and creativity are found only in relation to constitutional courts.

[34] See above p. 84.

[35] C. Guarnieri, *Magistratura e politica in Italia* (Bologna 1993), 27.

[36] Above p. 70.

A further important constraint is the extent of any change that judicial creativity introduces. Adjudication is a miniaturist process – it focuses on the particular problem in most cases. Only occasionally in relation to abstract constitutional review or some advisory opinions are courts invited to range widely over the field of law, rather than focus on specific problems. Adjudication lends itself to incremental and reactive, rather than systematic and proactive, law reform. Judges can contribute as one actor among many in offering advice in a pre-legislative process about wide-ranging reform, but their voices are not decisive. Their authority as more autonomous lawmakers is typically confined to making piecemeal changes in response to urgent problems that have come up. The discussion of the *Perruche* or *Bland* cases[37] illustrates that form of important lawmaking. Even in constitutional cases, there is usually scope for constitutional amendment to change the result.

As a result of these dynamics, historical patterns of creativity do change. The judiciary may well develop internally a sense of what is appropriate, especially through its internal leaders, but this is subject to comment and reaction within the legal community and in the wider political community.

Independence

As was stated in chapter 1, judicial independence is a response to previous experiences within a particular country, as well as an ideal of general application.[38] The past shapes the identification of threats to the independence of the judiciary. It also influences the institutional arrangements that are put in place to promote and safeguard it. The conceptions of judicial independence that come to the fore in the institutions and practices of the judiciary in a particular country can therefore differ from those of its neighbour. Each of the chapters has identified particular conceptions of judicial independence and the constraints imposed on judges and others to maintain it.

Stevens contrasts the personal independence of the individual English judge, free from dismissal and direction, with the bureaucratic continental judge who is only free in conducting the individual case, but is part of an institutionally dependent organisation.[39] His analysis focuses on the difference between an office-holder with an inherent authority and a member of a professional, but hierarchically integrated, corps. The

[37] Above pp. 70 and 336. [38] Above pp. 27 and 42.
[39] Stevens, *English Judge*, above n. 16, 79 and 20.

kind of independence from political authorities that is appropriate to the former is seen as less appropriate to the latter. But this dimension conveys only part of the picture. We have seen both that the English judiciary is more dependent as an organisation on ministries, and that there are ways in which continental judiciaries have achieved significant independence. Guarnieri and Pederzoli rightly argue that independence is always going to be relative – in a state under the rule of law one is naturally free from the pressure of the parties or of the state in the conduct of a particular case, but a judge has a responsibility to her superiors for her conduct and her overall performance.[40]

Total independence from government is neither desirable nor possible. In a system of responsible government, the different branches interact constantly.[41] The effective system of relationships will show appropriate mutual respect for the roles that each performs. There has to be a sense of responsible criticism combined with deference. The way of balancing these two features leads to controversy, particularly where the politicians are those who are subjects of the judicial decisions, such as in political corruption cases or where an administrative act or legislation is scrutinised. The French political class, like British governments, is perhaps more resistant than that of Germany to what it perceives as interference with its prerogatives. Spanish and German histories of excessive executive power, even dictatorship, have given the judges a higher standing. They have more formal freedom from politics. In many ways, the Swedish judiciary has the least by way of formal independence from the executive and the legislature. The balance of powers is very much in favour of the other branches of government. Yet the overall pattern is of co-operation, rather than confrontation, with an important role for the judiciary in the overall design of the legislative and governmental processes. The judiciary is independent, but in a different way from in Spain. The Swedish judiciary has an inherent authority, which is more similar to that of the English judiciary, a standing acquired over many years. Freedom from improper political interference is most readily accepted in the area of operational independence. Even then, the political nature of the law generates problems – can criminal prosecutions or sentences initiated or imposed on behalf of the community be totally outside the decision-making purview of politicians?

Two further areas of controversy where countries differ in their approaches to judicial independence are the appropriate involvement of

[40] Guarnieri and Pederzoli, 37.

[41] See Stevens, *English Judge*, above n. 16, 96.

judges in politically sensitive activity out of court and judicial accountability. While judges cannot avoid some of their judicial decisions being controversial, external activity is a different matter. At one extreme, Spanish judges are excluded from political activity and thereby are insulated from political controversy. Swedish and English judges, on the other hand, will often chair controversial inquiries into law reform or other matters. In both these countries, senior judges are public figures and, as such, are expected to perform public services that might sometimes appear to compromise their standing as neutral figures in society. In Spain, given its history, the public association of a judge with a contentious social issue is likely to harm the judiciary in a way that is thought to be less likely in countries that have not had such a turbulent recent history.

Judicial accountability is also a difficult area. For the most part in relation to individual decisions, judges have relied on giving reasons predominantly in a way that is understood within the legal community. This protects the judges in relation to individual outcomes, but is less satisfactory in terms of the way in which justice in general is delivered. Accountability for the pattern of lawmaking that emerges from the higher courts and the effectiveness of routine decisions in the lower courts are both important matters. As justice becomes conceived less as an act of state authority and more as a public service, so the demands for accountability for the system grow. Many higher courts on the continent produce annual reports, justifying and opening to scrutiny their effectiveness and key decisions. In many systems, however, the information is gathered internally by the Ministry of Justice and produced as a set of annual statistics without a serious attempt to produce a publicly available narrative explanation and justification for what has been happening. This is most clearly the case in France and Germany. On the whole, public accountability happens most explicitly in Spain and Sweden where an independent agency runs the judiciary. It has to operate within a framework set by a ministry or Parliament and respond to it. In a sense, judicial independence is maintained by explicitness on both sides about what is expected and what is being delivered. Without an agency, there is often less explicitness about both expectations and delivery.

The freedom of judges to enforce justice as they see it within the mission that they have been given is a relatively recent area of controversy. In part, this is because the judicial system was seen in the past as one of the natural areas of government activity, like lawmaking, policing and the military, expenditure on which required little justification. As the judicial system has been reconceived as one public service competing with others for a finite pot for public expenditure, at the same time as it has come under increasing demand, so the judiciary has perceived the need to be more forceful in arguing for control over what it perceives to be its necessary share of that pot. The creation of a Courts Administration Agency or even a Judicial Service Agency has been one response. In other systems, there has to be some other way of negotiating how resources are allocated.

Public office

The bureaucratic character of the judicial career is a typical European feature. It is very much a job to be performed professionally with the core value lying in the rule of law (or more precisely *l'état de droit* – the state acting in conformity with the law). Only at the most senior levels or among the lay judges is there a sense of the judiciary as a public office, an integral element of the separation of powers. The appeal of the notion of judicial independence draws on the constitutional role that the judiciary plays in safeguarding the individual in relation to the state, such as in the criminal process or in controlling administrative decisions. In these areas, the judge must be even-handed, whilst the executive is permitted to pursue its own agenda. The constitutional role of public office-holder gives the judge an independent legitimacy. The hierarchical model of the bureaucratic functionary offers an essentially instrumental legitimacy for the judge. The reactions in Spain and France to issues of political corruption show that judges were keen to be seen as upholding the standards of justice against even major political figures. This raised their profile with the public, but caused conflict with politicians. On the whole, there was broad popular support for this role, which reinforced the position of the judiciary.

It is easy to envisage the public office model as appropriate to the constitutional judge, whose appointment is usually the subject of distinct procedures and enquiries about legitimacy. It is harder to see this distinct legitimacy in relation to many other roles at lower levels in the system. Here the essential function of the judge is to give effect to what has been settled in the law with accuracy, due process, humanity and understanding.

Judges in different countries have specific standards of what it is to behave professionally as a judge. Few countries have a code of ethics for judges, though France is beginning to evolve one.[42] Usually, the standards are set by the tradition of the judicial community, reinforced by both training and discipline. Such standards set limits on what judges may properly undertake or how they may properly behave, but they also function positively to give judges a sense of their own identity.[43] Most of the standards are similar between jurisdictions, e.g. on deportment, honesty, diligence and so on. There are differences in some specific areas. Relations with the media are less prominent in Sweden and Germany than in France and Spain. Even then, there are significant differences among the types of judges, so there is not a universal practice even among judges within the same jurisdiction. Involvement in politics is also a variable. French judges are perhaps the most involved in politics among those studied here. This follows a general tradition among civil servants that this is proper, and judges may well end up as members of the legislature. This is less frequent in the other countries, where either civil service ethics are different, as in Britain, or the judiciary is now being made distinct from the civil service. The concept of professionalism depends on the approach of other reference groups.

Conjunctural events

Human structures are rarely simply the product of institutional planning.[44] There are often events that shape the direction of the institution. In recent times, the investigation of political corruption has placed many criminal judiciaries in conflict with politicians and has altered conceptions of judicial independence. In France, Italy and Spain, such prosecutions gave ordinary judges a social standing which gives them legitimacy in controlling the excesses of politicians.[45] Equally, public expenditure limits have provoked different reflections on how the resources for justice can be secured.

The traditional status of the continental judge has also been increased by an emphasis on fundamental rights and the control over the legislative power. In some countries, such changes have been planned. This has clearly been the case in Spain and Germany, where constitutional

42 See G. Canivet, 'The Responsibility of Judges in France' (2003) 5 *Cambridge Yearbook of European Legal Studies* 15.
43 Guarnieri, *Magistratura e politica*, above n. 35, 153.
44 See Goodin, *Institutional Design*, above n. 1, 31–3.
45 Above p. 28.

judges have been given a special status to achieve these objectives. Similarly, the Human Rights Act 1998 involved a deliberate re-education of the judges and civil servants. In France, the position has been less planned. The Conseil constitutionnel was not originally expected to be the guardian of fundamental rights, but arrogated to itself the control over the legislature without the structural advantages of integration into the rest of the judiciary. The conjunctural events of 1971, coming after the Fifth Republic had proved its stability by managing to survive the crisis of May 1968 and the succession to its founder, De Gaulle, in 1969, enabled the Conseil to acquire a major, if unplanned, role in the constitutional system.[46] In relation to human rights, the earlier incorporations in France and Germany were not accompanied by the same planning as in England, so that judges have developed their positions by way of an incremental response to the developing case-law of the Court in Strasbourg. These are not examples of planning, but of a gradual adjustment.

Adjustments in the absence of planning are a feature of the European dimensions of the judiciaries discussed here. The doctrines of direct effect and the supremacy of European Community law were not clearly stated in the original treaties of the European Communities or in the British accession through the European Communities Act 1972. It was therefore for the judges to adjust to the values put in place by the European Court of Justice in 1963–4.[47] Whereas the French Cour de cassation responded in 1975, the Conseil d'Etat and the Conseil constitutionnel both took until after the end of the Gaullist era and after the Single European Act of 1986 before they adopted more similar positions in 1989 and 1988 respectively.[48] The German courts had similar hesitations.[49] Developing a sense of direction in such changed circumstances requires a political sense among the judges of what is going to last. Developing such a collective sense among the members of a supreme court, let alone among the lower judges, requires much internal discussion. The decision is often prepared by what Lord Devlin called 'rumblings from Olympus' – there were musings that indicated a potential change of direction.[50] Without a formal debate, there was a gradual realisation of 'the spirit of the times', often coinciding with changes in key personnel.

[46] Above p. 96.

[47] Case 26/62, *Van Gend en Loos v. Nederlandse Administratie der Belastingen* [1963] ECR 1; Case 6/64, *Costa v. ENEL* [1964] ECR 585.

[48] Above p. 73. [49] Above pp. 166–7. [50] P. Devlin, *The Judge* (Oxford 1979), 11.

The implication of this discussion is that the judicial role is not just the product of planning and institutional design. It comes from the response of significant numbers of judges during the course of their work. In order to understand these changes of period style, it is not possible to confine oneself to the map of formal institutions and their authority in the process of legal development. It is also necessary to examine the informal systems by which the collective view is developed. This means that there has to be an account not just of the decisions of the courts, but also of the fora in which judges are able to discuss potential developments. In various collegial courts, there will be some opportunity for discussion at an informal level, though the degree of this will often depend on the size of the group and the ease of informal deliberation – if judges are mainly working from home, this may inhibit a degree of informal networking among them. On the whole, the studies in this book suggest that discussions within a specific court can be quite good, but that discussions between courts are more patchy, even if they are within the same hierarchical judicial system. The relationship between superior and inferior courts is more often based on hierarchy than on discussions. The previous discussion on the concept of leadership most aptly captures the way in which a collective view emerges – through the initiative of certain leaders within the judicial community to which other judges and the wider community respond.

External expectations

The analysis presented in earlier chapters suggests that judges of the various jurisdictions fit within the legal community and the wider social and political communities in different ways. As a result, they respond to external expectations in different ways and to different degrees.

Within the legal community, the senior judges have traditionally had a strong leadership role in England, Sweden and the French Conseil d'Etat. To these one can now add the judges of constitutional courts in Germany, France and Spain. They were recruited as an elite and have had the authority to be leaders in generating ideas. In Spain, Germany and French private law, professors have had a more influential role within the legal community, providing works that define the subject areas. In most of these countries, the professors have also had a role in practice and in law reform commissions, providing many informal routes of influence. Thus, in terms of judicial creativity, expectations depend on which of these two plays a leadership role, as well as on the degree of legislative activity. In many areas of law, such as crime and social welfare, the initiative is with the legislature and politicians. In more technical areas, or in areas of the control exercised over the executive and legislation, then the initiative will be with judges and professors, who will set the expectations for creativity in response to an analysis of the needs of the period.

Within most of the countries studied, advocates have not been a dominant group within the legal community. In some countries, such as Sweden, they have enjoyed a low status and in many others they have been fragmented into local bars or a diversity of professions. Competitive examinations were able to establish the quality of the judges, in contrast to the absence of bar entrance examinations in Sweden or Spain, or the lower marks typically achieved by advocates in the German state examinations. Some advocates exercised leadership as members of the legislature, but often relied on professors for advice on difficult issues. The French elite Avocats au Conseil d'Etat et à la Cour de cassation and the English Bar were exceptions. But these traditional descriptions have to be revised in the light of developments in the 1990s. The rise of national and international law firms, focused on commercial work, has diminished the attraction of the judicial career among the best young lawyers, and will in time lead to an adjustment in the balance of influence within the legal community and in relation to the legislature on issues of law reform.

The expectations of the wider community are mediated in a number of ways. The position of political superiors is important, but we have seen that the trend is for them to set global benchmarks for performance and even sentencing. This role of setting a framework is more common where the judiciary is governed by an executive or constitutional agency. Mechanisms of accountability rarely invite the senior judges to defend the performance of the judiciary in public, such as before a parliamentary select committee, which can transmit clear expectations about how the law should operate, though this has happened on occasion in England.[51] For the most part, community expectations are set out informally. The media may provide a forum for politicians to criticise aspects of the work of the judiciary and generate a debate, such as often happens in relation to sensitive issues of constitutional review.[52]

[51] A. Le Sueur, 'Developing Mechanisms for Judicial Accountability in the UK' (2004) 24 *Legal Studies* 73, 97–8.

[52] See above pp. 321 and 349.

In the criminal investigation process, it has been noted how French defence lawyers use the media to manage the image of their client, but this is becoming more widespread as a practice in other countries. Such public statements have the effect of putting pressure on the investigating judges and prosecutors. More reliably, community values and expectations are transmitted through the participation of lay people in the judicial process, particularly where they have high status, as in Sweden and England, and scope for exercising a distinct individual voice in the process, as happens with most lay judges, except those in a jury. It is often the influence of alternative views at the operational level of judicial activity that is most effective, but most difficult to identify or quantify.

Conclusion

The immediate focus of this research has been to examine the factors that shape the character of national judiciaries in Western Europe. The argument has been that there is a matrix of factors that work cumulatively to give a distinctive character to a particular national judiciary. Because there are a number of variables, it is easy to see how the character of the judiciary can change over time. It is also easy to see how there can be overlapping concerns among national judiciaries, but not a perfect coincidence of views, even on core concepts such as 'judicial independence'.

In terms of comparative method, the studies of the four continental countries show that bracketing them together as 'civilian' does not really help in understanding important features of those systems. Even to distinguish the Romano-Germanic from the Latin systems does not really help to detect the differences and the elements in common. Sources of private law rules might usefully be distinguished in this way, but to understand other features of a legal system, the categorisation of systems into 'legal families' demonstrates its limitations. A 'functional' approach suggests that there are common tasks to be performed in each legal system, but this again has its limitations. Despite the great similarities in tasks performed by judges in the different systems, there are also differences that go to the heart of where the judiciary fits within the scheme of government. The study of the judiciary as an institution made up of reflective professionals, but also influenced from the outside, enables one to identify the similarities and differences. The tools of analysis of organisational theory and in particular of institutional culture enable one to identify the features shaping particular judicial institutions. By immersing oneself in the way a judiciary works, one can identify the interplay of features, before then moving to compare. Of course, one's initial hypotheses are informed by initial comparative research, giving a pre-understanding of what might be useful from a comparative perspective and not merely to those from a particular jurisdiction. But that pre-understanding has to be revised in the light of further research. The reader will hopefully take this work as the starting point for her own pre-understanding and improve upon its analysis.

Index

CAMBRIDGE STUDIES IN INTERNATIONAL AND COMPARATIVE LAW

Books in the series

Judiciaries within Europe: A Comparative Review John Bell

Law in Times of Crisis: Emergency Powers in Theory and Practice Oren Gross and Fionnuala Ní Aoláin

Vessel-Source Marine Pollution: The Law and Politics of International Regulation Alan Tan

Enforcing Obligations Erga Omnes *in International Law* Christian J. Tams

Non-Governmental Organisations in International Law Anna-Karin Lindblom

Democracy, Minorities and International Law Steven Wheatley

Prosecuting International Crimes: Selectivity and the International Law Regime Robert Cryer

Compensation for Personal Injury in English, German and Italian Law: A Comparative Outline Basil Markesinis, Michael Coester, Guido Alpa and Augustus Ullstein

Dispute Settlement in the UN Convention on the Law of the Sea Natalie Klein

The International Protection of Internally Displaced Persons Catherine Phuong

Imperialism, Sovereignty and the Making of International Law Antony Anghie

Necessity, Proportionality and the Use of Force by States Judith Gardam

International Legal Argument in the Permanent Court of International Justice: The Rise of the International Judiciary Ole Spiermann

Great Powers and Outlaw States: Unequal Sovereigns in the International Legal Order Gerry Simpson

Local Remedies in International Law C. F. Amerasinghe

Reading Humanitarian Intervention: Human Rights and the Use of Force in International Law Anne Orford

Conflict of Norms in Public International Law: How WTO Law Relates to Other Rules of Law Joost Pauwelyn

Transboundary Damage in International Law Hanqin Xue

European Criminal Procedures Edited by Mireille Delmas-Marty and John Spencer

The Accountability of Armed Opposition Groups in International Law Liesbeth Zegveld

Sharing Transboundary Resources: International Law and Optimal Resource Use Eyal Benvenisti

International Human Rights and Humanitarian Law René Provost

Remedies Against International Organisations Karel Wellens

Diversity and Self-Determination in International Law Karen Knop

The Law of Internal Armed Conflict Lindsay Moir

International Commercial Arbitration and African States: Practice, Participation and Institutional Development Amazu A. Asouzu

The Enforceability of Promises in European Contract Law James Gordley

International Law in Antiquity David J. Bederman

Money Laundering: A New International Law Enforcement Model Guy Stessens

Good Faith in European Contract Law Reinhard Zimmermann and Simon Whittaker

On Civil Procedure J. A. Jolowicz

Trusts: A Comparative Study Maurizio Lupoi

The Right to Property in Commonwealth Constitutions Tom Allen

International Organizations Before National Courts August Reinisch

The Changing International Law of High Seas Fisheries Francisco Orrego Vicuña

Trade and the Environment: A Comparative Study of EC and US Law Damien Geradin

Unjust Enrichment: A Study of Private Law and Public Values Hanoch Dagan

Religious Liberty and International Law in Europe Malcolm D. Evans

Ethics and Authority in International Law Alfred P. Rubin

Sovereignty Over Natural Resources: Balancing Rights and Duties Nico Schrijver

The Polar Regions and the Development of International Law Donald R. Rothwell

Fragmentation and the International Relations of Micro-States: Self-Determination and Statehood Jorri Duursma

Principles of the Institutional Law of International Organizations C. F. Amerasinghe

For EU product safety concerns, contact us at Calle de José Abascal, 56–1°,
28003 Madrid, Spain or eugpsr@cambridge.org.

www.ingramcontent.com/pod-product-compliance
Lightning Source LLC
Chambersburg PA
CBHW061607180926
51615CB00006B/13
9780521172851